MW01680015

T-SQL Fundamentals, Third Edition

Itzik Ben-Gan

PHI Learning Private Limited
Delhi-110092
2017

This Indian Reprint—₹ 595.00
(Original U.S. Edition—₹ 3505.00)

T-SQL FUNDAMENTALS, 3rd ed.
by Itzik Ben-Gan

Authorized reprint from the English language edition, entitled T-SQL FUNDAMENTALS, 3rd Edition, 9781509302000 by BEN-GAN, ITZIK, published by Pearson Education, Inc, publishing as Microsoft Press, Copyright © 2016 by Itzik Ben-Gan.

All rights reserved. No part of this book may be reproduced or transmitted in any form or by any means, electronic or mechanical, including photocopying, recording or by any information storage retrieval system, without permission from Pearson Education, Inc. ENGLISH language edition published by PHI LEARNING PRIVATE LIMITED, Copyright © 2017.

ISBN-978-81-203-5296-4

This book is provided "as-is" and expresses the author's views and opinions. The views, opinions and information expressed in this book, including URL and other Internet website references, may change without notice.

Some examples depicted herein are provided for illustration only and are fictitious. No real association or connection is intended or should be inferred.

Microsoft and the trademarks listed at *http://www.microsoft.com* on the "Trademarks" webpage are trademarks of the Microsoft group of companies. All other marks are property of their respective owners.

This edition is authorised for sale in India, Pakistan, Bangladesh, Bhutan, Nepal, Sri Lanka, and the Maldives only.

The export rights of this book are vested solely with the publisher.

Published by Asoke K. Ghosh, PHI Learning Private Limited, Rimjhim House, 111, Patparganj Industrial Estate, Delhi-110092 and Printed by Syndicate Binders, A-20, Hosiery Complex, Noida, Phase-II Extension, Noida-201305 (N.C.R. Delhi).

To Dato,

To live in hearts we leave behind,
Is not to die.

—Thomas Campbell

Contents at a glance

Contents

What do you think of this book? We want to hear from you!

Microsoft is interested in hearing your feedback so we can improve our books and learning resources for you. To participate in a brief survey, please visit:

http://aka.ms/tellpress

What do you think of this book? We want to hear from you!

Microsoft is interested in hearing your feedback so we can improve our books and learning resources for you. To participate in a brief survey, please visit:

http://aka.ms/tellpress

Introduction

This book walks you through your first steps in T-SQL (also known as *Transact-SQL*), which is the Microsoft SQL Server dialect of the ISO and ANSI standards for SQL. You'll learn the theory behind T-SQL querying and programming and how to develop T-SQL code to query and modify data, and you'll get an overview of programmable objects.

Although this book is intended for beginners, it's not merely a set of procedures for readers to follow. It goes beyond the syntactical elements of T-SQL and explains the logic behind the language and its elements.

Occasionally, the book covers subjects that might be considered advanced for readers who are new to T-SQL; therefore, you should consider those sections to be optional reading. The text will indicate when a section is considered more advanced and is provided as optional reading. If you feel comfortable with the material discussed in the book up to that point, you might want to tackle these more advanced subjects; otherwise, feel free to skip those sections and return to them after you gain more experience.

Many aspects of SQL are unique to the language and very different from other programming languages. This book helps you adopt the right state of mind and gain a true understanding of the language elements. You learn how to think in relational terms and follow good SQL programming practices.

The book is not version specific; it does, however, cover language elements that were introduced in recent versions of SQL Server, including SQL Server 2016. When I discuss language elements that were introduced recently, I specify the version in which they were added.

Besides being available as a box product, SQL Server is also available as a cloud-based service called Microsoft Azure SQL Database, or in short, just SQL Database. The code samples in this book were tested against both a box SQL Server product and Azure SQL Database. The book's companion content (available at *http://aka.ms/T-SQLFund3e/downloads*) provides information about compatibility issues between the flavors.

To complement the learning experience, the book provides exercises you can use to practice what you learn. The book occasionally provides optional exercises that are more advanced. Those exercises are intended for readers who feel comfortable with the material and want to challenge themselves with more difficult problems. The optional exercises for advanced readers are labeled as such.

Who should read this book

This book is intended for T-SQL developers, database administrators (DBAs), business intelligence (BI) practitioners, data scientists, report writers, analysts, architects, and SQL Server power users who just started working with SQL Server and who need to write queries and develop code using Transact-SQL.

Assumptions

To get the most out of this book, you should have working experience with Microsoft Windows and with applications based on Windows. You should also be familiar with basic concepts of relational database management systems.

This book might not be for you if...

Not every book is aimed at every possible audience. This book covers fundamentals. It's mainly aimed at T-SQL practitioners with little or no experience. This book might not be for you if you're an advanced T-SQL practitioner with many years of experience. With that said, several readers of the previous editions of this book have mentioned that—even though they already had years of experience—they still found the book useful for filling gaps in their knowledge.

Organization of this book

This book starts with a theoretical background to T-SQL querying and programming in Chapter 1, laying the foundations for the rest of the book, and basic coverage of creating tables and defining data integrity. The book moves on to various aspects of querying and modifying data in Chapters 2 through 9, and then moves to a discussion of concurrency and transactions in Chapter 10. Finally, it provides an overview of programmable objects in Chapter 11.

Here's a list of the chapters along with a short description of the content in each chapter:

- Chapter 1, "Background to T-SQL querying and programming," provides the theoretical background for SQL, set theory, and predicate logic. It examines the relational model, describes SQL Server's architecture, and explains how to create tables and define data integrity.

- Chapter 2, "Single-table queries," covers various aspects of querying a single table by using the *SELECT* statement.
- Chapter 3, "Joins," covers querying multiple tables by using joins, including cross joins, inner joins, and outer joins.
- Chapter 4, "Subqueries," covers queries within queries, otherwise known as *subqueries*.
- Chapter 5, "Table expressions," covers derived tables, Common Table Expressions (CTEs), views, inline table-valued functions, and the *APPLY* operator.
- Chapter 6, "Set operators," covers the set operators *UNION*, *INTERSECT*, and *EXCEPT*.
- Chapter 7, "Beyond the fundamentals of querying," covers window functions, pivoting, unpivoting, and working with grouping sets.
- Chapter 8, "Data modification," covers inserting, updating, deleting, and merging data.
- Chapter 9, "Temporal tables," covers system-versioned temporal tables.
- Chapter 10, "Transactions and concurrency," covers concurrency of user connections that work with the same data simultaneously; it covers transactions, locks, blocking, isolation levels, and deadlocks.
- Chapter 11, "Programmable objects," provides an overview of the T-SQL programming capabilities in SQL Server.
- The book also provides an appendix, "Getting started," to help you set up your environment, download the book's source code, install the TSQLV4 sample database, start writing code against SQL Server, and learn how to get help by working with SQL Server Books Online.

System requirements

The Appendix, "Getting started," explains which editions of SQL Server 2016 you can use to work with the code samples included with this book. Each edition of SQL Server might have different hardware and software requirements, and those requirements are well documented in SQL Server Books Online under "Hardware and Software Requirements for Installing SQL Server 2016" at the following URL: *https://msdn.microsoft.com/en-us/library/ms143506.aspx*. The Appendix also explains how to work with SQL Server Books Online.

If you're connecting to Azure SQL Database, hardware and server software are handled by Microsoft, so those requirements are irrelevant in this case.

You will need SQL Server Management Studio (SSMS) to run the code samples against both SQL Server 2016 and Azure SQL Database. You can download SSMS and find information about the supported operating systems at the following URL: *https://msdn.microsoft.com/en-us/library/mt238290.aspx.*

Installing and using the source code

Most of the chapters in this book include exercises that let you interactively try out new material learned in the main text. All source code, including exercises and solutions, can be downloaded from the following webpage:

http://aka.ms/T-SQLFund3e/downloads

Follow the instructions to download the TSQLFundamentalsYYYYMMDD.zip file, where YYYYMMDD reflects the last update date of the source code.

Refer to the Appendix, "Getting started," for details about the source code.

Acknowledgments

A number of people contributed to making this book a reality, either directly or indirectly, and deserve thanks and recognition. It's certainly possible I omitted some names unintentionally, and I apologize for this ahead of time.

To Lilach: You're the one who makes me want to be good at what I do. Besides being my inspiration in life, you always take an active role in my books, helping to review the text for the first time.

To my mom, Mila, and to my siblings, Mickey and Ina: Thank you for the constant support and for accepting the fact that I'm away. To my dad, Gabi, who loved puzzles, logic, and numbers: I attribute my affinity to SQL to you; we all miss you a lot.

To the technical reviewer of the book, Bob Beauchemin: You've been around in the SQL Server community for many years. I was always impressed by your extensive knowledge and was happy that you agreed to work with me on this book.

To Steve Kass, Dejan Sarka, Gianluca Hotz, and Herbert Albert: Thanks for your valuable advice during the planning phases of the book. I had to make some hard decisions in terms of what to include and what not to include in the book, and your advice was very helpful.

Many thanks to the book's editors. To Devon Musgrave, who played the acquisitions editor role: You are the one who made this book a reality and handled all the initial stages. I realize that this book is likely one of many you were responsible for, and I'd like to thank you for dedicating the time and effort that you did. To Carol Dillingham, the book's developmental editor and project editor, many thanks for your excellent handling; I always enjoy working with you on my books. Also thanks to Roger LeBlanc for his fine copy edits, and to Christian Holdener for his project management.

To SolidQ, my company for over a decade: It's gratifying to be part of such a great company that evolved into what it is today. The members of this company are much more than colleagues to me; they are partners, friends, and family. To Fernando G. Guerrero, Antonio Soto, and Douglas McDowell: thanks for leading the company. To my many colleagues: It's an honor to be part of this amazingly talented group.

To members of the Microsoft SQL Server development team, past and present: Tobias Ternstrom, Lubor Kollar, Umachandar Jayachandran (UC), Boris Baryshnikov, Conor Cunningham, Kevin Farlee, Josde Bruijn, Marc Friedman, Drazen Sumic, Borko Novakovic, Milan Stojic, Milan Ruzic, Jovan Popovic, Lindsey Allen, Craig Freedman, Campbell Fraser, Eric Hanson, Mark Souza, Dave Campbell, César Galindo-Legaria, Pedro Lopes, and I'm sure many others. Thanks for creating such a great product, and thanks for all the time you spent meeting with me and responding to my emails, addressing my questions, and answering my requests for clarification.

To members of the SQL Server Pro editorial team, Tim Ford and Debra Donston-Miller: I've been writing for the magazine for almost two decades, and I'm grateful for the opportunity to share my knowledge with the magazine's readers.

To Data Platform MVPs, past and present: Paul White, Alejandro Mesa, Erland Sommarskog, Aaron Bertrand, Tibor Karaszi, Benjamin Nevarez, Simon Sabin, Darren Green, Allan Mitchell, Tony Rogerson, and many others—and to the Data Platform MVP lead, Jennifer Moser. This is a great program that I'm grateful for and proud to be part of. The level of expertise of this group is amazing, and I'm always excited when we all get to meet, both to share ideas and just to catch up at a personal level over beers.

Finally, to my students: Teaching about T-SQL is what drives me. It's my passion. Thanks for allowing me to fulfill my calling and for all the great questions that make me seek more knowledge.

Errata, updates, & book support

We've made every effort to ensure the accuracy of this book and its companion content. You can access updates to this book—in the form of a list of submitted errata and their related corrections—at:

http://aka.ms/T-SQLFund3e/errata

If you discover an error that is not already listed, please submit it to us at the same page.

If you need additional support, email Microsoft Press Book Support at *mspinput@microsoft.com*.

Please note that product support for Microsoft software and hardware is not offered through the previous addresses. For help with Microsoft software or hardware, go to *http://support.microsoft.com*.

Free ebooks from Microsoft Press

From technical overviews to in-depth information on special topics, the free ebooks from Microsoft Press cover a wide range of topics. These ebooks are available in PDF, EPUB, and Mobi for Kindle formats, ready for you to download at:

http://aka.ms/mspressfree

Check back often to see what is new!

We want to hear from you

At Microsoft Press, your satisfaction is our top priority, and your feedback our most valuable asset. Please tell us what you think of this book at:

http://aka.ms/tellpress

We know you're busy, so we've kept it short with just a few questions. Your answers go directly to the editors at Microsoft Press. (No personal information will be requested.) Thanks in advance for your input!

Stay in touch

Let's keep the conversation going! We're on Twitter: *http://twitter.com/MicrosoftPress*.

CHAPTER 1

Background to T-SQL querying and programming

You're about to embark on a journey to a land that is like no other—a land that has its own set of laws. If reading this book is your first step in learning Transact-SQL (T-SQL), you should feel like Alice—just before she started her adventures in Wonderland. For me, the journey has not ended; instead, it's an ongoing path filled with new discoveries. I envy you; some of the most exciting discoveries are still ahead of you!

I've been involved with T-SQL for many years: teaching, speaking, writing, and consulting about it. For me, T-SQL is more than just a language—it's a way of thinking. In my first few books about T-SQL, I've written extensively on advanced topics, and for years, I have postponed writing about fundamentals. This is not because T-SQL fundamentals are simple or easy—in fact, it's just the opposite. The apparent simplicity of the language is misleading. I could explain the language syntax elements in a superficial manner and have you writing queries within minutes. But that approach would only hold you back in the long run and make it harder for you to understand the essence of the language.

Acting as your guide while you take your first steps in this realm is a big responsibility. I wanted to make sure that I spent enough time and effort exploring and understanding the language before writing about fundamentals. T-SQL is deep; learning the fundamentals the right way involves much more than just understanding the syntax elements and coding a query that returns the right output. You pretty much need to forget what you know about other programming languages and start thinking in terms of T-SQL.

Theoretical background

SQL stands for *Structured Query Language*. SQL is a standard language that was designed to query and manage data in relational database management systems (RDBMSs). An RDBMS is a database management system based on the relational model (a semantic model for representing data), which in turn is based on two mathematical branches: set theory and predicate logic. Many other programming languages and various aspects of computing evolved pretty much as a result of intuition. In contrast, to the degree that SQL is based on the relational model, it is based on a firm foundation—applied mathematics. T-SQL thus sits on wide and solid shoulders. Microsoft provides T-SQL as a dialect of, or extension to, SQL in Microsoft SQL Server data-management software, its RDBMS.

This section provides a brief theoretical background about SQL, set theory and predicate logic, the relational model, and types of database systems. Because this book is neither a mathematics book nor a design/data-modeling book, the theoretical information provided here is informal and by no means complete. The goals are to give you a context for the T-SQL language and to deliver the key points that are integral to correctly understanding T-SQL later in the book.

Language independence

The relational model is language independent. That is, you can apply data management and manipulation following the relational model's principles with languages other than SQL—for example, with C# in an object model. Today it is common to see RDBMSs that support languages other than a dialect of SQL, such as the CLR integration in SQL Server, with which you can handle tasks that historically you handled mainly with SQL, such as data manipulation.

Also, you should realize from the start that SQL deviates from the relational model in several ways. Some even say that a new language—one that more closely follows the relational model—should replace SQL. But to date, SQL is the industrial language used by all leading RDBMSs in practice.

See Also *For details about the deviations of SQL from the relational model, as well as how to use SQL in a relational way, see this book on the topic:* SQL and Relational Theory: How to Write Accurate SQL Code, Third Edition *by C. J. Date (O'Reilly Media, 2015).*

SQL

SQL is both an ANSI and ISO standard language based on the relational model, designed for querying and managing data in an RDBMS.

In the early 1970s, IBM developed a language called SEQUEL (short for Structured English QUEry Language) for its RDBMS product called System R. The name of the language was later changed from SEQUEL to SQL because of a trademark dispute. SQL first became an ANSI standard in 1986, and then an ISO standard in 1987. Since 1986, the American National Standards Institute (ANSI) and the International Organization for Standardization (ISO) have been releasing revisions for the SQL standard every few years. So far, the following standards have been released: SQL-86 (1986), SQL-89 (1989), SQL-92 (1992), SQL:1999 (1999), SQL:2003 (2003), SQL:2006 (2006), SQL:2008 (2008), and SQL:2011 (2011). The SQL standard is made of multiple parts. Part 1 (Framework) and Part 2 (Foundation) pertain to the SQL language, whereas the other parts define standard extensions, such as SQL for XML and SQL-Java integration.

Interestingly, SQL resembles English and is also very logical. Unlike many programming languages, which use an imperative programming paradigm, SQL uses a declarative one. That is, SQL requires you to specify *what* you want to get and not *how* to get it, letting the RDBMS figure out the physical mechanics required to process your request.

SQL has several categories of statements, including Data Definition Language (DDL), Data Manipulation Language (DML), and Data Control Language (DCL). DDL deals with object definitions and includes statements such as *CREATE, ALTER,* and *DROP.* DML allows you to query and modify data and includes statements such as *SELECT, INSERT, UPDATE, DELETE, TRUNCATE,* and *MERGE.* It's a common misunderstanding that DML includes only data-modification statements, but as I mentioned, it also includes *SELECT.* Another common misunderstanding is that *TRUNCATE* is a DDL statement, but in fact it is a DML statement. DCL deals with permissions and includes statements such as *GRANT* and *REVOKE.* This book focuses on DML.

T-SQL is based on standard SQL, but it also provides some nonstandard/proprietary extensions. Moreover, T-SQL does not implement all of standard SQL. In other words, T-SQL is both a subset and a superset of SQL. When describing a language element for the first time, I'll typically mention whether it is standard.

Set theory

Set theory, which originated with the mathematician Georg Cantor, is one of the mathematical branches on which the relational model is based. Cantor's definition of a set follows:

> *By a "set" we mean any collection M into a whole of definite, distinct objects m (which are called the "elements" of M) of our perception or of our thought.*
>
> *—Joseph W. Dauben and Georg Cantor (Princeton University Press, 1990)*

Every word in the definition has a deep and crucial meaning. The definitions of a set and set membership are axioms that are not supported by proofs. Each element belongs to a universe, and either is or is not a member of the set.

Let's start with the word *whole* in Cantor's definition. A set should be considered a single entity. Your focus should be on the collection of objects as opposed to the individual objects that make up the collection. Later on, when you write T-SQL queries against tables in a database (such as a table of employees), you should think of the set of employees as a whole rather than the individual employees. This might sound trivial and simple enough, but apparently many programmers have difficulty adopting this way of thinking.

The word *distinct* means that every element of a set must be unique. Jumping ahead to tables in a database, you can enforce the uniqueness of rows in a table by defining key constraints. Without a key, you won't be able to uniquely identify rows, and therefore the table won't qualify as a set. Rather, the table would be a *multiset* or a *bag*.

The phrase *of our perception or of our thought* implies that the definition of a set is subjective. Consider a classroom: one person might perceive a set of people, whereas another might perceive a set of students and a set of teachers. Therefore, you have a substantial amount of freedom in defining sets. When you design a data model for your database, the design process should carefully consider the subjective needs of the application to determine adequate definitions for the entities involved.

As for the word *object*, the definition of a set is not restricted to physical objects, such as cars or employees, but rather is relevant to abstract objects as well, such as prime numbers or lines.

What Cantor's definition of a set leaves out is probably as important as what it includes. Notice that the definition doesn't mention any order among the set elements. The order in which set elements are listed is not important. The formal notation for listing set elements uses curly brackets: {a, b, c}. Because order has no relevance, you can express the same set as *{b, a, c}* or *{b, c, a}*. Jumping ahead to the set of attributes (called *columns* in SQL) that make up the heading of a relation (called a *table* in SQL), an element is supposed to be identified by name—not by ordinal position.

Similarly, consider the set of tuples (called *rows* by SQL) that make up the body of the relation; an element is identified by its key values—not by position. Many programmers have a hard time adapting to the idea that, with respect to querying tables, there is no order among the rows. In other words, a query against a table can return table rows in *any order* unless you explicitly request that the data be sorted in a specific way, perhaps for presentation purposes.

Predicate logic

Predicate logic, whose roots reach back to ancient Greece, is another branch of mathematics on which the relational model is based. Dr. Edgar F. Codd, in creating the relational model, had the insight to connect predicate logic to both the management and querying of data. Loosely speaking, a *predicate* is a property or an expression that either holds or doesn't hold—in other words, is either true or false. The relational model relies on predicates to maintain the logical integrity of the data and define its structure. One example of a predicate used to enforce integrity is a constraint defined in a table called *Employees* that allows only employees with a salary greater than zero to be stored in the table. The predicate is "salary greater than zero" (T-SQL expression: *salary > 0*).

You can also use predicates when filtering data to define subsets, and more. For example, if you need to query the *Employees* table and return only rows for employees from the sales department, you use the predicate "department equals sales" in your query filter (T-SQL expression: *department = 'sales'*).

In set theory, you can use predicates to define sets. This is helpful because you can't always define a set by listing all its elements (for example, infinite sets), and sometimes for brevity it's more convenient to define a set based on a property. As an example of an infinite set defined with a predicate, the set of all prime numbers can be defined with the following predicate: "*x* is a positive integer greater than 1 that is divisible only by 1 and itself." For any specified value, the predicate is either true or not true. The set of all prime numbers is the set of all elements for which the predicate is true. As an example of a finite set defined with a predicate, the set *{0, 1, 2, 3, 4, 5, 6, 7, 8, 9}* can be defined as the set of all elements for which the following predicate holds true: "*x* is an integer greater than or equal to 0 and smaller than or equal to 9."

The relational model

The relational model is a semantic model for data management and manipulation and is based on set theory and predicate logic. As mentioned earlier, it was created by Dr. Edgar F. Codd, and later explained and developed by Chris Date, Hugh Darwen, and others. The first version of the relational model was proposed by Codd in 1969 in an IBM research report called "Derivability, Redundancy, and

Consistency of Relations Stored in Large Data Banks." A revised version was proposed by Codd in 1970 in a paper called "A Relational Model of Data for Large Shared Data Banks," published in the journal *Communications of the ACM*.

The goal of the relational model is to enable consistent representation of data with minimal or no redundancy and without sacrificing completeness, and to define data integrity (enforcement of data consistency) as part of the model. An RDBMS is supposed to implement the relational model and provide the means to store, manage, enforce the integrity of, and query data. The fact that the relational model is based on a strong mathematical foundation means that given a certain data-model instance (from which a physical database will later be generated), you can tell with certainty when a design is flawed, rather than relying solely on intuition.

The relational model involves concepts such as propositions, predicates, relations, tuples, attributes, and more. For nonmathematicians, these concepts can be quite intimidating. The sections that follow cover some key aspects of the model in an informal, nonmathematical manner and explain how they relate to databases.

Propositions, predicates, and relations

The common belief that the term *relational* stems from relationships between tables is incorrect. "Relational" actually pertains to the mathematical term *relation*. In set theory, a relation is a representation of a set. In the relational model, a relation is a set of related information, with the counterpart in SQL being a table—albeit not an exact counterpart. A key point in the relational model is that a single relation should represent a single set (for example, *Customers*). Note that operations on relations (based on relational algebra) result in a relation (for example, a join between two relations).

Note The relational model distinguishes between a *relation* and a *relation variable*, but to keep things simple, I won't get into this distinction. Instead, I'll use the term *relation* for both cases. Also, a relation is made of a heading and a body. The heading consists of a set of attributes (called *columns* in SQL), where each element is identified by an attribute name and a type name. The body consists of a set of tuples (called *rows* in SQL), where each element is identified by a key. To keep things simple, I'll refer to a table as a set of rows.

When you design a data model for a database, you represent all data with relations (tables). You start by identifying propositions that you will need to represent in your database. A proposition is an assertion or a statement that must be true or false. For example, the statement, "Employee Itzik Ben-Gan was born on February 12, 1971, and works in the IT department" is a proposition. If this proposition is true, it will manifest itself as a row in a table of *Employees*. A false proposition simply won't manifest itself. This presumption is known as the *closed-world assumption (CWA)*.

The next step is to formalize the propositions. You do this by taking out the actual data (the body of the relation) and defining the structure (the heading of the relation)—for example, by creating predicates out of propositions. You can think of predicates as parameterized propositions. The heading of a relation comprises a set of attributes. Note the use of the term "set"; in the relational model, attributes are unordered and distinct. An attribute is identified by an attribute name and a type name. For example, the heading of an *Employees* relation might consist of the following attributes (expressed as pairs of attribute names and type names): *employeeid* integer, *firstname* character string, *lastname* character string, *birthdate* date, and *departmentid* integer.

A *type* is one of the most fundamental building blocks for relations. A type constrains an attribute to a certain set of possible or valid values. For example, the type *INT* is the set of all integers in the range –2,147,483,648 to 2,147,483,647. A type is one of the simplest forms of a predicate in a database because it restricts the attribute values that are allowed. For example, the database would not accept a proposition where an employee birth date is February 31, 1971 (not to mention a birth date stated as something like "abc!"). Note that types are not restricted to base types such as integers or character strings; a type also can be an enumeration of possible values, such as an enumeration of possible job positions. A type can be simple or complex. Probably the best way to think of a type is as a class—encapsulated data and the behavior supporting it. An example of a complex type is a geometry type that supports polygons.

Missing values

One aspect of the relational model is the source of many passionate debates—whether predicates should be restricted to two-valued logic. That is, in two-valued predicate logic, a predicate is either true or false. If a predicate is not true, it must be false. Use of two-valued predicate logic follows a mathematical law called "the law of excluded middle." However, some say that there's room for three-valued (or even four-valued) predicate logic, taking into account cases where values are missing. A predicate involving a missing value yields neither *true* nor *false*—it yields *unknown*.

Take, for example, a mobile phone attribute of an *Employees* relation. Suppose that a certain employee's mobile phone number is missing. How do you represent this fact in the database? In a three-valued logic implementation, the mobile phone attribute should allow the use of a special marker for a missing value. Then a predicate comparing the mobile phone attribute with some specific number will yield *unknown* for the case with the missing value. Three-valued predicate logic refers to the three possible logical values that can result from a predicate—*true*, *false*, and *unknown*.

Some people believe that three-valued predicate logic is nonrelational, whereas others believe that it is relational. Codd actually advocated for four-valued predicate logic, saying that there were two different cases of missing values: missing but applicable (A-Values marker), and missing but inapplicable (I-Values marker). An example of "missing but applicable" is when an employee has a mobile phone, but you don't know what the mobile phone number is. An example of "missing but inapplicable" is when an employee doesn't have a mobile phone at all. According to Codd, two special markers should be used to support these two cases of missing values. SQL implements three-valued predicate logic by supporting the *NULL* marker to signify the generic concept of a missing value. Support for *NULLs* and three-valued predicate logic in SQL is the source of a great deal of confusion and complexity, though one can argue that missing values are part of reality. In addition, the alternative—using only two-valued predicate logic—is no less problematic.

Note As mentioned, a *NULL* is not a value but rather a marker for a missing value. Therefore, though unfortunately it's common, the use of the terminology "*NULL* value" is incorrect. The correct terminology is "*NULL* marker" or just "*NULL*." In the book, I chose to use the latter because it's more common in the SQL community.

Constraints

One of the greatest benefits of the relational model is the ability to define data integrity as part of the model. Data integrity is achieved through rules called *constraints* that are defined in the data model and enforced by the RDBMS. The simplest methods of enforcing integrity are assigning an attribute type with its attendant "nullability" (whether it supports or doesn't support *NULLs*). Constraints are also enforced through the model itself; for example, the relation *Orders(orderid, orderdate, duedate, shipdate)* allows three distinct dates per order, whereas the relations *Employees(empid)* and *EmployeeChildren(empid, childname)* allow zero to countable infinity children per employee.

Other examples of constraints include *candidate keys,* which provide entity integrity, and *foreign keys,* which provide referential integrity. A candidate key is a key defined on one or more attributes that prevents more than one occurrence of the same tuple (*row* in SQL) in a relation. A predicate based on a candidate key can uniquely identify a row (such as an employee). You can define multiple candidate keys in a relation. For example, in an *Employees* relation, you can define candidate keys on *employeeid,* on *SSN* (Social Security number), and others. Typically, you arbitrarily choose one of the candidate keys as the *primary key* (for example, *employeeid* in the *Employees* relation) and use that as the preferred way to identify a row. All other candidate keys are known as *alternate keys*.

Foreign keys are used to enforce referential integrity. A foreign key is defined on one or more attributes of a relation (known as the *referencing relation*) and references a candidate key in another (or possibly the same) relation. This constraint restricts the values in the referencing relation's foreign-key attributes to the values that appear in the referenced relation's candidate-key attributes. For example, suppose that the *Employees* relation has a foreign key defined on the attribute *departmentid,* which references the primary-key attribute *departmentid* in the *Departments* relation. This means that the values in *Employees.departmentid* are restricted to the values that appear in *Departments.departmentid.*

Normalization

The relational model also defines *normalization rules* (also known as *normal forms*). Normalization is a formal mathematical process to guarantee that each entity will be represented by a single relation. In a normalized database, you avoid anomalies during data modification and keep redundancy to a minimum without sacrificing completeness. If you follow Entity Relationship Modeling (ERM), and represent each entity and its attributes, you probably won't need normalization; instead, you will apply normalization only to reinforce and ensure that the model is correct. You can find the definition of ERM in the following Wikipedia article: *https://en.wikipedia.org/wiki/Entity%E2%80%93relationship_model.*

The following sections briefly cover the first three normal forms (1NF, 2NF, and 3NF) introduced by Codd.

1NF The first normal form says that the tuples (rows) in the relation (table) must be unique and attributes should be atomic. This is a redundant definition of a relation; in other words, if a table truly represents a relation, it is already in first normal form.

You achieve unique rows in SQL by defining a unique key for the table.

You can operate on attributes only with operations that are defined as part of the attribute's type. Atomicity of attributes is subjective in the same way that the definition of a set is subjective. As an example, should an employee name in an *Employees* relation be expressed with one attribute (*fullname*), two (*firstname* and *lastname*), or three (*firstname*, *middlename*, and *lastname*)? The answer depends on the application. If the application needs to manipulate the parts of the employee's name separately (such as for search purposes), it makes sense to break them apart; otherwise, it doesn't.

In the same way that an attribute might not be atomic enough based on the needs of the applications that use it, an attribute might also be subatomic. For example, if an address attribute is considered atomic for the applications that use it, not including the city as part of the address would violate the first normal form.

This normal form is often misunderstood. Some people think that an attempt to mimic arrays violates the first normal form. An example would be defining a *YearlySales* relation with the following attributes: *salesperson*, *qty2014*, *qty2015*, and *qty2016*. However, in this example, you don't really violate the first normal form; you simply impose a constraint—restricting the data to three specific years: 2014, 2015, and 2016.

2NF The second normal form involves two rules. One rule is that the data must meet the first normal form. The other rule addresses the relationship between nonkey and candidate-key attributes. For every candidate key, every nonkey attribute has to be fully functionally dependent on the entire candidate key. In other words, a nonkey attribute cannot be fully functionally dependent on part of a candidate key. To put it more informally, if you need to obtain any nonkey attribute value, you need to provide the values of all attributes of a candidate key from the same tuple. You can find any value of any attribute of any tuple if you know all the attribute values of a candidate key.

As an example of violating the second normal form, suppose that you define a relation called *Orders* that represents information about orders and order lines. (See Figure 1-1.) The *Orders* relation contains the following attributes: *orderid*, *productid*, *orderdate*, *qty*, *customerid*, and *companyname*. The primary key is defined on *orderid* and *productid*.

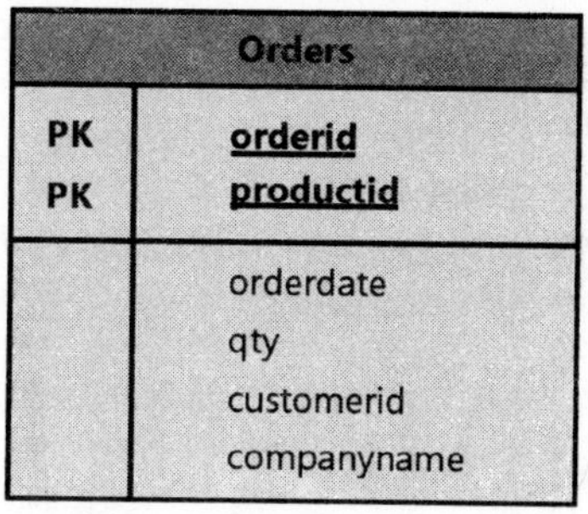

FIGURE 1-1 Data model before applying 2NF.

The second normal form is violated in Figure 1-1 because there are nonkey attributes that depend on only part of a candidate key (the primary key, in this example). For example, you can find the *orderdate* of an order, as well as *customerid* and *companyname*, based on the *orderid* alone.

To conform to the second normal form, you would need to split your original relation into two relations: *Orders* and *OrderDetails* (as shown in Figure 1-2). The *Orders* relation would include the attributes *orderid, orderdate, customerid,* and *companyname*, with the primary key defined on *orderid.* The *OrderDetails* relation would include the attributes *orderid, productid,* and *qty,* with the primary key defined on *orderid* and *productid.*

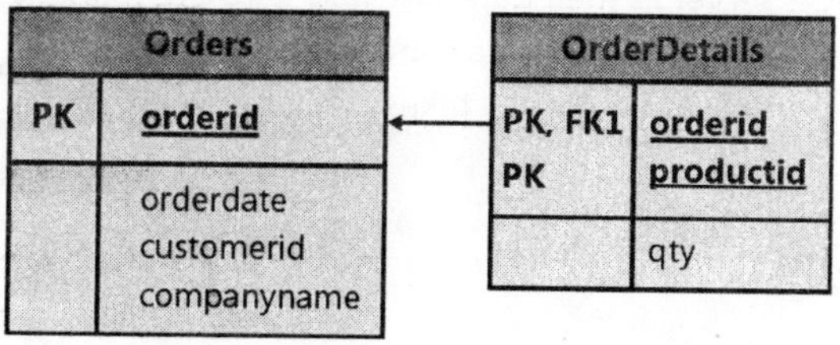

FIGURE 1-2 Data model after applying 2NF and before 3NF.

3NF The third normal form also has two rules. The data must meet the second normal form. Also, all nonkey attributes must be dependent on candidate keys nontransitively. Informally, this rule means that all nonkey attributes must be mutually independent. In other words, one nonkey attribute cannot be dependent on another nonkey attribute.

The *Orders* and *OrderDetails* relations described previously now conform to the second normal form. Remember that the *Orders* relation at this point contains the attributes *orderid, orderdate, customerid,* and *companyname*, with the primary key defined on *orderid.* Both *customerid* and *companyname* depend on the whole primary key—*orderid.* For example, you need the entire primary key to find the *customerid* representing the customer who placed the order. Similarly, you need the whole primary key to find the company name of the customer who placed the order. However, *customerid* and *companyname* are also dependent on each other. To meet the third normal form, you need to add a *Customers* relation (shown in Figure 1-3) with the attributes *customerid* (as the primary key) and *companyname.* Then you can remove the *companyname* attribute from the *Orders* relation.

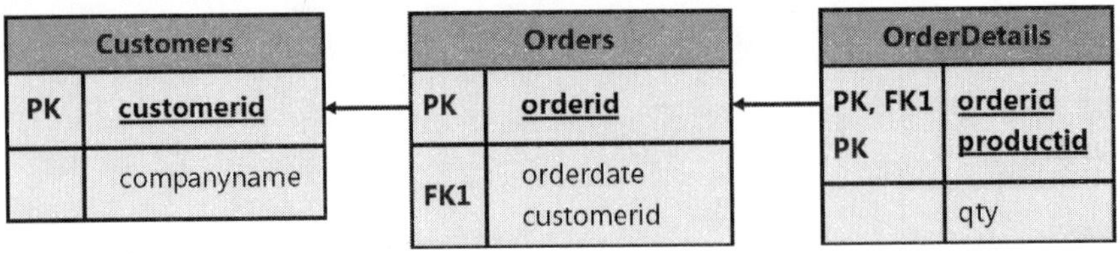

FIGURE 1-3 Data model after applying 3NF.

Informally, 2NF and 3NF are commonly summarized with the sentence, "Every non-key attribute is dependent on the key, the whole key, and nothing but the key—so help me Codd."

There are higher normal forms beyond Codd's original first three normal forms that involve compound primary keys and temporal databases, but they are outside the scope of this book.

> **Note** SQL, as well as T-SQL, permit violating all the normal forms in real tables. It's the data modeler's prerogative and responsibility to design a normalized model.

Types of database systems

Two main types of systems, or workloads, use SQL Server as their database and T-SQL to manage and manipulate the data: online transactional processing (OLTP) and data warehouses (DWs). Figure 1-4 illustrates those systems and the transformation process that usually takes place between them.

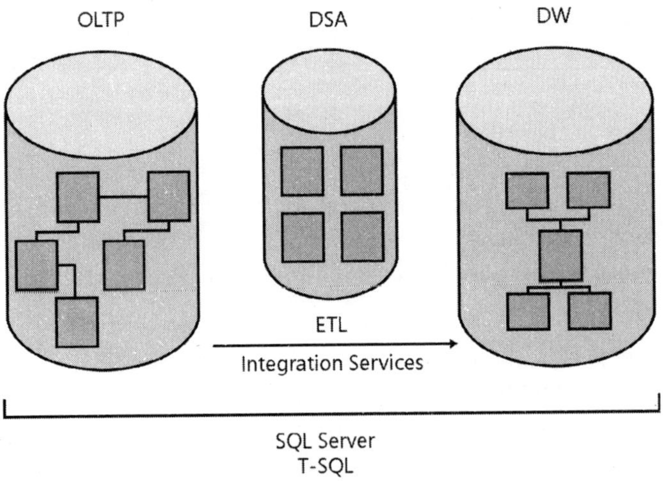

FIGURE 1-4 Classes of database systems.

Here's a quick description of what each acronym represents:

- OLTP: online transactional processing
- DSA: data-staging area
- DW: data warehouse
- ETL: extract, transform, and load

Online transactional processing

Data is entered initially into an online transactional processing system. The primary focus of an OLTP system is data entry and not reporting—transactions mainly insert, update, and delete data. The relational model is targeted primarily at OLTP systems, where a normalized model provides both good performance for data entry and data consistency. In a normalized environment, each table represents a single entity and keeps redundancy to a minimum. When you need to modify a fact, you need to modify it in only one place. This results in optimized performance for data modifications and little chance for error.

However, an OLTP environment is not suitable for reporting purposes because a normalized model usually involves many tables (one for each entity) with complex relationships. Even simple reports require joining many tables, resulting in complex and poorly performing queries.

You can implement an OLTP database in SQL Server and both manage it and query it with T-SQL.

Data warehouses

A *data warehouse* (DW) is an environment designed for data-retrieval and reporting purposes. When it serves an entire organization, such an environment is called a *data warehouse*; when it serves only part of the organization (such as a specific department) or a subject matter area in the organization, it is called a *data mart*. The data model of a data warehouse is designed and optimized mainly to support data-retrieval needs. The model has intentional redundancy, fewer tables, and simpler relationships, ultimately resulting in simpler and more efficient queries than an OLTP environment.

The simplest data-warehouse design is called a *star schema*. The star schema includes several dimension tables and a fact table. Each dimension table represents a subject by which you want to analyze the data. For example, in a system that deals with orders and sales, you will probably want to analyze data by dimensions such as customers, products, employees, and time.

In a star schema, each dimension is implemented as a single table with redundant data. For example, a product dimension could be implemented as a single *ProductDim* table instead of three normalized tables: *Products*, *ProductSubCategories*, and *ProductCategories*. If you normalize a dimension table, which results in multiple tables representing that dimension, you get what's known as a *snowflake dimension*. A schema that contains snowflake dimensions is known as a *snowflake schema*. A star schema is considered a special case of a snowflake schema.

The fact table holds the facts and measures, such as quantity and value, for each relevant combination of dimension keys. For example, for each relevant combination of customer, product, employee, and day, the fact table would have a row containing the quantity and value. Note that data in a data warehouse is typically preaggregated to a certain level of granularity (such as a day), unlike data in an OLTP environment, which is usually recorded at the transaction level.

Historically, early versions of SQL Server mainly targeted OLTP environments, but eventually SQL Server also started targeting data-warehouse systems and data-analysis needs. You can implement a data warehouse as a SQL Server database and manage and query it with T-SQL.

The process that pulls data from source systems (OLTP and others), manipulates it, and loads it into the data warehouse is called *extract, transform, and load*, or *ETL*. SQL Server provides a tool called Microsoft SQL Server Integration Services (SSIS) to handle ETL needs.

Often the ETL process will involve the use of a data-staging area (DSA) between the OLTP and the DW. The DSA usually resides in a relational database, such as a SQL Server database, and is used as the data-cleansing area. The DSA is not open to end users.

SQL Server architecture

This section will introduce you to the SQL Server architecture, the different RDBMS flavors that Microsoft offers, the entities involved—SQL Server instances, databases, schemas, and database objects—and the purpose of each entity.

The ABCs of Microsoft RDBMS flavors

Initially, Microsoft offered mainly one enterprise-level RDBMS—an on-premises flavor called Microsoft SQL Server. These days, Microsoft offers an overwhelming plethora of options as part of its data platform, which constantly keeps evolving. Within its data platform, Microsoft offers three main RDBMS flavors, which you can think of as the *ABC flavors*: A for Appliance, B for Box (on-premises), and C for Cloud.

Box

The box, or on-premises RDBMS flavor, that Microsoft offers is called Microsoft SQL Server, or just SQL Server. This is the traditional flavor, usually installed on the customer's premises. The customer is responsible for everything—getting the hardware, installing the software, patching, high availability and disaster recovery, security, and everything else.

The customer can install multiple instances of the product on the same server (more on this in the next section) and can write queries that interact with multiple databases. It is also possible to switch the connection between databases, unless one of them is a contained database (defined later).

The querying language used is T-SQL. You can run all the code samples and exercises in this book on an on-premises SQL Server implementation, if you want. See the Appendix for details about obtaining and installing an evaluation edition of SQL Server, as well as creating the sample database.

Appliance

The idea behind the appliance flavor is to provide the customer a complete turnkey solution with preconfigured hardware and software. Speed is achieved by things being co-located, with the storage being close to the processing. The appliance is hosted locally at the customer site. Microsoft partners with hardware vendors such as Dell and HP to provide the appliance offering. Experts from Microsoft and the hardware vendor handle the performance, security, and availability aspects for the customer.

There are several appliances available today, one of which is the Microsoft Analytics Platform System (APS), which focuses on data warehousing and big data technologies. This appliance includes a data-warehouse engine called Parallel Data Warehouse (PDW), which implements massively parallel processing (MPP) technology. It also includes HDInsight, which is Microsoft's Hadoop distribution (big data solution). APS also includes a querying technology called PolyBase, which allows using T-SQL queries across relational data from PDW and nonrelational data from HDInsight.

Cloud

Cloud computing provides computing resources on demand from a shared pool of resources. Microsoft's RDBMS technologies can be provided both as private-cloud and public-cloud services. A *private cloud* is cloud infrastructure that services a single organization and usually uses virtualization technology. It's typically hosted locally at the customer site, and maintained by the IT group in the organization. It's about self-service agility, allowing the users to deploy resources on demand. It provides standardization and usage metering. The database engine is usually a box engine (hence the same T-SQL is used to manage and manipulate the data).

As for the public cloud, the services are provided over the network and available to the public. Microsoft provides two forms of public RDBMS cloud services: infrastructure as a service (IaaS) and platform as a service (PaaS). With IaaS, you provision a virtual machine (VM) that resides in Microsoft's cloud infrastructure. As a starting point, you can choose between several preconfigured VMs that already have a certain version and edition of SQL Server (box engine) installed on them. The hardware is maintained by Microsoft, but you're responsible for maintaining and patching the software. It's essentially like maintaining your own SQL Server installation—one that happens to reside on Microsoft's hardware.

With PaaS, Microsoft provides the database cloud platform as a service. It's hosted in Microsoft's data centers. Hardware, software installation and maintenance, high availability and disaster recovery, and patching are all responsibilities of Microsoft. The customer is still responsible for index and query tuning, however.

Microsoft provides a number of PaaS database offerings. For OLTP systems, it offers the Azure SQL Database service. It's also referred to more shortly as just SQL Database. The customer can have multiple databases on the cloud server (a conceptual server, of course) but cannot switch between databases.

Interestingly, Microsoft uses the same code base for SQL Database and SQL Server. So most of the T-SQL language surface is exposed (eventually) in both environments in the same manner. Therefore, most of the T-SQL you'll learn about in this book is applicable to both environments. You can read about the differences that do exist here: *https://azure.microsoft.com/en-us/documentation/articles/sql-database-transact-sql-*

information. You should also note that the update and deployment rate of new versions of SQL Database are faster than that of the on-premises SQL Server. Therefore, some T-SQL features might be exposed in SQL Database before they show up in the on-premises SQL Server version.

Microsoft also provides a PaaS offering for data-warehouse systems called Microsoft Azure SQL Data Warehouse (also called Azure SQL Data Warehouse or just SQL Data Warehouse). This service is basically PDW/APS in the cloud. Microsoft uses the same code base for both the appliance and the cloud service. You manage and manipulate data in APS and SQL Data Warehouse with T-SQL, although it's not the same T-SQL surface as in SQL Server and SQL Database, yet.

Microsoft also offers other cloud data services, such as Data Lake for big data–related services, Azure DocumentDB for NoSQL document database services, and others.

Confused? If it's any consolation, you're not alone. Like I said, Microsoft provides an overwhelming plethora of database-related technologies. Curiously, the one thread that is common to many of them is T-SQL.

SQL Server instances

In the box product, an instance of SQL Server, as illustrated in Figure 1-5, is an installation of a SQL Server database engine or service. You can install multiple instances of on-premises SQL Server on the same computer. Each instance is completely independent of the others in terms of security and the data that it manages, and in all other respects. At the logical level, two different instances residing on the same computer have no more in common than two instances residing on two separate computers. Of course, same-computer instances do share the server's physical resources, such as CPU, memory, and disk.

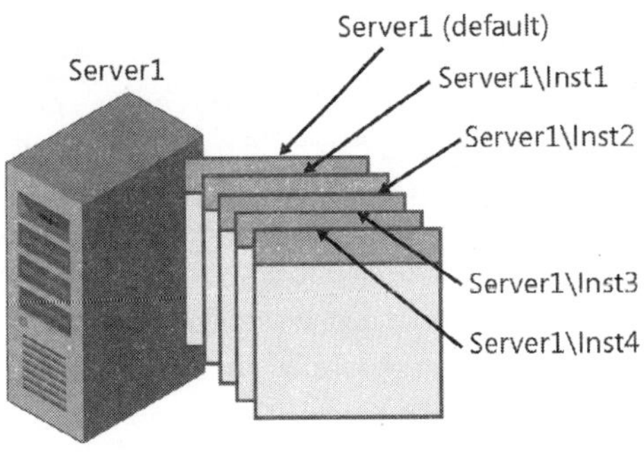

FIGURE 1-5 Multiple instances of SQL Server on the same computer.

You can set up one of the multiple instances on a computer as the *default instance*, whereas all others must be *named instances*. You determine whether an instance is the default or a named one upon installation; you cannot change that decision later. To connect to a default instance, a client application needs to specify the computer's name or IP address. To connect to a named instance, the client needs to specify the computer's name or IP address, followed by a backslash (\), followed by the instance name (as provided upon installation). For example, suppose you have two instances of SQL Server installed on a computer called *Server1*. One of these instances was installed as the default instance, and the other was installed as a named instance called *Inst1*. To connect to the default instance, you need to specify only *Server1* as the server name. However, to connect to the named instance, you need to specify both the server and the instance name: *Server1\Inst1*.

There are various reasons why you might want to install multiple instances of SQL Server on the same computer, but I'll mention only a couple here. One reason is to save on support costs. For example, to test the functionality of features in response to support calls or reproduce errors that users encounter in the production environment, the support department needs local installations of SQL Server that mimic the user's production environment in terms of version, edition, and service pack of SQL Server. If an organization has multiple user environments, the support department needs multiple installations of SQL Server. Rather than having multiple computers, each hosting a different installation of SQL Server that must be supported separately, the support department can have one computer with multiple installed instances. Of course, you can achieve a similar result by using multiple virtual machines.

As another example, consider people like me who teach and lecture about SQL Server. For us, it is convenient to be able to install multiple instances of SQL Server on the same laptop. This way, we can perform demonstrations against different versions of the product, showing differences in behavior between versions, and so on.

As a final example, providers of database services sometimes need to guarantee their customers complete security separation of their data from other customers' data. At least in the past, the database provider could have a very powerful data center hosting multiple instances of SQL Server, rather than needing to maintain multiple less-powerful computers, each hosting a different instance. More recently, cloud solutions and advanced virtualization technologies make it possible to achieve similar goals.

Databases

You can think of a database as a container of objects such as tables, views, stored procedures, and other objects. Each instance of SQL Server can contain multiple databases, as illustrated in Figure 1-6. When you install an on-premises flavor of SQL Server, the setup program creates several system databases that hold system data and serve internal purposes. After the installation of SQL Server, you can create your own user databases that will hold application data.

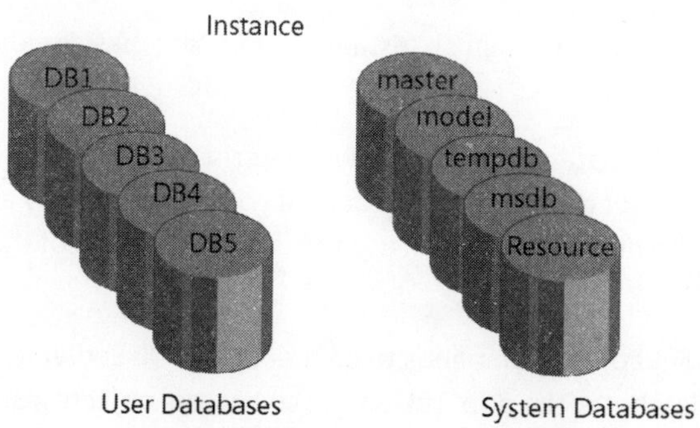

FIGURE 1-6 An example of multiple databases on a SQL Server instance.

The system databases that the setup program creates include *master*, *Resource*, *model*, *tempdb*, and *msdb*. A description of each follows:

- ***master*** The *master* database holds instance-wide metadata information, the server configuration, information about all databases in the instance, and initialization information.
- ***Resource*** The *Resource* database is a hidden, read-only database that holds the definitions of all system objects. When you query system objects in a database, they appear to reside in the *sys schema* of the local database, but in actuality their definitions reside in the *Resource* database.
- ***model*** The *model* database is used as a template for new databases. Every new database you create is initially created as a copy of *model*. So if you want certain objects (such as data types) to appear in all new databases you create, or certain database properties to be configured in a certain way in all new databases, you need to create those objects and configure those properties in the *model* database. Note that changes you apply to the *model* database will not affect existing databases—only new databases you create in the future.
- ***tempdb*** The *tempdb* database is where SQL Server stores temporary data such as work tables, sort and hash table data, row versioning information, and so on. With SQL Server, you can create temporary tables for your own use, and the physical location of those temporary tables is *tempdb*. Note that this database is destroyed and re-created as a copy of the *model* database every time you restart the instance of SQL Server.
- ***msdb*** The *msdb* database is used mainly by a service called SQL Server Agent to store its data. SQL Server Agent is in charge of automation, which includes entities such as jobs, schedules, and alerts. SQL Server Agent is also the service in charge of replication. The *msdb* database also holds information related to other SQL Server features, such as Database Mail, Service Broker, backups, and more.

In an on-premises installation of SQL Server, you can connect directly to the system databases *master*, *model*, *tempdb*, and *msdb*. In SQL Database, you can connect directly only to the system database *master*. If you create temporary tables or declare table variables (more on this topic in Chapter 11, "Programmable objects"), they are created in *tempdb*, but you cannot connect directly to *tempdb* and explicitly create user objects there.

You can create multiple user databases (up to 32,767) within an instance. A user database holds objects and data for an application.

You can define a property called *collation* at the database level that will determine default language support, case sensitivity, and sort order for character data in that database. If you do not specify a collation for the database when you create it, the new database will use the default collation of the instance (chosen upon installation).

To run T-SQL code against a database, a client application needs to connect to a SQL Server instance and be in the context of, or use, the relevant database. The application can still access objects from other databases by adding the database name as a prefix.

In terms of security, to be able to connect to a SQL Server instance, the database administrator (DBA) must create a *login* for you. The login can be tied to your Microsoft Windows credentials, in which case it is called a *Windows authenticated login*. With a Windows authenticated login, you can't provide login and password information when connecting to SQL Server because you already provided those when you logged on to Windows. The login can be independent of your Windows credentials, in which case it's called a *SQL Server authenticated login*. When connecting to SQL Server using a SQL Server authenticated login, you will need to provide both a login name and a password.

The DBA needs to map your login to a *database user* in each database you are supposed to have access to. The database user is the entity that is granted permissions to objects in the database.

SQL Server supports a feature called *contained databases* that breaks the connection between a database user and an instance-level login. The user (Windows or SQL authenticated) is fully contained within the specific database and is not tied to a login at the instance level. When connecting to SQL Server, the user needs to specify the database he or she is connecting to, and the user cannot subsequently switch to other user databases.

So far, I've mainly mentioned the logical aspects of databases. If you're using SQL Database, your only concern is that logical layer. You do not deal with the physical layout of the database data and log files, *tempdb*, and so on. But if you're using a box version of SQL Server, you are responsible for the physical layer as well. Figure 1-7 shows a diagram of the physical database layout.

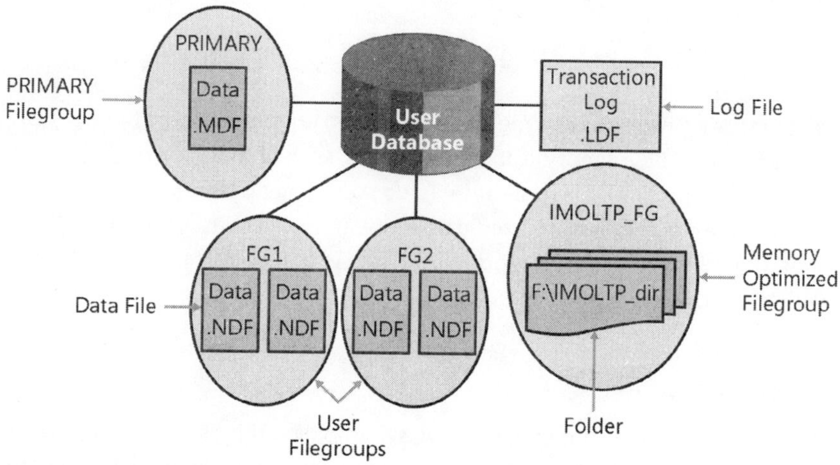

FIGURE 1-7 Database layout.

The database is made up of data files, transaction log files, and optionally checkpoint files holding memory-optimized data (part of a feature called *In-Memory OLTP*, which I describe shortly). When you create a database, you can define various properties for data and log files, including the file name, location, initial size, maximum size, and an autogrowth increment. Each database must have at least one data file and at least one log file (the default in SQL Server). The data files hold object data, and the log files hold information that SQL Server needs to maintain transactions.

Although SQL Server can write to multiple data files in parallel, it can write to only one log file at a time, in a sequential manner. Therefore, unlike with data files, having multiple log files does not result in a performance benefit. You might need to add log files if the disk drive where the log resides runs out of space.

Data files are organized in logical groups called *filegroups*. A filegroup is the target for creating an object, such as a table or an index. The object data will be spread across the files that belong to the target filegroup. Filegroups are your way of controlling the physical locations of your objects. A database must have at least one filegroup called *PRIMARY*, and it can optionally have other user filegroups as well. The *PRIMARY* filegroup contains the primary data file (which has an .mdf extension) for the database, and the database's system catalog. You can optionally add secondary data files (which have an .ndf extension) to *PRIMARY*. User filegroups contain only secondary data files. You can decide which filegroup is marked as the default filegroup. Objects are created in the default filegroup when the object creation statement does not explicitly specify a different target filegroup.

File extensions .mdf, .ldf, and .ndf

The database file extensions .mdf and .ldf are quite straightforward. The extension *.mdf* stands for *Master Data File* (not to be confused with the *master* database), and *.ldf* stands for *Log Data File*. According to one anecdote, when discussing the extension for the secondary data files, one of the developers suggested, humorously, using .ndf to represent "Not Master Data File," and the idea was accepted.

The SQL Server database engine includes a memory-optimized engine called In-Memory OLTP. You can use this feature to integrate memory-optimized objects, such as memory-optimized tables and natively compiled procedures, into your database. To do so, you need to create a filegroup in the database marked as containing memory-optimized data and, within it, at least one path to a folder. SQL Server stores checkpoint files with memory-optimized data in that folder, and it uses those to recover the data every time SQL Server is restarted.

Schemas and objects

When I said earlier that a database is a container of objects, I simplified things a bit. As illustrated in Figure 1-8, a database contains schemas, and schemas contain objects. You can think of a schema as a container of objects, such as tables, views, stored procedures, and others.

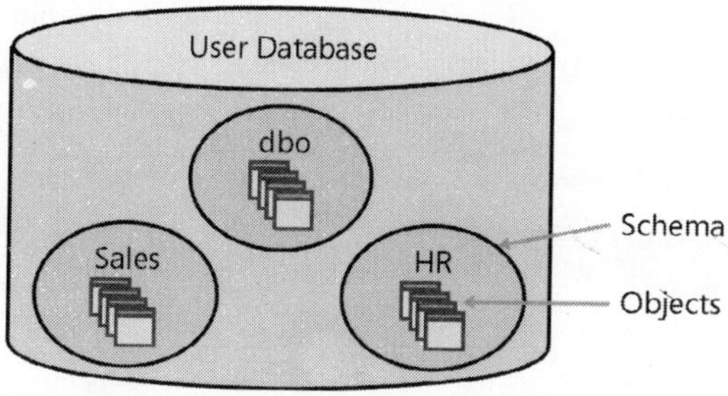

FIGURE 1-8 A database, schemas, and database objects.

You can control permissions at the schema level. For example, you can grant a user SELECT permissions on a schema, allowing the user to query data from all objects in that schema. So security is one of the considerations for determining how to arrange objects in schemas.

The schema is also a namespace—it is used as a prefix to the object name. For example, suppose you have a table named *Orders* in a schema named *Sales*. The schema-qualified object name (also known as the *two-part object name*) is *Sales.Orders*. You can refer to objects in other databases by adding the database name as a prefix (*three-part object name*), and to objects in other instances by adding the instance name as a prefix (*four-part object name*). If you omit the schema name when referring to an object, SQL Server will apply a process to resolve the schema name, such as checking whether the object exists in the user's default schema and, if the object doesn't exist, checking whether it exists in the *dbo* schema. Microsoft recommends that when you refer to objects in your code you always use the two-part object names. There are some relatively insignificant extra costs involved in resolving the schema name when you don't specify it explicitly. But as insignificant as this extra cost might be, why pay it? Also, if multiple objects with the same name exist in different schemas, you might end up getting a different object than the one you wanted.

Creating tables and defining data integrity

This section describes the fundamentals of creating tables and defining data integrity using T-SQL. Feel free to run the included code samples in your environment.

> **More Info** If you don't know yet how to run code against SQL Server, the Appendix will help you get started.

As mentioned earlier, DML rather than DDL is the focus of this book. Still, you need to understand how to create tables and define data integrity. I won't go into the explicit details here, but I'll provide a brief description of the essentials.

Before you look at the code for creating a table, remember that tables reside within schemas, and schemas reside within databases. The examples use the book's sample database, *TSQLV4*, and a schema called *dbo*.

More Info See the Appendix for details on creating the sample database.

The examples here use a schema named *dbo* that is created automatically in every database and is also used as the default schema for users who are not explicitly associated with a different schema.

Creating tables

The following code creates a table named *Employees* in the *dbo* schema in the *TSQLV4* database:

```
USE TSQLV4;

DROP TABLE IF EXISTS dbo.Employees;

CREATE TABLE dbo.Employees
(
  empid     INT         NOT NULL,
  firstname VARCHAR(30) NOT NULL,
  lastname  VARCHAR(30) NOT NULL,
  hiredate  DATE        NOT NULL,
  mgrid     INT         NULL,
  ssn       VARCHAR(20) NOT NULL,
  salary    MONEY       NOT NULL
);
```

The *USE* statement sets the current database context to that of *TSQLV4*. It is important to incorporate the *USE* statement in scripts that create objects to ensure that SQL Server creates the objects in the specified database. In an on-premises SQL Server implementation, the *USE* statement can actually change the database context from one to another. In SQL Database, you cannot switch between different databases, but the *USE* statement will not fail as long as you are already connected to the target database. So even in SQL Database, I recommend having the *USE* statement to ensure that you are connected to the right database when creating your objects.

The *DROP IF EXISTS* command drops the table if it already exists. Note that this command was introduced in SQL Server 2016. If you're using earlier versions of SQL Server, use the following statement instead:

```
IF OBJECT_ID(N'dbo.Employees', N'U') IS NOT NULL DROP TABLE dbo.Employees;
```

The *IF* statement invokes the *OBJECT_ID* function to check whether the *Employees* table already exists in the current database. The *OBJECT_ID* function accepts an object name and type as inputs. The type *U* represents a user table. This function returns the internal object ID if an object with the specified input name and type exists, and *NULL* otherwise. If the function returns a *NULL*, you know that the object doesn't exist. In our case, the code drops the table if it already exists and then creates a new one. Of course, you can choose a different treatment, such as simply not creating the object if it already exists.

The *CREATE TABLE* statement is in charge of defining what I referred to earlier as the heading of the relation. Here you specify the name of the table and, in parentheses, the definition of its attributes (columns).

Notice the use of the two-part name *dbo.Employees* for the table name, as recommended earlier. If you omit the schema name, for ad-hoc queries SQL Server will assume the default schema associated with the database user running the code. For queries in stored procedures, SQL Server will assume the schema associated with the procedure's owner.

For each attribute, you specify the attribute name, data type, and whether the value can be *NULL* (which is called *nullability*).

In the *Employees* table, the attributes *empid* (employee ID) and *mgrid* (manager ID) are each defined with the *INT* (four-byte integer) data type; the *firstname*, *lastname*, and *ssn* (US Social Security number) are defined as *VARCHAR* (variable-length character string with the specified maximum supported number of characters); and *hiredate* is defined as *DATE* and *salary* is defined as *MONEY*.

If you don't explicitly specify whether a column allows or disallows *NULLs*, SQL Server will have to rely on defaults. Standard SQL dictates that when a column's nullability is not specified, the assumption should be *NULL* (allowing *NULLs*), but SQL Server has settings that can change that behavior. I recommend that you be explicit and not rely on defaults. Also, I recommend defining a column as *NOT NULL* unless you have a compelling reason to support *NULLs*. If a column is not supposed to allow *NULLs* and you don't enforce this with a *NOT NULL* constraint, you can rest assured that *NULLs* will occur. In the *Employees* table, all columns are defined as *NOT NULL* except for the *mgrid* column. A *NULL* in the *mgrid* column would represent the fact that the employee has no manager, as in the case of the CEO of the organization.

Coding style

You should be aware of a few general notes regarding coding style, the use of white spaces (space, tab, new line, and so on), and semicolons. I'm not aware of any formal coding styles. My advice is that you use a style that you and your fellow developers feel comfortable with. What ultimately matters most is the consistency, readability, and maintainability of your code. I have tried to reflect these aspects in my code throughout the book.

T-SQL lets you use white spaces quite freely in your code. You can take advantage of white space to facilitate readability. For example, I could have written the code in the previous section as a single line. However, the code wouldn't have been as readable as when it is broken into multiple lines that use indentation.

The practice of using a semicolon to terminate statements is standard and, in fact, is a requirement in several other database platforms. SQL Server requires the semicolon only in particular cases—but in cases where a semicolon is not required, using one doesn't cause problems. I recommend that you adopt the practice of terminating all statements with a semicolon. Not only will doing this improve the readability of your code, but in some cases it can save you some grief. (When a semicolon is required and is *not* specified, the error message SQL Server produces is not always clear.)

> **Note** The SQL Server documentation indicates that not terminating T-SQL statements with a semicolon is a deprecated feature. This means that the long-term goal is to enforce use of the semicolon in a future version of the product. That's one more reason to get into the habit of terminating all your statements, even where it's currently not required.

Defining data integrity

As mentioned earlier, one of the great benefits of the relational model is that data integrity is an integral part of it. Data integrity enforced as part of the model—namely, as part of the table definitions—is considered *declarative data integrity*. Data integrity enforced with code—such as with stored procedures or triggers—is considered *procedural data integrity*.

Data type and nullability choices for attributes and even the data model itself are examples of declarative data integrity constraints. In this section, I will describe other examples of declarative constraints: primary key, unique, foreign key, check, and default constraints. You can define such constraints when creating a table as part of the *CREATE TABLE* statement, or you can define them for already-created tables by using an *ALTER TABLE* statement. All types of constraints except for default constraints can be defined as *composite constraints*—that is, based on more than one attribute.

Primary-key constraints

A primary-key constraint enforces the uniqueness of rows and also disallows *NULLs* in the constraint attributes. Each unique set of values in the constraint attributes can appear only once in the table—in other words, only in one row. An attempt to define a primary-key constraint on a column that allows *NULLs* will be rejected by the RDBMS. Each table can have only one primary key.

Here's an example of defining a primary-key constraint on the *empid* attribute in the *Employees* table that you created earlier:

```
ALTER TABLE dbo.Employees
  ADD CONSTRAINT PK_Employees
  PRIMARY KEY(empid);
```

With this primary key in place, you can be assured that all *empid* values will be unique and known. An attempt to insert or update a row such that the constraint would be violated will be rejected by the RDBMS and result in an error.

To enforce the uniqueness of the logical primary-key constraint, SQL Server will create a unique index behind the scenes. A *unique index* is a physical mechanism used by SQL Server to enforce uniqueness. Indexes (not necessarily unique ones) are also used to speed up queries by avoiding unnecessary full table scans (similar to indexes in books).

Unique constraints

A unique constraint enforces the uniqueness of rows, allowing you to implement the concept of alternate keys from the relational model in your database. Unlike with primary keys, you can define multiple unique constraints within the same table. Also, a unique constraint is not restricted to columns defined as *NOT NULL*.

The following code defines a unique constraint on the *ssn* column in the *Employees* table:

```
ALTER TABLE dbo.Employees
  ADD CONSTRAINT UNQ_Employees_ssn
  UNIQUE(ssn);
```

As with a primary-key constraint, SQL Server will create a unique index behind the scenes as the physical mechanism to enforce the logical unique constraint.

According to standard SQL, a column with a unique constraint is supposed to allow multiple *NULLs* (as if two *NULLs* were different from each other). However, SQL Server's implementation rejects duplicate *NULLs* (as if two *NULLs* were equal to each other). To emulate the standard unique constraint in SQL Server you can use a unique filtered index that filters only non-*NULL* values. For example, suppose that the column *ssn* allowed *NULLs,* and you wanted to create such an index instead of a unique constraint. You would have used the following code:

```
CREATE UNIQUE INDEX idx_ssn_notnull ON dbo.Employees(ssn) WHERE ssn IS NOT NULL;
```

The index is defined as a unique one, and the filter excludes *NULLs* from the index, so duplicate *NULLs* will be allowed, whereas duplicate non-*NULL* values won't be allowed.

Foreign-key constraints

A foreign-key enforces referential integrity. This constraint is defined on one or more attributes in what's called the *referencing* table and points to candidate-key (primary-key or unique-constraint) attributes in what's called the *referenced* table. Note that the referencing and referenced tables can be one and the same. The foreign key's purpose is to restrict the values allowed in the foreign-key columns to those that exist in the referenced columns.

The following code creates a table called *Orders* with a primary key defined on the *orderid* column:

```
DROP TABLE IF EXISTS dbo.Orders;

CREATE TABLE dbo.Orders
(
  orderid   INT          NOT NULL,
  empid     INT          NOT NULL,
  custid    VARCHAR(10)  NOT NULL,
  orderts   DATETIME2    NOT NULL,
  qty       INT          NOT NULL,
  CONSTRAINT PK_Orders
    PRIMARY KEY(orderid)
);
```

Suppose you want to enforce an integrity rule that restricts the values supported by the *empid* column in the *Orders* table to the values that exist in the *empid* column in the *Employees* table. You can achieve this by defining a foreign-key constraint on the *empid* column in the *Orders* table pointing to the *empid* column in the *Employees* table, like the following:

```
ALTER TABLE dbo.Orders
  ADD CONSTRAINT FK_Orders_Employees
  FOREIGN KEY(empid)
  REFERENCES dbo.Employees(empid);
```

Similarly, if you want to restrict the values supported by the *mgrid* column in the *Employees* table to the values that exist in the *empid* column of the same table, you can do so by adding the following foreign key:

```
ALTER TABLE dbo.Employees
  ADD CONSTRAINT FK_Employees_Employees
  FOREIGN KEY(mgrid)
  REFERENCES dbo.Employees(empid);
```

Note that *NULLs* are allowed in the foreign-key columns (*mgrid* in the last example) even if there are no *NULLs* in the referenced candidate-key columns.

The preceding two examples are basic definitions of foreign keys that enforce a referential action called *no action*. No action means that attempts to delete rows from the referenced table or update the referenced candidate-key attributes will be rejected if related rows exist in the referencing table. For example, if you try to delete an employee row from the *Employees* table when there are related orders in the *Orders* table, the RDBMS will reject such an attempt and produce an error.

You can define the foreign key with actions that will compensate for such attempts (to delete rows from the referenced table or update the referenced candidate-key attributes when related rows exist in the referencing table). You can define the options *ON DELETE* and *ON UPDATE* with actions such as *CASCADE*, *SET DEFAULT*, and *SET NULL* as part of the foreign-key definition. *CASCADE* means that the operation (delete or update) will be cascaded to related rows. For example, *ON DELETE CASCADE* means that when you delete a row from the referenced table, the RDBMS will delete the related rows from the referencing table. *SET DEFAULT* and *SET NULL* mean that the compensating action will set the foreign-key attributes of the related rows to the column's default value or *NULL*, respectively. Note that regardless of which action you choose, the referencing table will have only orphaned rows in the case of the exception with *NULLs* that I mentioned earlier. Parents with no children are always allowed.

Check constraints

You can use a *check constraint* to define a predicate that a row must meet to be entered into the table or to be modified. For example, the following check constraint ensures that the salary column in the *Employees* table will support only positive values:

```
ALTER TABLE dbo.Employees
  ADD CONSTRAINT CHK_Employees_salary
  CHECK(salary > 0.00);
```

An attempt to insert or update a row with a nonpositive salary value will be rejected by the RDBMS. Note that a check constraint rejects an attempt to insert or update a row when the predicate evaluates to *FALSE*. The modification will be accepted when the predicate evaluates to either *TRUE* or *UNKNOWN*. For example, salary –1000 will be rejected, whereas salaries 50000 and *NULL* will both be accepted (if the column allowed *NULLs*). As mentioned earlier, SQL is based on three-valued logic, which results in two actual actions. With a check constraint, the row is either accepted or rejected.

When adding check and foreign-key constraints, you can specify an option called *WITH NOCHECK* that tells the RDBMS you want it to bypass constraint checking for existing data. This is considered a bad practice because you cannot be sure your data is consistent. You can also disable or enable existing check and foreign-key constraints.

Default constraints

A default constraint is associated with a particular attribute. It's an expression that is used as the default value when an explicit value is not specified for the attribute when you insert a row. For example, the following code defines a default constraint for the *orderts* attribute (representing the order's time stamp):

```
ALTER TABLE dbo.Orders
  ADD CONSTRAINT DFT_Orders_orderts
  DEFAULT(SYSDATETIME()) FOR orderts;
```

The default expression invokes the *SYSDATETIME* function, which returns the current date and time value. After this default expression is defined, whenever you insert a row in the *Orders* table and do not explicitly specify a value in the *orderts* attribute, SQL Server will set the attribute value to *SYSDATETIME*.

When you're done, run the following code for cleanup:

```
DROP TABLE IF EXISTS dbo.Orders, dbo.Employees;
```

Conclusion

This chapter provided a brief background to T-SQL querying and programming. It presented a theoretical background, explaining the strong foundations that T-SQL is based on. It gave an overview of the SQL Server architecture and concluded with sections that demonstrated how to use T-SQL to create tables and define data integrity. I hope that by now you see that there's something special about SQL, and that it's not just a language that can be learned as an afterthought. This chapter equipped you with fundamental concepts—the actual journey is just about to begin.

CHAPTER 2

Single-table queries

This chapter introduces you to the fundamentals of the *SELECT* statement, focusing for now on queries against a single table. The chapter starts by describing logical query processing—namely, the series of logical phases involved in producing the correct result set of a particular *SELECT* query. The chapter then covers other aspects of single-table queries, including predicates and operators, *CASE* expressions, *NULLs*, all-at-once operations, manipulating character data and date and time data, and querying metadata. Many of the code samples and exercises in this book use a sample database called *TSQLV4*. You can find the instructions for downloading and installing this sample database in the Appendix, "Getting started."

Elements of the *SELECT* statement

The purpose of a *SELECT* statement is to query tables, apply some logical manipulation, and return a result. In this section, I talk about the phases involved in logical query processing. I describe the logical order in which the different query clauses are processed and what happens in each phase.

Note that by "logical query processing," I'm referring to the conceptual way in which standard SQL defines how a query should be processed and the final result achieved. Don't be alarmed if some logical processing phases that I describe here seem inefficient. The database engine doesn't have to follow logical query processing to the letter; rather, it is free to physically process a query differently by rearranging processing phases, as long as the final result would be the same as that dictated by logical query processing. The database engine's query optimizer can—and in fact, often does—make many shortcuts in the physical processing of a query as a result of query optimization.

To describe logical query processing and the various *SELECT* query clauses, I use the query in Listing 2-1 as an example.

LISTING 2-1 Sample query

```
USE TSQLV4;

SELECT empid, YEAR(orderdate) AS orderyear, COUNT(*) AS numorders
FROM Sales.Orders
WHERE custid = 71
GROUP BY empid, YEAR(orderdate)
HAVING COUNT(*) > 1
ORDER BY empid, orderyear;
```

This query filters orders that were placed by customer 71, groups those orders by employee and order year, and filters only groups of employees and years that have more than one order. For the remaining groups, the query presents the employee ID, order year, and count of orders, sorted by the employee ID and order year. For now, don't worry about understanding how this query does what it does; I'll explain the query clauses one at a time and gradually build this query.

The code starts with a *USE* statement that ensures that the database context of your session is the *TSQLV4* sample database. If your session is already in the context of the database you need to query, the *USE* statement is not required.

Before I get into the details of each phase of the *SELECT* statement, notice the order in which the query clauses are logically processed. In most programming languages, the lines of code are processed in the order that they are written. In SQL, things are different. Even though the *SELECT* clause appears first in the query, it is logically processed almost last. The clauses are logically processed in the following order:

1. *FROM*
2. *WHERE*
3. *GROUP BY*
4. *HAVING*
5. *SELECT*
6. *ORDER BY*

So even though syntactically the sample query in Listing 2-1 starts with a *SELECT* clause, logically its clauses are processed in the following order:

```
FROM Sales.Orders
WHERE custid = 71
GROUP BY empid, YEAR(orderdate)
HAVING COUNT(*) > 1
SELECT empid, YEAR  (orderdate) AS orderyear, COUNT(*) AS numorders
ORDER BY empid, orderyear
```

Or, to present it in a more readable manner, here's what the statement does:

1. Queries the rows *from* the *Sales.Orders* table
2. Filters only orders *where* the customer ID is equal to 71
3. *Groups* the orders *by* employee ID and order year
4. Filters only groups (employee ID and order year) *having* more than one order
5. *Selects* (returns) for each group the employee ID, order year, and number of orders
6. *Orders* (sorts) the rows in the output *by* employee ID and order year

You cannot write the query in correct logical order. You have to start with the *SELECT* clause, as shown in Listing 2-1. There's reason behind this discrepancy between the keyed-in order and the logical processing order of the clauses. The designers of SQL envisioned a declarative language with which you provide your request in an English-like manner. Consider an instruction made by one human to another in English, such as, "Bring me the car keys from the top-left drawer in the kitchen." Notice that you start the instruction with the object and then indicate the location where the object resides. But if you were to express the same instruction to a robot, or a computer program, you would have to start with the location before indicating what can be obtained from that location. Your instruction might have been something like, "Go to the kitchen; open the top-left drawer; grab the car keys; bring them to me." The keyed-in order of the query clauses is similar to English—it starts with the *SELECT* clause. Logical query processing order is similar to how you provide instructions to a computer program—with the *FROM* clause processed first.

Now that you understand the order in which the query clauses are logically processed, the next sections explain the details of each phase.

When discussing logical query processing, I refer to query *clauses* and query *phases* (the *WHERE* clause and the *WHERE* phase, for example). A query clause is a syntactical component of a query, so when discussing the syntax of a query element I usually use the term *clause*—for example, "In the *WHERE* clause, you specify a predicate." When discussing the logical manipulation taking place as part of logical query processing, I usually use the term *phase*—for example, "The *WHERE* phase returns rows for which the predicate evaluates to *TRUE*."

Recall my recommendation from the previous chapter regarding the use of a semicolon to terminate statements. At the moment, Microsoft SQL Server doesn't require you to terminate all statements with a semicolon. This is a requirement only in particular cases where the parsing of the code might otherwise be ambiguous. However, I recommend you terminate all statements with a semicolon because it is standard, it improves the code readability, and it is likely that SQL Server will require this in more—if not all—cases in the future. Currently, when a semicolon is not required, adding one doesn't interfere.

The *FROM* clause

The *FROM* clause is the very first query clause that is logically processed. In this clause, you specify the names of the tables you want to query and table operators that operate on those tables. This chapter doesn't get into table operators; I describe those in Chapters 3, 5, and 7. For now, you can just consider the *FROM* clause to be simply where you specify the name of the table you want to query. The sample query in Listing 2-1 queries the *Orders* table in the *Sales* schema, finding 830 rows.

```
FROM Sales.Orders
```

Recall the recommendation I gave in the previous chapter to always schema-qualify object names in your code. When you don't specify the schema name explicitly, SQL Server must resolve it implicitly based on its implicit name-resolution rules. This creates some minor cost and can result in SQL Server choosing a different object than the one you intended. By being explicit, your code is safer in the sense you ensure that you get the object you intended to get. Plus, you don't pay any unnecessary penalties.

To return all rows from a table with no special manipulation, all you need is a query with a *FROM* clause in which you specify the table you want to query, and a *SELECT* clause in which you specify the attributes you want to return. For example, the following statement queries all rows from the *Orders* table in the *Sales* schema, selecting the attributes *orderid, custid, empid, orderdate,* and *freight*.

```
SELECT orderid, custid, empid, orderdate, freight
FROM Sales.Orders;
```

The output of this statement is shown here in abbreviated form:

```
orderid     custid      empid       orderdate  freight
----------- ----------- ----------- ---------- ---------------------
10248       85          5           2014-07-04 32.38
10249       79          6           2014-07-05 11.61
10250       34          4           2014-07-08 65.83
10251       84          3           2014-07-08 41.34
10252       76          4           2014-07-09 51.30
10253       34          3           2014-07-10 58.17
10254       14          5           2014-07-11 22.98
10255       68          9           2014-07-12 148.33
10256       88          3           2014-07-15 13.97
10257       35          4           2014-07-16 81.91
...

(830 row(s) affected)
```

Although it might seem that the output of the query is returned in a particular order, this is not guaranteed. I'll elaborate on this point later in this chapter, in the sections "The *SELECT* clause" and "The *ORDER BY* clause."

Delimiting identifier names

As long as the identifiers in your query comply with rules for the format of regular identifiers, you don't need to delimit the identifier names used for schemas, tables, and columns. The rules for the format of regular identifiers can be found in SQL Server Books Online at the following URL: *http://msdn.microsoft.com/en-us/library/ms175874*. If an identifier is irregular—for example, if it has embedded spaces or special characters, starts with a digit, or is a reserved keyword—you have to delimit it. You can delimit identifiers in SQL Server in a couple of ways. The standard SQL form is to use double quotes—for example, *"Order Details"*. The form specific to T-SQL is to use square brackets—for example, *[Order Details]*—but T-SQL also supports the standard form.

With identifiers that do comply with the rules for the format of regular identifiers, delimiting is optional. For example, a table called *OrderDetails* residing in the *Sales* schema can be referred to as *Sales.OrderDetails* or *"Sales"."OrderDetails"* or *[Sales].[OrderDetails]*. My personal preference is not to use delimiters when they are not required, because they tend to clutter the code. Also, when you're in charge of assigning identifiers, I recommend always using regular ones—for example, *OrderDetails* instead of *Order Details*.

The *WHERE* clause

In the *WHERE* clause, you specify a predicate or logical expression to filter the rows returned by the *FROM* phase. Only rows for which the logical expression evaluates to *TRUE* are returned by the *WHERE* phase to the subsequent logical query processing phase. In the sample query in Listing 2-1, the *WHERE* phase filters only orders placed by customer 71:

```
FROM Sales.Orders
WHERE custid = 71
```

Out of the 830 rows returned by the *FROM* phase, the *WHERE* phase filters only the 31 rows where the customer ID is equal to 71. To see which rows you get back after applying the filter *custid = 71*, run the following query:

```
SELECT orderid, empid, orderdate, freight
FROM Sales.Orders
WHERE custid = 71;
```

This query generates the following output:

```
orderid     empid       orderdate  freight
----------- ----------- ---------- --------
10324       9           2014-10-08 214.27
10393       1           2014-12-25 126.56
10398       2           2014-12-30 89.16
10440       4           2015-02-10 86.53
10452       8           2015-02-20 140.26
10510       6           2015-04-18 367.63
10555       6           2015-06-02 252.49
10603       8           2015-07-18 48.77
10607       5           2015-07-22 200.24
10612       1           2015-07-28 544.08
10627       8           2015-08-11 107.46
10657       2           2015-09-04 352.69
10678       7           2015-09-23 388.98
10700       3           2015-10-10 65.10
10711       5           2015-10-21 52.41
10713       1           2015-10-22 167.05
10714       5           2015-10-22 24.49
10722       8           2015-10-29 74.58
10748       3           2015-11-20 232.55
10757       6           2015-11-27 8.19
10815       2           2016-01-05 14.62
10847       4           2016-01-22 487.57
10882       4           2016-02-11 23.10
10894       1           2016-02-18 116.13
10941       7           2016-03-11 400.81
10983       2           2016-03-27 657.54
10984       1           2016-03-30 211.22
11002       4           2016-04-06 141.16
11030       7           2016-04-17 830.75
11031       6           2016-04-17 227.22
11064       1           2016-05-01 30.09

(31 row(s) affected)
```

The *WHERE* clause has significance when it comes to query performance. Based on what you have in the filter expression, SQL Server evaluates the use of indexes to access the required data. By using indexes, SQL Server can sometimes get the required data with much less work compared to applying full table scans. Query filters also reduce the network traffic created by returning all possible rows to the caller and filtering on the client side.

Earlier, I mentioned that only rows for which the logical expression evaluates to *TRUE* are returned by the *WHERE* phase. Always keep in mind that T-SQL uses three-valued predicate logic, where logical expressions can evaluate to *TRUE, FALSE,* or *UNKNOWN.* With three-valued logic, saying "returns *TRUE*" is not the same as saying "does not return *FALSE*." The *WHERE* phase returns rows for which the logical expression evaluates to *TRUE,* and it doesn't return rows for which the logical expression evaluates to *FALSE* or *UNKNOWN.* I elaborate on this point later in this chapter in the section "*NULLs.*"

The *GROUP BY* clause

You can use the *GROUP BY* phase to arrange the rows returned by the previous logical query processing phase in groups. The groups are determined by the elements you specify in the *GROUP BY* clause. For example, the *GROUP BY* clause in the query in Listing 2-1 has the elements *empid* and *YEAR(orderdate)*:

```
FROM Sales.Orders
WHERE custid = 71
GROUP BY empid, YEAR(orderdate)
```

This means that the *GROUP BY* phase produces a group for each unique combination of employee-ID and order-year values that appears in the data returned by the *WHERE* phase. The expression *YEAR(orderdate)* invokes the *YEAR* function to return only the year part from the *orderdate* column.

The *WHERE* phase returned 31 rows, within which there are 16 unique combinations of employee-ID and order-year values, as shown here:

```
empid       YEAR(orderdate)
----------- ---------------
1           2014
1           2015
1           2016
2           2014
2           2015
2           2016
3           2015
4           2015
4           2016
5           2015
6           2015
6           2016
7           2015
7           2016
8           2015
9           2014
```

Thus, the *GROUP BY* phase creates 16 groups and associates each of the 31 rows returned from the *WHERE* phase with the relevant group.

If the query involves grouping, all phases subsequent to the *GROUP BY* phase—including *HAVING*, *SELECT*, and *ORDER BY*—must operate on groups as opposed to operating on individual rows. Each group is ultimately represented by a single row in the final result of the query. This implies that all expressions you specify in clauses that are processed in phases subsequent to the *GROUP BY* phase are required to guarantee returning a scalar (single value) per group.

Expressions based on elements that participate in the *GROUP BY* clause meet the requirement because, by definition, each group has only one unique occurrence of each *GROUP BY* element. For example, in the group for employee ID 8 and order year 2015, there's only one unique employee-ID value and only one unique order-year value. Therefore, you're allowed to refer to the expressions *empid* and *YEAR(orderdate)* in clauses that are processed in phases subsequent to the *GROUP BY* phase, such as the *SELECT* clause. The following query, for example, returns 16 rows for the 16 groups of employee-ID and order-year values:

```
SELECT empid, YEAR(orderdate) AS orderyear
FROM Sales.Orders
WHERE custid = 71
GROUP BY empid, YEAR(orderdate);
```

This query returns the following output:

```
empid       orderyear
----------- -----------
1           2014
1           2015
1           2016
2           2014
2           2015
2           2016
3           2015
4           2015
4           2016
5           2015
6           2015
6           2016
7           2015
7           2016
8           2015
9           2014

(16 row(s) affected)
```

Elements that do not participate in the *GROUP BY* clause are allowed only as inputs to an aggregate function such as *COUNT*, *SUM*, *AVG*, *MIN*, or *MAX*. For example, the following query returns the total freight and number of orders per employee and order year:

```
SELECT
  empid,
  YEAR(orderdate) AS orderyear,
```

```
  SUM(freight) AS totalfreight,
  COUNT(*) AS numorders
FROM Sales.Orders
WHERE custid = 71
GROUP BY empid, YEAR(orderdate);
```

This query generates the following output:

```
empid       orderyear   totalfreight          numorders
----------- ----------- --------------------- -----------
1           2014        126.56                1
2           2014        89.16                 1
9           2014        214.27                1
1           2015        711.13                2
2           2015        352.69                1
3           2015        297.65                2
4           2015        86.53                 1
5           2015        277.14                3
6           2015        628.31                3
7           2015        388.98                1
8           2015        371.07                4
1           2016        357.44                3
2           2016        672.16                2
4           2016        651.83                3
6           2016        227.22                1
7           2016        1231.56               2

(16 row(s) affected)
```

The expression *SUM(freight)* returns the sum of all freight values in each group, and the function *COUNT(*)* returns the count of rows in each group—which in this case means the number of orders. If you try to refer to an attribute that does not participate in the *GROUP BY* clause (such as *freight*) and not as an input to an aggregate function in any clause that is processed after the *GROUP BY* clause, you get an error—in such a case, there's no guarantee that the expression will return a single value per group. For example, the following query will fail:

```
SELECT empid, YEAR(orderdate) AS orderyear, freight
FROM Sales.Orders
WHERE custid = 71
GROUP BY empid, YEAR(orderdate);
```

SQL Server produces the following error:

```
Msg 8120, Level 16, State 1, Line 1
Column  Sales.Orders.freight' is invalid in the select list because it is not contained in
either an aggregate function or the GROUP BY clause.
```

Note that all aggregate functions ignore *NULLs*, with one exception—*COUNT(*)*. For example, consider a group of five rows with the values *30, 10, NULL, 10, 10* in a column called *qty*. The expression *COUNT(*)* returns 5 because there are five rows in the group, whereas *COUNT(qty)* returns 4 because there are four known values. If you want to handle only distinct occurrences of known values, specify the *DISTINCT* keyword before the input expression to the aggregate function. For example, the expression *COUNT(DISTINCT qty)* returns 2, because there are two distinct known values (30 and 10). The

DISTINCT keyword can be used with other functions as well. For example, although the expression *SUM(qty)* returns 60, the expression *SUM(DISTINCT qty)* returns 40. The expression *AVG(qty)* returns 15, whereas the expression *AVG(DISTINCT qty)* returns 20. As an example of using the *DISTINCT* option with an aggregate function in a complete query, the following code returns the number of distinct (unique) customers handled by each employee in each order year:

```
SELECT
  empid,
  YEAR(orderdate) AS orderyear,
  COUNT(DISTINCT custid) AS numcusts
FROM Sales.Orders
GROUP BY empid, YEAR(orderdate);
```

This query generates the following output:

```
empid       orderyear   numcusts
----------- ----------- -----------
1           2014        22
2           2014        15
3           2014        16
4           2014        26
5           2014        10
6           2014        15
7           2014        11
8           2014        19
9           2014        5
1           2015        40
2           2015        35
3           2015        46
4           2015        57
5           2015        13
6           2015        24
7           2015        30
8           2015        36
9           2015        16
1           2016        32
2           2016        34
3           2016        30
4           2016        33
5           2016        11
6           2016        17
7           2016        21
8           2016        23
9           2016        16

(27 row(s) affected)
```

The *HAVING* clause

Whereas the *WHERE* clause is a row filter, the *HAVING* clause is a group filter. Only groups for which the *HAVING* predicate evaluates to *TRUE* are returned by the *HAVING* phase to the next logical query processing phase. Groups for which the predicate evaluates to *FALSE* or *UNKNOWN* are discarded.

Because the *HAVING* clause is processed after the rows have been grouped, you can refer to aggregate functions in the logical expression. For example, in the query from Listing 2-1, the *HAVING* clause has the logical expression *COUNT(*) > 1*, meaning that the *HAVING* phase filters only groups (employee and order year) with more than one row. The following fragment of the Listing 2-1 query shows the steps that have been processed so far:

```
FROM Sales.Orders
WHERE custid = 71
GROUP BY empid, YEAR(orderdate)
HAVING COUNT(*) > 1
```

Recall that the *GROUP BY* phase created 16 groups of employee ID and order year. Seven of those groups have only one row, so after the *HAVING* clause is processed, nine groups remain. Run the following query to return those nine groups:

```
SELECT empid, YEAR(orderdate) AS orderyear
FROM Sales.Orders
WHERE custid = 71
GROUP BY empid, YEAR(orderdate)
HAVING COUNT(*) > 1;
```

This query returns the following output:

```
empid       orderyear
----------- -----------
1           2015
3           2015
5           2015
6           2015
8           2015
1           2016
2           2016
4           2016
7           2016

(9 row(s) affected)
```

The *SELECT* clause

The *SELECT* clause is where you specify the attributes (columns) you want to return in the result table of the query. You can base the expressions in the *SELECT* list on attributes from the queried tables, with or without further manipulation.

For example, the *SELECT* list in Listing 2-1 has the following expressions: *empid*, *YEAR(orderdate)*, and *COUNT(*)*. If an expression refers to an attribute with no manipulation, such as *empid*, the name of the target attribute is the same as the name of the source attribute. You can optionally assign your own name to the target attribute by using the *AS* clause—for example, *empid AS employee_id*. Expressions that do apply manipulation, such as *YEAR(orderdate)*, or that are not based on a source attribute, such as a call to the function *SYSDATETIME*, won't have a name unless you alias them. T-SQL allows a query to return result columns with no names in certain cases, but the relational model doesn't. I recommend you alias such expressions as *YEAR(orderdate) AS orderyear* so that all result attributes have names. In this respect, the result table returned from the query would be considered relational.

In addition to supporting the *AS* clause, T-SQL supports a couple of other forms with which you can alias expressions. To me, the *AS* clause seems the most readable and intuitive form; therefore, I recommend using it. I will cover the other forms for the sake of completeness and also to describe an elusive bug related to one of them.

In addition to supporting the form *<expression> AS <alias>*, T-SQL also supports the forms *<alias>* = *<expression>* ("alias equals expression") and *<expression> <alias>* ("expression space alias"). An example of the former is *orderyear = YEAR(orderdate)*, and an example of the latter is *YEAR(orderdate) orderyear*. I find the latter particularly unclear and recommend avoiding it, although unfortunately this form is very common in people's code.

Note that if by mistake you miss a comma between two column names in the *SELECT* list, your code won't fail. Instead, SQL Server will assume the second name is an alias for the first column name. As an example, suppose you want to query the columns *orderid* and *orderdate* from the *Sales.Orders* table and you miss the comma between them, as follows:

```
SELECT orderid orderdate
FROM Sales.Orders;
```

This query is considered syntactically valid, as if you intended to alias the *orderid* column as *orderdate*. In the output, you will get only one column holding the order IDs, with the alias *orderdate*:

```
orderdate
-----------
10248
10249
10250
10251
10252
...

(830 row(s) affected)
```

If you're accustomed to using the syntax with the space between an expression and its alias, it will be harder for you to detect such bugs.

With the addition of the *SELECT* phase, the following query clauses from the query in Listing 2-1 have been processed so far:

```
SELECT empid, YEAR(orderdate) AS orderyear, COUNT(*) AS numorders
FROM Sales.Orders
WHERE custid = 71
GROUP BY empid, YEAR(orderdate)
HAVING COUNT(*) > 1
```

The *SELECT* clause produces the result table of the query. In the case of the query in Listing 2-1, the heading of the result table has the attributes *empid*, *orderyear*, and *numorders*, and the body has nine rows (one for each group). Run the following query to return those nine rows:

```
SELECT empid, YEAR(orderdate) AS orderyear, COUNT(*) AS numorders
FROM Sales.Orders
WHERE custid = 71
GROUP BY empid, YEAR(orderdate)
HAVING COUNT(*) > 1;
```

This query generates the following output:

```
empid       orderyear   numorders
----------- ----------- -----------
1           2015        2
3           2015        2
5           2015        3
6           2015        3
8           2015        4
1           2016        3
2           2016        2
4           2016        3
7           2016        2

(9 row(s) affected)
```

Remember that the *SELECT* clause is processed after the *FROM*, *WHERE*, *GROUP BY*, and *HAVING* clauses. This means that aliases assigned to expressions in the *SELECT* clause do not exist as far as clauses that are processed before the *SELECT* clause are concerned. It's a typical mistake to try and refer to expression aliases in clauses that are processed before the *SELECT* clause, such as in the following example in which the attempt is made in the WHERE clause:

```
SELECT orderid, YEAR(orderdate) AS orderyear
FROM Sales.Orders
WHERE orderyear > 2015;
```

At first glance, this query might seem valid, but if you consider that the column aliases are created in the *SELECT* phase—which is processed after the *WHERE* phase—you can see that the reference to the *orderyear* alias in the *WHERE* clause is invalid. In fact, SQL Server produces the following error:

```
Msg 207, Level 16, State 1, Line 3
Invalid column name 'orderyear'.
```

Amusingly, a lecture attendee once asked me in all seriousness when Microsoft is going to fix this bug. As you can gather from this chapter, this behavior is not a bug; rather, it is by design. Also, it was not defined by Microsoft; rather, it was defined by the SQL standard.

One way around this problem is to repeat the expression *YEAR(orderdate)* in both the *WHERE* and *SELECT* clauses:

```
SELECT orderid, YEAR(orderdate) AS orderyear
FROM Sales.Orders
WHERE YEAR(orderdate) > 2015;
```

A similar problem can happen if you try to refer to an expression alias in the *HAVING* clause, which is also processed before the *SELECT* clause:

```
SELECT empid, YEAR(orderdate) AS orderyear, COUNT(*) AS numorders
FROM Sales.Orders
WHERE custid = 71
GROUP BY empid, YEAR(orderdate)
HAVING numorders > 1;
```

This query fails with an error saying that the column name *numorders* is invalid. Just like in the previous example, the workaround here is to repeat the expression *COUNT(*)* in both clauses:

```
SELECT empid, YEAR(orderdate) AS orderyear, COUNT(*) AS numorders
FROM Sales.Orders
WHERE custid = 71
GROUP BY empid, YEAR(orderdate)
HAVING COUNT(*) > 1;
```

In the relational model, operations on relations are based on relational algebra and result in a relation. Recall that a relation's body is a set of tuples, and a set has no duplicates. Unlike the relational model, which is based on mathematical set theory, SQL is based on multiset theory. The mathematical term *multiset*, or *bag*, is similar in some aspects to a set but does allow duplicates. A table in SQL isn't required to have a key. Without a key, the table can have duplicate rows and therefore isn't relational. Even if the table does have a key, a *SELECT* query against the table can still return duplicate rows. SQL query results do not have keys. As an example, the *Orders* table does have a primary key defined on *orderid* column. Still, the query in Listing 2-2 against the *Orders* table returns duplicate rows.

LISTING 2-2 Query returning duplicate rows

```
SELECT empid, YEAR(orderdate) AS orderyear
FROM Sales.Orders
WHERE custid = 71;
```

This query generates the following output:

```
empid       orderyear
----------- -----------
9           2014
1           2014
2           2014
4           2015
8           2015
6           2015
6           2015
8           2015
5           2015
1           2015
8           2015
2           2015
7           2015
3           2015
5           2015
1           2015
5           2015
```

```
8           2015
3           2015
6           2015
2           2016
4           2016
4           2016
1           2016
7           2016
2           2016
1           2016
4           2016
7           2016
6           2016
1           2016

(31 row(s) affected)
```

SQL provides the means to remove duplicates using the *DISTINCT* clause (as shown in Listing 2-3) and, in this sense, return a relational result.

LISTING 2-3 Query with a *DISTINCT* clause

```
SELECT DISTINCT empid, YEAR(orderdate) AS orderyear
FROM Sales.Orders
WHERE custid = 71;
```

This query generates the following output:

```
empid       orderyear
----------- -----------
1           2014
1           2015
1           2016
2           2014
2           2015
2           2016
3           2015
4           2015
4           2016
5           2015
6           2015
6           2016
7           2015
7           2016
8           2015
9           2014

(16 row(s) affected)
```

Of the 31 rows in the multiset returned by the query in Listing 2-2, 16 rows are in the set returned by the query in Listing 2-3 after the removal of duplicates.

SQL allows specifying an asterisk (*) in the *SELECT* list to request all attributes from the queried tables instead of listing them explicitly, as in the following example:

```
SELECT *
FROM Sales.Shippers;
```

Such use of an asterisk is considered a bad programming practice in most cases. It is recommended that you explicitly list all attributes you need. Unlike with the relational model, SQL keeps ordinal positions for columns based on the order in which you specified them in the *CREATE TABLE* statement. By specifying *SELECT **, you're guaranteed to get the columns ordered in the output based on their ordinal positions. Client applications can refer to columns in the result by their ordinal positions (a bad practice in its own right) instead of by name. Then any schema changes applied to the table—such as adding or removing columns, rearranging their order, and so on—might result in failures in the client application or, even worse, in application bugs that will go unnoticed. By explicitly specifying the attributes you need, you always get the right ones, as long as the columns exist in the table. If a column referenced by the query was dropped from the table, you get an error and can fix your code accordingly.

People often wonder whether there's any performance difference between specifying an asterisk and explicitly listing column names. There is some extra work involved in resolving column names when the asterisk is used, but the cost is negligible compared to other costs involved in the processing of a query. Because listing column names explicitly is the recommended practice anyway, it's a win-win situation.

Curiously, you are not allowed to refer to column aliases created in the *SELECT* clause in other expressions within the same *SELECT* clause. That's the case even if the expression that tries to use the alias appears to the right of the expression that created it. For example, the following attempt is invalid:

```
SELECT orderid,
  YEAR(orderdate) AS orderyear,
  orderyear + 1 AS nextyear
FROM Sales.Orders;
```

I'll explain the reason for this restriction later in this chapter, in the section, "All-at-Once Operations." As explained earlier in this section, one of the ways around this problem is to repeat the expression:

```
SELECT orderid,
  YEAR(orderdate) AS orderyear,
  YEAR(orderdate) + 1 AS nextyear
FROM Sales.Orders;
```

The *ORDER BY* clause

You use the *ORDER BY* clause to sort the rows in the output for presentation purposes. In terms of logical query processing, *ORDER BY* is the very last clause to be processed. The sample query shown in Listing 2-4 sorts the rows in the output by employee ID and order year.

LISTING 2-4 Query demonstrating the *ORDER BY* clause

```
SELECT empid, YEAR(orderdate) AS orderyear, COUNT(*) AS numorders
FROM Sales.Orders
WHERE custid = 71
GROUP BY empid, YEAR(orderdate)
HAVING COUNT(*) > 1
ORDER BY empid, orderyear;
```

This query generates the following output:

```
empid       orderyear   numorders
----------- ----------- -----------
1           2015        2
1           2016        3
2           2016        2
3           2015        2
4           2016        3
5           2015        3
6           2015        3
7           2016        2
8           2015        4

(9 row(s) affected)
```

This time, presentation ordering in the output is guaranteed—unlike with queries that don't have a presentation *ORDER BY* clause.

One of the most important points to understand about SQL is that a table—be it an existing table in the database or a table result returned by a query—has no guaranteed order. That's because a table is supposed to represent a set of rows (or multiset, if it has duplicates), and a set has no order. This means that when you query a table without specifying an *ORDER BY* clause, SQL Server is free to return the rows in the output in any order. The only way for you to guarantee the presentation order in the result is with an *ORDER BY* clause. However, you should realize that if you do specify an *ORDER BY* clause, the result can't qualify as a table because it is ordered. Standard SQL calls such a result a *cursor*.

You're probably wondering why it matters whether a query returns a table or a cursor. Some language elements and operations in SQL expect to work with table results of queries and not with cursors. Examples include table expressions and set operators, which I cover in detail in Chapter 5, "Table expressions," and in Chapter 6, "Set operators."

Notice in the query in Listing 2-4 that the *ORDER BY* clause refers to the column alias *orderyear*, which was created in the *SELECT* phase. The *ORDER BY* phase is the only phase in which you can refer to column aliases created in the *SELECT* phase, because it is the only phase processed after the *SELECT* phase. Note that if you define a column alias that is the same as an underlying column name, as in *1 - col1 AS col1*, and refer to that alias in the *ORDER BY* clause, the new column is the one considered for ordering.

When you want to sort by an expression in ascending order, you either specify *ASC* right after the expression, as in *orderyear ASC*, or don't specify anything after the expression, because *ASC* is the default. If you want to sort in descending order, you need to specify *DESC* after the expression, as in *orderyear DESC*.

With T-SQL, you can specify ordinal positions of columns in the *ORDER BY* clause, based on the order in which the columns appear in the *SELECT* list. For example, in the query in Listing 2-4, instead of using

```
ORDER BY empid, orderyear
```

you could use

```
ORDER BY 1, 2
```

However, this is considered bad programming practice for a couple of reasons. First, in the relational model, attributes don't have ordinal positions and need to be referred to by name. Second, when you make revisions to the *SELECT* clause, you might forget to make the corresponding revisions in the *ORDER BY* clause. When you use column names, your code is safe from this type of mistake.

With T-SQL, you also can specify elements in the *ORDER BY* clause that do not appear in the *SELECT* clause, meaning you can sort by something you don't necessarily want to return. The big drawback for this is that you can't check your sorted results by looking at the query output. For example, the following query sorts the employee rows by hire date without returning the *hiredate* attribute:

```
SELECT empid, firstname, lastname, country
FROM HR.Employees
ORDER BY hiredate;
```

However, when the *DISTINCT* clause is specified, you are restricted in the *ORDER BY* list only to elements that appear in the *SELECT* list. The reasoning behind this restriction is that when *DISTINCT* is specified, a single result row might represent multiple source rows; therefore, it might not be clear which of the values in the multiple rows should be used. Consider the following invalid query:

```
SELECT DISTINCT country
FROM HR.Employees
ORDER BY empid;
```

There are nine employees in the *Employees* table—five from the United States and four from the United Kingdom. If you omit the invalid *ORDER BY* clause from this query, you get two rows back—one for each distinct country. Because each country appears in multiple rows in the source table, and each such row has a different employee ID, the meaning of *ORDER BY empid* is not really defined.

The *TOP* and *OFFSET-FETCH* filters

Earlier in this chapter I covered the filtering clauses *WHERE* and *HAVING*, which are based on predicates. In this section I cover the filtering clauses *TOP* and *OFFSET-FETCH*, which are based on number of rows and ordering.

The *TOP* filter

The *TOP* filter is a proprietary T-SQL feature you can use to limit the number or percentage of rows your query returns. It relies on two elements as part of its specification: one is the number or percent of rows to return, and the other is the ordering. For example, to return from the *Orders* table the five most recent orders, you specify *TOP (5)* in the *SELECT* clause and *orderdate DESC* in the *ORDER BY* clause, as shown in Listing 2-5.

LISTING 2-5 Query demonstrating the *TOP* filter

```
SELECT TOP (5) orderid, orderdate, custid, empid
FROM Sales.Orders
ORDER BY orderdate DESC;
```

This query returns the following output:

```
orderid     orderdate  custid      empid
----------- ---------- ----------- -----------
11077       2016-05-06 65          1
11076       2016-05-06 9           4
11075       2016-05-06 68          8
11074       2016-05-06 73          7
11073       2016-05-05 58          2

(5 row(s) affected)
```

Remember that the *ORDER BY* clause is evaluated after the *SELECT* clause, which includes the *DISTINCT* option. The same is true with the *TOP* filter, which relies on the *ORDER BY* specification to give it its filtering-related meaning. This means that if *DISTINCT* is specified in the *SELECT* clause, the *TOP* filter is evaluated after duplicate rows have been removed.

Also note that when the *TOP* filter is specified, the *ORDER BY* clause serves a dual purpose in the query. One purpose is to define the presentation ordering for the rows in the query result. Another purpose is to define for the *TOP* option which rows to filter. For example, the query in Listing 2-5 returns the five rows with the most recent *orderdate* values and presents the rows in the output in *orderdate DESC* ordering.

If you're confused about whether a *TOP* query returns a table result or a cursor, you have every reason to be. Normally, a query with an *ORDER BY* clause returns a cursor—not a relational result. But what if you need to filter rows with the *TOP* option based on some ordering but still return a relational result? Also, what if you need to filter rows with the *TOP* option based on one order but present the output rows in another order?

To achieve this, you have to use a table expression, but I'll save the discussion about table expressions for Chapter 5. All I want to say for now is that if the design of the *TOP* filter seems confusing, there's a good reason. In other words, it's not you—it's the feature's design. It would have been nice if the *TOP* filter had its own ordering specification that was separate from the presentation ordering specification in the query. Unfortunately, that ship has sailed already.

You can use the *TOP* option with the *PERCENT* keyword, in which case SQL Server calculates the number of rows to return based on a percentage of the number of qualifying rows, rounded up. For example, the following query requests the top 1 percent of the most recent orders:

```
SELECT TOP (1) PERCENT orderid, orderdate, custid, empid
FROM Sales.Orders
ORDER BY orderdate DESC;
```

This query generates the following output:

```
orderid     orderdate  custid      empid
----------- ---------- ----------- -----------
11074       2016-05-06 73          7
11075       2016-05-06 68          8
11076       2016-05-06 9           4
11077       2016-05-06 65          1
11070       2016-05-05 44          2
11071       2016-05-05 46          1
11072       2016-05-05 20          4
11073       2016-05-05 58          2
11067       2016-05-04 17          1

(9 row(s) affected)
```

The query returns nine rows because the *Orders* table has 830 rows, and 1 percent of 830, rounded up, is 9.

In the query in Listing 2-5, you might have noticed that the *ORDER BY* list is not unique (because no primary key or unique constraint is defined on the *orderdate* column). Multiple rows can have the same order date. In such a case, the ordering among rows with the same order date is undefined. This fact makes the query nondeterministic—more than one result can be considered correct. In case of ties, SQL Server filters rows based on physical access order.

Note that you can even use the *TOP* filter in a query without an *ORDER BY* clause. In such a case, the ordering is completely undefined—SQL Server returns whichever *n* rows it happens to physically access first, where *n* is the requested number of rows.

Notice in the output for the query in Listing 2-5 that the minimum order date in the rows returned is May 5, 2016, and one row in the output has that date. Other rows in the table might have the same order date, and with the existing non-unique *ORDER BY* list, there is no guarantee which one will be returned.

If you want the query to be deterministic, you need to make the *ORDER BY* list unique; in other words, add a tiebreaker. For example, you can add *orderid DESC* to the *ORDER BY* list as shown in Listing 2-6 so that, in case of ties, the row with the greater order ID value will be preferred.

LISTING 2-6 Query demonstrating *TOP* with unique *ORDER BY* list

```
SELECT TOP (5) orderid, orderdate, custid, empid
FROM Sales.Orders
ORDER BY orderdate DESC, orderid DESC;
```

This query returns the following output:

```
orderid     orderdate  custid      empid
----------- ---------- ----------- -----------
11077       2016-05-06 65          1
11076       2016-05-06 9           4
11075       2016-05-06 68          8
11074       2016-05-06 73          7
11073       2016-05-05 58          2

(5 row(s) affected)
```

If you examine the results of the queries from Listings 2-5 and 2-6, you'll notice that they seem to be the same. The important difference is that the result shown in the query output for Listing 2-5 is one of several possible valid results for this query, whereas the result shown in the query output for Listing 2-6 is the only possible valid result.

Instead of adding a tiebreaker to the *ORDER BY* list, you can request to return all ties. For example, you can ask that, in addition to the five rows you get back from the query in Listing 2-5, all other rows from the table be returned that have the same sort value (order date, in this case) as the last one found (May 5, 2016, in this case). You achieve this by adding the *WITH TIES* option, as shown in the following query:

```
SELECT TOP (5) WITH TIES orderid, orderdate, custid, empid
FROM Sales.Orders
ORDER BY orderdate DESC;
```

This query returns the following output:

```
orderid     orderdate  custid      empid
----------- ---------- ----------- -----------
11077       2016-05-06 65          1
11076       2016-05-06 9           4
11075       2016-05-06 68          8
11074       2016-05-06 73          7
11073       2016-05-05 58          2
11072       2016-05-05 20          4
11071       2016-05-05 46          1
11070       2016-05-05 44          2

(8 row(s) affected)
```

Notice that the output has eight rows, even though you specified *TOP (5)*. SQL Server first returned the *TOP (5)* rows based on *orderdate DESC* ordering, and it also returned all other rows from the table that had the same *orderdate* value as in the last of the five rows that were accessed. Using the WITH TIES option, the selection of rows is deterministic, but the presentation order among rows with the same order date isn't.

The *OFFSET-FETCH* filter

The *TOP* filter is very practical, but it has two shortcomings—it's not standard, and it doesn't support a skipping capability. T-SQL also supports a standard, *TOP*-like filter, called *OFFSET-FETCH*, which does support a skipping option. This makes it very useful for ad-hoc paging purposes.

The *OFFSET-FETCH* filter is considered an extension to the *ORDER BY* clause. With the *OFFSET* clause you indicate how many rows to skip, and with the *FETCH* clause you indicate how many rows to filter after the skipped rows. As an example, consider the following query:

```
SELECT orderid, orderdate, custid, empid
FROM Sales.Orders
ORDER BY orderdate, orderid
OFFSET 50 ROWS FETCH NEXT 25 ROWS ONLY;
```

The query orders the rows from the *Orders* table based on the *orderdate* and *orderid* attributes (from least recent to most recent, with *orderid* as the tiebreaker). Based on this ordering, the *OFFSET* clause skips the first 50 rows and the *FETCH* clause filters the next 25 rows only.

Note that a query that uses *OFFSET-FETCH* must have an *ORDER BY* clause. Also, T-SQL doesn't support the *FETCH* clause without the *OFFSET* clause. If you do not want to skip any rows but do want to filter rows with the *FETCH* clause, you must indicate that by using *OFFSET 0 ROWS*. However, *OFFSET* without *FETCH* is allowed. In such a case, the query skips the indicated number of rows and returns all remaining rows in the result.

There are interesting language aspects to note about the syntax for the *OFFSET-FETCH* filter. The singular and plural forms *ROW* and *ROWS* are interchangeable. The idea behind this is to allow you to phrase the filter in an intuitive English-like manner. For example, suppose you want to fetch only one row; though it would be syntactically valid, it would nevertheless look strange if you specified *FETCH 1 ROWS*. Therefore, you're allowed to use the form *FETCH 1 ROW*. The same principle applies to the *OFFSET* clause. Also, if you're not skipping any rows (*OFFSET 0 ROWS*), you might find the term "first" more suitable than "next." Hence, the forms *FIRST* and *NEXT* are interchangeable.

As you can see, the *OFFSET-FETCH* filter is more flexible than the *TOP* filter in the sense that it supports a skipping capability. However, at the date of this writing (the year 2016), the T-SQL implementation of the *OFFSET-FETCH* filter doesn't yet support the *PERCENT* and *WITH TIES* options that *TOP* does. Curiously, the SQL standard specification for the *OFFSET-FETCH* filter does support these options.

A quick look at window functions

A window function is a function that, for each row in the underlying query, operates on a window (set) of rows that is derived from the underlying query result, and computes a scalar (single) result value. The window of rows is defined with an *OVER* clause. Window functions are profound; you can use them to address a wide variety of needs, such as to perform data-analysis calculations. T-SQL supports several categories of window functions, and each category has several functions. Window functions are a SQL standard, but T-SQL supports a subset of the features from the standard.

At this point in the book, it could be premature to get into too much detail. For now, I'll just provide a glimpse into the concept and demonstrate it by using the *ROW_NUMBER* window function. Later in the book (in Chapter 7, "Beyond the fundamentals of querying"), I provide more details.

As mentioned, a window function operates on a set of rows exposed to it by the *OVER* clause. For each row in the underlying query, the *OVER* clause exposes to the function a subset of the rows from the underlying query's result set. The *OVER* clause can restrict the rows in the window by using a window partition subclause (*PARTITION BY*). It can define ordering for the calculation (if relevant) using a window order subclause (*ORDER BY*)—not to be confused with the query's presentation *ORDER BY* clause.

Consider the following query as an example:

```
SELECT orderid, custid, val,
  ROW_NUMBER() OVER(PARTITION BY custid
                    ORDER BY val) AS rownum
FROM Sales.OrderValues
ORDER BY custid, val;
```

This query generates the following output:

```
orderid     custid      val                                     rownum
----------- ----------- --------------------------------------- --------------------
10702       1           330.00                                  1
10952       1           471.20                                  2
10643       1           814.50                                  3
10835       1           845.80                                  4
10692       1           878.00                                  5
11011       1           933.50                                  6
10308       2           88.80                                   1
10759       2           320.00                                  2
10625       2           479.75                                  3
10926       2           514.40                                  4
10682       3           375.50                                  1
...

(830 row(s) affected)
```

The *ROW_NUMBER* function assigns unique, sequential, incrementing integers to the rows in the result within the respective partition, based on the indicated ordering. The *OVER* clause in this example function partitions the window by the *custid* attribute; hence, the row numbers are unique to each customer. The *OVER* clause also defines ordering in the window by the *val* attribute, so the sequential row numbers are incremented within the partition based on the values in this attribute.

Note that the *ROW_NUMBER* function must produce unique values within each partition. This means that even when the ordering value doesn't increase, the row number still must increase. Therefore, if the *ROW_NUMBER* function's *ORDER BY* list is non-unique, as in the preceding example, the query is nondeterministic. That is, more than one correct result is possible. If you want to make a row number calculation deterministic, you must add elements to the *ORDER BY* list to make it unique. For example, in our sample query you can achieve this by adding the *orderid* attribute as a tiebreaker.

Window ordering should not be confused with presentation ordering; it does not prevent the result from being relational. Also, specifying window ordering in a window function doesn't give you any presentation-ordering guarantees. If you need to guarantee presentation ordering, you must add a presentation *ORDER BY* clause, as I did in the last query.

Note that expressions in the *SELECT* list are evaluated before the *DISTINCT* clause (if one exists). This rule also applies to expressions based on window functions that appear in the *SELECT* list. I explain the significance of this fact in Chapter 7.

To put it all together, the following list presents the logical order in which all clauses discussed so far are processed:

- *FROM*
- *WHERE*
- *GROUP BY*
- *HAVING*
- *SELECT*
  - Expressions
  - *DISTINCT*
- *ORDER BY*
  - TOP/OFFSET-FETCH

Predicates and operators

T-SQL has language elements in which predicates can be specified—for example, query filters such as *WHERE* and *HAVING*, *CHECK* constraints, and others. Remember that predicates are logical expressions that evaluate to *TRUE*, *FALSE*, or *UNKNOWN*. You can combine predicates by using logical operators such as *AND* (forming a combination known as a *conjunction of predicates*) and *OR* (known as a *disjunction of predicates*). You can also involve other types of operators, such as comparison operators, in your expressions.

Examples of predicates supported by T-SQL include *IN*, *BETWEEN*, and *LIKE*. You use the *IN* predicate to check whether a value, or scalar expression, is equal to at least one of the elements in a set. For example, the following query returns orders in which the order ID is equal to 10248, 10249, or 10250:

```
SELECT orderid, empid, orderdate
FROM Sales.Orders
WHERE orderid IN(10248, 10249, 10250);
```

You use the *BETWEEN* predicate to check whether a value is in a specified range, inclusive of the two specified delimiters. For example, the following query returns all orders in the inclusive range 10300 through 10310:

```
SELECT orderid, empid, orderdate
FROM Sales.Orders
WHERE orderid BETWEEN 10300 AND 10310;
```

With the *LIKE* predicate, you can check whether a character string value meets a specified pattern. For example, the following query returns employees whose last names start with the letter *D*:

```
SELECT empid, firstname, lastname
FROM HR.Employees
WHERE lastname LIKE N'D%';
```

Later in this chapter, I'll elaborate on pattern matching and the *LIKE* predicate.

Notice the use of the letter *N* to prefix the string *'D%'*; it stands for *National* and is used to denote that a character string is of a Unicode data type (*NCHAR* or *NVARCHAR*), as opposed to a regular character data type (*CHAR* or *VARCHAR*). Because the data type of the *lastname* attribute is *NVARCHAR(40)*, the letter *N* is used to prefix the string. Later in this chapter, in the section "Working with character data," I elaborate on the treatment of character strings.

T-SQL supports the following comparison operators: =, >, <, >=, <=, <>, !=, !>, !<, of which the last three are not standard. Because the nonstandard operators have standard alternatives (such as <> instead of !=), I recommend you avoid using nonstandard operators. For example, the following query returns all orders placed on or after January 1, 2016:

```
SELECT orderid, empid, orderdate
FROM Sales.Orders
WHERE orderdate >= '20160101';
```

If you need to combine logical expressions, you can use the logical operators *OR* and *AND*. If you want to negate an expression, you can use the *NOT* operator. For example, the following query returns orders placed on or after January 1, 2016, that were handled by one of the employees whose ID is 1, 3, or 5:

```
SELECT orderid, empid, orderdate
FROM Sales.Orders
WHERE orderdate >= '20160101'
  AND empid IN(1, 3, 5);
```

T-SQL supports the four obvious arithmetic operators: +, –, *, and /. It also supports the % operator (modulo), which returns the remainder of integer division. For example, the following query calculates the net value as a result of arithmetic manipulation of the *quantity*, *unitprice*, and *discount* attributes:

```
SELECT orderid, productid, qty, unitprice, discount,
  qty * unitprice * (1 - discount) AS val
FROM Sales.OrderDetails;
```

Note that the data type of a scalar expression involving two operands is determined in T-SQL by the higher of the two in terms of data-type precedence. If both operands are of the same data type, the result of the expression is of the same data type as well. For example, a division between two integers (*INT*) yields an integer. The expression 5/2 returns the integer 2 and not the numeric 2.5. This is not a problem when you are dealing with constants, because you can always specify the values as numeric ones with a decimal point. But when you are dealing with, say, two integer columns, as in *col1/col2*, you need to cast the operands to the appropriate type if you want the calculation to be a numeric one: *CAST(col1 AS NUMERIC(12, 2))/CAST(col2 AS NUMERIC(12, 2))*. The data type *NUMERIC(12, 2)* has a precision of 12 and a scale of 2, meaning that it has 12 digits in total, 2 of which are after the decimal point.

If the two operands are of different types, the one with the lower precedence is promoted to the one that is higher. For example, in the expression 5/2.0, the first operand is *INT* and the second is *NUMERIC*. Because *NUMERIC* is considered higher than *INT*, the *INT* operand 5 is implicitly converted to the *NUMERIC* 5.0 before the arithmetic operation, and you get the result 2.5.

You can find the precedence order among types in SQL Server Books Online under "Data Type Precedence."

When multiple operators appear in the same expression, SQL Server evaluates them based on operator precedence rules. The following list describes the precedence among operators, from highest to lowest:

1. ( ) (Parentheses)
2. * (Multiplication), / (Division), % (Modulo)
3. + (Positive), – (Negative), + (Addition), + (Concatenation), – (Subtraction)
4. =, >, <, >=, <=, <>, !=, !>, !< (Comparison operators)
5. *NOT*
6. *AND*
7. *BETWEEN, IN, LIKE, OR*
8. = (Assignment)

For example, in the following query, *AND* has precedence over *OR*:

```
SELECT orderid, custid, empid, orderdate
FROM Sales.Orders
WHERE
        custid = 1
    AND empid IN(1, 3, 5)
    OR  custid = 85
    AND empid IN(2, 4, 6);
```

The query returns orders that were either "placed by customer 1 and handled by employees 1, 3, or 5" or "placed by customer 85 and handled by employees 2, 4, or 6."

Parentheses have the highest precedence, so they give you full control. For the sake of other people who need to review or maintain your code and for readability purposes, it's a good practice to use parentheses even when they are not required. The same is true with indentation. For example, the following query is the logical equivalent of the previous query, only its logic is much clearer:

```
SELECT orderid, custid, empid, orderdate
FROM Sales.Orders
WHERE
      (custid = 1
        AND empid IN(1, 3, 5))
    OR
      (custid = 85
        AND empid IN(2, 4, 6));
```

Using parentheses to force precedence with logical operators is similar to using parentheses with arithmetic operators. For example, without parentheses in the following expression, multiplication precedes addition:

```
SELECT 10 + 2 * 3;
```

Therefore, this expression returns 16. You can use parentheses to force the addition to be calculated first:

```
SELECT (10 + 2) * 3;
```

This time, the expression returns 36.

CASE expressions

A *CASE* expression is a scalar expression that returns a value based on conditional logic. It is based on the SQL standard. Note that *CASE* is an expression and not a statement; that is, it doesn't take action such as controlling the flow of your code. Instead, it returns a value. Because *CASE* is a scalar expression, it is allowed wherever scalar expressions are allowed, such as in the *SELECT*, *WHERE*, *HAVING*, and *ORDER BY* clauses and in *CHECK* constraints.

There are two forms of *CASE* expressions: *simple* and *searched*. You use the simple form to compare one value or scalar expression with a list of possible values and return a value for the first match. If no value in the list is equal to the tested value, the *CASE* expression returns the value that appears in the *ELSE* clause (if one exists). If the *CASE* expression doesn't have an *ELSE* clause, it defaults to *ELSE NULL*.

For example, the following query against the *Production.Products* table uses a *CASE* expression in the *SELECT* clause to produce the description of the *categoryid* column value:

```
SELECT productid, productname, categoryid,
  CASE categoryid
    WHEN 1 THEN 'Beverages'
    WHEN 2 THEN 'Condiments'
    WHEN 3 THEN 'Confections'
    WHEN 4 THEN 'Dairy Products'
    WHEN 5 THEN 'Grains/Cereals'
    WHEN 6 THEN 'Meat/Poultry'
    WHEN 7 THEN 'Produce'
    WHEN 8 THEN 'Seafood'
    ELSE 'Unknown Category'
  END AS categoryname
FROM Production.Products;
```

This query produces the following output, shown in abbreviated form:

```
productid   productname    categoryid  categoryname
----------- -------------- ----------- ----------------
1           Product HHYDP  1           Beverages
2           Product RECZE  1           Beverages
3           Product IMEHJ  2           Condiments
```

```
4           Product KSBRM  2          Condiments
5           Product EPEIM  2          Condiments
6           Product VAIIV  2          Condiments
7           Product HMLNI  7          Produce
8           Product WVJFP  2          Condiments
9           Product AOZBW  6          Meat/Poultry
10          Product YHXGE  8          Seafood
...

(77 row(s) affected)
```

Note that this query is used for illustration purposes. Normally you maintain the product categories in a table and join that table with the *Products* table when you need to get the category descriptions. In fact, the *TSQLV4* database has just such a *Categories* table.

The simple *CASE* form has a single test value or expression right after the *CASE* keyword that is compared with a list of possible values in the *WHEN* clauses. The searched *CASE* form is more flexible in the sense you can specify predicates in the *WHEN* clauses rather than being restricted to using equality comparisons. The searched *CASE* expression returns the value in the *THEN* clause that is associated with the first *WHEN* predicate that evaluates to *TRUE*. If none of the *WHEN* predicates evaluates to *TRUE*, the *CASE* expression returns the value that appears in the *ELSE* clause (or *NULL* if an *ELSE* clause is not present). For example, the following query produces a value category description based on whether the value is less than 1,000.00, between 1,000.00 and 3,000.00, or greater than 3,000.00:

```
SELECT orderid, custid, val,
  CASE
    WHEN val < 1000.00                   THEN 'Less than 1000'
    WHEN val BETWEEN 1000.00 AND 3000.00 THEN 'Between 1000 and 3000'
    WHEN val > 3000.00                   THEN 'More than 3000'
    ELSE 'Unknown'
  END AS valuecategory
FROM Sales.OrderValues;
```

This query generates the following output:

```
orderid     custid      val      valuecategory
----------- ----------- -------- ---------------------
10248       85          440.00   Less than 1000
10249       79          1863.40  Between 1000 and 3000
10250       34          1552.60  Between 1000 and 3000
10251       84          654.06   Less than 1000
10252       76          3597.90  More than 3000
10253       34          1444.80  Between 1000 and 3000
10254       14          556.62   Less than 1000
10255       68          2490.50  Between 1000 and 3000
10256       88          517.80   Less than 1000
10257       35          1119.90  Between 1000 and 3000
...

(830 row(s) affected)
```

You can see that every simple *CASE* expression can be converted to the searched *CASE* form, but the reverse is not true.

T-SQL supports some functions you can consider as abbreviations of the *CASE* expression: *ISNULL*, *COALESCE*, *IIF*, and *CHOOSE*. Note that of the four, only *COALESCE* is standard.

The *ISNULL* function accepts two arguments as input and returns the first that is not *NULL*, or *NULL* if both are *NULL*. For example *ISNULL(col1, '')* returns the *col1* value if it isn't *NULL* and an empty string if it is *NULL*. The *COALESCE* function is similar, only it supports two or more arguments and returns the first that isn't *NULL*, or *NULL* if all are *NULL*.

See Also *It's a common question whether you should use* ISNULL *or* COALESCE. *I cover the topic in detail in my* SQL Server Pro *magazine column in the following article: http://sqlmag.com/t-sql/coalesce-vs-isnull.*

The nonstandard *IIF* and *CHOOSE* functions were added to T-SQL to support easier migrations from Microsoft Access. The function *IIF(<logical_expression>, <expr1>, <expr2>)* returns *expr1* if *logical_expression* is *TRUE*, and it returns *expr2* otherwise. For example, the expression *IIF(col1 <> 0, col2/col1, NULL)* returns the result of *col2/col1* if *col1* is not zero; otherwise, it returns a *NULL*. The function *CHOOSE(<index>, <expr1>, <expr2>, ..., <exprn>)* returns the expression from the list in the specified index. For example, the expression *CHOOSE(3, col1, col2, col3)* returns the value of *col3*. Of course, actual expressions that use the *CHOOSE* function tend to be more dynamic—for example, relying on user input.

So far, I've just used a few examples to familiarize you with the *CASE* expression and related functions. Even though it might not be apparent at this point from these examples, the *CASE* expression is an extremely powerful and useful language element.

NULLs

As explained in Chapter 1, "Background to T-SQL querying and programming," SQL supports the *NULL* marker to represent missing values and uses three-valued predicate logic, meaning that predicates can evaluate to *TRUE*, *FALSE*, or *UNKNOWN*. T-SQL follows the standard in this respect. Treatment of *NULLs* and *UNKNOWN* in SQL can be confusing because intuitively people are more accustomed to thinking in terms of two-valued logic (*TRUE* and *FALSE*). To add to the confusion, different language elements in SQL treat *NULLs* and *UNKNOWN* inconsistently.

Let's start with three-valued predicate logic. A logical expression involving only non-*NULL* values evaluates to either *TRUE* or *FALSE*. When the logical expression involves a missing value, it evaluates to *UNKNOWN*. For example, consider the predicate *salary > 0*. When *salary* is equal to 1,000, the expression evaluates to *TRUE*. When *salary* is equal to –1,000, the expression evaluates to *FALSE*. When *salary* is *NULL*, the expression evaluates to *UNKNOWN*.

SQL treats *TRUE* and *FALSE* in an intuitive and probably expected manner. For example, if the predicate *salary > 0* appears in a query filter (such as in a *WHERE* or *HAVING* clause), rows or groups for which the expression evaluates to *TRUE* are returned, whereas those for which the expression evaluates to *FALSE* are discarded. Similarly, if the predicate *salary > 0* appears in a *CHECK* constraint in a table, *INSERT* or *UPDATE* statements for which the expression evaluates to *TRUE* for all rows are accepted, whereas those for which the expression evaluates to *FALSE* for any row are rejected.

SQL has different treatments for *UNKNOWN* in different language elements (and for some people, not necessarily the expected treatments). The treatment SQL has for query filters is "accept *TRUE*," meaning that both *FALSE* and *UNKNOWN* are discarded. Conversely, the definition of the treatment SQL has for *CHECK* constraints is "reject FALSE," meaning that both *TRUE* and *UNKNOWN* are accepted. Had SQL used two-valued predicate logic, there wouldn't have been a difference between the definitions "accept *TRUE*" and "reject *FALSE*." But with three-valued predicate logic, "accept *TRUE*" rejects *UNKNOWN*, whereas "reject *FALSE*" accepts it. With the predicate *salary > 0* from the previous example, a *NULL* salary would cause the expression to evaluate to *UNKNOWN*. If this predicate appears in a query's *WHERE* clause, a row with a *NULL* salary will be discarded. If this predicate appears in a *CHECK* constraint in a table, a row with a *NULL* salary will be accepted.

One of the tricky aspects of the logical value *UNKNOWN* is that when you negate it, you still get *UNKNOWN*. For example, given the predicate *NOT (salary > 0)*, when salary is *NULL*, *salary > 0* evaluates to *UNKNOWN*, and *NOT UNKNOWN* remains *UNKNOWN*.

What some people find surprising is that an expression comparing two *NULLs* (*NULL = NULL*) evaluates to *UNKNOWN*. The reasoning for this from SQL's perspective is that a *NULL* represents a missing value, and you can't really tell whether one missing value is equal to another. Therefore, SQL provides you with the predicates *IS NULL* and *IS NOT NULL*, which you should use instead of *= NULL* and *<> NULL*.

To make things a bit more tangible, I'll demonstrate the ramifications of three-valued logic with an example. The *Sales.Customers* table has three attributes, called *country*, *region*, and *city*, where the customer's location information is stored. All locations have existing countries and cities. Some have existing regions (such as *country*: USA, *region*: WA, *city*: Seattle), yet for some the *region* element is missing but inapplicable (such as *country*: UK, *region*: NULL, *city*: London). Consider the following query, which attempts to return all customers where the region is equal to WA:

```
SELECT custid, country, region, city
FROM Sales.Customers
WHERE region = N'WA';
```

This query generates the following output:

```
custid      country         region          city
----------- --------------- --------------- ---------------
43          USA             WA              Walla Walla
82          USA             WA              Kirkland
89          USA             WA              Seattle
```

Out of the 91 rows in the *Customers* table, the query returns the three rows where the *region* attribute is equal to WA. The query returns neither rows in which the value in the *region* attribute is present and different than WA (the predicate evaluates to *FALSE*) nor those where the *region* attribute is *NULL* (the predicate evaluates to *UNKNOWN*). Most people would consider this result as the expected one.

The following query attempts to return all customers for whom the region is different than WA:

```
SELECT custid, country, region, city
FROM Sales.Customers
WHERE region <> N'WA';
```

This query generates the following output:

```
custid      country         region          city
----------- --------------- --------------- ---------------
10          Canada          BC              Tsawassen
15          Brazil          SP              Sao Paulo
21          Brazil          SP              Sao Paulo
31          Brazil          SP              Campinas
32          USA             OR              Eugene
33          Venezuela       DF              Caracas
34          Brazil          RJ              Rio de Janeiro
35          Venezuela       Táchira         San Cristóbal
36          USA             OR              Elgin
37          Ireland         Co. Cork        Cork
38          UK              Isle of Wight   Cowes
42          Canada          BC              Vancouver
45          USA             CA              San Francisco
46          Venezuela       Lara            Barquisimeto
47          Venezuela       Nueva Esparta   I. de Margarita
48          USA             OR              Portland
51          Canada          Québec          Montréal
55          USA             AK              Anchorage
61          Brazil          RJ              Rio de Janeiro
62          Brazil          SP              Sao Paulo
65          USA             NM              Albuquerque
67          Brazil          RJ              Rio de Janeiro
71          USA             ID              Boise
75          USA             WY              Lander
77          USA             OR              Portland
78          USA             MT              Butte
81          Brazil          SP              Sao Paulo
88          Brazil          SP              Resende

(28 row(s) affected)
```

If you expected to get 88 rows back (91 rows in the table minus 3 returned by the previous query), you might find this result (with just 28 rows) surprising. But remember, a query filter "accepts *TRUE*," meaning that it rejects both *FALSE* and *UNKNOWN*. So this query returned rows in which the *region* value was present and different than WA. It returned neither rows in which the *region* value was equal to WA nor rows in which *region* was *NULL*. You will get the same output if you use the predicate *NOT (region = N'WA')*. That's because in the rows where *region* is *NULL* the expression *region = N'WA'* evaluates to *UNKNOWN*, and *NOT (region = N'WA')* evaluates to *UNKNOWN* also.

If you want to return all rows for which *region* is *NULL*, do not use the predicate *region = NULL*, because the expression evaluates to *UNKNOWN* in all rows—both those in which the value is present and those in which the value is missing (is *NULL*). The following query returns an empty set:

```
SELECT custid, country, region, city
FROM Sales.Customers
WHERE region = NULL;
```

```
custid      country         region          city
----------- --------------- --------------- ---------------

(0 row(s) affected)
```

Instead, you should use the *IS NULL* predicate:

```
SELECT custid, country, region, city
FROM Sales.Customers
WHERE region IS NULL;
```

This query generates the following output, shown in abbreviated form:

```
custid      country         region          city
----------- --------------- --------------- ---------------
1           Germany         NULL            Berlin
2           Mexico          NULL            México D.F.
3           Mexico          NULL            México D.F.
4           UK              NULL            London
5           Sweden          NULL            Luleå
6           Germany         NULL            Mannheim
7           France          NULL            Strasbourg
8           Spain           NULL            Madrid
9           France          NULL            Marseille
11          UK              NULL            London
...

(60 row(s) affected)
```

If you want to return all rows for which the *region* attribute is different than WA, including those in which the value is missing, you need to include an explicit test for *NULLs*, like this:

```
SELECT custid, country, region, city
FROM Sales.Customers
WHERE region <> N'WA'
   OR region IS NULL;
```

This query generates the following output, shown in abbreviated form:

```
custid      country         region          city
----------- --------------- --------------- ---------------
1           Germany         NULL            Berlin
2           Mexico          NULL            México D.F.
3           Mexico          NULL            México D.F.
4           UK              NULL            London
5           Sweden          NULL            Luleå
6           Germany         NULL            Mannheim
7           France          NULL            Strasbourg
8           Spain           NULL            Madrid
9           France          NULL            Marseille
10          Canada          BC              Tsawassen
...

(88 row(s) affected)
```

SQL also treats *NULLs* inconsistently in different language elements for comparison and sorting purposes. Some elements treat two *NULLs* as equal to each other, and others treat them as different.

For example, for grouping and sorting purposes, two *NULLs* are considered equal. That is, the *GROUP BY* clause arranges all *NULLs* in one group just like present values, and the *ORDER BY* clause sorts all *NULLs* together. Standard SQL leaves it to the product implementation to determine whether *NULLs* sort before present values or after them, but it must be consistent within the implementation. T-SQL sorts *NULLs* before present values.

As mentioned earlier, query filters "accept *TRUE*." An expression comparing two *NULLs* yields *UNKNOWN*; therefore, such a row is filtered out.

For the purposes of enforcing a *UNIQUE* constraint, standard SQL treats *NULLs* as different from each other (allowing multiple *NULLs*). Conversely, in T-SQL, a *UNIQUE* constraint considers two *NULLs* as equal (allowing only one *NULL*).

The complexity in handling *NULLs* often results in logical errors. Therefore, you should think about them in every query you write. If the default treatment is not what you want, you must intervene explicitly; otherwise, just ensure that the default behavior is, in fact, what you want.

All-at-once operations

SQL supports a concept called *all-at-once operations*, which means that all expressions that appear in the same logical query processing phase are evaluated logically at the same point in time. The reason for this is that all expressions that appear in the same logical phase are treated as a set, and as mentioned earlier, a set has no order to its elements.

This concept explains why, for example, you cannot refer to column aliases assigned in the *SELECT* clause within the same *SELECT* clause. Consider the following query:

```
SELECT
  orderid,
  YEAR(orderdate) AS orderyear,
  orderyear + 1 AS nextyear
FROM Sales.Orders;
```

The reference to the column alias *orderyear* in the third expression in the *SELECT* list is invalid, even though the referencing expression appears to the right of the one in which the alias is assigned. The reason is that logically there is no order of evaluation of the expressions in the *SELECT* clause—it is a set of expressions. Conceptually, all the expressions are evaluated at the same point in time. Therefore, this query generates the following error:

```
Msg 207, Level 16, State 1, Line 4
Invalid column name 'orderyear'.
```

Here's another example for the ramifications of all-at-once operations: Suppose you have a table called *T1* with two integer columns called *col1* and *col2*, and you want to return all rows for which *col2/col1* is greater than 2. Because there might be rows in the table in which *col1* is zero, you need to ensure that the division doesn't take place in those cases—otherwise, the query would fail because of a divide-by-zero error. So you write a query using the following format:

```
SELECT col1, col2
FROM dbo.T1
WHERE col1 <> 0 AND col2/col1 > 2;
```

You might very well assume SQL Server evaluates the expressions from left to right, and that if the expression *col1 <> 0* evaluates to *FALSE*, SQL Server will short-circuit—that is, that it won't bother to evaluate the expression *10/col1 > 2* because at this point it is known that the whole expression is *FALSE*. So you might think that this query should never produce a divide-by-zero error.

SQL Server does support short circuits, but because of the all-at-once operations concept, it is free to process the expressions in the *WHERE* clause in any order. SQL Server usually makes decisions like this based on cost estimations. You can see that if SQL Server decides to process the expression *10/col1 > 2* first, this query might fail because of a divide-by-zero error.

You have several ways to avoid a failure here. For example, the order in which the *WHEN* clauses of a *CASE* expression are evaluated is guaranteed. So you could revise the query as follows:

```
SELECT col1, col2
FROM dbo.T1
WHERE
  CASE
    WHEN col1 = 0 THEN 'no' -- or 'yes' if row should be returned
    WHEN col2/col1 > 2 THEN 'yes'
    ELSE 'no'
  END = 'yes';
```

In rows where *col1* is equal to zero, the first *WHEN* clause evaluates to *TRUE* and the *CASE* expression returns the string *'no'*. (Replace *'no'* with *'yes'* if you want to return the row when *col1* is equal to zero.) Only if the first *CASE* expression does not evaluate to *TRUE*—meaning that *col1* is not 0—does the second *WHEN* clause check whether the expression *col2/col1 > 2* evaluates to *TRUE*. If it does, the *CASE* expression returns the string *'yes.'* In all other cases, the *CASE* expression returns the string *'no.'* The predicate in the *WHERE* clause returns *TRUE* only when the result of the *CASE* expression is equal to the string *'yes'*. This means that there will never be an attempt here to divide by zero.

This workaround turned out to be quite convoluted. In this particular case, you can use a mathematical workaround that avoids division altogether:

```
SELECT col1, col2
FROM dbo.T1
WHERE (col1 > 0 AND col2 > 2*col1) OR (col1 < 0 AND col2 < 2*col1);
```

I included this example to explain the unique and important concept of all-at-once operations and to elaborate on the fact that SQL Server guarantees the processing order of the *WHEN* clauses in a *CASE* expression.

Working with character data

In this section, I cover query manipulation of character data—including data types, collation, and operators and functions—and pattern matching.

Data types

SQL Server supports two kinds of character data types: regular and Unicode. Regular data types include *CHAR* and *VARCHAR*, and Unicode data types include *NCHAR* and *NVARCHAR*. Regular characters use 1 byte of storage for each character, whereas Unicode data requires 2 bytes per character, and in cases in which a surrogate pair is needed, 4 bytes are required. (For details on surrogate pairs, see *https://msdn.microsoft.com/en-us/library/windows/desktop/dd374069.*) If you choose a regular character type for a column, you are restricted to only one language in addition to English. The language support for the column is determined by the column's effective collation, which I'll describe shortly. With Unicode data types, multiple languages are supported. So if you store character data in multiple languages, make sure that you use Unicode character types and not regular ones.

The two kinds of character data types also differ in the way in which literals are expressed. When expressing a regular character literal, you simply use single quotes: *'This is a regular character string literal'*. When expressing a Unicode character literal, you need to specify the character *N* (for *National*) as a prefix: *N'This is a Unicode character string literal'*.

Any data type without the *VAR* element (*CHAR*, *NCHAR*) in its name has a fixed length, which means that SQL Server preserves space in the row based on the column's defined size and not on the actual number of characters in the character string. For example, when a column is defined as *CHAR(25)*, SQL Server preserves space for 25 characters in the row regardless of the length of the stored character string. Because no expansion of the row is required when the strings are expanded, fixed-length data types are more suited for write-focused systems. But because storage consumption is not optimal with fixed-length strings, you pay more when reading data.

A data type with the *VAR* element (*VARCHAR*, *NVARCHAR*) in its name has a variable length, which means that SQL Server uses as much storage space in the row as required to store the characters that appear in the character string, plus two extra bytes for offset data. For example, when a column is defined as *VARCHAR(25)*, the maximum number of characters supported is 25, but in practice, the actual number of characters in the string determines the amount of storage. Because storage consumption for these data types is less than that for fixed-length types, read operations are faster. However, updates might result in row expansion, which might result in data movement outside the current page. Therefore, updates of data having variable-length data types are less efficient than updates of data having fixed-length data types.

> **Note** If compression is used, the storage requirements change. For details about compression, see "Data Compression" in SQL Server Books Online at *http://msdn.microsoft.com/en-us/library/cc280449.aspx.*

You can also define the variable-length data types with the *MAX* specifier instead of a maximum number of characters. When the column is defined with the *MAX* specifier, any value with a size up to a certain threshold (8,000 bytes by default) can be stored inline in the row (as long as it can fit in the row). Any value with a size above the threshold is stored external to the row as a large object (LOB).

Later in this chapter, in the "Querying metadata" section, I explain how you can obtain metadata information about objects in the database, including the data types of columns.

Collation

Collation is a property of character data that encapsulates several aspects: language support, sort order, case sensitivity, accent sensitivity, and more. To get the set of supported collations and their descriptions, you can query the table function *fn_helpcollations* as follows:

```
SELECT name, description
FROM sys.fn_helpcollations();
```

For example, the following list explains the collation *Latin1_General_CI_AS*:

- ***Latin1_General*** Code page 1252 is used. (This supports English and German characters, as well as characters used by most Western European countries.)
- **Dictionary sorting** Sorting and comparison of character data are based on dictionary order (A and a < B and b).

  You can tell that dictionary order is used because that's the default when no other ordering is defined explicitly. More specifically, the element *BIN* doesn't explicitly appear in the collation name. If the element *BIN* appeared, it would mean that the sorting and comparison of character data was based on the binary representation of characters (A < B < a < b).
- ***CI*** The data is case insensitive (a = A).
- ***AS*** The data is accent sensitive (à <> ä).

In an on-premises SQL Server implementation, collation can be defined at four different levels: instance, database, column, and expression. The lowest effective level is the one that should be used. In Azure SQL Database, collation can be defined at the database, column, and expression levels. There are some specialized aspects of collation in contained databases. (For details, see *https://msdn.microsoft.com/en-GB/library/ff929080.aspx*.)

The collation of the instance is chosen as part of the setup program. It determines the collations of all system databases and is used as the default for user databases.

When you create a user database, you can specify a collation for the database by using the *COLLATE* clause. If you don't, the instance's collation is assumed by default.

The database collation determines the collation of the metadata of objects in the database and is used as the default for user table columns. I want to emphasize the importance of the fact that the database collation determines the collation of the metadata, including object and column names.

For example, if the database collation is case insensitive, you can't create two tables called *T1* and *t1* within the same schema, but if the database collation is case sensitive, you can do that. Note, though, that the collation aspects of variable and parameter identifiers are determined by the instance and not the database collation, regardless of the database you are connected to when declaring them. For example, if your instance has a case-insensitive collation and your database has a case-sensitive collation, you won't be able to define two variables or parameters named *@p* and *@P* in the same scope. Such an attempt will result in an error saying that the variable name has already been declared.

You can explicitly specify a collation for a column as part of its definition by using the *COLLATE* clause. If you don't, the database collation is assumed by default.

You can convert the collation of an expression by using the *COLLATE* clause. For example, in a case-insensitive environment, the following query uses a case-insensitive comparison:

```
SELECT empid, firstname, lastname
FROM HR.Employees
WHERE lastname = N'davis';
```

The query returns the row for Sara Davis, even though the casing doesn't match, because the effective casing is insensitive:

```
empid       firstname  lastname
----------- ---------- --------------------
1           Sara       Davis
```

If you want to make the filter case sensitive even though the column's collation is case insensitive, you can convert the collation of the expression:

```
SELECT empid, firstname, lastname
FROM HR.Employees
WHERE lastname COLLATE Latin1_General_CS_AS = N'davis';
```

This time the query returns an empty set because no match is found when a case-sensitive comparison is used.

Quoted identifiers

In standard SQL, single quotes are used to delimit literal character strings (for example, *'literal'*) and double quotes are used to delimit irregular identifiers such as table or column names that include a space or start with a digit (for example, *"Irregular Identifier"*). In SQL Server, there's a setting called *QUOTED_IDENTIFIER* that controls the meaning of double quotes. You can apply this setting either at the database level by using the *ALTER DATABASE* command or at the session level by using the *SET* command. When the setting is turned on, the behavior is determined according to standard SQL, meaning that double quotes are used to delimit identifiers. When the setting is turned off, the behavior is nonstandard, and double quotes are used to delimit literal character strings. It is strongly recommended that you follow best practices and use standard behavior (with the setting on). Most database interfaces, including OLE DB and ODBC, turn this setting on by default.

Tip As an alternative to using double quotes to delimit identifiers, T-SQL also supports square brackets (for example, *[Irregular Identifier]*).

Regarding single quotes that are used to delimit literal character strings, if you want to incorporate a single quote character as part of the string, you need to specify two single quotes. For example, to express the literal *abc'de*, specify **'abc''de'**.

Operators and functions

This section covers string concatenation and functions that operate on character strings. For string concatenation, T-SQL provides the plus-sign (+) operator and the *CONCAT* function. For other operations on character strings, T-SQL provides several functions, including *SUBSTRING, LEFT, RIGHT, LEN, DATALENGTH, CHARINDEX, PATINDEX, REPLACE, REPLICATE, STUFF, UPPER, LOWER, RTRIM, LTRIM, FORMAT, COMPRESS, DECOMPRESS*, and *STRING_SPLIT*. In the following sections, I describe these commonly used operators and functions. Note that there is no SQL standard functions library—they are all implementation-specific.

String concatenation (plus-sign [+] operator and *CONCAT* function)

T-SQL provides the plus-sign (+) operator and the *CONCAT* function to concatenate strings. For example, the following query against the *Employees* table produces the *fullname* result column by concatenating *firstname*, a space, and *lastname*:

```
SELECT empid, firstname + N' ' + lastname AS fullname
FROM HR.Employees;
```

This query produces the following output:

```
empid       fullname
----------- -------------------------------
1           Sara Davis
2           Don Funk
3           Judy Lew
4           Yael Peled
5           Sven Mortensen
6           Paul Suurs
7           Russell King
8           Maria Cameron
9           Patricia Doyle
```

Standard SQL dictates that a concatenation with a *NULL* should yield a *NULL*. This is the default behavior of T-SQL. For example, consider the query against the *Customers* table shown in Listing 2-7.

LISTING 2-7 Query demonstrating string concatenation

```
SELECT custid, country, region, city,
  country + N',' + region + N',' + city AS location
FROM Sales.Customers;
```

Some of the rows in the *Customers* table have a *NULL* in the region column. For those, SQL Server returns by default a *NULL* in the location result column:

```
custid      country         region  city            location
----------- --------------- ------- --------------- --------------------
1           Germany         NULL    Berlin          NULL
2           Mexico          NULL    México D.F.     NULL
3           Mexico          NULL    México D.F.     NULL
4           UK              NULL    London          NULL
5           Sweden          NULL    Luleå           NULL
6           Germany         NULL    Mannheim        NULL
7           France          NULL    Strasbourg      NULL
8           Spain           NULL    Madrid          NULL
9           France          NULL    Marseille       NULL
10          Canada          BC      Tsawwassen      Canada,BC,Tsawwassen
11          UK              NULL    London          NULL
12          Argentina       NULL    Buenos Aires    NULL
13          Mexico          NULL    México D.F.     NULL
14          Switzerland     NULL    Bern            NULL
15          Brazil          SP      Sao Paulo       Brazil,SP,Sao Paulo
16          UK              NULL    London          NULL
17          Germany         NULL    Aachen          NULL
18          France          NULL    Nantes          NULL
19          UK              NULL    London          NULL
20          Austria         NULL    Graz            NULL
...

(91 row(s) affected)
```

To treat a *NULL* as an empty string—or more accurately, to substitute a *NULL* with an empty string—you can use the *COALESCE* function. This function accepts a list of input values and returns the first that is not *NULL*. Here's how you can revise the query from Listing 2-7 to programmatically substitute *NULLs* with empty strings:

```
SELECT custid, country, region, city,
  country + COALESCE( N',' + region, N'') + N',' + city AS location
FROM Sales.Customers;
```

T-SQL supports a function called *CONCAT* that accepts a list of inputs for concatenation and automatically substitutes NULLs with empty strings. For example, the expression *CONCAT('a', NULL, 'b')* returns the string 'ab'.

Here's how to use the *CONCAT* function to concatenate the customer's location elements, replacing *NULLs* with empty strings:

```
SELECT custid, country, region, city,
```

```
  CONCAT(country, N',' + region, N',' + city) AS location
FROM Sales.Customers;
```

The *SUBSTRING* function

The *SUBSTRING* function extracts a substring from a string.

Syntax

SUBSTRING(*string, start, length*)

This function operates on the input *string* and extracts a substring starting at position *start* that is *length* characters long. For example, the following code returns the output 'abc':

```
SELECT SUBSTRING('abcde', 1, 3);
```

If the value of the third argument exceeds the end of the input string, the function returns everything until the end without raising an error. This can be convenient when you want to return everything from a certain point until the end of the string—you can simply specify the maximum length of the data type or a value representing the full length of the input string.

The *LEFT* and *RIGHT* functions

The *LEFT* and *RIGHT* functions are abbreviations of the *SUBSTRING* function, returning a requested number of characters from the left or right end of the input string.

Syntax

LEFT(*string, n*), RIGHT(*string, n*)

The first argument, *string*, is the string the function operates on. The second argument, *n*, is the number of characters to extract from the left or right end of the string. For example, the following code returns the output 'cde':

```
SELECT RIGHT('abcde', 3);
```

The *LEN* and *DATALENGTH* functions

The *LEN* function returns the number of characters in the input string.

Syntax

LEN(*string*)

Note that this function returns the number of characters in the input string and not necessarily the number of bytes. With regular characters, both numbers are the same because each character requires 1 byte of storage. With Unicode characters, each character requires at least 2 bytes of storage (in most cases, at least); therefore, the number of characters is half the number of bytes. To get the number of bytes, use the *DATALENGTH* function instead of *LEN*. For example, the following code returns 5:

```
SELECT LEN(N'abcde');
```

The following code returns 10:

```
SELECT DATALENGTH(N'abcde');
```

Another difference between *LEN* and *DATALENGTH* is that the former excludes trailing blanks but the latter doesn't.

The *CHARINDEX* function

The *CHARINDEX* function returns the position of the first occurrence of a substring within a string.

Syntax

CHARINDEX(*substring*, *string*[, *start_pos*])

This function returns the position of the first argument, *substring*, within the second argument, *string*. You can optionally specify a third argument, *start_pos*, to tell the function the position from which to start looking. If you don't specify the third argument, the function starts looking from the first character. If the substring is not found, the function returns 0. For example, the following code returns the first position of a space in *'Itzik Ben-Gan'*, so it returns the output 6:

```
SELECT CHARINDEX(' ','Itzik Ben-Gan');
```

The *PATINDEX* function

The *PATINDEX* function returns the position of the first occurrence of a pattern within a string.

Syntax

PATINDEX(*pattern*, *string*)

The argument *pattern* uses similar patterns to those used by the *LIKE* predicate in T-SQL. I'll explain patterns and the *LIKE* predicate later in this chapter, in "The *LIKE* predicate" section. Even though I haven't explained yet how patterns are expressed in T-SQL, I include the following example here to show how to find the position of the first occurrence of a digit within a string:

```
SELECT PATINDEX('%[0-9]%', 'abcd123efgh');
```

This code returns the output 5.

The *REPLACE* function

The *REPLACE* function replaces all occurrences of a substring with another.

Syntax

REPLACE(*string*, *substring1*, *substring2*)

The function replaces all occurrences of *substring1* in *string* with *substring2*. For example, the following code substitutes all occurrences of a dash in the input string with a colon:

```
SELECT REPLACE('1-a 2-b', '-', ':');
```

This code returns the output: '1:a 2:b'.

You can use the *REPLACE* function to count the number of occurrences of a character within a string. To do this, you replace all occurrences of the character with an empty string (zero characters) and calculate the original length of the string minus the new length. For example, the following query returns, for each employee, the number of times the character *e* appears in the *lastname* attribute:

```
SELECT empid, lastname,
  LEN(lastname) - LEN(REPLACE(lastname, 'e', '')) AS numoccur
FROM HR.Employees;
```

This query generates the following output:

```
empid       lastname             numoccur
----------- -------------------- -----------
8           Cameron              1
1           Davis                0
9           Doyle                1
2           Funk                 0
7           King                 0
3           Lew                  1
5           Mortensen            2
4           Peled                2
6           Suurs                0
```

The *REPLICATE* function

The *REPLICATE* function replicates a string a requested number of times.

Syntax

REPLICATE(*string*, *n*)

For example, the following code replicates the string 'abc' three times, returning the string 'abcabcabc':

```
SELECT REPLICATE('abc', 3);
```

The next example demonstrates the use of the *REPLICATE* function, along with the *RIGHT* function and string concatenation. The following query against the *Production.Suppliers* table generates a 10-digit string representation of the supplier ID integer with leading zeros:

```
SELECT supplierid,
  RIGHT(REPLICATE('0', 9) + CAST(supplierid AS VARCHAR(10)), 10) AS strsupplierid
FROM Production.Suppliers;
```

The expression producing the result column *strsupplierid* replicates the character *0* nine times (producing the string '000000000') and concatenates the string representation of the supplier ID. The

CAST function converts the original integer supplier ID to a string data type (*VARCHAR*). Finally, the *RIGHT* function extracts the 10 rightmost characters of the result string. Here's the output of this query, shown in abbreviated form:

```
supplierid  strsupplierid
----------- -------------
29          0000000029
28          0000000028
4           0000000004
21          0000000021
2           0000000002
22          0000000022
14          0000000014
11          0000000011
25          0000000025
7           0000000007
...

(29 row(s) affected)
```

Note that T-SQL supports a function called *FORMAT* that you can use to achieve such formatting needs much more easily, though at a higher cost. I'll describe it later in this section.

The *STUFF* function

You use the *STUFF* function to remove a substring from a string and insert a new substring instead.

Syntax

STUFF(*string, pos, delete_length, insert_string*)

This function operates on the input parameter *string*. It deletes as many characters as the number specified in the *delete_length* parameter, starting at the character position specified in the *pos* input parameter. The function inserts the string specified in the *insert_string* parameter in position *pos*. For example, the following code operates on the string 'xyz', removes one character from the second character, and inserts the substring 'abc' instead:

```
SELECT STUFF('xyz', 2, 1, 'abc');
```

The output of this code is 'xabcz'.

If you just want to insert a string and not delete anything, you can specify a length of 0 as the third argument.

The *UPPER* and *LOWER* functions

The *UPPER* and *LOWER* functions return the input string with all uppercase or lowercase characters, respectively.

Syntax

UPPER(*string*), LOWER(*string*)

For example, the following code returns 'ITZIK BEN-GAN':

```
SELECT UPPER('Itzik Ben-Gan');
```

The following code returns 'itzik ben-gan':

```
SELECT LOWER('Itzik Ben-Gan');
```

The *RTRIM* and *LTRIM* functions

The *RTRIM* and *LTRIM* functions return the input string with leading or trailing spaces removed.

Syntax

RTRIM(*string*), LTRIM(*string*)

If you want to remove both leading and trailing spaces, use the result of one function as the input to the other. For example, the following code removes both leading and trailing spaces from the input string, returning 'abc':

```
SELECT RTRIM(LTRIM('   abc   '));
```

The *FORMAT* function

You use the *FORMAT* function to format an input value as a character string based on a Microsoft .NET format string and an optional culture specification.

Syntax

FORMAT(*input* , *format_string*, *culture*)

There are numerous possibilities for formatting inputs using both standard and custom format strings. The MSDN article at *http://go.microsoft.com/fwlink/?LinkId=211776* provides more information. But just as a simple example, recall the convoluted expression used earlier to format a number as a 10-digit string with leading zeros. By using *FORMAT*, you can achieve the same task with either the custom format string '0000000000' or the standard one, 'd10'. As an example, the following code returns '0000001759':

```
SELECT FORMAT(1759, '000000000');
```

> **Note** The FORMAT function is usually more expensive than alternative T-SQL functions that you use to format values. You should generally refrain from using it unless you are willing to accept the performance penalty. As an example, I ran a query against a table with 1,000,000 rows to compute the 10-digit string representation of one of the integer columns. The query took close to a minute to complete on my computer with the *FORMAT* function compared to under a second with the alternative method using the *REPLICATE* and *RIGHT* functions.

The COMPRESS and DECOMPRESS functions

The *COMPRESS* and *DECOMPRESS* functions use the GZIP algorithm to compress and decompress the input, respectively. Both functions were introduced in SQL Server 2016.

Syntax

COMPRESS(*string*), DECOMPRESS(*string*)

The *COMPRESS* function accepts a character or binary string as input and returns a compressed *VARBINARY(MAX)* typed value. Here's an example for using the function with a constant as input:

```
SELECT COMPRESS(N'This is my cv. Imagine it was much longer.');
```

The result is a binary value holding the compressed form of the input string.

If you want to store the compressed form of input values in a column in a table, you need to apply the *COMPRESS* function to the input value and store the result in the table. You can do this as part of the *INSERT* statement that adds the row to the target table. (For information about data modification, see Chapter 8.) For example, suppose you have a table called *EmployeeCVs* in your database, with columns called *empid* and *cv*. The column *cv* holds the compressed form of the employee's resume and is defined as *VARBINARY(MAX)*. Suppose you have a stored procedure called *AddEmpCV* that accepts input parameters called *@empid* and *@cv*. (For information about stored procedures, see Chapter 11.) The parameter *@cv* is the uncompressed form of the input employee's resume and is defined as *NVARCHAR(MAX)*. The procedure is responsible for inserting a new row into the table with the compressed employee resume information. The *INSERT* statement within the stored procedure might look like this:

```
INSERT INTO dbo.EmployeeCVs( empid, cv ) VALUES( @empid, COMPRESS(@cv) );
```

The *DECOMPRESS* function accepts a binary string as input and returns a decompressed *VARBINARY(MAX)* typed value. Note that if the value you originally compressed was of a character string type, you will need to explicitly cast the result of the *DECOMPRESS* function to the target type. As an example, the following code doesn't return the original input value; rather, it returns a binary value:

```
SELECT DECOMPRESS(COMPRESS(N'This is my cv. Imagine it was much longer.'));
```

To get the original value, you need to cast the result to the target character string type, like so:

```
SELECT
  CAST(
    DECOMPRESS(COMPRESS(N'This is my cv. Imagine it was much longer.'))
      AS NVARCHAR(MAX));
```

Consider the *EmployeeCVs* table from the earlier example. To return the uncompressed form of the employee resumes, you use the following query (don't run this code because this table doesn't actually exist):

```
SELECT empid, CAST(DECOMPRESS(cv) AS NVARCHAR(MAX)) AS cv
FROM dbo.EmployeeCVs;
```

The *STRING_SPLIT* function

The *STRING_SPLIT* table function splits an input string with a separated list of values into the individual elements. This function was introduced in SQL Server 2016.

Syntax

SELECT value FROM STRING_SPLIT(*string, separator*);

Unlike the string functions described so far, which are all scalar functions, the *STRING_SPLIT* function is a table function. It accepts as inputs a string with a separated list of values plus a separator, and it returns a table result with a string column called *val* with the individual elements. If you need the elements to be returned with a data type other than a character string, you will need to cast the *val* column to the target type. For example, the following code accepts the input string '10248,10249,10250' and separator ',' and it returns a table result with the individual elements:

```
SELECT CAST(value AS INT) AS myvalue
FROM STRING_SPLIT('10248,10249,10250', ',') AS S;
```

In this example, the input list contains values representing order IDs. Because the IDs are supposed to be integers, the query converts the *val* column to the *INT* data type. Here's the output of this code:

```
myvalue
-----------
10248
10249
10250
```

A common use case for such splitting logic is passing a separated list of values representing keys, such as order IDs, to a stored procedure or user-defined function and returning the rows from some table, such as Orders, that have the input keys. This is achieved by joining the *STRING_SPLIT* function with the target table and matching the keys from both sides.

The *LIKE* predicate

T-SQL provides a predicate called *LIKE* that you can use to check whether a character string matches a specified pattern. Similar patterns are used by the *PATINDEX* function described earlier. The following section describes the wildcards supported in the patterns and demonstrates their use.

The % (percent) wildcard

The percent sign represents a string of any size, including an empty string. For example, the following query returns employees where the last name starts with *D*:

```
SELECT empid, lastname
FROM HR.Employees
WHERE lastname LIKE N'D%';
```

This query returns the following output:

```
empid       lastname
----------- --------------------
1           Davis
9           Doyle
```

Note that often you can use functions such as *SUBSTRING* and *LEFT* instead of the *LIKE* predicate to represent the same meaning. But the *LIKE* predicate tends to get optimized better—especially when the pattern starts with a known prefix.

The _ (underscore) wildcard

An underscore represents a single character. For example, the following query returns employees where the second character in the last name is *e*:

```
SELECT empid, lastname
FROM HR.Employees
WHERE lastname LIKE N'_e%';
```

This query returns the following output:

```
empid       lastname
----------- --------------------
3           Lew
4           Peled
```

The [<*list of characters*>] wildcard

Square brackets with a list of characters (such as *[ABC]*) represent a single character that must be one of the characters specified in the list. For example, the following query returns employees where the first character in the last name is *A*, *B*, or *C*:

```
SELECT empid, lastname
FROM HR.Employees
WHERE lastname LIKE N'[ABC]%';
```

This query returns the following output:

```
empid       lastname
----------- --------------------
8           Cameron
```

The [<*character*>-<*character*>] wildcard

Square brackets with a character range (such as *[A-E]*) represent a single character that must be within the specified range. For example, the following query returns employees where the first character in the last name is a letter in the range *A* through *E*, inclusive, taking the collation into account:

```
SELECT empid, lastname
FROM HR.Employees
WHERE lastname LIKE N'[A-E]%';
```

This query returns the following output:

```
empid       lastname
----------- --------------------
8           Cameron
1           Davis
9           Doyle
```

The [^<*character list or range*>] wildcard

Square brackets with a caret sign (^) followed by a character list or range (such as *[^A-E]*) represent a single character that is not in the specified character list or range. For example, the following query returns employees where the first character in the last name is not a letter in the range *A* through *E*:

```
SELECT empid, lastname
FROM HR.Employees
WHERE lastname LIKE N'[^A-E]%';
```

This query returns the following output:

```
empid       lastname
----------- --------------------
2           Funk
7           King
3           Lew
5           Mortensen
4           Peled
6           Suurs
```

The *ESCAPE* character

If you want to search for a character that is also used as a wildcard (such as %, _, [, or]), you can use an escape character. Specify a character that you know for sure doesn't appear in the data as the escape character in front of the character you are looking for, and specify the keyword *ESCAPE* followed by the escape character right after the pattern. For example, to check whether a column called *col1* contains an underscore, use *col1 LIKE '%!_%' ESCAPE '!'*.

For the wildcards %, _, and [, you can use square brackets instead of an escape character. For example, instead of *col1 LIKE '%!_%' ESCAPE '!'*, you can use *col1 LIKE '%[_]%'*.

Working with date and time data

Working with date and time data in SQL Server is not trivial. You will face several challenges in this area, such as expressing literals in a language-neutral manner and working with date and time separately.

In this section, I first introduce the date and time data types supported by SQL Server; then I explain the recommended way to work with those types; and finally I cover date- and time-related functions.

Date and time data types

T-SQL supports six date and time data types: two legacy types called *DATETIME* and *SMALLDATETIME*, and four later additions (since SQL Server 2008) called *DATE, TIME, DATETIME2,* and *DATETIMEOFFSET*. The legacy types *DATETIME* and *SMALLDATETIME* include date and time components that are inseparable. The two types differ in their storage requirements, their supported date range, and their precision. The *DATE* and *TIME* data types provide a separation between the date and time components if you need it. The *DATETIME2* data type has a bigger date range and better precision than the legacy types. The *DATETIMEOFFSET* data type is similar to *DATETIME2*, but it also includes the offset from UTC.

Table 2-1 lists details about date and time data types, including storage requirements, supported date range, precision, and recommended entry format.

TABLE 2-1 Date and time data types

Data type	Storage (bytes)	Date range	Accuracy	Recommended entry format and example
DATETIME	8	January 1, 1753, through December 31, 9999	3 1/3 milliseconds	'YYYYMMDD hh:mm:ss.nnn' '20160212 12:30:15.123'
SMALLDATETIME	4	January 1, 1900, through June 6, 2079	1 minute	"YYYYMMDD hh:mm' '20160212 12:30'
DATE	3	January 1, 0001, through December 31, 9999	1 day	'YYYY-MM-DD' '2016-02-12'
TIME	3 to 5	N/A	100 nanoseconds	'hh:mm:ss.nnnnnnn' '12:30:15.1234567'
DATETIME2	6 to 8	January 1, 0001, through December 31, 9999	100 nanoseconds	'YYYY-MM-DD hh:mm:ss.nnnnnnn' '2016-02-12 12:30:15.1234567'
DATETIMEOFFSET	8 to 10	January 1, 0001, through December 31, 9999	100 nanoseconds	'YYYY-MM-DD hh:mm:ss.nnnnnnn [+|-] hh:mm' '2016-02-12 12:30:15.1234567 +02:00'

The storage requirements for the last three data types in Table 2-1 (*TIME, DATETIME2,* and *DATETIMEOFFSET*) depend on the precision you choose. You specify a fractional-second precision as an integer in the range 0 to 7. For example, *TIME(0)* means 0 fractional-second precision—in other words, one-second precision. *TIME(3)* means one-millisecond precision, and *TIME(7)* means 100-nanosecond precision. If you don't specify a fractional-second precision, SQL Server assumes 7 by default. When converting a value to a data type with a lower precision, it gets rounded to the closest expressible value in the target precision.

Literals

When you need to specify a literal (constant) of a date and time data type, you should consider several things. First, though it might sound a bit strange, T-SQL doesn't provide the means to express a date and time literal; instead, you can specify a literal of a different type that can be converted—explicitly or implicitly—to a date and time data type. It is a best practice to use character strings to express date and time values, as shown in the following example:

```
SELECT orderid, custid, empid, orderdate
FROM Sales.Orders
WHERE orderdate = '20160212';
```

SQL Server recognizes the literal '20160212' as a character-string literal and not as a date and time literal, but because the expression involves operands of two different types, one operand needs to be implicitly converted to the other's type. Normally, implicit conversion between types is based on what's called *data-type precedence*. SQL Server defines precedence among data types and will usually implicitly convert the operand that has a lower data-type precedence to the one that has higher precedence. In this example, the character-string literal is converted to the column's data type (*DATETIME*) because character strings are considered lower in terms of data-type precedence with respect to date and time data types. Implicit conversion rules are not always that simple. In fact, different rules are applied with filters and in other expressions, but for the purposes of this discussion, I'll keep things simple. For the complete description of data-type precedence, see "Data Type Precedence" in SQL Server Books Online.

The point I'm trying to make is that in the preceding example, implicit conversion takes place behind the scenes. This query is logically equivalent to the following one, which explicitly converts the character string to a *DATE* data type:

```
SELECT orderid, custid, empid, orderdate
FROM Sales.Orders
WHERE orderdate = CAST('20160212' AS DATE);
```

Note that some character-string formats of date and time literals are language dependent, meaning that when you convert them to a date and time data type, SQL Server might interpret the value differently based on the language setting in effect in the session. Each login defined by the database administrator has a default language associated with it, and unless it is changed explicitly, that language becomes the effective language in the session. You can overwrite the default language in your session by using the *SET LANGUAGE* command, but this is generally not recommended because some aspects of the code might rely on the user's default language.

The effective language in the session sets several language-related settings behind the scenes. Among them is one called *DATEFORMAT*, which determines how SQL Server interprets the literals you enter when they are converted from a character-string type to a date and time type. The *DATEFORMAT* setting is expressed as a combination of the characters *d*, *m*, and *y*. For example, the *us_english* language setting sets the *DATEFORMAT* to *mdy*, whereas the *British* language setting sets the *DATEFORMAT* to *dmy*. You can override the *DATEFORMAT* setting in your session by using the *SET DATEFORMAT* command, but as mentioned earlier, changing language-related settings is generally not recommended.

Consider, for example, the literal '02/12/2016'. SQL Server can interpret the date as either February 12, 2016 or December 2, 2016 when you convert this literal to one of the following types: *DATETIME*, *SMALLDATETIME*, *DATE*, *DATETIME2*, or *DATETIMEOFFSET*. The effective *LANGUAGE/DATEFORMAT* setting is the determining factor. To demonstrate different interpretations of the same character-string literal, run the following code:

```
SET LANGUAGE British;
SELECT CAST('02/12/2016' AS DATE);

SET LANGUAGE us_english;
SELECT CAST('02/12/2016' AS DATE);
```

Notice in the output that the literal was interpreted differently in the two different language environments:

```
Changed language setting to British.

----------
2016-12-02

Changed language setting to us_english.

----------
2016-02-12
```

Note that the *LANGUAGE/DATEFORMAT* setting affects only the way the values you enter are interpreted; these settings have no impact on the format used in the output for presentation purposes. Output format is determined by the database interface used by the client tool (such as ODBC) and not by the *LANGUAGE/DATEFORMAT* setting. For example, OLE DB and ODBC present *DATE* values in the format *'YYYY-MM-DD'*.

Because the code you write might end up being used by international users with different language settings for their logins, understanding that some formats of literals are language dependent is crucial. It is strongly recommended that you phrase your literals in a language-neutral manner. Language-neutral formats are always interpreted by SQL Server the same way and are not affected by language-related settings.

Table 2-2 provides literal formats that are considered neutral for each of the date and time types.

TABLE 2-2 Language-neutral date and time data type formats

Data type	Accuracy	Recommended entry format and example
DATETIME	'YYYYMMDD hh:mm:ss.nnn' 'YYYY-MM-DDThh:mm:ss.nnn' 'YYYYMMDD'	'20160212 12:30:15.123' '2016-02-12T12:30:15.123' '20160212'
SMALLDATETIME	'YYYYMMDD hh:mm' 'YYYY-MM-DDThh:mm' 'YYYYMMDD'	'20160212 12:30' '2016-02-12T12:30' '20160212'
DATE	'YYYYMMDD' 'YYYY-MM-DD'	'20160212' '2016-02-12'
DATETIME2	'YYYYMMDD hh:mm:ss.nnnnnnn' 'YYYY-MM-DD hh:mm:ss.nnnnnnn' 'YYYY-MM-DDThh:mm:ss.nnnnnnn' 'YYYYMMDD' 'YYYY-MM-DD'	'20160212 12:30:15.1234567' '2016-02-12 12:30:15.1234567' '2016-02-12T12:30:15.1234567' '20160212' '2016-02-12'
DATETIMEOFFSET	'YYYYMMDD hh:mm:ss.nnnnnnn [+|-]hh:mm' 'YYYY-MM-DD hh:mm:ss.nnnnnnn [+|-]hh:mm' 'YYYYMMDD' 'YYYY-MM-DD'	'20160212 12:30:15.1234567 +02:00' '2016-02-12 12:30:15.1234567 +02:00' '20160212' '2016-02-12'
TIME	'hh:mm:ss.nnnnnnn'	'12:30:15.1234567'

Note a couple of things about Table 2-2. With all types that include both date and time components, if you don't specify a time part in your literal, SQL Server assumes midnight. If you don't specify an offset from UTC, SQL Server assumes 00:00. Also note that the formats 'YYYY-MM-DD' and 'YYYY-

MM-DD hh:mm...' are language dependent when converted to *DATETIME* or *SMALLDATETIME* and language neutral when converted to *DATE*, *DATETIME2*, and *DATETIMEOFFSET*.

For example, notice in the following code that the language setting has no impact on how a literal expressed with the format 'YYYYMMDD' is interpreted when it is converted to *DATE*:

```
SET LANGUAGE British;
SELECT CAST('20160212' AS DATE);

SET LANGUAGE us_english;
SELECT CAST('20160212' AS DATE);
```

The output shows that the literal was interpreted in both cases as February 12, 2016:

```
Changed language setting to British.

----------
2016-02-12

Changed language setting to us_english.

----------
2016-02-12
```

I probably can't emphasize enough that using language-neutral formats such as 'YYYYMMDD' is a best practice, because such formats are interpreted the same way regardless of the *LANGUAGE/DATEFORMAT* settings.

If you insist on using a language-dependent format to express literals, there are two options available to you. One is to use the *CONVERT* function to explicitly convert the character-string literal to the requested data type and, in the third argument, specify a number representing the style you used. SQL Server Books Online has a table with all the style numbers and the formats they represent. You can find it under the topic "The *CAST* and *CONVERT* Functions." For example, if you want to specify the literal '02/12/2016' with the format *MM/DD/YYYY*, use style number 101, as shown here:

```
SELECT CONVERT(DATE, '02/12/2016', 101);
```

The literal is interpreted as February 12, 2016, regardless of the language setting that is in effect.

If you want to use the format *DD/MM/YYYY*, use style number 103:

```
SELECT CONVERT(DATE, '02/12/2016', 103);
```

This time, the literal is interpreted as December 2, 2016.

Another option is to use the *PARSE* function. By using this function, you can parse a value as a requested type and indicate the culture. For example, the following is the equivalent of using *CONVERT* with style 101 (US English):

```
SELECT PARSE('02/12/2016' AS DATE USING 'en-US');
```

The following is equivalent to using *CONVERT* with style 103 (British English):

```
SELECT PARSE('02/12/2016' AS DATE USING 'en-GB');
```

> **Note** The *PARSE* function is significantly more expensive than the *CONVERT* function; therefore, it is generally recommended you refrain from using it.

Working with date and time separately

If you need to work with only dates or only times, it's recommended that you use the *DATE* and *TIME* data types, respectively. Adhering to this guideline can become challenging if you need to restrict yourself to using only the legacy types *DATETIME* and *SMALLDATETIME* for reasons such as compatibility with older systems. The challenge is that the legacy types contain both the date and time components. The best practice in such a case says that when you want to work only with dates, you store the date with a value of midnight in the time part. When you want to work only with times, you store the time with the base date January 1, 1900.

To demonstrate working with date and time separately, I'll use a table called *Sales.Orders2*, which has a column called *orderdate* of a *DATETIME* data type. Run the following code to create the *Sales.Orders2* table by copying data from the *Sales.Orders* table and casting the source *orderdate* column, which is of a *DATE* type, to *DATETIME*:

```
DROP TABLE IF EXISTS Sales.Orders2;

SELECT orderid, custid, empid, CAST(orderdate AS DATETIME) AS orderdate
INTO Sales.Orders2
FROM Sales.Orders;
```

Don't worry if you're not familiar yet with the *SELECT INTO* statement. I describe it in Chapter 8, "Data modifications."

As mentioned, the *orderdate* column in the *Sales.Orders2* table is of a *DATETIME* data type, but because only the date component is actually relevant, all values contain midnight as the time. When you need to filter only orders from a certain date, you don't have to use a range filter. Instead, you can use the equality operator like this:

```
SELECT orderid, custid, empid, orderdate
FROM Sales.Orders2
WHERE orderdate = '20160212';
```

When SQL Server converts a character-string literal that has only a date to *DATETIME*, it assumes midnight by default. Because all values in the *orderdate* column contain midnight in the time component, all orders placed on the requested date will be returned. Note that you can use a *CHECK* constraint to ensure that only midnight is used as the time part:

```
ALTER TABLE Sales.Orders2
  ADD CONSTRAINT CHK_Orders2_orderdate
```

```
CHECK( CONVERT(CHAR(12), orderdate, 114) = '00:00:00:000' );
```

The *CONVERT* function extracts the time-only portion of the *orderdate* value as a character string using style 114. The *CHECK* constraint verifies that the string represents midnight.

If the time component is stored with nonmidnight values, you can use a range filter like this:

```
SELECT orderid, custid, empid, orderdate
FROM Sales.Orders2
WHERE orderdate >= '20160212'
  AND orderdate < '20160213';
```

If you want to work only with times using the legacy types, you can store all values with the base date of January 1, 1900. When SQL Server converts a character-string literal that contains only a time component to *DATETIME* or *SMALLDATETIME*, SQL Server assumes that the date is the base date. For example, run the following code:

```
SELECT CAST('12:30:15.123' AS DATETIME);
```

You get the following output:

```
-----------------------
1900-01-01 12:30:15.123
```

Suppose you have a table with a column called *tm* of a *DATETIME* data type and you store all values by using the base date. Again, this can be enforced with a *CHECK* constraint. To return all rows for which the time value is 12:30:15.123, you use the filter *WHERE tm = '12:30:15.123'*. Because you did not specify a date component, SQL Server assumes the date is the base date when it implicitly converts the character string to a *DATETIME* data type.

If you want to work only with dates or only with times using the legacy types, but the input values you get include both date and time components, you need to apply some manipulation to the input values to "zero" the irrelevant part. That is, set the time component to midnight if you want to work only with dates, and set the date component to the base date if you want to work only with times. I'll explain how you can achieve this shortly, in the "Date and Time functions" section.

Run the following code for cleanup:

```
DROP TABLE IF EXISTS Sales.Orders2;
```

Filtering date ranges

When you need to filter a range of dates, such as a whole year or a whole month, it seems natural to use functions such as *YEAR* and *MONTH*. For example, the following query returns all orders placed in the year 2015:

```
SELECT orderid, custid, empid, orderdate
FROM Sales.Orders
WHERE YEAR(orderdate) = 2015;
```

However, you should be aware that in most cases, when you apply manipulation on the filtered column, SQL Server cannot use an index in an efficient manner. This is probably hard to understand without some background about indexes and performance, which are outside the scope of this book. For now, just keep this general point in mind: To have the potential to use an index efficiently, you shouldn't manipulate the filtered column. To achieve this, you can revise the filter predicate from the last query like this:

```
SELECT orderid, custid, empid, orderdate
FROM Sales.Orders
WHERE orderdate >= '20150101' AND orderdate < '20160101';
```

Similarly, instead of using functions to filter orders placed in a particular month, like this:

```
SELECT orderid, custid, empid, orderdate
FROM Sales.Orders
WHERE YEAR(orderdate) = 2016 AND MONTH(orderdate) = 2;
```

use a range filter, like the following:

```
SELECT orderid, custid, empid, orderdate
FROM Sales.Orders
WHERE orderdate >= '20160201' AND orderdate < '20160301';
```

Date and time functions

In this section, I describe functions that operate on date and time data types, including *GETDATE, CURRENT_TIMESTAMP, GETUTCDATE, SYSDATETIME, SYSUTCDATETIME, SYSDATETIMEOFFSET, CAST, CONVERT, SWITCHOFFSET, AT TIME ZONE, TODATETIMEOFFSET, DATEADD, DATEDIFF* and *DATEDIFF_BIG, DATEPART, YEAR, MONTH, DAY, DATENAME*, various *FROMPARTS* functions, and *EOMONTH*.

Current date and time

The following *niladic* (parameterless) functions return the current date and time values in the system where the SQL Server instance resides: *GETDATE, CURRENT_TIMESTAMP, GETUTCDATE, SYSDATETIME, SYSUTCDATETIME*, and *SYSDATETIMEOFFSET*.

Table 2-3 provides the description of these functions.

TABLE 2-3 Functions returning current date and time

Function	Return type	Description
GETDATE	*DATETIME*	Current date and time
CURRENT_TIMESTAMP	*DATETIME*	Same as GETDATE but ANSI SQL–compliant
GETUTCDATE	*DATETIME*	Current date and time in UTC
SYSDATETIME	*DATETIME2*	Current date and time
SYSUTCDATETIME	*DATETIME2*	Current date and time in UTC
SYSDATETIMEOFFSET	*DATETIMEOFFSET*	Current date and time, including the offset from UTC

Note that you need to specify empty parentheses with all functions that should be specified without parameters, except the standard function *CURRENT_TIMESTAMP*. Also, because *CURRENT_TIMESTAMP* and *GETDATE* return the same thing but only the former is standard, it is recommended that you use the former. This is a practice I try to follow in general—when I have several options that do the same thing with no functional or performance difference, and one is standard but others aren't, my preference is to use the standard option.

The following code demonstrates using the current date and time functions:

```
SELECT
  GETDATE()              AS [GETDATE],
  CURRENT_TIMESTAMP      AS [CURRENT_TIMESTAMP],
  GETUTCDATE()           AS [GETUTCDATE],
  SYSDATETIME()          AS [SYSDATETIME],
  SYSUTCDATETIME()       AS [SYSUTCDATETIME],
  SYSDATETIMEOFFSET() AS [SYSDATETIMEOFFSET];
```

As you probably noticed, none of the functions return only the current system date or only the current system time. However, you can get those easily by converting *CURRENT_TIMESTAMP* or *SYSDATETIME* to *DATE* or *TIME* like this:

```
SELECT
  CAST(SYSDATETIME() AS DATE) AS [current_date],
  CAST(SYSDATETIME() AS TIME) AS [current_time];
```

The *CAST*, *CONVERT*, and *PARSE* functions and their *TRY_* counterparts

The *CAST*, *CONVERT*, and *PARSE* functions are used to convert an input value to some target type. If the conversion succeeds, the functions return the converted value; otherwise, they cause the query to fail. The three functions have counterparts called *TRY_CAST*, *TRY_CONVERT*, and *TRY_PARSE*, respectively. Each version with the prefix TRY_ accepts the same input as its counterpart and applies the same conversion; the difference is that if the input isn't convertible to the target type, the function returns a *NULL* instead of failing the query.

Syntax

CAST(*value* AS *datatype*)

TRY_CAST(*value* AS *datatype*)

CONVERT (*datatype*, *value* [, *style_number*])

TRY_CONVERT (*datatype*, *value* [, *style_number*])

PARSE (*value* AS *datatype* [USING *culture*])

TRY_PARSE (*value* AS *datatype* [USING *culture*])

All three base functions convert the input *value* to the specified target *datatype*. In some cases, *CONVERT* has a third argument with which you can specify the style of the conversion. For example, when you are converting from a character string to one of the date and time data types (or the other way around), the style number indicates the format of the string. For example, style 101 indicates 'MM/DD/YYYY', and style 103 indicates 'DD/MM/YYYY'. You can find the full list of style numbers and their meanings in SQL Server Books Online under "*CAST* and *CONVERT*." Similarly, where applicable, the *PARSE* function supports the indication of a culture—for example, *'en-US'* for U.S. English and *'en-GB'* for British English.

As mentioned earlier, when you are converting from a character string to one of the date and time data types, some of the string formats are language dependent. I recommend either using one of the language-neutral formats or using the *CONVERT* function and explicitly specifying the style number. This way, your code is interpreted the same way regardless of the language of the login running it.

Note that *CAST* is standard and *CONVERT* and *PARSE* aren't, so unless you need to use the style number or culture, it is recommended that you use the *CAST* function.

Following are a few examples of using the *CAST*, *CONVERT*, and *PARSE* functions with date and time data types. The following code converts the character string literal '20160212' to a *DATE* data type:

```
SELECT CAST('20160212' AS DATE);
```

The following code converts the current system date and time value to a *DATE* data type, practically extracting only the current system date:

```
SELECT CAST(SYSDATETIME() AS DATE);
```

The following code converts the current system date and time value to a *TIME* data type, practically extracting only the current system time:

```
SELECT CAST(SYSDATETIME() AS TIME);
```

As suggested earlier, if you need to work with the *DATETIME* or *SMALLEDATETIME* types (for example, to be compatible with legacy systems) and want to represent only a date or only a time, you can set the irrelevant part to a specific value. To work only with dates, you set the time to midnight. To work only with time, you set the date to the base date January 1, 1900.

The following code converts the current date and time value to *CHAR(8)* by using style 112 ('YYYYMMDD'):

```
SELECT CONVERT(CHAR(8), CURRENT_TIMESTAMP, 112);
```

For example, if the current date is February 12, 2016, this code returns '20160212'. You then convert the character string back to *DATETIME* and get the current date at midnight:

```
SELECT CONVERT(DATETIME, CONVERT(CHAR(8), CURRENT_TIMESTAMP, 112), 112);
```

Similarly, to zero the date portion to the base date, you can first convert the current date and time value to *CHAR(12)* by using style 114 ('hh:mm:ss.nnn'):

```
SELECT CONVERT(CHAR(12), CURRENT_TIMESTAMP, 114);
```

When the code is converted back to *DATETIME*, you get the current time on the base date:

```
SELECT CONVERT(DATETIME, CONVERT(CHAR(12), CURRENT_TIMESTAMP, 114), 114);
```

As for using the *PARSE* function, here are a couple of examples:

```
SELECT PARSE('02/12/2016' AS DATETIME USING 'en-US');
SELECT PARSE('02/12/2016' AS DATETIME USING 'en-GB');
```

The first example parses the input string by using a U.S. English culture, and the second one does so by using a British English culture.

As a reminder, the *PARSE* function is significantly more expensive than the *CONVERT* function; therefore, I recommend you use the latter.

The *SWITCHOFFSET* function

The *SWITCHOFFSET* function adjusts an input *DATETIMEOFFSET* value to a specified target offset from UTC.

Syntax

SWITCHOFFSET(*datetimeoffset_value, UTC_offset*)

For example, the following code adjusts the current system *datetimeoffset* value to offset –05:00.

```
SELECT SWITCHOFFSET(SYSDATETIMEOFFSET(), '-05:00');
```

So if the current system *datetimeoffset* value is February 12, 2016 10:00:00.0000000 –08:00, this code returns the value February 12, 2016 13:00:00.0000000 –05:00.

The following code adjusts the current *datetimeoffset* value to UTC:

```
SELECT SWITCHOFFSET(SYSDATETIMEOFFSET(), '+00:00');
```

Assuming the aforementioned current *datetimeoffset* value, this code returns the value February 12, 2016 18:00:00.0000000 +00:00.

The *TODATETIMEOFFSET* function

The *TODATETIMEOFFSET* function constructs a *DATETIMEOFFSET* typed value from a local date and time value and an offset from UTC.

Syntax

TODATETIMEOFFSET(*local_date_and_time_value, UTC_offset*)

This function is different from *SWITCHOFFSET* in that its first input is a local date and time value without an offset component. This function simply merges the input date and time value with the specified offset to create a new *datetimeoffset* value.

You will typically use this function when migrating non-offset-aware data to offset-aware data. Imagine you have a table holding local date and time values in an attribute called *dt* of a *DATETIME2* or

DATETIME data type and holding the offset in an attribute called *theoffset*. You then decide to merge the two to one offset-aware attribute called *dto*. You alter the table and add the new attribute. Then you update it to the result of the expression *TODATETIMEOFFSET(dt, theoffset)*. Then you can drop the two existing attributes *dt* and *theoffset*.

The *AT TIME ZONE* function

The *AT TIME ZONE* function accepts an input date and time value and converts it to a *datetimeoffset* value that corresponds to the specified target time zone. This function was introduced in SQL Server 2016.

Syntax

dt_val AT TIME ZONE *time_zone*

The input *dt_val* can be of the following data types: *DATETIME, SMALLDATETIME, DATETIME2*, and *DATETIMEOFFSET*. The input *time_zone* can be any of the supported Windows time-zone names as they appear in the *name* column in the *sys.time_zone_info* view. Use the following query to see the available time zones, their current offset from UTC and whether it's currently Daylight Savings Time (DST):

```
SELECT name, current_utc_offset, is_currently_dst
FROM sys.time_zone_info;
```

Regarding *dt_val*: when using any of the three non-*datetimeoffset* types (*DATETIME, SMALLDATE-TIME*, and *DATETIME2*), the *AT TIME ZONE* function assumes the input value is already in the target time zone. As a result, it behaves similar to the *TODATETIMEOFFSET* function, except the offset isn't necessarily fixed. It depends on whether DST applies. Take the time zone Pacific Standard Time as an example. When it's not DST, the offset from UTC is –08:00; when it is DST, the offset is –07:00. The following code demonstrates the use of this function with non-*datetimeoffset* inputs:

```
SELECT
  CAST('20160212 12:00:00.0000000' AS DATETIME2)
    AT TIME ZONE 'Pacific Standard Time' AS val1,
  CAST('20160812 12:00:00.0000000' AS DATETIME2)
    AT TIME ZONE 'Pacific Standard Time' AS val2;
```

This code generates the following output:

```
val1                               val2
---------------------------------- ----------------------------------
2016-02-12 12:00:00.0000000 -08:00 2016-08-12 12:00:00.0000000 -07:00
```

The first value happens when DST doesn't apply; hence, offset –08:00 is assumed. The second value happens during DST; hence, offset –07:00 is assumed. Here there's no ambiguity.

There are two tricky cases: when switching to DST and when switching from DST. For example, in Pacific Standard Time, when switching to DST the clock is advanced by an hour, so there's an hour that doesn't exist. If you specify a nonexisting time during that hour, the offset before the change (–08:00) is assumed. When switching from DST, the clock retreats by an hour, so there's an hour that repeats itself. If you specify a time during that hour, starting at the bottom of the hour, non-DST is assumed (that is, the offset –08:00 is used).

When the input *dt_val* is a *datetimeoffset* value, the *AT TIME ZONE* function behaves more similarly to the *SWITCHOFFSET* function. Again, however, the target offset isn't necessarily fixed. T-SQL uses the Windows time-zone-conversion rules to apply the conversion. The following code demonstrates the use of the function with *datetimeoffset* inputs:

```
SELECT
  CAST('20160212 12:00:00.0000000 -05:00' AS DATETIMEOFFSET)
    AT TIME ZONE 'Pacific Standard Time' AS val1,
  CAST('20160812 12:00:00.0000000 -04:00' AS DATETIMEOFFSET)
    AT TIME ZONE 'Pacific Standard Time' AS val2;
```

The input values reflect the time zone Eastern Standard Time. Both have noon in the time component. The first value occurs when DST doesn't apply (offset is –05:00), and the second one occurs when DST does apply (that is, the offset is –04:00). Both values are converted to the time zone Pacific Standard Time (the offset –08:00 when DST doesn't apply and –07:00 when it does). In both cases, the time needs to retreat by three hours to 9:00 AM. You get the following output:

```
val1                               val2
---------------------------------- ----------------------------------
2016-02-12 09:00:00.0000000 -08:00 2016-08-12 09:00:00.0000000 -07:00
```

The *DATEADD* function

You use the *DATEADD* function to add a specified number of units of a specified date part to an input date and time value.

Syntax

DATEADD(*part, n, dt_val*)

Valid values for the *part* input include *year, quarter, month, dayofyear, day, week, weekday, hour, minute, second, millisecond, microsecond,* and *nanosecond*. You can also specify the part in abbreviated form, such as *yy* instead of *year*. Refer to SQL Server Books Online for details.

The return type for a date and time input is the same type as the input's type. If this function is given a string literal as input, the output is *DATETIME*.

For example, the following code adds one year to February 12, 2016:

```
SELECT DATEADD(year, 1, '20160212');
```

This code returns the following output:

```
-----------------------
2017-02-12 00:00:00.000
```

The *DATEDIFF* and *DATEDIFF_BIG* Functions

The *DATEDIFF* and *DATEDIFF_BIG* functions return the difference between two date and time values in terms of a specified date part. The former returns a value typed as *INT* (a 4-byte integer), and the latter returns a value typed as *BIGINT* (an 8-byte integer). The function *DATEDIFF_BIG* was introduced in SQL Server 2016.

Syntax

DATEDIFF(*part*, *dt_val1*, *dt_val2*), DATEDIFF_BIG(*part*, *dt_val1*, *dt_val2*)

For example, the following code returns the difference in terms of days between two values:

```
SELECT DATEDIFF(day, '20150212', '20160212');
```

This code returns the output 366.

There are certain differences that result in an integer that is greater than the maximum INT value (2,147,483,647). For example, the difference in milliseconds between January 1, 0001 and February 12, 2016 is 63,590,832,000,000. You can't use the *DATEDIFF* function to compute such a difference, but you can achieve this with the *DATEDIFF_BIG* function:

```
SELECT DATEDIFF_BIG(millisecond, '00010101', '20160212');
```

If you need to compute the beginning of the day that corresponds to an input date and time value, you can simply cast the input value to the *DATE* type and then cast the result to the target type. But with a bit more sophisticated use of the *DATEADD* and *DATEDIFF* functions, you can compute the beginning or end of different parts (day, month, quarter, year) that correspond to the input value. For example, use the following code to compute the beginning of the day that corresponds to the input date and time value:

```
SELECT
  DATEADD(
    day,
    DATEDIFF(day, '19000101', SYSDATETIME()), '19000101');
```

This is achieved by first using the *DATEDIFF* function to calculate the difference in terms of whole days between an anchor date at midnight ('19000101' in this case) and the current date and time (call that difference *diff*). Then the *DATEADD* function is used to add *diff* days to the anchor. You get the current system date at midnight.

If you use this expression with a month part instead of a day, and make sure to use an anchor that is the first day of a month (as in this example), you get the first day of the current month:

```
SELECT
  DATEADD(
    month,
    DATEDIFF(month, '19000101', SYSDATETIME()), '19000101');
```

Similarly, by using a year part and an anchor that is the first day of a year, you get back the first day of the current year.

If you want the last day of the month or year, simply use an anchor that is the last day of a month or year. For example, the following expression returns the last day of the current year:

```
SELECT
  DATEADD(
    year,
    DATEDIFF(year, '18991231', SYSDATETIME()), '18991231');
```

Using a similar expression with the month part, you can get the last day of the month, but it's much easier to achieve this using the function *EOMONTH* instead. Unfortunately, there are no similar functions to get the end of quarter and year, so you will need to use a computation for those such as the one just shown.

The *DATEPART* function

The *DATEPART* function returns an integer representing a requested part of a date and time value.

Syntax

DATEPART(*part*, *dt_val*)

Valid values for the *part* argument include *year*, *quarter*, *month*, *dayofyear*, *day*, *week*, *weekday*, *hour*, *minute*, *second*, *millisecond*, *microsecond*, *nanosecond*, *TZoffset*, and *ISO_WEEK*. As mentioned, you can use abbreviations for the date and time parts, such as *yy* instead of *year*, *mm* instead of *month*, *dd* instead of *day*, and so on.

For example, the following code returns the month part of the input value:

```
SELECT DATEPART(month, '20160212');
```

This code returns the integer 2.

The *YEAR*, *MONTH*, and *DAY* functions

The *YEAR*, *MONTH*, and *DAY* functions are abbreviations for the *DATEPART* function returning the integer representation of the year, month, and day parts of an input date and time value.

Syntax

YEAR(*dt_val*)

MONTH(*dt_val*)

DAY(*dt_val*)

For example, the following code extracts the day, month, and year parts of an input value:

```
SELECT
  DAY('20160212') AS theday,
  MONTH('20160212') AS themonth,
  YEAR('20160212') AS theyear;
```

This code returns the following output:

```
theday      themonth    theyear
----------- ----------- -----------
12          2           2016
```

The *DATENAME* function

The *DATENAME* function returns a character string representing a part of a date and time value.

Syntax

DATENAME(*dt_val, part*)

This function is similar to *DATEPART* and, in fact, has the same options for the *part* input. However, when relevant, it returns the name of the requested part rather than the number. For example, the following code returns the month name of the given input value:

```
SELECT DATENAME(month, '20160212');
```

Recall that *DATEPART* returned the integer 2 for this input. *DATENAME* returns the name of the month, which is language dependent. If your session's language is one of the English languages (such as U.S. English or British English), you get back the value 'February'. If your session's language is Italian, you get back the value 'febbraio'. If a part is requested that has no name, and only a numeric value (such as *year*), the *DATENAME* function returns its numeric value as a character string. For example, the following code returns '2016':

```
SELECT DATENAME(year, '20160212');
```

The *ISDATE* function

The *ISDATE* function accepts a character string as input and returns 1 if it is convertible to a date and time data type and 0 if it isn't.

Syntax

ISDATE(*string*)

For example, the following code returns 1:

```
SELECT ISDATE('20160212');
```

And the following code returns 0:

```
SELECT ISDATE('20160230');
```

The *FROMPARTS* functions

The *FROMPARTS* functions accept integer inputs representing parts of a date and time value and construct a value of the requested type from those parts.

Syntax

DATEFROMPARTS (*year, month, day*)

DATETIME2FROMPARTS (*year, month, day, hour, minute, seconds, fractions, precision*)

DATETIMEFROMPARTS (*year, month, day, hour, minute, seconds, milliseconds*)

DATETIMEOFFSETFROMPARTS (*year, month, day, hour, minute, seconds, fractions, hour_offset, minute_offset, precision*)

SMALLDATETIMEFROMPARTS (*year, month, day, hour, minute*)

TIMEFROMPARTS (*hour, minute, seconds, fractions, precision*)

These functions make it easier for programmers to construct date and time values from the different components, and they also simplify migrating code from other environments that already support similar functions. The following code demonstrates the use of these functions:

```
SELECT
  DATEFROMPARTS(2016, 02, 12),
  DATETIME2FROMPARTS(2016, 02, 12, 13, 30, 5, 1, 7),
  DATETIMEFROMPARTS(2016, 02, 12, 13, 30, 5, 997),
  DATETIMEOFFSETFROMPARTS(2016, 02, 12, 13, 30, 5, 1, -8, 0, 7),
  SMALLDATETIMEFROMPARTS(2016, 02, 12, 13, 30),
  TIMEFROMPARTS(13, 30, 5, 1, 7);
```

The *EOMONTH* function

The *EOMONTH* function accepts an input date and time value and returns the respective end-of-month date as a *DATE* typed value. The function also supports an optional second argument indicating how many months to add (or subtract, if negative).

Syntax

EOMONTH(*input* [, *months_to_add*])

For example, the following code returns the end of the current month:

```
SELECT EOMONTH(SYSDATETIME());
```

The following query returns orders placed on the last day of the month:

```
SELECT orderid, orderdate, custid, empid
FROM Sales.Orders
WHERE orderdate = EOMONTH(orderdate);
```

Querying metadata

SQL Server provides tools for getting information about the metadata of objects, such as information about tables in a database and columns in a table. Those tools include catalog views, information schema views, and system stored procedures and functions. This area is documented well in SQL

Server Books Online in the "Querying the SQL Server System Catalog" section, so I won't cover it in great detail here. I'll just give a couple of examples of each metadata tool to give you a sense of what's available and get you started.

Catalog views

Catalog views provide detailed information about objects in the database, including information that is specific to SQL Server. For example, if you want to list the tables in a database along with their schema names, you can query the *sys.tables* view as follows:

```
USE TSQLV4;

SELECT SCHEMA_NAME(schema_id) AS table_schema_name, name AS table_name
FROM sys.tables;
```

The *SCHEMA_NAME* function is used to convert the schema ID integer to its name. This query returns the following output:

```
table_schema_name  table_name
------------------ --------------
HR                 Employees
Production         Suppliers
Production         Categories
Production         Products
Sales              Customers
Sales              Shippers
Sales              Orders
Sales              OrderDetails
Stats              Tests
Stats              Scores
dbo                Nums
```

To get information about columns in a table, you can query the *sys.columns* table. For example, the following code returns information about columns in the *Sales.Orders* table, including column names, data types (with the system type ID translated to a name by using the *TYPE_NAME* function), maximum length, collation name, and nullability:

```
SELECT
  name AS column_name,
  TYPE_NAME(system_type_id) AS column_type,
  max_length,
  collation_name,
  is_nullable
FROM sys.columns
WHERE object_id = OBJECT_ID(N'Sales.Orders');
```

This query returns the following output:

```
column_name     column_type  max_length collation_name        is_nullable
--------------- ------------ ---------- --------------------- -----------
orderid         int          4          NULL                  0
custid          int          4          NULL                  1
```

```
empid           int        4    NULL                  0
orderdate       date       3    NULL                  0
requireddate    date       3    NULL                  0
shippeddate     date       3    NULL                  1
shipperid       int        4    NULL                  0
freight         money      8    NULL                  0
shipname        nvarchar   80   Latin1_General_CI_AS  0
shipaddress     nvarchar   120  Latin1_General_CI_AS  0
shipcity        nvarchar   30   Latin1_General_CI_AS  0
shipregion      nvarchar   30   Latin1_General_CI_AS  1
shippostalcode  nvarchar   20   Latin1_General_CI_AS  1
shipcountry     nvarchar   30   Latin1_General_CI_AS  0
```

Information schema views

An information schema view is a set of views that resides in a schema called *INFORMATION_SCHEMA* and provides metadata information in a standard manner. That is, the views are defined in the SQL standard, so naturally they don't cover metadata aspects or objects specific to SQL Server (such as indexing).

For example, the following query against the *INFORMATION_SCHEMA.TABLES* view lists the user tables in the current database along with their schema names:

```
SELECT TABLE_SCHEMA, TABLE_NAME
FROM INFORMATION_SCHEMA.TABLES
WHERE TABLE_TYPE = N'BASE TABLE';
```

The following query against the *INFORMATION_SCHEMA.COLUMNS* view provides most of the available information about columns in the *Sales.Orders* table:

```
SELECT
  COLUMN_NAME, DATA_TYPE, CHARACTER_MAXIMUM_LENGTH,
  COLLATION_NAME, IS_NULLABLE
FROM INFORMATION_SCHEMA.COLUMNS
WHERE TABLE_SCHEMA = N'Sales'
  AND TABLE_NAME = N'Orders';
```

System stored procedures and functions

System stored procedures and functions internally query the system catalog and give you back more "digested" metadata information. Again, you can find the full list of objects and their detailed descriptions in SQL Server Books Online, but here are a few examples.

The *sp_tables* stored procedure returns a list of objects (such as tables and views) that can be queried in the current database:

```
EXEC sys.sp_tables;
```

The *sp_help* procedure accepts an object name as input and returns multiple result sets with general information about the object, and also information about columns, indexes, constraints, and more. For example, the following code returns detailed information about the *Orders* table:

```
EXEC sys.sp_help
  @objname = N'Sales.Orders';
```

The *sp_columns* procedure returns information about columns in an object. For example, the following code returns information about columns in the *Orders* table:

```
EXEC sys.sp_columns
  @table_name = N'Orders',
  @table_owner = N'Sales';
```

The *sp_helpconstraint* procedure returns information about constraints in an object. For example, the following code returns information about constraints in the *Orders* table:

```
EXEC sys.sp_helpconstraint
  @objname = N'Sales.Orders';
```

One set of functions returns information about properties of entities such as the SQL Server instance, database, object, column, and so on. The *SERVERPROPERTY* function returns the requested property of the current instance. For example, the following code returns the product level (such as RTM, SP1, SP2, and so on) of the current instance:

```
SELECT
  SERVERPROPERTY('ProductLevel');
```

The *DATABASEPROPERTYEX* function returns the requested property of the specified database name. For example, the following code returns the collation of the TSQLV4 database:

```
SELECT
  DATABASEPROPERTYEX(N'TSQLV4', 'Collation');
```

The *OBJECTPROPERTY* function returns the requested property of the specified object name. For example, the output of the following code indicates whether the *Orders* table has a primary key:

```
SELECT
  OBJECTPROPERTY(OBJECT_ID(N'Sales.Orders'), 'TableHasPrimaryKey');
```

Notice the nesting of the function *OBJECT_ID* within *OBJECTPROPERTY*. The *OBJECTPROPERTY* function expects an object ID and not a name, so the *OBJECT_ID* function is used to return the ID of the *Orders* table.

The *COLUMNPROPERTY* function returns the requested property of a specified column. For example, the output of the following code indicates whether the *shipcountry* column in the *Orders* table is nullable:

```
SELECT
  COLUMNPROPERTY(OBJECT_ID(N'Sales.Orders'), N'shipcountry', 'AllowsNull');
```

Conclusion

This chapter introduced you to the *SELECT* statement, logical query processing, and various other aspects of single-table queries. I covered quite a few subjects here, including many new and unique concepts. If you're new to T-SQL, you might feel overwhelmed at this point. But remember, this chapter introduces some of the most important points about SQL that might be hard to digest at the beginning. If some of the concepts weren't completely clear, you might want to revisit sections from this chapter later on, after you've had a chance to sleep on it.

For an opportunity to practice what you learned and absorb the material better, I recommend going over the chapter exercises.

Exercises

This section provides exercises to help you familiarize yourself with the subjects discussed in Chapter 2. Solutions to the exercises appear in the section that follows.

You can find instructions for downloading and installing the *TSQLV4* sample database in the Appendix.

Exercise 1

Write a query against the *Sales.Orders* table that returns orders placed in June 2015:

- Tables involved: *TSQLV4* database and the *Sales.Orders* table
- Desired output (abbreviated):

```
orderid     orderdate  custid      empid
----------- ---------- ----------- -----------
10555       2015-06-02 71          6
10556       2015-06-03 73          2
10557       2015-06-03 44          9
10558       2015-06-04 4           1
10559       2015-06-05 7           6
10560       2015-06-06 25          8
10561       2015-06-06 24          2
10562       2015-06-09 66          1
10563       2015-06-10 67          2
10564       2015-06-10 65          4
...

(30 row(s) affected)
```

Exercise 2

Write a query against the *Sales.Orders* table that returns orders placed on the last day of the month:

- Tables involved: *TSQLV4* database and the *Sales.Orders* table
- Desired output (abbreviated):

```
orderid     orderdate  custid      empid
----------- ---------- ----------- -----------
10269       2014-07-31 89          5
10317       2014-09-30 48          6
10343       2014-10-31 44          4
10399       2014-12-31 83          8
10432       2015-01-31 75          3
10460       2015-02-28 24          8
10461       2015-02-28 46          1
10490       2015-03-31 35          7
10491       2015-03-31 28          8
10522       2015-04-30 44          4
...

(26 row(s) affected)
```

Exercise 3

Write a query against the *HR.Employees* table that returns employees with a last name containing the letter *e* twice or more:

- Tables involved: *TSQLV4* database and the *HR.Employees* table
- Desired output:

```
empid       firstname  lastname
----------- ---------- --------------------
4           Yael       Peled
5           Sven       Mortensen

(2 row(s) affected)
```

Exercise 4

Write a query against the *Sales.OrderDetails* table that returns orders with a total value (quantity * unitprice) greater than 10,000, sorted by total value:

- Tables involved: *TSQLV4* database and the *Sales.OrderDetails* table
- Desired output:

```
orderid     totalvalue
----------- ---------------------
10865       17250.00
11030       16321.90
10981       15810.00
10372       12281.20
10424       11493.20
10817       11490.70
```

```
10889        11380.00
10417        11283.20
10897        10835.24
10353        10741.60
10515        10588.50
10479        10495.60
10540        10191.70
10691        10164.80

(14 row(s) affected)
```

Exercise 5

To check the validity of the data, write a query against the *HR.Employees* table that returns employees with a last name that starts with a lowercase English letter in the range a through z. Remember that the collation of the sample database is case insensitive (*Latin1_General_CI_AS*):

- Tables involved: *TSQLV4* database and the *HR.Employees* table
- Desired output is an empty set:

```
empid       lastname
----------- --------------------

(0 row(s) affected))
```

Exercise 6

Explain the difference between the following two queries:

```
-- Query 1
SELECT empid, COUNT(*) AS numorders
FROM Sales.Orders
WHERE orderdate < '20160501'
GROUP BY empid;

-- Query 2
SELECT empid, COUNT(*) AS numorders
FROM Sales.Orders
GROUP BY empid
HAVING MAX(orderdate) < '20160501';
```

- Tables involved: *TSQLV4* database and the *Sales.Orders* table

Exercise 7

Write a query against the *Sales.Orders* table that returns the three shipped-to countries with the highest average freight in 2015:

- Tables involved: *TSQLV4* database and the *Sales.Orders* table

- Desired output:

```
shipcountry     avgfreight
--------------- ---------------------
Austria         178.3642
Switzerland     117.1775
Sweden          105.16

(3 row(s) affected)
```

Exercise 8

Write a query against the *Sales.Orders* table that calculates row numbers for orders based on order date ordering (using the order ID as the tiebreaker) for each customer separately:

- Tables involved: *TSQLV4* database and the *Sales.Orders* table
- Desired output (abbreviated):

```
custid      orderdate  orderid     rownum
----------- ---------- ----------- --------------------
1           2015-08-25 10643       1
1           2015-10-03 10692       2
1           2015-10-13 10702       3
1           2016-01-15 10835       4
1           2016-03-16 10952       5
1           2016-04-09 11011       6
2           2014-09-18 10308       1
2           2015-08-08 10625       2
2           2015-11-28 10759       3
2           2016-03-04 10926       4
...

(830 row(s) affected)
```

Exercise 9

Using the *HR.Employees* table, write a *SELECT* statement that returns for each employee the gender based on the title of courtesy. For 'Ms.' and 'Mrs.' return 'Female'; for 'Mr.' return 'Male'; and in all other cases (for example, 'Dr.') return 'Unknown':

- Tables involved: *TSQLV4* database and the *HR.Employees* table
- Desired output:

```
empid       firstname  lastname             titleofcourtesy           gender
----------- ---------- -------------------- ------------------------- -------
1           Sara       Davis                Ms.                       Female
2           Don        Funk                 Dr.                       Unknown
3           Judy       Lew                  Ms.                       Female
4           Yael       Peled                Mrs.                      Female
5           Sven       Mortensen            Mr.                       Male
6           Paul       Suurs                Mr.                       Male
```

```
7           Russell    King               Mr.                  Male
8           Maria      Cameron            Ms.                  Female
9           Patricia   Doyle              Ms.                  Female

(9 row(s) affected)
```

Exercise 10

Write a query against the *Sales.Customers* table that returns for each customer the customer ID and region. Sort the rows in the output by region, having *NULLs* sort last (after non-*NULL* values). Note that the default sort behavior for *NULLs* in T-SQL is to sort first (before non-*NULL* values):

- Tables involved: *TSQLV4* database and the *Sales.Customers* table
- Desired output (abbreviated):

```
custid      region
----------- ---------------
55          AK
10          BC
42          BC
45          CA
37          Co. Cork
33          DF
71          ID
38          Isle of Wight
46          Lara
78          MT
...
1           NULL
2           NULL
3           NULL
4           NULL
5           NULL
6           NULL
7           NULL
8           NULL
9           NULL
11          NULL
...

(91 row(s) affected)
```

Solutions

This section provides the solutions to the exercises for this chapter, accompanied by explanations where needed.

Exercise 1

You might have considered using the *YEAR* and *MONTH* functions in the *WHERE* clause of your solution query, like this:

```
USE TSQLV4;

SELECT orderid, orderdate, custid, empid
FROM Sales.Orders
WHERE YEAR(orderdate) = 2015 AND MONTH(orderdate) = 6;
```

This solution is valid and returns the correct result. However, I explained that if you apply manipulation to the filtered column, in most cases SQL Server can't use an index efficiently. Therefore, I advise using a range filter instead:

```
SELECT orderid, orderdate, custid, empid
FROM Sales.Orders
WHERE orderdate >= '20150601'
  AND orderdate < '20150701';
```

Exercise 2

You can use the *EOMONTH* function to address this task, like this:

```
SELECT orderid, orderdate, custid, empid
FROM Sales.Orders
WHERE orderdate = EOMONTH(orderdate);
```

I also provided an alternative expression for computing the last day of the month that corresponds to the input date value:

```
DATEADD(month, DATEDIFF(month, '18991231', date_val), '18991231')
```

It is a more complex technique, but it has the advantage that you can use it to compute the beginning or end of other parts (day, month, quarter, year).

This expression first calculates the difference in terms of whole months between an anchor last day of some month (December 31, 1899, in this case) and the specified date. Call this difference *diff*. By adding *diff* months to the anchor date, you get the last day of the target month. Here's the full solution query, returning only orders that were placed on the last day of the month:

```
SELECT orderid, orderdate, custid, empid
FROM Sales.Orders
WHERE orderdate = DATEADD(month, DATEDIFF(month, '18991231', orderdate), '18991231');
```

Exercise 3

This exercise involves using pattern matching with the *LIKE* predicate. Remember that the percent sign (%) represents a character string of any size, including an empty string. Therefore, you can use the pattern *'%e%e%'* to express at least two occurrences of the character *e* anywhere in the string. Here's the full solution query:

```
SELECT empid, firstname, lastname
FROM HR.Employees
WHERE lastname LIKE '%e%e%';
```

Exercise 4

This exercise is quite tricky, and if you managed to solve it correctly, you should be proud of yourself. A subtle requirement in the request might be overlooked or interpreted incorrectly. Observe that the request said "return orders with *total value* greater than 10,000" and not "return orders with *value* greater than 10,000." In other words, it's not the individual order detail row that is supposed to meet the requirement. Instead, the group of all order details within the order should meet the requirement. This means that the query shouldn't have a filter in the *WHERE* clause like this:

```
WHERE quantity * unitprice > 10000
```

Rather, the query should group the data by the *orderid* attribute and have a filter in the *HAVING* clause like this:

```
HAVING SUM(quantity*unitprice) > 10000
```

Here's the complete solution query:

```
SELECT orderid, SUM(qty*unitprice) AS totalvalue
FROM Sales.OrderDetails
GROUP BY orderid
HAVING SUM(qty*unitprice) > 10000
ORDER BY totalvalue DESC;
```

Exercise 5

You might have tried addressing the task using a query such as the following:

```
SELECT empid, lastname
FROM HR.Employees
WHERE lastname COLLATE Latin1_General_CS_AS LIKE N'[a-z]%';
```

The expression in the *WHERE* clause uses the *COLLATE* clause to convert the current case-insensitive collation of the *lastname* column to a case-sensitive one. The *LIKE* predicate then checks that the case-sensitive last name starts with a letter in the range a through z. The tricky part here is that the specified collation uses dictionary sort order, in which the lowercase and uppercase forms of each letter appear next to each other and not in separate groups. The sort order looks like this:

```
a
```

```
A
b
B
c
C
...
x
X
y
Y
z
Z
```

You realize that all the lowercase letters a through z, as well as the uppercase letters A through Y (excluding Z), qualify. Therefore, if you run the preceding query, you get the following output:

```
empid       lastname
----------- --------------------
8           Cameron
1           Davis
9           Doyle
2           Funk
7           King
3           Lew
5           Mortensen
4           Peled
6           Suurs
```

To look only for the lowercase letters a through z, one solution is to list them explicitly in the LIKE pattern like this:

```
SELECT empid, lastname
FROM HR.Employees
WHERE lastname COLLATE Latin1_General_CS_AS LIKE N'[abcdefghijklmnopqrstuvwxyz]%';
```

Naturally, there are other possible solutions.

I'd like to thank Paul White who enlightened me when I fell into this trap myself in the past.

Exercise 6

The *WHERE* clause is a row filter, whereas the *HAVING* clause is a group filter. Query 1 filters only orders placed before May 2016, groups them by the employee ID, and returns the number of orders each employee handled among the filtered ones. In other words, it computes how many orders each employee handled prior to May 2016. The query doesn't include orders placed in May 2016 or later in the count. An employee will show up in the output as long as he or she handled orders prior to May 2016, regardless of whether the employee handled orders since May 2016. Here's the output of Query 1:

```
empid       numorders
----------- -----------
9           43
3           127
6           67
```

```
7           70
1           118
4           154
5           42
2           94
8           101
```

Query 2 groups all orders by the employee ID, and then filters only groups having a maximum date of activity prior to May 2016. Then it computes the order count in each employee group. The query discards the entire employee group if the employee handled any orders since May 2016. In a sentence, this query returns for employees who didn't handle any orders since May 2016 the total number of orders they handled. This query generates the following output:

```
empid       numorders
----------- -----------
9           43
3           127
6           67
5           42
```

Take employee 1 as an example. This employee had activity both before and since May 2016. The first query result includes this employee, but the order count reflects only the orders the employee handled prior to May 2016. The second query result doesn't include this employee at all.

Exercise 7

Because the request involves activity in the year 2015, the query should have a *WHERE* clause with the appropriate date-range filter (*orderdate >= '20150101' AND orderdate < '20160101'*). Because the request involves average freight values per shipping country and the table can have multiple rows per country, the query should group the rows by country and calculate the average freight. To get the three countries with the highest average freights, the query should specify *TOP (3)*, based on the order of average freight descending. Here's the complete solution query:

```
SELECT TOP (3) shipcountry, AVG(freight) AS avgfreight
FROM Sales.Orders
WHERE orderdate >= '20150101' AND orderdate < '20160101'
GROUP BY shipcountry
ORDER BY avgfreight DESC;
```

Remember that you can use the standard *OFFSET-FETCH* filter instead of the proprietary *TOP* filter. Here's the revised solution using *OFFSET-FETCH*:

```
SELECT shipcountry, AVG(freight) AS avgfreight
FROM Sales.Orders
WHERE orderdate >= '20150101' AND orderdate < '20160101'
GROUP BY shipcountry
ORDER BY avgfreight DESC
OFFSET 0 ROWS FETCH NEXT 3 ROWS ONLY;
```

Exercise 8

Because the exercise requests that the row number calculation be done for each customer separately, the expression should partition the window by *custid* (*PARTITION BY custid*). In addition, the request was to use ordering based on the *orderdate* column, with the *orderid* column as a tiebreaker (*ORDER BY orderdate, orderid*). Here's the complete solution query:

```
SELECT custid, orderdate, orderid,
  ROW_NUMBER() OVER(PARTITION BY custid ORDER BY orderdate, orderid) AS rownum
FROM Sales.Orders
ORDER BY custid, rownum;
```

Exercise 9

You can handle the conditional logic in this exercise with a *CASE* expression. Using the simple *CASE* expression form, you specify the *titleofcourtesy* attribute right after the *CASE* keyword; list each possible title of courtesy in a separate *WHEN* clause followed by the *THEN* clause and the gender; and in the *ELSE* clause, specify *'Unknown'*.

```
SELECT empid, firstname, lastname, titleofcourtesy,
  CASE titleofcourtesy
    WHEN 'Ms.'  THEN 'Female'
    WHEN 'Mrs.' THEN 'Female'
    WHEN 'Mr.'  THEN 'Male'
    ELSE             'Unknown'
  END AS gender
FROM HR.Employees;
```

You can also use the searched *CASE* form with two predicates—one to handle all cases where the gender is female and one for all cases where the gender is male—and an *ELSE* clause with *'Unknown'*.

```
SELECT empid, firstname, lastname, titleofcourtesy,
  CASE
    WHEN titleofcourtesy IN('Ms.', 'Mrs.') THEN 'Female'
    WHEN titleofcourtesy = 'Mr.'           THEN 'Male'
    ELSE                                        'Unknown'
  END AS gender
FROM HR.Employees;
```

Exercise 10

By default, SQL Server sorts *NULLs* before non-*NULL* values. To get *NULLs* to sort last, you can use a *CASE* expression that returns 1 when the *region* column is *NULL* and 0 when it is not *NULL*. Specify this *CASE* expression as the first sort column and the *region* column as the second. This way, non-*NULLs* sort correctly among themselves first followed by *NULLs*. Here's the complete solution query:

```
SELECT custid, region
FROM Sales.Customers
ORDER BY
  CASE WHEN region IS NULL THEN 1 ELSE 0 END, region;
```

CHAPTER 3

Joins

The *FROM* clause of a query is the first clause to be logically processed, and within the *FROM* clause, table operators operate on input tables. T-SQL supports four table operators: *JOIN*, *APPLY*, *PIVOT*, and *UNPIVOT*. The *JOIN* table operator is standard, whereas *APPLY*, *PIVOT*, and *UNPIVOT* are T-SQL extensions to the standard. Each table operator acts on tables provided to it as input, applies a set of logical query processing phases, and returns a table result. This chapter focuses on the *JOIN* table operator. The *APPLY* operator will be covered in Chapter 5, "Table expressions," and the *PIVOT* and *UNPIVOT* operators will be covered in Chapter 7, "Beyond the fundamentals of querying."

A *JOIN* table operator operates on two input tables. The three fundamental types of joins are cross joins, inner joins, and outer joins. These three types of joins differ in how they apply their logical query processing phases; each type applies a different set of phases. A cross join applies only one phase—Cartesian Product. An inner join applies two phases—Cartesian Product and Filter. An outer join applies three phases—Cartesian Product, Filter, and Add Outer Rows. This chapter explains in detail each of the join types and the phases involved.

Logical query processing describes a generic series of logical steps that for any specified query produces the correct result, whereas *physical query processing* is the way the query is processed by the RDBMS engine in practice. Some phases of logical query processing of joins might sound inefficient, but remember that the query will be optimized by the physical implementation. It's important to stress the term *logical* in *logical query processing*. The steps in the process apply operations to the input tables based on relational algebra. The database engine does not have to follow logical query processing phases literally, as long as it can guarantee that the result that it produces is the same as that dictated by logical query processing. The query optimizer often applies shortcuts when it knows it can still produce the correct result. Even though this book's focus is on understanding the logical aspects of querying, I want to stress this point to avoid performance-related concerns.

Cross joins

The cross join is the simplest type of join. It implements only one logical query processing phase—a Cartesian Product. This phase operates on the two tables provided as inputs and produces a Cartesian product of the two. That is, each row from one input is matched with all rows from the other. So if you have *m* rows in one table and *n* rows in the other, you get $m \times n$ rows in the result.

T-SQL supports two standard syntaxes for cross joins: the ISO/ANSI SQL-92 and ISO/ANSI SQL-89 syntaxes. I recommend you use the SQL 92 syntax for reasons I'll describe shortly. It's also the main syntax I use throughout the book. For the sake of completeness, I describe both syntaxes in this section.

ISO/ANSI SQL-92 syntax

The following query applies a cross join between the *Customers* and *Employees* tables (using the SQL-92 syntax) in the *TSQLV4* database, and returns the *custid* and *empid* attributes in the result set:

```
USE TSQLV4;

SELECT C.custid, E.empid
FROM Sales.Customers AS C
  CROSS JOIN HR.Employees AS E;
```

Because there are 91 rows in the *Customers* table and 9 rows in the *Employees* table, this query produces a result set with 819 rows, as shown here in abbreviated form:

```
custid      empid
----------- -----------
1           2
2           2
3           2
4           2
5           2
6           2
7           2
8           2
9           2
11          2
...

(819 row(s) affected)
```

When you use the SQL-92 syntax, you specify the CROSS JOIN keywords between the two tables involved in the join.

Notice that in the *FROM* clause of the preceding query, I assigned the aliases *C* and *E* to the *Customers* and *Employees* tables, respectively. The result set produced by the cross join is a virtual table with attributes that originate from both sides of the join. Because I assigned aliases to the source tables, the names of the columns in the virtual table are prefixed by the table aliases (for example, *C.custid*, *E.empid*). The column prefixes do not appear in the final query result. If you do not assign aliases to the tables in the *FROM* clause, the names of the columns in the virtual table are prefixed by the full source-table names (for example, *Customers.custid*, *Employees.empid*). The purpose of the prefixes is to facilitate the identification of columns in an unambiguous manner when the same column name appears in both tables. The aliases of the tables are assigned for brevity. Note that you are required to use column prefixes only when referring to ambiguous column names (column names that appear in more than one table); in unambiguous cases, column prefixes are optional. However, it's a good practice to always use column prefixes for the sake of clarity. Also note that if you assign an alias to a table, it's invalid to use the full table name as a column prefix; in ambiguous cases, you have to use the table alias as a prefix.

ISO/ANSI SQL-89 syntax

T-SQL also supports an older syntax for cross joins that was introduced in SQL-89. In this syntax, you simply specify a comma between the table names, like this:

```
SELECT C.custid, E.empid
FROM Sales.Customers AS C, HR.Employees AS E;
```

There is no logical or performance difference between the two syntaxes. Both are integral parts of the SQL standard, and both are fully supported by T-SQL. I'm not aware of any plans to deprecate the older syntax in the SQL standard or in T-SQL. However, I recommend using the SQL-92 syntax for reasons that will become clear after I explain inner and outer joins.

Self cross joins

You can join multiple instances of the same table. This capability is known as a *self join* and is supported with all fundamental join types (cross joins, inner joins, and outer joins). For example, the following query performs a self cross join between two instances of the *Employees* table:

```
SELECT
  E1.empid, E1.firstname, E1.lastname,
  E2.empid, E2.firstname, E2.lastname
FROM HR.Employees AS E1
  CROSS JOIN HR.Employees AS E2;
```

This query produces all possible combinations of pairs of employees. Because the *Employees* table has 9 rows, this query returns 81 rows, as shown here in abbreviated form:

```
empid       firstname  lastname             empid       firstname  lastname
----------- ---------- -------------------- ----------- ---------- --------------------
1           Sara       Davis                1           Sara       Davis
2           Don        Funk                 1           Sara       Davis
3           Judy       Lew                  1           Sara       Davis
4           Yael       Peled                1           Sara       Davis
5           Sven       Mortensen            1           Sara       Davis
6           Paul       Suurs                1           Sara       Davis
7           Russell    King                 1           Sara       Davis
8           Maria      Cameron              1           Sara       Davis
9           Patricia   Doyle                1           Sara       Davis
1           Sara       Davis                2           Don        Funk
2           Don        Funk                 2           Don        Funk
3           Judy       Lew                  2           Don        Funk
4           Yael       Peled                2           Don        Funk
5           Sven       Mortensen            2           Don        Funk
6           Paul       Suurs                2           Don        Funk
7           Russell    King                 2           Don        Funk
8           Maria      Cameron              2           Don        Funk
9           Patricia   Doyle                2           Don        Funk
...

(81 row(s) affected)
```

In a self join, aliasing tables is not optional. Without table aliases, all column names in the result of the join would be ambiguous.

Producing tables of numbers

One situation in which cross joins can be handy is when they are used to produce a result set with a sequence of integers (1, 2, 3, and so on). Such a sequence of numbers is an extremely powerful tool that I use for many purposes. By using cross joins, you can produce the sequence of integers in a very efficient manner.

You can start by creating a table called *Digits* with a column called *digit*, and populate the table with 10 rows with the digits 0 through 9. Run the following code to create the *Digits* table in the *TSQLV4* database and populate it with the 10 digits:

```
USE TSQLV4;

DROP TABLE IF EXISTS dbo.Digits;

CREATE TABLE dbo.Digits(digit INT NOT NULL PRIMARY KEY);

INSERT INTO dbo.Digits(digit)
  VALUES (0),(1),(2),(3),(4),(5),(6),(7),(8),(9);

SELECT digit FROM dbo.Digits;
```

This code also uses an *INSERT* statement to populate the *Digits* table. If you're not familiar with the syntax of the *INSERT* statement, see Chapter 8, "Data modification," for details.

This code generates the following output:

```
digit
-----------
0
1
2
3
4
5
6
7
8
9
```

Suppose you need to write a query that produces a sequence of integers in the range 1 through 1,000. You apply cross joins between three instances of the *Digits* table, each representing a different power of 10 (1, 10, 100). By multiplying three instances of the same table, each instance with 10 rows, you get a result set with 1,000 rows. To produce the actual number, multiply the digit from each instance by the power of 10 it represents, sum the results, and add 1. Here's the complete query:

```
SELECT D3.digit * 100 + D2.digit * 10 + D1.digit + 1 AS n
FROM         dbo.Digits AS D1
  CROSS JOIN dbo.Digits AS D2
```

```
  CROSS JOIN dbo.Digits AS D3
ORDER BY n;
```

This query returns the following output, shown here in abbreviated form:

```
n
-----------
1
2
3
4
5
6
7
8
9
10
...
998
999
1000

(1000 row(s) affected)
```

This was an example that produces a sequence of 1,000 integers. If you need more numbers, you can add more instances of the *Digits* table to the query. For example, if you need to produce a sequence of 1,000,000 rows, you need to join six instances.

Inner joins

An inner join applies two logical query processing phases—it applies a Cartesian product between the two input tables like in a cross join, and then it filters rows based on a predicate you specify. Like cross joins, inner joins have two standard syntaxes: SQL-92 and SQL-89.

ISO/ANSI SQL-92 syntax

Using the SQL-92 syntax, you specify the INNER JOIN keywords between the table names. The INNER keyword is optional, because an inner join is the default. So you can specify the JOIN keyword alone. You specify the predicate that is used to filter rows in a designated clause called *ON*. This predicate is also known as the *join condition*.

For example, the following query performs an inner join between the *Employees* and *Orders* tables in the *TSQLV4* database, matching employees and orders based on the predicate *E.empid = O.empid*:

```
USE TSQLV4;

SELECT E.empid, E.firstname, E.lastname, O.orderid
FROM HR.Employees AS E
  INNER JOIN Sales.Orders AS O
    ON E.empid = O.empid;
```

This query produces the following result set, shown here in abbreviated form:

```
empid       firstname  lastname             orderid
----------- ---------- -------------------- -----------
1           Sara       Davis                10258
1           Sara       Davis                10270
1           Sara       Davis                10275
1           Sara       Davis                10285
1           Sara       Davis                10292
...
2           Don        Funk                 10265
2           Don        Funk                 10277
2           Don        Funk                 10280
2           Don        Funk                 10295
2           Don        Funk                 10300
...

(830 row(s) affected)
```

For most people, the easiest way to think of such an inner join is as matching each employee row with all order rows that have the same employee ID as in the employee row. This is a simplified way to think of the join. The more formal way to think of it is based on relational algebra. First, the join performs a Cartesian product between the two tables (9 employee rows × 830 order rows = 7,470 rows). Then, the join filters rows based on the predicate *E.empid = O.empid*, eventually returning 830 rows. As mentioned earlier, that's just the logical way that the join is processed; in practice, physical processing of the query by the database engine can be different.

Recall the discussion from previous chapters about the three-valued predicate logic used by SQL. As with the *WHERE* and *HAVING* clauses, the *ON* clause also returns only rows for which the predicate returns *TRUE*, and it does not return rows for which the predicate evaluates to *FALSE* or *UNKNOWN*.

In the *TSQLV4* database, all employees have related orders, so all employees show up in the output. However, had there been employees with no related orders, they would have been discarded by the filter phase. The same would apply to orders with no related employees, although a foreign-key relationship forbids those in our sample database.

ISO/ANSI SQL-89 syntax

Similar to cross joins, inner joins can be expressed by using the SQL-89 syntax. You specify a comma between the table names just as in a cross join, and you specify the join condition in the query's *WHERE* clause, like this:

```
SELECT E.empid, E.firstname, E.lastname, O.orderid
FROM HR.Employees AS E, Sales.Orders AS O
WHERE E.empid = O.empid;
```

Note that the SQL-89 syntax has no *ON* clause.

Again, both syntaxes are standard, fully supported by T-SQL, and interpreted in the same way by the database engine, so you shouldn't expect any performance difference between them. But one syntax is safer, as explained in the next section.

Inner join safety

I strongly recommend that you stick to the SQL-92 join syntax because it's less prone to errors. Suppose you intend to write an inner join query, and by mistake you forget to specify the join condition. With the SQL-92 syntax, the query becomes invalid, and the parser generates an error. For example, try to run the following code:

```
SELECT E.empid, E.firstname, E.lastname, O.orderid
FROM HR.Employees AS E
  INNER JOIN Sales.Orders AS O;
```

You get the following error:

```
Msg 102, Level 15, State 1, Line 74
Incorrect syntax near ';'.
```

Even though it might not be immediately obvious from the error message that the error involves a missing join condition, you will figure it out eventually and fix the query. However, if you forget to specify the join condition when you're using the SQL-89 syntax, you get a valid query that performs a cross join:

```
SELECT E.empid, E.firstname, E.lastname, O.orderid
FROM HR.Employees AS E, Sales.Orders AS O;
```

Because the query doesn't fail, the logical error might go unnoticed for a while, and users of your application might end up relying on incorrect results. It's unlikely that a programmer would forget to specify the join condition with such short and simple queries; however, most production queries are much more complicated and have multiple tables, filters, and other query elements. In those cases, the likelihood of forgetting to specify a join condition increases.

If I've convinced you that it's important to use the SQL-92 syntax for inner joins, you might wonder whether the recommendation holds for cross joins. Because no join condition is involved, you might think that both syntaxes are just as good for cross joins. However, I recommend staying with the SQL-92 syntax with cross joins for a couple of reasons—one being consistency. Also, suppose you do use the SQL-89 syntax. Even if you intended to write a cross join, when other developers need to review or maintain your code, how will they know whether you intended to write a cross join or intended to write an inner join and forgot to specify the join condition?

More join examples

This section covers a few join examples that are known by specific names: composite joins, non-equi joins, and multi-join queries.

Composite joins

A *composite join* is simply a join where you need to match multiple attributes from each side. You usually need such a join when a primary key–foreign key relationship is based on more than one attribute. For example, suppose you have a foreign key defined on *dbo.Table2*, columns *col1, col2*, referencing *dbo.Table1*, columns *col1, col2*, and you need to write a query that joins the two based on this relationship. The *FROM* clause of the query would look like this:

```
FROM dbo.Table1 AS T1
  INNER JOIN dbo.Table2 AS T2
    ON T1.col1 = T2.col1
    AND T1.col2 = T2.col2
```

For a more tangible example, suppose you need to audit updates to column values against the *OrderDetails* table in the *TSQLV4* database. You create a custom auditing table called *OrderDetailsAudit*:

```
USE TSQLV4;

DROP TABLE IF EXISTS Sales.OrderDetailsAudit;

CREATE TABLE Sales.OrderDetailsAudit
(
  lsn        INT NOT NULL IDENTITY,
  orderid    INT NOT NULL,
  productid  INT NOT NULL,
  dt         DATETIME NOT NULL,
  loginname  sysname NOT NULL,
  columnname sysname NOT NULL,
  oldval     SQL_VARIANT,
  newval     SQL_VARIANT,
  CONSTRAINT PK_OrderDetailsAudit PRIMARY KEY(lsn),
  CONSTRAINT FK_OrderDetailsAudit_OrderDetails
    FOREIGN KEY(orderid, productid)
    REFERENCES Sales.OrderDetails(orderid, productid)
);
```

Each audit row stores a log serial number (*lsn*), the key of the modified row (*orderid, productid*), the name of the modified column (*columnname*), the old value (*oldval*), the new value (*newval*), when the change took place (*dt*), and who made the change (*loginname*). The table has a foreign key defined on the attributes *orderid, productid*, referencing the primary key of the *OrderDetails* table, which is defined on the attributes *orderid, productid*. Assume you already have in place the process that logs changes in the *OrderDetailsAudit* table whenever columns are updated in the *OrderDetails* table.

You need to write a query against the *OrderDetails* and *OrderDetailsAudit* tables that returns information about all value changes that took place in the column *qty*. In each result row, you need to return the current value from the *OrderDetails* table and the values before and after the change from the *OrderDetailsAudit* table. You need to join the two tables based on a primary key–foreign key relationship, like this:

```
SELECT OD.orderid, OD.productid, OD.qty,
  ODA.dt, ODA.loginname, ODA.oldval, ODA.newval
FROM Sales.OrderDetails AS OD
```

```
  INNER JOIN Sales.OrderDetailsAudit AS ODA
    ON OD.orderid = ODA.orderid
    AND OD.productid = ODA.productid
WHERE ODA.columnname = N'qty';
```

Because the relationship is based on multiple attributes, the join condition is composite.

Non-equi joins

When a join condition involves only an equality operator, the join is said to be an *equi join*. When a join condition involves any operator besides equality, the join is said to be a *non-equi join*.

> **Note** Standard SQL supports a concept called *natural join*, which represents an inner join based on a match between columns with the same name in both sides. For example, *T1 NATURAL JOIN T2* joins the rows between *T1* and *T2* based on a match between the columns with the same names on both sides. T-SQL doesn't have an implementation of a natural join. A join that has an explicit join predicate that is based on a binary operator (equality or inequality) is known as a *theta join*. So both equi joins and non-equi joins are types of theta joins.

As an example of a non-equi join, the following query joins two instances of the *Employees* table to produce unique pairs of employees:

```
SELECT
  E1.empid, E1.firstname, E1.lastname,
  E2.empid, E2.firstname, E2.lastname
FROM HR.Employees AS E1
  INNER JOIN HR.Employees AS E2
    ON E1.empid < E2.empid;
```

Notice the predicate specified in the *ON* clause. The purpose of the query is to produce unique pairs of employees. Had a cross join been used, the result would have included self pairs (for example, 1 with 1) and also mirrored pairs (for example, 1 with 2 and also 2 with 1). Using an inner join with a join condition that says the key on the left side must be smaller than the key on the right side eliminates the two inapplicable cases. Self pairs are eliminated because both sides are equal. With mirrored pairs, only one of the two cases qualifies because, of the two cases, only one will have a left key that is smaller than the right key. In this example, of the 81 possible pairs of employees a cross join would have returned, this query returns the 36 unique pairs shown here:

```
empid       firstname  lastname             empid       firstname  lastname
----------- ---------- -------------------- ----------- ---------- --------------------
1           Sara       Davis                2           Don        Funk
1           Sara       Davis                3           Judy       Lew
2           Don        Funk                 3           Judy       Lew
1           Sara       Davis                4           Yael       Peled
2           Don        Funk                 4           Yael       Peled
3           Judy       Lew                  4           Yael       Peled
1           Sara       Davis                5           Sven       Mortensen
```

```
2           Don       Funk            5           Sven      Mortensen
3           Judy      Lew             5           Sven      Mortensen
4           Yael      Peled           5           Sven      Mortensen
1           Sara      Davis           6           Paul      Suurs
2           Don       Funk            6           Paul      Suurs
3           Judy      Lew             6           Paul      Suurs
4           Yael      Peled           6           Paul      Suurs
5           Sven      Mortensen       6           Paul      Suurs
1           Sara      Davis           7           Russell   King
2           Don       Funk            7           Russell   King
3           Judy      Lew             7           Russell   King
4           Yael      Peled           7           Russell   King
5           Sven      Mortensen       7           Russell   King
6           Paul      Suurs           7           Russell   King
1           Sara      Davis           8           Maria     Cameron
2           Don       Funk            8           Maria     Cameron
3           Judy      Lew             8           Maria     Cameron
4           Yael      Peled           8           Maria     Cameron
5           Sven      Mortensen       8           Maria     Cameron
6           Paul      Suurs           8           Maria     Cameron
7           Russell   King            8           Maria     Cameron
1           Sara      Davis           9           Patricia  Doyle
2           Don       Funk            9           Patricia  Doyle
3           Judy      Lew             9           Patricia  Doyle
4           Yael      Peled           9           Patricia  Doyle
5           Sven      Mortensen       9           Patricia  Doyle
6           Paul      Suurs           9           Patricia  Doyle
7           Russell   King            9           Patricia  Doyle
8           Maria     Cameron         9           Patricia  Doyle

(36 row(s) affected)
```

If it's still not clear to you what this query does, try to process it one step at a time with a smaller set of employees. For example, suppose the *Employees* table contained only employees 1, 2, and 3. First, produce the Cartesian product of two instances of the table:

```
E1.empid      E2.empid
------------- -------------
1             1
1             2
1             3
2             1
2             2
2             3
3             1
3             2
3             3
```

Next, filter the rows based on the predicate *E1.empid < E2.empid*, and you are left with only three rows:

```
E1.empid      E2.empid
------------- -------------
1             2
1             3
2             3
```

Multi-join queries

A join table operator operates only on two tables, but a single query can have multiple joins. In general, when more than one table operator appears in the *FROM* clause, the table operators are logically processed from left to right. That is, the result table of the first table operator is treated as the left input to the second table operator; the result of the second table operator is treated as the left input to the third table operator; and so on. So if there are multiple joins in the *FROM* clause, the first join operates on two base tables, but all other joins get the result of the preceding join as their left input. With cross joins and inner joins, the database engine can (and often does) internally rearrange join ordering for optimization purposes because it won't have an impact on the correctness of the result of the query.

As an example, the following query joins the *Customers* and *Orders* tables to match customers with their orders, and then it joins the result of the first join with the *OrderDetails* table to match orders with their order lines:

```
SELECT
  C.custid, C.companyname, O.orderid,
  OD.productid, OD.qty
FROM Sales.Customers AS C
  INNER JOIN Sales.Orders AS O
    ON C.custid = O.custid
  INNER JOIN Sales.OrderDetails AS OD
    ON O.orderid = OD.orderid;
```

This query returns the following output, shown here in abbreviated form:

```
custid      companyname       orderid     productid   qty
----------- ----------------- ----------- ----------- ------
85          Customer ENQZT    10248       11          12
85          Customer ENQZT    10248       42          10
85          Customer ENQZT    10248       72          5
79          Customer FAPSM    10249       14          9
79          Customer FAPSM    10249       51          40
34          Customer IBVRG    10250       41          10
34          Customer IBVRG    10250       51          35
34          Customer IBVRG    10250       65          15
84          Customer NRCSK    10251       22          6
84          Customer NRCSK    10251       57          15
...

(2155 row(s) affected)
```

Outer joins

Compared to the other types of joins, outer joins are usually harder for people to grasp. First I will describe the fundamentals of outer joins. If by the end of the "Fundamentals of outer joins" section you feel ready for more advanced content, you can proceed to the optional section "Beyond the fundamentals of outer joins." Otherwise, feel free to skip that part and return to it when you feel more comfortable with the material.

Fundamentals of outer joins

Outer joins were introduced in SQL-92 and, unlike inner joins and cross joins, have only one standard syntax—the one in which the JOIN keyword is specified between the table names and the join condition is specified in the *ON* clause. Outer joins apply the two logical processing phases that inner joins apply (Cartesian Product and the *ON* filter), plus a third phase called Adding Outer Rows that is unique to this type of join.

In an outer join, you mark a table as a "preserved" table by using the keywords LEFT OUTER JOIN, RIGHT OUTER JOIN, or FULL OUTER JOIN between the table names. The OUTER keyword is optional. The LEFT keyword means that the rows of the left table (the one to the left of the JOIN keyword) are preserved; the RIGHT keyword means that the rows in the right table are preserved; and the FULL keyword means that the rows in both the left and right tables are preserved. The third logical query processing phase of an outer join identifies the rows from the preserved table that did not find matches in the other table based on the *ON* predicate. This phase adds those rows to the result table produced by the first two phases of the join, and it uses *NULLs* as placeholders for the attributes from the nonpreserved side of the join in those outer rows.

A good way to understand outer joins is through an example. The following query joins the *Customers* and *Orders* tables, based on a match between the customer's customer ID and the order's customer ID, to return customers and their orders. The join type is a left outer join; therefore, the query also returns customers who did not place any orders:

```
SELECT C.custid, C.companyname, O.orderid
FROM Sales.Customers AS C
  LEFT OUTER JOIN Sales.Orders AS O
    ON C.custid = O.custid;
```

This query returns the following output, shown here in abbreviated form:

```
custid      companyname    orderid
----------- -------------- -----------
1           Customer NRZBB 10643
1           Customer NRZBB 10692
1           Customer NRZBB 10702
1           Customer NRZBB 10835
1           Customer NRZBB 10952
...
21          Customer KIDPX 10414
21          Customer KIDPX 10512
21          Customer KIDPX 10581
21          Customer KIDPX 10650
21          Customer KIDPX 10725
22          Customer DTDMN NULL
23          Customer WVFAF 10408
23          Customer WVFAF 10480
23          Customer WVFAF 10634
23          Customer WVFAF 10763
23          Customer WVFAF 10789
...
56          Customer QNIVZ 10684
56          Customer QNIVZ 10766
```

```
56          Customer QNIVZ  10833
56          Customer QNIVZ  10999
56          Customer QNIVZ  11020
57          Customer WVAXS  NULL
58          Customer AHXHT  10322
58          Customer AHXHT  10354
58          Customer AHXHT  10474
58          Customer AHXHT  10502
58          Customer AHXHT  10995
...
91          Customer CCFIZ  10792
91          Customer CCFIZ  10870
91          Customer CCFIZ  10906
91          Customer CCFIZ  10998
91          Customer CCFIZ  11044

(832 row(s) affected)
```

Two customers in the *Customers* table did not place any orders. Their IDs are 22 and 57. Observe that in the output of the query, both customers are returned with *NULLs* in the attributes from the *Orders* table. Logically, the rows for these two customers were discarded by the second phase of the join (the filter based on the *ON* predicate), but the third phase added those as outer rows. Had the join been an inner join, these two rows would not have been returned. These two rows are added to preserve all the rows of the left table.

It might help to think of the result of an outer join as having two kinds of rows with respect to the preserved side—inner rows and outer rows. Inner rows are rows that have matches on the other side based on the *ON* predicate, and outer rows are rows that don't. An inner join returns only inner rows, whereas an outer join returns both inner and outer rows.

A common question about outer joins that is the source of a lot of confusion is whether to specify a predicate in the *ON* or *WHERE* clause of a query. You can see that with respect to rows from the preserved side of an outer join, the filter based on the *ON* predicate is not final. In other words, the *ON* predicate does not determine whether a row will show up in the output, only whether it will be matched with rows from the other side. So when you need to express a predicate that is not final—meaning a predicate that determines which rows to match from the nonpreserved side—specify the predicate in the *ON* clause. When you need a filter to be applied after outer rows are produced, and you want the filter to be final, specify the predicate in the *WHERE* clause. The *WHERE* clause is processed after the *FROM* clause—specifically, after all table operators have been processed and (in the case of outer joins) after all outer rows have been produced. Also, the *WHERE* clause is final with respect to rows that it filters out, unlike the *ON* clause. To recap, in the *ON* clause you specify nonfinal, or matching, predicates. In the *WHERE* clause you specify final, or filtering, predicates.

Suppose you need to return only customers who did not place any orders or, more technically speaking, you need to return only outer rows. You can use the previous query as your basis, adding a *WHERE* clause that filters only outer rows. Remember that outer rows are identified by the *NULLs* in the attributes from the nonpreserved side of the join. So you can filter only the rows in which one of the attributes on the nonpreserved side of the join is *NULL*, like this:

```
SELECT C.custid, C.companyname
FROM Sales.Customers AS C
  LEFT OUTER JOIN Sales.Orders AS O
    ON C.custid = O.custid
WHERE O.orderid IS NULL;
```

This query returns only two rows, with the customers 22 and 57:

```
custid      companyname
----------- ---------------
22          Customer DTDMN
57          Customer WVAXS

(2 row(s) affected)
```

Notice a couple of important things about this query. Recall the discussions about *NULLs* earlier in the book: When looking for a *NULL*, you should use the operator *IS NULL* and not an equality operator. You do this because when an equality operator compares something with a *NULL*, it always returns *UNKNOWN*—even when it's comparing two *NULLs*. Also, the choice of which attribute from the nonpreserved side of the join to filter is important. You should choose an attribute that can have only a *NULL* when the row is an outer row and not otherwise (for example, not a *NULL* originating from the base table). For this purpose, three cases are safe to consider: a primary key column, a join column, and a column defined as *NOT NULL*. A primary key column cannot be *NULL*; therefore, a *NULL* in such a column can only mean that the row is an outer row. If a row has a *NULL* in the join column, that row is filtered out by the second phase of the join, so a *NULL* in such a column can only mean that it's an outer row. And obviously, a *NULL* in a column that is defined as *NOT NULL* can only mean that the row is an outer row.

To practice what you learned and get a better grasp of outer joins, make sure you perform the exercises for this chapter.

Beyond the fundamentals of outer joins

This section covers more advanced aspects of outer joins and is provided as optional reading for when you feel comfortable with the fundamentals of outer joins.

Including missing values

You can use outer joins to identify and include missing values when querying data. For example, suppose you need to query all orders from the *Orders* table in the *TSQLV4* database. You need to ensure that you get at least one row in the output for each date in the range January 1, 2014 through December 31, 2016. You don't want to do anything special with dates within the range that have orders, but you do want the output to include the dates with no orders, with *NULLs* as placeholders in the attributes of the order.

To solve the problem, you can first write a query that returns a sequence of all dates in the requested period. You can then perform a left outer join between that set and the *Orders* table. This way, the result also includes the missing dates.

To produce a sequence of dates in a given range, I usually use an auxiliary table of numbers. I create a table called *dbo.Nums* with a column called *n*, and populate it with a sequence of integers (1, 2, 3, and so on). I find that an auxiliary table of numbers is an extremely powerful general-purpose tool I end up using to solve many problems. You need to create it only once in the database and populate it with as many numbers as you might need. The *TSQLV4* sample database already has such an auxiliary table.

As the first step in the solution, you need to produce a sequence of all dates in the requested range. You can achieve this by querying the *Nums* table and filtering as many numbers as the number of days in the requested date range. You can use the *DATEDIFF* function to calculate that number. By adding *n – 1* days to the starting point of the date range (January 1, 2014), you get the actual date in the sequence. Here's the solution query:

```
SELECT DATEADD(day, n-1, CAST('20140101' AS DATE)) AS orderdate
FROM dbo.Nums
WHERE n <= DATEDIFF(day, '20140101', '20161231') + 1
ORDER BY orderdate;
```

This query returns a sequence of all dates in the range January 1, 2014 through December 31, 2016, as shown here in abbreviated form:

```
orderdate
-----------
2014-01-01
2014-01-02
2014-01-03
2014-01-04
2014-01-05
...
2016-12-27
2016-12-28
2016-12-29
2016-12-30
2016-12-31

(1096 row(s) affected)
```

The next step is to extend the previous query, adding a left outer join between *Nums* and the *Orders* tables. The join condition compares the order date produced from the *Nums* table and the *orderdate* from the *Orders* table by using the expression *DATEADD(day, Nums.n – 1, CAST('20140101' AS DATE))* like this:

```
SELECT DATEADD(day, Nums.n - 1, CAST('20140101' AS DATE)) AS orderdate,
  O.orderid, O.custid, O.empid
FROM dbo.Nums
  LEFT OUTER JOIN Sales.Orders AS O
    ON DATEADD(day, Nums.n - 1, CAST('20140101' AS DATE)) = O.orderdate
WHERE Nums.n <= DATEDIFF(day, '20140101', '20161231') + 1
ORDER BY orderdate;
```

This query produces the following output, shown here in abbreviated form:

```
orderdate   orderid     custid      empid
----------- ----------- ----------- -----------
2014-01-01  NULL        NULL        NULL
2014-01-02  NULL        NULL        NULL
2014-01-03  NULL        NULL        NULL
2014-01-04  NULL        NULL        NULL
2014-01-05  NULL        NULL        NULL
...
2014-06-29  NULL        NULL        NULL
2014-06-30  NULL        NULL        NULL
2014-07-01  NULL        NULL        NULL
2014-07-02  NULL        NULL        NULL
2014-07-03  NULL        NULL        NULL
2014-07-04  10248       85          5
2014-07-05  10249       79          6
2014-07-06  NULL        NULL        NULL
2014-07-07  NULL        NULL        NULL
2014-07-08  10250       34          4
2014-07-08  10251       84          3
2014-07-09  10252       76          4
2014-07-10  10253       34          3
2014-07-11  10254       14          5
2014-07-12  10255       68          9
2014-07-13  NULL        NULL        NULL
2014-07-14  NULL        NULL        NULL
2014-07-15  10256       88          3
2014-07-16  10257       35          4
...
2008-12-2  NULL        NULL        NULL
2008-12-2  NULL        NULL        NULL
2008-12-2  NULL        NULL        NULL
2008-12-3  NULL        NULL        NULL
2008-12-3  NULL        NULL        NULL

(1446 row(s) affected)
```

Dates that do not appear as order dates in the *Orders* table appear in the output of the query with *NULLs* in the order attributes.

Filtering attributes from the nonpreserved side of an outer join

When you need to review code involving outer joins to look for logical bugs, one of the things you should examine is the *WHERE* clause. If the predicate in the *WHERE* clause refers to an attribute from the nonpreserved side of the join using an expression in the form *<attribute> <operator> <value>*, it's usually an indication of a bug. This is because attributes from the nonpreserved side of the join are *NULLs* in outer rows, and an expression in the form *NULL <operator> <value>* yields *UNKNOWN* (unless it's the *IS NULL* operator explicitly looking for *NULLs*). Recall that a *WHERE* clause filters *UNKNOWN* out. Such a predicate in the *WHERE* clause causes all outer rows to be filtered out, effectively nullifying the outer join. Effectively, the join becomes an inner join. So the programmer either made a mistake in the join type or in the predicate.

If this is not clear yet, the following example might help. Consider the following query:

```
SELECT C.custid, C.companyname, O.orderid, O.orderdate
FROM Sales.Customers AS C
  LEFT OUTER JOIN Sales.Orders AS O
    ON C.custid = O.custid
WHERE O.orderdate >= '20160101';
```

The query performs a left outer join between the *Customers* and *Orders* tables. Prior to applying the *WHERE* filter, the join operator returns inner rows for customers who placed orders and outer rows for customers who didn't place orders, with *NULLs* in the order attributes. The predicate *O.orderdate >= '20160101'* in the *WHERE* clause evaluates to *UNKNOWN* for all outer rows, because those have a *NULL* in the *O.orderdate* attribute. All outer rows are eliminated by the *WHERE* filter, as you can see in the output of the query, shown here in abbreviated form:

```
custid      companyname     orderid     orderdate
----------- --------------- ----------- ----------
1           Customer NRZBB  10835       2016-01-15
1           Customer NRZBB  10952       2016-03-16
1           Customer NRZBB  11011       2016-04-09
2           Customer MLTDN  10926       2016-03-04
3           Customer KBUDE  10856       2016-01-28
...
90          Customer XBBVR  10910       2016-02-26
91          Customer CCFIZ  10906       2016-02-25
91          Customer CCFIZ  10870       2016-02-04
91          Customer CCFIZ  10998       2016-04-03
91          Customer CCFIZ  11044       2016-04-23

(270 row(s) affected)
```

This means that the use of an outer join here was futile. The programmer either made a mistake in using an outer join or in specifying the predicate in the *WHERE* clause.

Using outer joins in a multi-join query

Recall the discussion about all-at-once operations in Chapter 2, "Single-table queries." The concept describes the fact that all expressions that appear in the same logical query processing phase are evaluated as a set, at the same point in time. However, this concept is not applicable to the processing of table operators in the *FROM* phase. Table operators are logically evaluated from left to right. Rearranging the order in which outer joins are processed might result in different output, so you cannot rearrange them at will.

Some interesting bugs have to do with the logical order in which outer joins are processed. For example, a common bug could be considered a variation of the bug in the previous section. Suppose you write a multi-join query with an outer join between two tables, followed by an inner join with a third table. If the predicate in the inner join's *ON* clause compares an attribute from the nonpreserved side of the outer join and an attribute from the third table, all outer rows are discarded. Remember that outer rows have *NULLs* in the attributes from the nonpreserved side of the join, and comparing a *NULL* with anything yields *UNKNOWN*. *UNKNOWN* is filtered out by the *ON* filter. In other words, such a predicate nullifies the outer join, effectively turning it into an inner join. For example, consider the following query:

```
SELECT C.custid, O.orderid, OD.productid, OD.qty
FROM Sales.Customers AS C
  LEFT OUTER JOIN Sales.Orders AS O
    ON C.custid = O.custid
  INNER JOIN Sales.OrderDetails AS OD
    ON O.orderid = OD.orderid;
```

The first join is an outer join returning customers and their orders and also customers who did not place any orders. The outer rows representing customers with no orders have *NULLs* in the order attributes. The second join matches order lines from the *OrderDetails* table with rows from the result of the first join, based on the predicate *O.orderid = OD.orderid*; however, in the rows representing customers with no orders, the *O.orderid* attribute is *NULL*. Therefore, the predicate evaluates to *UNKNOWN*, and those rows are discarded. The output shown here in abbreviated form doesn't contain the customers 22 and 57, the two customers who did not place orders:

```
custid      orderid     productid   qty
----------- ----------- ----------- ------
85          10248       11          12
85          10248       42          10
85          10248       72          5
79          10249       14          9
79          10249       51          40
...
65          11077       64          2
65          11077       66          1
65          11077       73          2
65          11077       75          4
65          11077       77          2

(2155 row(s) affected)
```

Generally, outer rows are dropped whenever any kind of outer join (left, right, or full) is followed by a subsequent inner join or right outer join. That's assuming, of course, that the join condition compares the *NULLs* from the left side with something from the right side.

There are several ways to get around the problem if you want to return customers with no orders in the output. One option is to use a left outer join in the second join as well:

```
SELECT C.custid, O.orderid, OD.productid, OD.qty
FROM Sales.Customers AS C
  LEFT OUTER JOIN Sales.Orders AS O
    ON C.custid = O.custid
  LEFT OUTER JOIN Sales.OrderDetails AS OD
    ON O.orderid = OD.orderid;
```

This way, the outer rows produced by the first join aren't filtered out, as you can see in the output shown here in abbreviated form:

```
custid      orderid     productid   qty
----------- ----------- ----------- ------
85          10248       11          12
85          10248       42          10
85          10248       72          5
79          10249       14          9
79          10249       51          40
...
65          11077       64          2
65          11077       66          1
65          11077       73          2
65          11077       75          4
65          11077       77          2
22          NULL        NULL        NULL
57          NULL        NULL        NULL

(2157 row(s) affected)
```

This solution is usually not a good one because it preserves all rows from *Orders*. What if there were rows in *Orders* that didn't have matches in *OrderDetails*, and you wanted those rows to be discarded. What you want is an inner join between *Orders* and *OrderDetails*.

A second option is to use an inner join between *Orders* and *OrderDetails*, and then join the result with the *Customers* table using a right outer join:

```
SELECT C.custid, O.orderid, OD.productid, OD.qty
FROM Sales.Orders AS O
  INNER JOIN Sales.OrderDetails AS OD
    ON O.orderid = OD.orderid
  RIGHT OUTER JOIN Sales.Customers AS C
     ON O.custid = C.custid;
```

This way, the outer rows are produced by the last join and are not filtered out.

A third option is to use parentheses to turn the inner join between *Orders* and *OrderDetails* into an independent unit. This way, you can apply a left outer join between the *Customers* table and that unit. The query would look like this:

```
SELECT C.custid, O.orderid, OD.productid, OD.qty
FROM Sales.Customers AS C
  LEFT OUTER JOIN
      (Sales.Orders AS O
         INNER JOIN Sales.OrderDetails AS OD
           ON O.orderid = OD.orderid)
    ON C.custid = O.custid;
```

Using the *COUNT* aggregate with outer joins

Another common bug involves using *COUNT* with outer joins. When you group the result of an outer join and use the *COUNT(*)* aggregate, the aggregate takes into consideration both inner rows and outer rows, because it counts rows regardless of their contents. Usually, you're not supposed to take outer rows into consideration for the purposes of counting. For example, the following query is supposed to return the count of orders for each customer:

```
SELECT C.custid, COUNT(*) AS numorders
FROM Sales.Customers AS C
  LEFT OUTER JOIN Sales.Orders AS O
    ON C.custid = O.custid
GROUP BY C.custid;
```

Customers such as 22 and 57 who did not place orders, each have an outer row in the result of the join; therefore, they show up in the output with a count of 1:

```
custid      numorders
----------- -----------
1           6
2           4
3           7
4           13
5           18
...
22          1
...
57          1
...
87          15
88          9
89          14
90          7
91          7

(91 row(s) affected)
```

The *COUNT(*)* aggregate function cannot detect whether a row really represents an order. To fix the problem, you should use *COUNT(<column>)* instead of *COUNT(*)* and provide a column from the nonpreserved side of the join. This way, the *COUNT()* aggregate ignores outer rows because they have a *NULL* in that column. Remember to use a column that can only be *NULL* in case the row is an outer row—for example, the primary key column *orderid*:

```
SELECT C.custid, COUNT(O.orderid) AS numorders
FROM Sales.Customers AS C
  LEFT OUTER JOIN Sales.Orders AS O
    ON C.custid = O.custid
GROUP BY C.custid;
```

Notice in the output that the customers 22 and 57 now show up with a count of 0:

```
custid      numorders
----------- -----------
1           6
2           4
3           7
4           13
5           18
...
22          0
...
57          0
...
```

```
87          15
88          9
89          14
90          7
91          7

(91 row(s) affected)
```

Conclusion

This chapter covered the *JOIN* table operator. It described the logical query processing phases involved in the three fundamental types of joins: cross joins, inner joins, and outer joins. The chapter also covered further join examples, including composite joins, non-equi joins, and multi-join queries. The chapter concluded with an optional reading section covering more advanced aspects of outer joins. To practice what you learned, go over the exercises for this chapter.

Exercises

This section provides exercises to help you familiarize yourself with the subjects discussed in this chapter. All exercises involve querying objects in the *TSQLV4* database.

Exercise 1-1

Write a query that generates five copies of each employee row:

- Tables involved: *HR.Employees* and *dbo.Nums*
- Desired output:

```
empid       firstname  lastname             n
----------- ---------- -------------------- -----------
1           Sara       Davis                1
2           Don        Funk                 1
3           Judy       Lew                  1
4           Yael       Peled                1
5           Sven       Mortensen            1
6           Paul       Suurs                1
7           Russell    King                 1
8           Maria      Cameron              1
9           Patricia   Doyle                1
1           Sara       Davis                2
2           Don        Funk                 2
3           Judy       Lew                  2
4           Yael       Peled                2
5           Sven       Mortensen            2
6           Paul       Suurs                2
7           Russell    King                 2
8           Maria      Cameron              2
9           Patricia   Doyle                2
```

```
1           Sara       Davis           3
2           Don        Funk            3
3           Judy       Lew             3
4           Yael       Peled           3
5           Sven       Mortensen       3
6           Paul       Suurs           3
7           Russell    King            3
8           Maria      Cameron         3
9           Patricia   Doyle           3
1           Sara       Davis           4
2           Don        Funk            4
3           Judy       Lew             4
4           Yael       Peled           4
5           Sven       Mortensen       4
6           Paul       Suurs           4
7           Russell    King            4
8           Maria      Cameron         4
9           Patricia   Doyle           4
1           Sara       Davis           5
2           Don        Funk            5
3           Judy       Lew             5
4           Yael       Peled           5
5           Sven       Mortensen       5
6           Paul       Suurs           5
7           Russell    King            5
8           Maria      Cameron         5
9           Patricia   Doyle           5

(45 row(s) affected)
```

Exercise 1-2 (optional, advanced)

Write a query that returns a row for each employee and day in the range June 12, 2016 through June 16, 2016:

- Tables involved: *HR.Employees* and *dbo.Nums*
- Desired output:

```
empid       dt
----------- -----------
1           2016-06-12
1           2016-06-13
1           2016-06-14
1           2016-06-15
1           2016-06-16
2           2016-06-12
2           2016-06-13
2           2016-06-14
2           2016-06-15
2           2016-06-16
3           2016-06-12
3           2016-06-13
3           2016-06-14
3           2016-06-15
```

```
3           2016-06-16
4           2016-06-12
4           2016-06-13
4           2016-06-14
4           2016-06-15
4           2016-06-16
5           2016-06-12
5           2016-06-13
5           2016-06-14
5           2016-06-15
5           2016-06-16
6           2016-06-12
6           2016-06-13
6           2016-06-14
6           2016-06-15
6           2016-06-16
7           2016-06-12
7           2016-06-13
7           2016-06-14
7           2016-06-15
7           2016-06-16
8           2016-06-12
8           2016-06-13
8           2016-06-14
8           2016-06-15
8           2016-06-16
9           2016-06-12
9           2016-06-13
9           2016-06-14
9           2016-06-15
9           2016-06-16

(45 row(s) affected)
```

Exercise 2

Explain what's wrong in the following query, and provide a correct alternative:

```
SELECT Customers.custid, Customers.companyname, Orders.orderid, Orders.orderdate
FROM Sales.Customers AS C
  INNER JOIN Sales.Orders AS O
    ON Customers.custid = Orders.custid;
```

Exercise 3

Return US customers, and for each customer return the total number of orders and total quantities:

- Tables involved: *Sales.Customers*, *Sales.Orders*, and *Sales.OrderDetails*
- Desired output:

```
custid      numorders   totalqty
----------- ----------- -----------
32          11          345
36          5           122
43          2           20
45          4           181
48          8           134
55          10          603
65          18          1383
71          31          4958
75          9           327
77          4           46
78          3           59
82          3           89
89          14          1063

(13 row(s) affected)
```

Exercise 4

Return customers and their orders, including customers who placed no orders:

- Tables involved: *Sales.Customers* and *Sales.Orders*
- Desired output (abbreviated):

```
custid      companyname     orderid     orderdate
----------- --------------- ----------- -----------
85          Customer ENQZT  10248       2014-07-04
79          Customer FAPSM  10249       2014-07-05
34          Customer IBVRG  10250       2014-07-08
84          Customer NRCSK  10251       2014-07-08
...
73          Customer JMIKW  11074       2016-05-06
68          Customer CCKOT  11075       2016-05-06
9           Customer RTXGC  11076       2016-05-06
65          Customer NYUHS  11077       2016-05-06
22          Customer DTDMN  NULL        NULL
57          Customer WVAXS  NULL        NULL

(832 row(s) affected)
```

Exercise 5

Return customers who placed no orders:

- Tables involved: *Sales.Customers* and *Sales.Orders*
- Desired output:

```
custid      companyname
----------- ---------------
22          Customer DTDMN
57          Customer WVAXS

(2 row(s) affected)
```

Exercise 6

Return customers with orders placed on February 12, 2016, along with their orders:

- Tables involved: *Sales.Customers* and *Sales.Orders*
- Desired output:

```
custid      companyname     orderid     orderdate
----------- --------------- ----------- ----------
48          Customer DVFMB  10883       2016-02-12
45          Customer QXPPT  10884       2016-02-12
76          Customer SFOGW  10885       2016-02-12

(3 row(s) affected)
```

Exercise 7 (optional, advanced)

Write a query that returns all customers in the output, but matches them with their respective orders only if they were placed on February 12, 2016:

- Tables involved: *Sales.Customers* and *Sales.Orders*
- Desired output (abbreviated):

```
custid      companyname     orderid     orderdate
----------- --------------- ----------- ----------
72          Customer AHPOP  NULL        NULL
58          Customer AHXHT  NULL        NULL
25          Customer AZJED  NULL        NULL
18          Customer BSVAR  NULL        NULL
91          Customer CCFIZ  NULL        NULL
68          Customer CCKOT  NULL        NULL
49          Customer CQRAA  NULL        NULL
24          Customer CYZTN  NULL        NULL
22          Customer DTDMN  NULL        NULL
48          Customer DVFMB  10883       2016-02-12
10          Customer EEALV  NULL        NULL
40          Customer EFFTC  NULL        NULL
85          Customer ENQZT  NULL        NULL
82          Customer EYHKM  NULL        NULL
79          Customer FAPSM  NULL        NULL
...
51          Customer PVDZC  NULL        NULL
52          Customer PZNLA  NULL        NULL
56          Customer QNIVZ  NULL        NULL
8           Customer QUHWH  NULL        NULL
67          Customer QVEPD  NULL        NULL
45          Customer QXPPT  10884       2016-02-12
7           Customer QXVLA  NULL        NULL
60          Customer QZURI  NULL        NULL
19          Customer RFNQC  NULL        NULL
9           Customer RTXGC  NULL        NULL
76          Customer SFOGW  10885       2016-02-12
69          Customer SIUIH  NULL        NULL
```

```
86          Customer SNXOJ  NULL        NULL
88          Customer SRQVM  NULL        NULL
54          Customer TDKEG  NULL        NULL
20          Customer THHDP  NULL        NULL
...

(91 row(s) affected)
```

Exercise 8 (optional, advanced)

Explain why the following query isn't a correct solution query for Exercise 7:

```
SELECT C.custid, C.companyname, O.orderid, O.orderdate
FROM Sales.Customers AS C
  LEFT OUTER JOIN Sales.Orders AS O
    ON O.custid = C.custid
WHERE O.orderdate = '20160212'
   OR O.orderid IS NULL;
```

Exercise 9 (optional, advanced)

Return all customers, and for each return a Yes/No value depending on whether the customer placed orders on February 12, 2016:

- Tables involved: *Sales.Customers* and *Sales.Orders*
- Desired output (abbreviated):

```
custid      companyname     HasOrderOn20160212
----------- --------------- ------------------
...
40          Customer EFFTC  No
41          Customer XIIWM  No
42          Customer IAIJK  No
43          Customer UISOJ  No
44          Customer OXFRU  No
45          Customer QXPPT  Yes
46          Customer XPNIK  No
47          Customer PSQUZ  No
48          Customer DVFMB  Yes
49          Customer CQRAA  No
50          Customer JYPSC  No
51          Customer PVDZC  No
52          Customer PZNLA  No
53          Customer GCJSG  No
...

(91 row(s) affected)
```

Solutions

This section provides solutions to the exercises for this chapter.

Exercise 1-1

Producing multiple copies of rows can be achieved with a cross join. If you need to produce five copies of each employee row, you need to perform a cross join between the *Employees* table and a table that has five rows; alternatively, you can perform a cross join between *Employees* and a table that has more than five rows, but filter only five from that table in the *WHERE* clause. The *Nums* table is convenient for this purpose. Simply join *Employees* and *Nums*, and filter from *Nums* as many rows as the number of requested copies (five, in this case). Here's the solution query:

```
SELECT E.empid, E.firstname, E.lastname, N.n
FROM HR.Employees AS E
  CROSS JOIN dbo.Nums AS N
WHERE N.n <= 5
ORDER BY n, empid;
```

Exercise 1-2

This exercise is an extension of the previous exercise. Instead of being asked to produce a predetermined constant number of copies of each employee row, you are asked to produce a copy for each day in a certain date range. So here you need to calculate the number of days in the requested date range by using the *DATEDIFF* function, and refer to the result of that expression in the query's *WHERE* clause instead of referring to a constant. To produce the dates, simply add *n – 1* days to the date that starts the requested range. Here's the solution query:

```
SELECT E.empid,
  DATEADD(day, D.n - 1, CAST('20160612' AS DATE)) AS dt
FROM HR.Employees AS E
  CROSS JOIN dbo.Nums AS D
WHERE D.n <= DATEDIFF(day, '20160612', '20160616') + 1
ORDER BY empid, dt;
```

The *DATEDIFF* function returns *4* because there is a four-day difference between June 12, 2016 and June 16, 2016. Add 1 to the result, and you get 5 for the five days in the range. So the *WHERE* clause filters five rows from *Nums* where *n* is less than or equal to 5. By adding *n – 1* days to June 12, 2016, you get all dates in the range June 12, 2016 through June 16, 2016.

Exercise 2

The first step in the processing of the JOIN table operator assigns to the *Customers* and *Orders* tables the shorter aliases *C* and *O*, respectively. The aliasing effectively renames the tables for the purposes of the query. In all subsequent phases of logical query processing, the original table names are not accessible, rather only the shorter aliases are. You have two options to fix the query. One is to avoid aliasing and use the original table names as prefixes, like so:

```
SELECT Customers.custid, Customers.companyname, Orders.orderid, Orders.orderdate
FROM Sales.Customers
  INNER JOIN Sales.Orders
    ON Customers.custid = Orders.custid;
```

Another solution is to keep the aliases, but to make sure to use the aliases as prefixes, like so:

```
SELECT C.custid, C.companyname, O.orderid, O.orderdate
FROM Sales.Customers AS C
  INNER JOIN Sales.Orders AS O
    ON C.custid = O.custid;
```

Exercise 3

This exercise requires you to write a query that joins three tables: *Customers*, *Orders*, and *OrderDetails*. The query should use the *WHERE* clause to filter only rows where the customer's country is the United States. Because you are asked to return aggregates per customer, the query should group the rows by customer ID. You need to resolve a tricky issue here to return the right number of orders for each customer. Because of the join between *Orders* and *OrderDetails*, you don't get only one row per order—you get one row per order line. So if you use the *COUNT(*)* function in the *SELECT* list, you get back the number of order lines for each customer and not the number of orders.

To resolve this issue, you need to take each order into consideration only once. You can do this by using *COUNT(DISTINCT O.orderid)* instead of *COUNT(*)*. The total quantities don't create any special issues because the quantity is associated with the order line and not the order. Here's the solution query:

```
SELECT C.custid, COUNT(DISTINCT O.orderid) AS numorders, SUM(OD.qty) AS totalqty
FROM Sales.Customers AS C
  INNER JOIN Sales.Orders AS O
    ON O.custid = C.custid
  INNER JOIN Sales.OrderDetails AS OD
    ON OD.orderid = O.orderid
WHERE C.country = N'USA'
GROUP BY C.custid;
```

Exercise 4

To get both customers who placed orders and customers who didn't place orders in the result, you need to use an outer join, like this:

```
SELECT C.custid, C.companyname, O.orderid, O.orderdate
FROM Sales.Customers AS C
  LEFT OUTER JOIN Sales.Orders AS O
    ON O.custid = C.custid;
```

This query returns 832 rows (including the customers 22 and 57, who didn't place orders). An inner join between the tables would return only 830 rows, without those customers.

Exercise 5

This exercise is an extension of the previous one. To return only customers who didn't place orders, you need to add a *WHERE* clause to the query that filters only outer rows—namely, rows that represent customers with no orders. Outer rows have *NULLs* in the attributes from the nonpreserved side of the join (*Orders*). But to make sure that the *NULL* is a placeholder for an outer row and not a *NULL* that originated from the table, it's recommended that you refer to an attribute that is the primary key, or the join column, or one defined as not allowing *NULLs*. Here's the solution query, which refers to the primary key of the *Orders* table in the *WHERE* clause:

```
SELECT C.custid, C.companyname
FROM Sales.Customers AS C
  LEFT OUTER JOIN Sales.Orders AS O
    ON O.custid = C.custid
WHERE O.orderid IS NULL;
```

This query returns only two rows, for customers 22 and 57, who didn't place orders.

Exercise 6

This exercise involves writing a query that performs an inner join between *Customers* and *Orders* and filters only rows in which the order date is February 12, 2016:

```
SELECT C.custid, C.companyname, O.orderid, O.orderdate
FROM Sales.Customers AS C
  INNER JOIN Sales.Orders AS O
    ON O.custid = C.custid
WHERE O.orderdate = '20160212';
```

The *WHERE* clause filtered out customers who didn't place orders on February 12, 2016, but that was the request.

Exercise 7

This exercise builds on the previous one. The trick here is to realize two things. First, you need an outer join because you are supposed to preserve all customers, even if they don't have matching orders. Second, the predicate based on the order date is a nonfinal matching predicate; as such it must appear in the *ON* clause and not the *WHERE* clause. Remember that the *WHERE* clause is a final filter that is applied after outer rows are added. Your goal is to match orders to customers only if the order was placed by the customer on February 12, 2016. You still want to get customers who didn't place orders on that date in the output. Hence, the *ON* clause should match customers and orders based on both an equality between the customer's customer ID and the order's customer ID, and on the order date being February 12, 2016. Here's the solution query:

```
SELECT C.custid, C.companyname, O.orderid, O.orderdate
FROM Sales.Customers AS C
  LEFT OUTER JOIN Sales.Orders AS O
    ON O.custid = C.custid
    AND O.orderdate = '20160212';
```

Exercise 8

The outer join matches all customers with their respective orders, and it preserves also customers who didn't place any orders. Customers without orders have *NULLs* in the order attributes. Then the *WHERE* filter keeps only rows where the order date is February 12, 2016 or the order ID is NULL (a customer without orders at all). The filter discards customers who didn't place orders on February 12, 2016 but did place orders on other dates, and according to Exercise 7 the query is supposed to return all customers. Here's the output of the incorrect query:

```
custid      companyname     orderid     orderdate
----------- --------------- ----------- ----------
48          Customer DVFMB  10883       2016-02-12
45          Customer QXPPT  10884       2016-02-12
76          Customer SFOGW  10885       2016-02-12
22          Customer DTDMN  NULL        NULL
57          Customer WVAXS  NULL        NULL

(5 row(s) affected)
```

The first three rows represent orders that were placed on February 12, 2016. The last two rows represent customers who didn't place orders at all. Observe that many of the 91 customers from the *Customers* table are missing. As mentioned, those are customers who didn't place orders on February 12, 2016, but did place orders on other dates.

Exercise 9

This exercise is an extension of Exercise 7. Here, instead of returning matching orders, you just need to return a Yes/No value indicating whether there is a matching order. Remember that in an outer join, a nonmatch is identified as an outer row with *NULLs* in the attributes of the nonpreserved side. So you can use a simple *CASE* expression that checks whether the current row is not an outer one, in which case it returns *Yes*; otherwise, it returns *No*. Because technically you can have more than one match per customer, you should add a *DISTINCT* clause to the *SELECT* list. This way, you get only one row back for each customer. Here's the solution query:

```
SELECT DISTINCT C.custid, C.companyname,
  CASE WHEN O.orderid IS NOT NULL THEN 'Yes' ELSE 'No' END AS HasOrderOn20160212
FROM Sales.Customers AS C
  LEFT OUTER JOIN Sales.Orders AS O
    ON O.custid = C.custid
    AND O.orderdate = '20160212';
```

CHAPTER 4

Subqueries

SQL supports writing queries within queries, or *nesting* queries. The outermost query is a query whose result set is returned to the caller and is known as the *outer query*. The inner query is a query whose result is used by the outer query and is known as a *subquery*. The inner query acts in place of an expression that is based on constants or variables and is evaluated at run time. Unlike the results of expressions that use constants, the result of a subquery can change, because of changes in the queried tables. When you use subqueries, you avoid the need for separate steps in your solutions that store intermediate query results in variables.

A subquery can be either self-contained or correlated. A self-contained subquery has no dependency on tables from the outer query, whereas a correlated subquery does. A subquery can be single-valued, multivalued, or table-valued. That is, a subquery can return a single value, multiple values, or a whole table result.

This chapter focuses on subqueries that return a single value (scalar subqueries) and subqueries that return multiple values (multivalued subqueries). I'll cover subqueries that return whole tables (table subqueries) later in the book in Chapter 5, "Table expressions."

Both self-contained and correlated subqueries can return a scalar or multiple values. I'll first describe self-contained subqueries and demonstrate both scalar and multivalued examples. Then I'll describe correlated subqueries.

Again, exercises at the end of the chapter can help you practice what you learned.

Self-contained subqueries

Every subquery has an outer query that contains it. Self-contained subqueries are subqueries that are independent of the tables in the outer query. Self-contained subqueries are convenient to debug, because you can always highlight the inner query, run it, and ensure that it does what it's supposed to do. Logically, the subquery code is evaluated only once before the outer query is evaluated, and then the outer query uses the result of the subquery. The following sections take a look at some concrete examples of self-contained subqueries.

Self-contained scalar subquery examples

A scalar subquery is a subquery that returns a single value. Such a subquery can appear anywhere in the outer query where a single-valued expression can appear (such as *WHERE* or *SELECT*).

For example, suppose you need to query the *Orders* table in the *TSQLV4* database and return information about the order that has the maximum order ID in the table. You could accomplish the task by using a variable. The code could retrieve the maximum order ID from the *Orders* table and store the result in a variable. Then the code could query the *Orders* table and filter the order where the order ID is equal to the value stored in the variable. The following code demonstrates this technique:

```
USE TSQLV4;

DECLARE @maxid AS INT = (SELECT MAX(orderid)
                         FROM Sales.Orders);

SELECT orderid, orderdate, empid, custid
FROM Sales.Orders
WHERE orderid = @maxid;
```

This query returns the following output:

```
orderid     orderdate  empid       custid
----------- ---------- ----------- ----------
11077       2016-05-06 1           65
```

You can substitute the variable with a scalar self-contained subquery, like so:

```
SELECT orderid, orderdate, empid, custid
FROM Sales.Orders
WHERE orderid = (SELECT MAX(O.orderid)
                 FROM Sales.Orders AS O);
```

For a scalar subquery to be valid, it must return no more than one value. If a scalar subquery returns more than one value, it fails at run time. With the sample data in the *TSQLV4* database, the following query runs successfully:

```
SELECT orderid
FROM Sales.Orders
WHERE empid =
  (SELECT E.empid
   FROM HR.Employees AS E
   WHERE E.lastname LIKE N'C%');
```

The purpose of this query is to return orders placed by employees whose last name starts with the letter *C*. The subquery returns employee IDs of all employees whose last names start with the letter *C*. The outer query returns the orders where the employee ID is equal to the result of the subquery. Because an equality operator expects scalar operands on both sides, the subquery is considered scalar. Because the subquery can potentially return more than one value, the choice of using an equality predicate here is wrong. If the subquery returns more than one value, the query fails.

This query happens to run without failure because currently the *Employees* table contains only one employee whose last name starts with *C* (Maria Cameron with employee ID 8). This query returns the following output, shown here in abbreviated form:

```
orderid
-----------
10262
10268
10276
10278
10279
...
11054
11056
11065
11068
11075

(104 row(s) affected)
```

If the subquery returns more than one value, the query fails. For example, try running the query with employees whose last names start with *D*:

```
SELECT orderid
FROM Sales.Orders
WHERE empid =
  (SELECT E.empid
   FROM HR.Employees AS E
   WHERE E.lastname LIKE N'D%');
```

Apparently, two employees have a last name starting with *D* (Sara Davis and Patricia Doyle). Therefore, the query fails at run time with the following error:

```
Msg 512, Level 16, State 1, Line 40
Subquery returned more than 1 value. This is not permitted when the subquery follows =, !=, <,
<= , >, >= or when the subquery is used as an expression.
```

If a scalar subquery returns no value, the empty result is converted to a *NULL*. Recall that a comparison with a *NULL* yields *UNKNOWN* and that query filters do not return a row for which the filter expression evaluates to *UNKNOWN*. For example, the *Employees* table currently has no employees whose last names start with *A*; therefore, the following query returns an empty set:

```
SELECT orderid
FROM Sales.Orders
WHERE empid =
  (SELECT E.empid
   FROM HR.Employees AS E
   WHERE E.lastname LIKE N'A%');
```

Self-contained multivalued subquery examples

A multivalued subquery is a subquery that returns multiple values as a single column. Some predicates, such as the *IN* predicate, operate on a multivalued subquery.

> **Note** SQL supports other predicates that operate on a multivalued subquery; those are *SOME*, *ANY*, and *ALL*. They are rarely used and therefore not covered in this book.

The form of the *IN* predicate is

<scalar_expression> IN (<multivalued subquery>)

The predicate evaluates to *TRUE* if *scalar_expression* is equal to any of the values returned by the subquery. Recall the request in the previous section—returning orders that were handled by employees with a last name starting with a certain letter. Because more than one employee can have a last name starting with the same letter, this request should be handled with the *IN* predicate not with an equality operator. For example, the following query returns orders placed by employees with a last name starting with *D*:

```
SELECT orderid
FROM Sales.Orders
WHERE empid IN
  (SELECT E.empid
   FROM HR.Employees AS E
   WHERE E.lastname LIKE N'D%');
```

Because this solution uses the *IN* predicate, this query is valid with any number of values returned—none, one, or more. This query returns the following output, shown here in abbreviated form:

```
orderid
-----------
10258
10270
10275
10285
10292
...
10978
11016
11017
11022
11058

(166 row(s) affected)
```

You might wonder why you don't implement this task by using a join instead of subqueries, like this:

```
SELECT O.orderid
FROM HR.Employees AS E
  INNER JOIN Sales.Orders AS O
    ON E.empid = O.empid
WHERE E.lastname LIKE N'D%';
```

Similarly, you're likely to stumble into many other querying problems you can solve with either subqueries or joins. I don't know of a reliable rule of thumb that says a subquery is better than a join or the other way around. In some cases the database engine optimizes both the same way, sometimes joins perform better, and sometimes subqueries perform better. My approach is to first write a solution query that is intuitive and then, if performance is not satisfactory, try query revisions among other tuning methods. Such query revisions might include using joins instead of subqueries or the other way around. Also, consider keeping the different query rewrites; future changes in the database engine or the data might result in a different query being faster.

As another example of using multivalued subqueries, suppose you need to write a query that returns orders placed by customers from the United States. You can write a query against the *Orders* table that returns orders where the customer ID is in the set of customer IDs of customers from the United States. You can implement the last part in a self-contained, multivalued subquery. Here's the complete solution query:

```
SELECT custid, orderid, orderdate, empid
FROM Sales.Orders
WHERE custid IN
  (SELECT C.custid
   FROM Sales.Customers AS C
   WHERE C.country = N'USA');
```

This query returns the following output, shown here in abbreviated form:

```
custid      orderid     orderdate  empid
----------- ----------- ---------- -----------
65          10262       2014-07-22 8
89          10269       2014-07-31 5
75          10271       2014-08-01 6
65          10272       2014-08-02 6
65          10294       2014-08-30 4
...
32          11040       2016-04-22 4
32          11061       2016-04-30 4
71          11064       2016-05-01 1
89          11066       2016-05-01 7
65          11077       2016-05-06 1

(122 row(s) affected)
```

As with any other predicate, you can negate the *IN* predicate with the *NOT* operator. For example, the following query returns customers who did not place any orders:

```
SELECT custid, companyname
FROM Sales.Customers
WHERE custid NOT IN
  (SELECT O.custid
   FROM Sales.Orders AS O);
```

Note that it's considered a best practice to qualify the subquery to exclude *NULLs*. I didn't do this here because I didn't explain the reason for this recommendation. I'll explain it later in the section "*NULL* trouble."

The subquery returns the IDs of all customers that appear in the *Orders* table. In other words, it returns only the IDs of customers who placed orders. The outer query returns customers with IDs that do not appear in the result of the subquery—in other words, customers who did not place orders. This query returns the following output:

```
custid      companyname
----------- ----------------
22          Customer DTDMN
57          Customer WVAXS
```

You might wonder whether specifying a *DISTINCT* clause in the subquery can help performance, because the same customer ID can occur more than once in the *Orders* table. The database engine is smart enough to consider removing duplicates without you asking it to do so explicitly, so this isn't something you need to worry about.

The last example in this section demonstrates the use of multiple self-contained subqueries in the same query—both single-valued and multivalued. Before I describe the task, run the following code to create a table called *dbo.Orders* in the *TSQLV4* database, and populate it with even-numbered order IDs from the *Sales.Orders* table:

```
USE TSQLV4;
DROP TABLE IF EXISTS dbo.Orders;
CREATE TABLE dbo.Orders(orderid INT NOT NULL CONSTRAINT PK_Orders PRIMARY KEY);

INSERT INTO dbo.Orders(orderid)
  SELECT orderid
  FROM Sales.Orders
  WHERE orderid % 2 = 0;
```

I describe the *INSERT* statement in more detail in Chapter 8, "Data modification," so don't worry if you're not familiar with it yet.

You need to write a query that returns all individual order IDs that are missing between the minimum and maximum ones in the table. It can be quite complicated to solve this problem with a query without any helper tables. You might find the *Nums* table introduced in Chapter 3, "Joins," useful here. Remember that the *Nums* table contains a sequence of integers, starting with 1, with no gaps. To return all missing order IDs, query the *Nums* table and filter only numbers that are between the minimum and maximum ones in the *dbo.Orders* table, and that do not appear as order IDs in the *Orders* table. You can use scalar self-contained subqueries to return the minimum and maximum order IDs and a multivalued self-contained subquery to return the set of all existing order IDs. Here's the complete solution query:

```
SELECT n
FROM dbo.Nums
WHERE n BETWEEN (SELECT MIN(O.orderid) FROM dbo.Orders AS O)
            AND (SELECT MAX(O.orderid) FROM dbo.Orders AS O)
  AND n NOT IN (SELECT O.orderid FROM dbo.Orders AS O);
```

Because the code that populated the *dbo.Orders* table filtered only even-numbered order IDs, this query returns all odd-numbered values between the minimum and maximum order IDs in the *Orders* table. The output of this query is shown here in abbreviated form:

```
n
-----------
10249
10251
10253
10255
10257
...
11067
11069
11071
11073
11075

(414 row(s) affected)
```

When you're done, run the following code for cleanup:

```
DROP TABLE IF EXISTS dbo.Orders;
```

Correlated subqueries

Correlated subqueries are subqueries that refer to attributes from the tables that appear in the outer query. This means the subquery is dependent on the outer query and cannot be invoked independently. Logically, the subquery is evaluated separately for each outer row. For example, the query in Listing 4-1 returns orders with the maximum order ID for each customer.

LISTING 4-1 Correlated subquery

```
USE TSQLV4;

SELECT custid, orderid, orderdate, empid
FROM Sales.Orders AS O1
WHERE orderid =
  (SELECT MAX(O2.orderid)
   FROM Sales.Orders AS O2
   WHERE O2.custid = O1.custid);
```

The outer query is issued against an instance of the *Orders* table called *O1*; it filters orders where the order ID is equal to the value returned by the subquery. The subquery filters orders from a second instance of the *Orders* table called *O2*, where the inner customer ID is equal to the outer customer ID, and returns the maximum order ID from those filtered orders. In other words, for each row in *O1*, the subquery returns the maximum order ID for the current customer. If the outer order ID and the order

ID returned by the subquery match, the query returns the outer row. This query returns the following output, shown here in abbreviated form:

```
custid      orderid     orderdate  empid
----------- ----------- ---------- -----------
91          11044       2016-04-23 4
90          11005       2016-04-07 2
89          11066       2016-05-01 7
88          10935       2016-03-09 4
87          11025       2016-04-15 6
...
5           10924       2016-03-04 3
4           11016       2016-04-10 9
3           10856       2016-01-28 3
2           10926       2016-03-04 4
1           11011       2016-04-09 3

(89 row(s) affected)
```

Because of the dependency on the outer query, correlated subqueries are usually harder to figure out than self-contained subqueries. To simplify things, I suggest you focus your attention on a single row in the outer table and think about the logical processing that takes place in the inner query for that row. For example, focus your attention on the following row from the table in the outer query, which has order ID 10248:

```
custid      orderid     orderdate                 empid
----------- ----------- ------------------------- -----------
85          10248       2014-07-04 00:00:00.000   5
```

When the subquery is evaluated for this row, the correlation to *O1.custid* means *85*. If you substitute the correlation manually with *85*, you get the following:

```
SELECT MAX(O2.orderid)
FROM Sales.Orders AS O2
WHERE O2.custid = 85;
```

This query returns the order ID 10739. The outer row's order ID—10248—is compared with the inner one—10739—and because there's no match in this case, the outer row is filtered out. The subquery returns the same value for all rows in *O1* with the same customer ID, and only in one case is there a match—when the outer row's order ID is the maximum for the current customer. Thinking in such terms will make it easier for you to grasp the concept of correlated subqueries.

The fact that correlated subqueries are dependent on the outer query makes it harder to troubleshoot problems with them compared to self-contained subqueries. You can't just highlight the subquery portion and run it. For example, if you try to highlight and run the subquery portion in Listing 4-1, you get the following error:

```
Msg 4104, Level 16, State 1, Line 119
The multi-part identifier "O1.custid" could not be bound.
```

This error indicates that the identifier *O1.custid* cannot be bound to an object in the query, because *O1* is not defined in the query. It is defined only in the context of the outer query. To troubleshoot correlated subqueries, you need to substitute the correlation with a constant, and after ensuring the code is correct, substitute the constant with the correlation.

As another example, suppose you need to query the *Sales.OrderValues* view and return for each order the percentage of the current order value out of the customer total. In Chapter 7, "Beyond the fundamentals of querying," I provide a solution to this problem that uses window functions; here I'll explain how to solve the problem by using subqueries. It's always a good idea to try to come up with several solutions to each problem, because the different solutions will usually vary in complexity and performance.

You can write an outer query against one instance of the *OrderValues* view called *O1*. In the *SELECT* list, divide the current value by the result of a correlated subquery against a second instance of *OrderValues* called *O2* that returns the current customer's total. Here's the complete solution query:

```
SELECT orderid, custid, val,
  CAST(100. * val / (SELECT SUM(O2.val)
                     FROM Sales.OrderValues AS O2
                     WHERE O2.custid = O1.custid)
       AS NUMERIC(5,2)) AS pct
FROM Sales.OrderValues AS O1
ORDER BY custid, orderid;
```

The *CAST* function is used to convert the datatype of the expression to *NUMERIC* with a precision of 5 (the total number of digits) and a scale of 2 (the number of digits after the decimal point).

This query returns the following output:

```
orderid     custid      val        pct
----------- ----------- ---------- ------
10643       1           814.50     19.06
10692       1           878.00     20.55
10702       1           330.00     7.72
10835       1           845.80     19.79
10952       1           471.20     11.03
11011       1           933.50     21.85
10308       2           88.80      6.33
10625       2           479.75     34.20
10759       2           320.00     22.81
10926       2           514.40     36.67
...

(830 row(s) affected)
```

The *EXISTS* predicate

T-SQL supports a predicate called *EXISTS* that accepts a subquery as input and returns *TRUE* if the subquery returns any rows and *FALSE* otherwise. For example, the following query returns customers from Spain who placed orders:

```
SELECT custid, companyname
FROM Sales.Customers AS C
WHERE country = N'Spain'
```

```
  AND EXISTS
    (SELECT * FROM Sales.Orders AS O
     WHERE O.custid = C.custid);
```

The outer query against the *Customers* table filters only customers from Spain for whom the *EXISTS* predicate returns *TRUE*. The *EXISTS* predicate returns *TRUE* if the current customer has related orders in the *Orders* table.

One of the benefits of using the *EXISTS* predicate is that you can intuitively phrase queries that sound like English. For example, this query can be read just as you would say it in ordinary English: Return customers from Spain if they have any orders where the order's customer ID is the same as the customer's customer ID.

This query returns the following output:

```
custid      companyname
----------- ----------------
8           Customer QUHWH
29          Customer MDLWA
30          Customer KSLQF
69          Customer SIUIH
```

As with other predicates, you can negate the *EXISTS* predicate with the *NOT* operator. For example, the following query returns customers from Spain who did not place orders:

```
SELECT custid, companyname
FROM Sales.Customers AS C
WHERE country = N'Spain'
  AND NOT EXISTS
    (SELECT * FROM Sales.Orders AS O
     WHERE O.custid = C.custid);
```

This query returns the following output:

```
custid      companyname
----------- ----------------
22          Customer DTDMN
```

Even though this book's focus is on logical query processing and not performance, I thought you might be interested to know that the *EXISTS* predicate lends itself to good optimization. That is, the database engine knows that it's enough to determine whether the subquery returns at least one row or none, and it doesn't need to process all qualifying rows. You can think of this capability as a kind of short-circuit evaluation. The same applies to the *IN* predicate.

Even though in most cases the use of star (*) is considered a bad practice, with *EXISTS* it isn't. The predicate cares only about the existence of matching rows, regardless of what you have in the *SELECT* list. The database engine knows this and—for example, for index selection purposes—ignores the subquery's *SELECT* list. Some minor extra cost might be incurred in the resolution process, where Microsoft SQL Server expands the * against metadata info—for example, to check that you have permissions to query all columns. But this cost is so minor you'll probably barely notice it. My opinion is that queries should be natural and intuitive unless there's a compelling reason to sacrifice this aspect of the code. I find the form

*EXISTS(SELECT * FROM . . .)* much more intuitive than *EXISTS(SELECT 1 FROM . . .)*. Saving the minor extra cost associated with the resolution of * is something that is not worth the cost of sacrificing the readability of the code.

Finally, another aspect of *EXISTS* that is worth mentioning is that, unlike most predicates in T-SQL, *EXISTS* uses two-valued logic and not three-valued logic. If you think about it, there's no situation where it's unknown whether a query returns any rows.

Beyond the fundamentals of subqueries

This section covers aspects of subqueries you might consider to be beyond the fundamentals. I provide it as optional reading in case you feel very comfortable with the material covered so far in this chapter.

Returning previous or next values

Suppose you need to query the *Orders* table in the *TSQLV4* database and return, for each order, information about the current order and also the previous order ID. The tricky part is that the concept of "previous" implies order, and rows in a table have no order. One way to achieve this objective is with a T-SQL expression that means "the maximum value that is smaller than the current value." You could use the following T-SQL expression, which is based on a correlated subquery, for this:

```
SELECT orderid, orderdate, empid, custid,
  (SELECT MAX(O2.orderid)
   FROM Sales.Orders AS O2
   WHERE O2.orderid < O1.orderid) AS prevorderid
FROM Sales.Orders AS O1;
```

This query produces the following output, shown here in abbreviated form:

```
orderid     orderdate   empid       custid      prevorderid
----------- ----------- ----------- ----------- -----------
10248       2014-07-04  5           85          NULL
10249       2014-07-05  6           79          10248
10250       2014-07-08  4           34          10249
10251       2014-07-08  3           84          10250
10252       2014-07-09  4           76          10251
...
11073       2016-05-05  2           58          11072
11074       2016-05-06  7           73          11073
11075       2016-05-06  8           68          11074
11076       2016-05-06  4           9           11075
11077       2016-05-06  1           65          11076

(830 row(s) affected)
```

Notice that because there's no order before the first order, the subquery returned a *NULL* for the first order.

Similarly, you can phrase the concept of "next" as "the minimum value that is greater than the current value." Here's a query that returns for each order the next order ID:

```
SELECT orderid, orderdate, empid, custid,
  (SELECT MIN(O2.orderid)
   FROM Sales.Orders AS O2
   WHERE O2.orderid > O1.orderid) AS nextorderid
FROM Sales.Orders AS O1;
```

This query produces the following output, shown here in abbreviated form:

```
orderid     orderdate   empid       custid      nextorderid
----------- ----------- ----------- ----------- -----------
10248       2014-07-04  5           85          10249
10249       2014-07-05  6           79          10250
10250       2014-07-08  4           34          10251
10251       2014-07-08  3           84          10252
10252       2014-07-09  4           76          10253
...
11073       2016-05-05  2           58          11074
11074       2016-05-06  7           73          11075
11075       2016-05-06  8           68          11076
11076       2016-05-06  4           9           11077
11077       2016-05-06  1           65          NULL

(830 row(s) affected)
```

Notice that because there's no order after the last order, the subquery returned a *NULL* for the last order.

Note that T-SQL supports window functions called *LAG* and *LEAD* that you use to obtain elements from a previous or next row much more easily. I will cover these and other window functions in Chapter 7.

Using running aggregates

Running aggregates are aggregates that accumulate values based on some order. In this section, I use the *Sales.OrderTotalsByYear* view to demonstrate a technique that calculates those. The view has total order quantities by year. Query the view to examine its contents:

```
SELECT orderyear, qty
FROM Sales.OrderTotalsByYear;
```

You get the following output:

```
orderyear   qty
----------- -----------
2016        16247
2014        9581
2015        25489
```

Suppose you need to compute for each year the running total quantity up to and including that year's. For the earliest year recorded in the view (2014), the running total is equal to that year's quantity. For the second year (2015), the running total is the sum of the first year plus the second year, and so on.

You query one instance of the view (call it *O1*) to return for each year the current year and quantity. You use a correlated subquery against a second instance of the view (call it *O2*) to calculate the running-total quantity. The subquery should filter all rows in *O2* where the order year is smaller than or equal to the current year in *O1*, and sum the quantities from *O2*. Here's the solution query:

```
SELECT orderyear, qty,
  (SELECT SUM(O2.qty)
   FROM Sales.OrderTotalsByYear AS O2
   WHERE O2.orderyear <= O1.orderyear) AS runqty
FROM Sales.OrderTotalsByYear AS O1
ORDER BY orderyear;
```

This query returns the following output:

```
orderyear   qty         runqty
----------- ----------- -----------
2014        9581        9581
2015        25489       35070
2016        16247       51317
```

Note that T-SQL supports window aggregate functions, which you can use to compute running totals much more easily and efficiently. As mentioned, I will discuss those in Chapter 7.

Dealing with misbehaving subqueries

This section introduces cases in which the use of subqueries involves bugs, and it provides best practices that can help you avoid those bugs.

NULL trouble

Remember that T-SQL uses three-valued logic because of its support for *NULLs*. In this section, I discuss problems that can evolve when you forget about *NULLs* and the three-valued logic.

Consider the following query, which is supposed to return customers who did not place orders:

```
SELECT custid, companyname
FROM Sales.Customers
WHERE custid NOT IN(SELECT O.custid
                    FROM Sales.Orders AS O);
```

With the current sample data in the *Orders* table, the query seems to work the way you expect it to, and indeed, it returns the following two customers:

```
custid      companyname
----------- ----------------
22          Customer DTDMN
57          Customer WVAXS
```

Next, run the following code to insert a new order into the *Orders* table with a *NULL* customer ID:

```
INSERT INTO Sales.Orders
  (custid, empid, orderdate, requireddate, shippeddate, shipperid,
   freight, shipname, shipaddress, shipcity, shipregion,
   shippostalcode, shipcountry)
  VALUES(NULL, 1, '20160212', '20160212',
         '20160212', 1, 123.00, N'abc', N'abc', N'abc',
         N'abc', N'abc', N'abc');
```

Next, run the previous query again:

```
SELECT custid, companyname
FROM Sales.Customers
WHERE custid NOT IN(SELECT O.custid
                    FROM Sales.Orders AS O);
```

This time, the query returns an empty set. Keeping in mind what you read in the section about *NULLs* in Chapter 2, "Single-table queries," try to explain why this query returns an empty set. Also try to think of ways to get customers 22 and 57 in the output.

Obviously, the culprit here is the *NULL* customer ID you added to the *Orders* table. The *NULL* is one of the elements returned by the subquery.

Let's start with the part that does behave like you expect it to. The *IN* predicate returns *TRUE* for a customer who placed orders (for example, customer 85), because such a customer is returned by the subquery. The *NOT* operator negates the *IN* predicate; hence, the *NOT TRUE* becomes *FALSE*, and the customer is discarded. The expected behavior here is that if a customer ID is known to appear in the Orders table, you know with certainty that you do not want to return it. However (take a deep breath), if a customer ID from *Customers* doesn't appear in the set of non-*NULL* customer IDs in *Orders*, and there's also a *NULL* customer ID in *Orders*, you can't tell with certainty that the customer is there—and similarly you can't tell with certainty that it's not there. Confused? I hope I can clarify this explanation with an example.

The *IN* predicate returns *UNKNOWN* for a customer such as 22 that does not appear in the set of known customer IDs in *Orders*. That's because when you compare it with known customer IDs you get *FALSE*, and when you compare it with a *NULL* you get *UNKNOWN*. *FALSE OR UNKNOWN* yields *UNKNOWN*. Consider the expression *22 NOT IN (1, 2, <other non-22 values>, NULL)*. This expression can be rephrased as *NOT 22 IN (1, 2, ..., NULL)*. You can expand this expression to *NOT (22 = 1 OR 22 = 2 OR ... OR 22 = NULL)*. Evaluate each individual expression in the parentheses to its truth value and you get *NOT (FALSE OR FALSE OR ... OR UNKNOWN)*, which translates to *NOT UNKNOWN*, which evaluates to *UNKNOWN*.

The logical meaning of *UNKNOWN* here, before you apply the *NOT* operator, is that it can't be determined whether the customer ID appears in the set, because the *NULL* could represent that customer ID. The tricky part here is that negating the *UNKNOWN* with the *NOT* operator still yields *UNKNOWN*. This means that in a case where it is unknown whether a customer ID appears in a set, it is also unknown whether it doesn't appear in the set. Remember that a query filter discards rows that get *UNKNOWN* in the result of the predicate.

In short, when you use the *NOT IN* predicate against a subquery that returns at least one *NULL*, the query always returns an empty set. So, what practices can you follow to avoid such trouble? First, when a column is not supposed to allow *NULLs*, be sure to define it as *NOT NULL*. Second, in all queries you write, you should consider *NULLs* and the three-valued logic. Think explicitly about whether the query might process *NULLs*, and if so, whether SQL's treatment of *NULLs* is correct for you. When it isn't, you need to intervene. For example, our query returns an empty set because of the comparison with the *NULL*. If you want to check whether a customer ID appears only in the set of known values, you should exclude the *NULLs*—either explicitly or implicitly. To exclude them explicitly, add the predicate *O.custid IS NOT NULL* to the subquery, like this:

```
SELECT custid, companyname
FROM Sales.Customers
WHERE custid NOT IN(SELECT O.custid
                    FROM Sales.Orders AS O
                    WHERE O.custid IS NOT NULL);
```

You can also exclude the *NULLs* implicitly by using the *NOT EXISTS* predicate instead of *NOT IN*, like this:

```
SELECT custid, companyname
FROM Sales.Customers AS C
WHERE NOT EXISTS
  (SELECT *
   FROM Sales.Orders AS O
   WHERE O.custid = C.custid);
```

Recall that unlike *IN*, *EXISTS* uses two-valued predicate logic. *EXISTS* always returns *TRUE* or *FALSE* and never *UNKNOWN*. When the subquery stumbles into a *NULL* in *O.custid*, the expression evaluates to *UNKNOWN* and the row is filtered out. As far as the *EXISTS* predicate is concerned, the *NULL* cases are eliminated naturally, as though they weren't there. So *EXISTS* ends up handling only known customer IDs. Therefore, it's safer to use *NOT EXISTS* than *NOT IN*.

When you're done, run the following code for cleanup:

```
DELETE FROM Sales.Orders WHERE custid IS NULL;
```

Substitution errors in subquery column names

Logical bugs in your code can sometimes be elusive. In this section, I cover a bug related to an innocent substitution error in a subquery column name. After explaining the bug, I provide best practices that can help you avoid it.

The examples in this section query a table called *MyShippers* in the *Sales* schema. Run the following code to create and populate this table:

```
DROP TABLE IF EXISTS Sales.MyShippers;

CREATE TABLE Sales.MyShippers
(
  shipper_id  INT          NOT NULL,
```

```
  companyname NVARCHAR(40) NOT NULL,
  phone       NVARCHAR(24) NOT NULL,
  CONSTRAINT PK_MyShippers PRIMARY KEY(shipper_id)
);

INSERT INTO Sales.MyShippers(shipper_id, companyname, phone)
  VALUES(1, N'Shipper GVSUA', N'(503) 555-0137'),
        (2, N'Shipper ETYNR', N'(425) 555-0136'),
        (3, N'Shipper ZHISN', N'(415) 555-0138');
```

Consider the following query, which is supposed to return shippers who shipped orders to customer 43:

```
SELECT shipper_id, companyname
FROM Sales.MyShippers
WHERE shipper_id IN
  (SELECT shipper_id
   FROM Sales.Orders
   WHERE custid = 43);
```

This query produces the following output:

```
shipper_id  companyname
----------- ---------------
1           Shipper GVSUA
2           Shipper ETYNR
3           Shipper ZHISN
```

Only shippers 2 and 3 shipped orders to customer 43, but for some reason this query returned all shippers from the *MyShippers* table. Examine the query carefully and also the schemas of the tables involved, and see if you can explain what's going on.

It turns out that the column name in the *Orders* table holding the shipper ID is not called *shipper_id*, rather *shipperid* (no underscore). The column in the *MyShippers* table is called *shipper_id* with an underscore. The resolution, or binding, of nonprefixed column names works in the context of a subquery from the inner scope outward. In our example, SQL Server first looks for the column *shipper_id* in the table in the inner query, *Orders*. Such a column is not found there, so SQL Server looks for it in the table in the outer query, *MyShippers*. Such a column is found in *MyShippers*, so that is the one used.

You can see that what was supposed to be a self-contained subquery unintentionally became a correlated subquery. As long as the *Orders* table has at least one row, all rows from the *MyShippers* table find a match when comparing the outer shipper ID with the very same shipper ID.

Some argue that this behavior is a bug in SQL Server. It is not. This behavior is by design in the SQL standard, and Microsoft just followed the standard here. The thinking in the standard is to allow you to refer to column names from the outer table without a prefix as long as they are unambiguous (that is, as long as they appear only in one of the tables).

This problem is more common in environments that do not use consistent attribute names across tables. Sometimes the names are only slightly different, as in this case—*shipperid* in one table and *shipper_id* in another. That's enough for the bug to manifest itself.

You can follow a couple of best practices to avoid such problems:

- Use consistent attribute names across tables.
- Prefix column names in subqueries with the source table name or alias (if you assigned one).

This way, the resolution process looks for the column only in the specified table. If it doesn't exist there, you get a resolution error. For example, try running the following code:

```
SELECT shipper_id, companyname
FROM Sales.MyShippers
WHERE shipper_id IN
  (SELECT O.shipper_id
   FROM Sales.Orders AS O
   WHERE O.custid = 43);
```

You get the following resolution error:

```
Msg 207, Level 16, State 1, Line 274
Invalid column name 'shipper_id'.
```

After getting this error, you identify the problem and correct the query:

```
SELECT shipper_id, companyname
FROM Sales.MyShippers
WHERE shipper_id IN
  (SELECT O.shipperid
   FROM Sales.Orders AS O
   WHERE O.custid = 43);
```

This time, the query returns the expected result:

```
shipper_id  companyname
----------- ---------------
2           Shipper ETYNR
3           Shipper ZHISN
```

When you're done, run the following code for cleanup:

```
DROP TABLE IF EXISTS Sales.MyShippers;
```

Conclusion

This chapter covered subqueries. It discussed self-contained subqueries, which are independent of their outer queries, and correlated subqueries, which are dependent on their outer queries. Regarding the results of subqueries, I discussed scalar and multivalued subqueries. I also provided a more advanced section as optional reading, in which I covered returning previous and next values, using running aggregates, and dealing with misbehaving subqueries. Remember to always think about the three-valued logic and the importance of prefixing column names in subqueries with the source table alias.

The next chapter focuses on table subqueries, also known as *table expressions*.

Exercises

This section provides exercises to help you familiarize yourself with the subjects discussed in this chapter. The sample database *TSQLV4* is used in all exercises in this chapter.

Exercise 1

Write a query that returns all orders placed on the last day of activity that can be found in the *Orders* table:

- Table involved: *Sales.Orders*
- Desired output:

```
orderid     orderdate   custid      empid
----------- ----------- ----------- -----------
11077       2016-05-06  65          1
11076       2016-05-06  9           4
11075       2016-05-06  68          8
11074       2016-05-06  73          7
```

Exercise 2 (optional, advanced)

Write a query that returns all orders placed by the customer(s) who placed the highest number of orders. Note that more than one customer might have the same number of orders:

- Table involved: *Sales.Orders*
- Desired output:

```
custid      orderid     orderdate  empid
----------- ----------- ---------- -----------
71          10324       2014-10-08 9
71          10393       2014-12-25 1
71          10398       2014-12-30 2
71          10440       2015-02-10 4
71          10452       2015-02-20 8
71          10510       2015-04-18 6
71          10555       2015-06-02 6
71          10603       2015-07-18 8
71          10607       2015-07-22 5
71          10612       2015-07-28 1
71          10627       2015-08-11 8
71          10657       2015-09-04 2
71          10678       2015-09-23 7
71          10700       2015-10-10 3
71          10711       2015-10-21 5
71          10713       2015-10-22 1
71          10714       2015-10-22 5
71          10722       2015-10-29 8
71          10748       2015-11-20 3
71          10757       2015-11-27 6
```

```
71          10815       2016-01-05 2
71          10847       2016-01-22 4
71          10882       2016-02-11 4
71          10894       2016-02-18 1
71          10941       2016-03-11 7
71          10983       2016-03-27 2
71          10984       2016-03-30 1
71          11002       2016-04-06 4
71          11030       2016-04-17 7
71          11031       2016-04-17 6
71          11064       2016-05-01 1

(31 row(s) affected)
```

Exercise 3

Write a query that returns employees who did not place orders on or after May 1, 2016:

- Tables involved: *HR.Employees* and *Sales.Orders*
- Desired output:

```
empid       FirstName  lastname
----------- ---------- --------------------
3           Judy       Lew
5           Sven       Mortensen
6           Paul       Suurs
9           Patricia   Doyle
```

Exercise 4

Write a query that returns countries where there are customers but not employees:

- Tables involved: *Sales.Customers* and *HR.Employees*
- Desired output:

```
country
---------------
Argentina
Austria
Belgium
Brazil
Canada
Denmark
Finland
France
Germany
Ireland
Italy
Mexico
Norway
Poland
Portugal
```

```
Spain
Sweden
Switzerland
Venezuela

(19 row(s) affected)
```

Exercise 5

Write a query that returns for each customer all orders placed on the customer's last day of activity:

- Table involved: *Sales.Orders*
- Desired output:

```
custid      orderid     orderdate   empid
----------- ----------- ----------- -----------
1           11011       2016-04-09  3
2           10926       2016-03-04  4
3           10856       2016-01-28  3
4           11016       2016-04-10  9
5           10924       2016-03-04  3
...
87          11025       2016-04-15  6
88          10935       2016-03-09  4
89          11066       2016-05-01  7
90          11005       2016-04-07  2
91          11044       2016-04-23  4

(90 row(s) affected)
```

Exercise 6

Write a query that returns customers who placed orders in 2015 but not in 2016:

- Tables involved: *Sales.Customers* and *Sales.Orders*
- Desired output:

```
custid      companyname
----------- ----------------
21          Customer KIDPX
23          Customer WVFAF
33          Customer FVXPQ
36          Customer LVJSO
43          Customer UISOJ
51          Customer PVDZC
85          Customer ENQZT

(7 row(s) affected)
```

Exercise 7 (optional, advanced)

Write a query that returns customers who ordered product 12:

- Tables involved: *Sales.Customers*, *Sales.Orders*, and *Sales.OrderDetails*
- Desired output:

```
custid      companyname
----------- ----------------
48          Customer DVFMB
39          Customer GLLAG
71          Customer LCOUJ
65          Customer NYUHS
44          Customer OXFRU
51          Customer PVDZC
86          Customer SNXOJ
20          Customer THHDP
90          Customer XBBVR
46          Customer XPNIK
31          Customer YJCBX
87          Customer ZHYOS

(12 row(s) affected)
```

Exercise 8 (optional, advanced)

Write a query that calculates a running-total quantity for each customer and month:

- Table involved: *Sales.CustOrders*
- Desired output:

```
custid      ordermonth  qty         runqty
----------- ----------- ----------- -----------
1           2015-08-01  38          38
1           2015-10-01  41          79
1           2016-01-01  17          96
1           2016-03-01  18          114
1           2016-04-01  60          174
2           2014-09-01  6           6
2           2015-08-01  18          24
2           2015-11-01  10          34
2           2016-03-01  29          63
3           2014-11-01  24          24
3           2015-04-01  30          54
3           2015-05-01  80          134
3           2015-06-01  83          217
3           2015-09-01  102         319
3           2016-01-01  40          359
...

(636 row(s) affected)
```

Exercise 9

Explain the difference between *IN* and *EXISTS*.

Exercise 10 (optional, advanced)

Write a query that returns for each order the number of days that passed since the same customer's previous order. To determine recency among orders, use *orderdate* as the primary sort element and *orderid* as the tiebreaker:

- Table involved: *Sales.Orders*
- Desired output:

```
custid      orderdate  orderid     diff
----------- ---------- ----------- -----------
1           2015-08-25 10643       NULL
1           2015-10-03 10692       39
1           2015-10-13 10702       10
1           2016-01-15 10835       94
1           2016-03-16 10952       61
1           2016-04-09 11011       24
2           2014-09-18 10308       NULL
2           2015-08-08 10625       324
2           2015-11-28 10759       112
2           2016-03-04 10926       97
...

(830 row(s) affected)
```

Solutions

This section provides solutions to the exercises in the preceding section.

Exercise 1

You can write a self-contained subquery that returns the maximum order date from the *Orders* table. You can refer to the subquery in the *WHERE* clause of the outer query to return all orders that were placed on the last day of activity. Here's the solution query:

```
USE TSQLV4;

SELECT orderid, orderdate, custid, empid
FROM Sales.Orders
WHERE orderdate =
  (SELECT MAX(O.orderdate) FROM Sales.Orders AS O);
```

Exercise 2

This problem is best solved in multiple steps. First, you can write a query that returns the customer or customers who placed the highest number of orders. You can achieve this by grouping the orders by customer, ordering the customers by *COUNT(*)* descending, and using the *TOP (1) WITH TIES* option to return the IDs of the customers who placed the highest number of orders. If you don't remember how to use the *TOP* option, refer to Chapter 2. Here's the query that solves the first step:

```
SELECT TOP (1) WITH TIES O.custid
FROM Sales.Orders AS O
GROUP BY O.custid
ORDER BY COUNT(*) DESC;
```

This query returns customer ID 71, which is the ID of the customer who placed the highest number of orders, 31. With the sample data stored in the *Orders* table, only one customer placed the maximum number of orders. But the query uses the *WITH TIES* option to return all IDs of customers who placed the maximum number of orders, in case there is more than one.

The next step is to write a query against the *Orders* table, returning all orders where the customer ID appears in the result of the subquery:

```
SELECT custid, orderid, orderdate, empid
FROM Sales.Orders
WHERE custid IN
  (SELECT TOP (1) WITH TIES O.custid
   FROM Sales.Orders AS O
   GROUP BY O.custid
   ORDER BY COUNT(*) DESC);
```

Exercise 3

You can write a self-contained subquery against the *Orders* table that filters orders placed on or after May 1, 2016, and returns only the employee IDs from those orders. Write an outer query against the *Employees* table returning employees whose IDs do not appear in the result of the subquery. Here's the complete solution query:

```
SELECT empid, FirstName, lastname
FROM HR.Employees
WHERE empid NOT IN
  (SELECT O.empid
   FROM Sales.Orders AS O
   WHERE O.orderdate >= '20160501');
```

Exercise 4

You can write a self-contained subquery against the *Employees* table, returning the country column. Write an outer query against the *Customers* table that filters only customers with a country that does not appear in the result of the subquery. In the *SELECT* list of the outer query, specify *DISTINCT country* to remove duplicates. Here's the complete solution query:

```
SELECT DISTINCT country
FROM Sales.Customers
WHERE country NOT IN
  (SELECT E.country FROM HR.Employees AS E);
```

Exercise 5

This exercise is similar to Exercise 1, except that in that exercise, you were asked to return orders placed on the last day of activity in general; in this exercise, you were asked to return orders placed on the last day of activity for the customer. The solutions for both exercises are similar, but here you need to correlate the subquery to match the inner customer ID with the outer customer ID, like this:

```
SELECT custid, orderid, orderdate, empid
FROM Sales.Orders AS O1
WHERE orderdate =
  (SELECT MAX(O2.orderdate)
   FROM Sales.Orders AS O2
   WHERE O2.custid = O1.custid)
ORDER BY custid;
```

You're not comparing the outer row's order date with the general maximum order date; instead, you're comparing it with the maximum order date for the current customer.

Exercise 6

You can solve this problem by querying the *Customers* table and using *EXISTS* and *NOT EXISTS* predicates with correlated subqueries. The *EXISTS* predicate returns *TRUE* if orders were placed by the current customer in 2015. The *NOT EXISTS* predicate returns *TRUE* only if no orders were placed by the current customer in 2016. Here's the complete solution query:

```
SELECT custid, companyname
FROM Sales.Customers AS C
WHERE EXISTS
  (SELECT *
   FROM Sales.Orders AS O
   WHERE O.custid = C.custid
     AND O.orderdate >= '20150101'
     AND O.orderdate < '20160101')
  AND NOT EXISTS
  (SELECT *
   FROM Sales.Orders AS O
   WHERE O.custid = C.custid
     AND O.orderdate >= '20160101'
     AND O.orderdate < '20170101');
```

Exercise 7

You can solve this exercise by nesting *EXISTS* predicates with correlated subqueries. You write the outermost query against the *Customers* table. In the *WHERE* clause of the outer query, you can use the *EXISTS* predicate with a correlated subquery against the *Orders* table to filter only the current customer's orders. In the filter of the subquery against the *Orders* table, you can use a nested *EXISTS* predicate with a subquery against the *OrderDetails* table that filters only order details with product ID 12. This way, only customers who placed orders that contain product 12 in their order details are returned. Here's the complete solution query:

```
SELECT custid, companyname
FROM Sales.Customers AS C
WHERE EXISTS
  (SELECT *
   FROM Sales.Orders AS O
   WHERE O.custid = C.custid
     AND EXISTS
       (SELECT *
        FROM Sales.OrderDetails AS OD
        WHERE OD.orderid = O.orderid
          AND OD.ProductID = 12));
```

Exercise 8

You can handle this task with a correlated subquery. Use the outer query against *CustOrders* (aliased as *O1*) to return the current customer, month, and quantity information. Use the correlated subquery against a second instance of *CustOrders* (aliased as *O2*). Aggregate all quantities from *O2* for the current customer in *O1* where the month from *O2* is on or before the current month in *O1*. Here's the complete solution query:

```
SELECT custid, ordermonth, qty,
  (SELECT SUM(O2.qty)
   FROM Sales.CustOrders AS O2
   WHERE O2.custid = O1.custid
     AND O2.ordermonth <= O1.ordermonth) AS runqty
FROM Sales.CustOrders AS O1
ORDER BY custid, ordermonth;
```

Exercise 9

Whereas the *IN* predicate uses three-valued logic, the *EXISTS* predicate uses two-valued logic. When no *NULLs* are involved in the data, *IN* and *EXISTS* give you the same meaning in both their positive and negative forms (with *NOT*). When *NULLs* are involved, *IN* and *EXISTS* give you the same meaning in their positive form but not in their negative form. In the positive form, when looking for a value that appears in the set of known values in the subquery, both return *TRUE*, and when looking for a value that doesn't appear in the set of known values, both return *FALSE*. In the negative forms (with *NOT*), when looking for a value that appears in the set of known values, both return *FALSE; however,* when looking for a value that doesn't appear in the set of known values, *NOT IN* returns *UNKNOWN* (outer row is discarded), whereas *NOT EXISTS* returns *TRUE* (outer row returned).

This is best understood through an example. See the section "*NULL* trouble" earlier in this chapter for a good example.

Exercise 10

You can handle the task in two steps:

1. Write a query that computes the date of the customer's previous order.
2. Compute the difference between the date returned by the first step and the current order date.

Here's the solution query that handles the first step:

```
SELECT custid, orderdate, orderid,
  (SELECT TOP (1) O2.orderdate
   FROM Sales.Orders AS O2
   WHERE O2.custid = O1.custid
     AND (    O2.orderdate = O1.orderdate AND O2.orderid < O1.orderid
           OR O2.orderdate < O1.orderdate )
   ORDER BY O2.orderdate DESC, O2.orderid DESC) AS prevdate
FROM Sales.Orders AS O1
ORDER BY custid, orderdate, orderid;
```

To get a previous order date, the solution uses a correlated subquery with the TOP filter. The subquery filters only orders where the inner customer ID is equal to the outer customer ID. It also filters only orders where either "the inner order date is equal to the outer order date and the inner order ID is smaller than the outer order ID," or "the inner order date is earlier than the outer order date." The remaining orders are the ones considered earlier than the current customer's order. Using the *TOP (1)* filter based on the ordering of *orderdate DESC, orderid DESC*, you get the date of the customer's previous order. This step returns the following output:

```
custid      orderdate  orderid     prevdate
----------- ---------- ----------- ----------
1           2015-08-25 10643       NULL
1           2015-10-03 10692       2015-08-25
1           2015-10-13 10702       2015-10-03
1           2016-01-15 10835       2015-10-13
1           2016-03-16 10952       2016-01-15
1           2016-04-09 11011       2016-03-16
2           2014-09-18 10308       NULL
2           2015-08-08 10625       2014-09-18
2           2015-11-28 10759       2015-08-08
2           2016-03-04 10926       2015-11-28
...

(830 row(s) affected)
```

If you're wondering why you don't rely on only *orderid* ordering, the reason is that companies typically support a concept of *late arrivals*. That's when an order was placed in the past but registered in the system at a later point. When the order is added to the system, it gets the highest order ID at that point but it doesn't have the most recent order date. So recency is determined first based on orderdate ordering, and then order ID is used as the tiebreaker. That's why the subquery's *WHERE* clause is so complex, and why the TOP filter's ordering is based on *orderdate DESC, orderid DESC* and not just *orderid DESC*.

As the second step, use the *DATEDIFF* function to compute the difference in terms of days between the previous order date returned by the subquery and the current order date. Here's the complete solution query:

```
SELECT custid, orderdate, orderid,
  DATEDIFF(day,
    (SELECT TOP (1) O2.orderdate
     FROM Sales.Orders AS O2
     WHERE O2.custid = O1.custid
       AND (     O2.orderdate = O1.orderdate AND O2.orderid < O1.orderid
             OR O2.orderdate < O1.orderdate )
     ORDER BY O2.orderdate DESC, O2.orderid DESC),
    orderdate) AS diff
FROM Sales.Orders AS O1
ORDER BY custid, orderdate, orderid;
```

CHAPTER 5

Table expressions

A table expression is a named query expression that represents a valid relational table. You can use table expressions in data-manipulation statements much like you use other tables. T-SQL supports four types of table expressions: derived tables, common table expressions (CTEs), views, and inline table-valued functions (inline TVFs). The focus of this chapter is on using SELECT queries against table expressions; Chapter 8, "Data modification," covers modifications against table expressions.

Table expressions are not physically materialized anywhere—they are virtual. When you query a table expression, the inner query gets unnested. In other words, the outer query and the inner query are merged into one query directly against the underlying objects. The benefits of using table expressions are typically related to logical aspects of your code and not to performance. For example, you can use table expressions to simplify your solutions by using a modular approach. Table expressions also help you circumvent certain restrictions in the language, such as the inability to refer to column aliases assigned in the *SELECT* clause in query clauses that are logically processed before the *SELECT* clause.

This chapter also introduces the *APPLY* table operator as it is used in conjunction with a table expression. I explain how to use this operator to apply a table expression to each row of another table.

Derived tables

Derived tables (also known as *table subqueries*) are defined in the *FROM* clause of an outer query. Their scope of existence is the outer query. As soon as the outer query is finished, the derived table is gone.

You specify the query that defines the derived table within parentheses, followed by the *AS* clause and the derived table name. For example, the following code defines a derived table called *USACusts* based on a query that returns all customers from the United States, and the outer query selects all rows from the derived table:

```
USE TSQLV4;

SELECT *
FROM (SELECT custid, companyname
      FROM Sales.Customers
      WHERE country = N'USA') AS USACusts;
```

In this particular case, which is a simple example of the basic syntax, a derived table is not needed because the outer query doesn't apply any manipulation.

The code in this basic example returns the following output:

```
custid      companyname
----------- ---------------
32          Customer YSIQX
36          Customer LVJSO
43          Customer UISOJ
45          Customer QXPPT
48          Customer DVFMB
55          Customer KZQZT
65          Customer NYUHS
71          Customer LCOUJ
75          Customer XOJYP
77          Customer LCYBZ
78          Customer NLTYP
82          Customer EYHKM
89          Customer YBQTI
```

With all types of table expressions, a query must meet three requirements to be a valid inner query in a table-expression definition:

- **Order is not guaranteed.** A table expression is supposed to represent a relational table, and the rows in a relational table have no guaranteed order. Recall that this aspect of a relation stems from set theory. For this reason, standard SQL disallows an *ORDER BY* clause in queries that are used to define table expressions, unless the *ORDER BY* serves a purpose other than presentation. An example for such an exception is when the query uses the *OFFSET-FETCH* filter. T-SQL enforces similar restrictions, with similar exceptions—when *TOP* or *OFFSET-FETCH* is also specified. In the context of a query with the *TOP* or *OFFSET-FETCH* filter, the *ORDER BY* clause serves as part of the specification of the filter. If you use a query with *TOP* or *OFFSET-FETCH* and *ORDER BY* to define a table expression, *ORDER BY* is guaranteed to serve only the filtering-related purpose and not the usual presentation purpose. If the outer query against the table expression does not have a presentation *ORDER BY*, the output is not guaranteed to be returned in any particular order. See the "Views and the *ORDER BY* clause" section later in this chapter for more detail on this item (which applies to all types of table expressions).

- **All columns must have names.** All columns in a table must have names; therefore, you must assign column aliases to all expressions in the *SELECT* list of the query that is used to define a table expression.

- **All column names must be unique.** All column names in a table must be unique; therefore, a table expression that has multiple columns with the same name is invalid. Having multiple columns with the same name might happen when the query defining the table expression joins two tables that have a column with the same name. If you need to incorporate both columns in your table expression, they must have different column names. You can resolve this issue by assigning different column aliases to the two columns.

All three requirements are related to the fact that the table expression is supposed to represent a relation. All relation attributes must have names; all attribute names must be unique; and, because the relation's body is a set of tuples, there's no order.

Assigning column aliases

One of the benefits of using table expressions is that, in any clause of the outer query, you can refer to column aliases that were assigned in the *SELECT* clause of the inner query. This behavior helps you get around the fact that you can't refer to column aliases assigned in the *SELECT* clause in query clauses that are logically processed prior to the *SELECT* clause (for example, *WHERE* or *GROUP BY*).

For example, suppose you need to write a query against the *Sales.Orders* table and return the number of distinct customers handled in each order year. The following attempt is invalid because the *GROUP BY* clause refers to a column alias that was assigned in the *SELECT* clause, and the *GROUP BY* clause is logically processed prior to the *SELECT* clause:

```
SELECT
  YEAR(orderdate) AS orderyear,
  COUNT(DISTINCT custid) AS numcusts
FROM Sales.Orders
GROUP BY orderyear;
```

If you try running this query, you get the following error:

```
Msg 207, Level 16, State 1, Line 5
Invalid column name 'orderyear'.
```

You can solve the problem by referring to the expression *YEAR(orderdate)* in both the *GROUP BY* and *SELECT* clauses, but this is an example with a short expression. What if the expression was much longer and you wanted to avoid the repetition of the code? You can achieve this with a table expression like the one shown in Listing 5-1.

LISTING 5-1 Query with a derived table using inline aliasing form

```
SELECT orderyear, COUNT(DISTINCT custid) AS numcusts
FROM (SELECT YEAR(orderdate) AS orderyear, custid
      FROM Sales.Orders) AS D
GROUP BY orderyear;
```

This query returns the following output:

```
orderyear   numcusts
----------- -----------
2014        67
2015        86
2016        81
```

This code defines a derived table called *D* based on a query against the *Orders* table that returns the order year and customer ID from all rows. The *SELECT* list of the inner query uses the inline aliasing form to assign the alias *orderyear* to the expression *YEAR(orderdate)*. The outer query can refer to the *orderyear* column alias in both the *GROUP BY* and *SELECT* clauses, because as far as the outer query is concerned, it queries a table called *D* with columns called *orderyear* and *custid*.

As I mentioned earlier, Microsoft SQL Server expands the definition of the table expression and accesses the underlying objects directly. After expansion, the query in Listing 5-1 looks like the following:

```
SELECT YEAR(orderdate) AS orderyear, COUNT(DISTINCT custid) AS numcusts
FROM Sales.Orders
GROUP BY YEAR(orderdate);
```

I present this example just to emphasize that you usually use table expressions for logical (not performance-related) reasons. Generally speaking, table expressions have neither a positive nor negative impact on performance when compared to the expanded query without the table expression.

Listing 5-1 uses the inline aliasing form to assign column aliases to expressions. The syntax for inline aliasing is *<expression> [AS] <alias>*. Note that the word *AS* is optional in the syntax for inline aliasing; however, I find that it helps the readability of the code and recommend using it.

In some cases, you might prefer to use a second aliasing form, which you can think of as external aliasing. With this form, you do not assign column aliases following the expressions in the *SELECT* list—you specify all target column names in parentheses following the table expression's name, like so:

```
SELECT orderyear, COUNT(DISTINCT custid) AS numcusts
FROM (SELECT YEAR(orderdate), custid
      FROM Sales.Orders) AS D(orderyear, custid)
GROUP BY orderyear;
```

Each form has its advantages. I'll start with the advantages of inline aliasing. If you need to debug the code when using the inline form, when you highlight the query defining the table expression and run it, the columns in the result appear with the aliases you assigned. With the external form, you cannot include the target column names when you highlight the table expression query, so the result appears with no column names in the case of the unnamed expressions. Also, when the table expression query is lengthy, using the external form can make it quite difficult to figure out which column alias belongs to which expression.

Then again, the external aliasing form has its advantages—for example, when the query defining the table expression won't undergo any further revisions and you want to treat it like a "black box." You want to focus your attention on the table-expression name followed by the target-column list when you look at the outer query. To use terminology from traditional programming, you can use external aliasing to specify a contract interface between the outer query and the table expression.

Using arguments

In the query that defines a derived table, you can refer to arguments. The arguments can be local variables and input parameters to a routine, such as a stored procedure or function. For example, the following code declares and initializes a variable called *@empid*, and the query in the derived table *D* refers to that variable in the *WHERE* clause:

```
DECLARE @empid AS INT = 3;

SELECT orderyear, COUNT(DISTINCT custid) AS numcusts
FROM (SELECT YEAR(orderdate) AS orderyear, custid
```

```
    FROM Sales.Orders
    WHERE empid = @empid) AS D
GROUP BY orderyear;
```

This query returns the number of distinct customers per year whose orders were handled by the input employee (the employee whose ID is stored in the variable *@empid*). Here's the output of this query:

```
orderyear   numcusts
----------- -----------
2014        16
2015        46
2016        30
```

Nesting

If you need to define a derived table based on a query that itself is based on a derived table, you can nest those. Nesting tends to complicate the code and reduces its readability.

As an example, Listing 5-2 returns order years and the number of customers handled in each year only for years in which more than 70 customers were handled.

LISTING 5-2 Query with nested derived tables

```
SELECT orderyear, numcusts
FROM (SELECT orderyear, COUNT(DISTINCT custid) AS numcusts
      FROM (SELECT YEAR(orderdate) AS orderyear, custid
            FROM Sales.Orders) AS D1
      GROUP BY orderyear) AS D2
WHERE numcusts > 70;
```

This code returns the following output:

```
orderyear   numcusts
----------- -----------
2015        86
2016        81
```

The purpose of the innermost derived table, *D1*, is to assign the column alias *orderyear* to the expression *YEAR(orderdate)*. The query against *D1* refers to *orderyear* in both the *GROUP BY* and *SELECT* clauses and assigns the column alias *numcusts* to the expression *COUNT(DISTINCT custid)*. The query against *D1* is used to define the derived table *D2*. The query against *D2* refers to *numcusts* in the *WHERE* clause to filter order years in which more than 70 customers were handled.

The whole purpose of using table expressions here is to simplify the code by reusing column aliases. However, with the complexity added by the nesting, I'm not sure this solution is really simpler than the alternative without table expressions:

```
SELECT YEAR(orderdate) AS orderyear, COUNT(DISTINCT custid) AS numcusts
FROM Sales.Orders
GROUP BY YEAR(orderdate)
HAVING COUNT(DISTINCT custid) > 70;
```

Multiple references

Another problematic aspect of derived tables is related to cases where you need to join multiple instances of the same one. A join treats its two inputs as a set and, as you know, a set has no order to its elements. This means that if you define a derived table and alias it as one input of the join, you can't refer to the same alias in the other input of the join. The query in Listing 5-3 illustrates this point.

LISTING 5-3 Multiple derived tables based on the same query

```
SELECT Cur.orderyear,
  Cur.numcusts AS curnumcusts, Prv.numcusts AS prvnumcusts,
  Cur.numcusts - Prv.numcusts AS growth
FROM (SELECT YEAR(orderdate) AS orderyear,
        COUNT(DISTINCT custid) AS numcusts
      FROM Sales.Orders
      GROUP BY YEAR(orderdate)) AS Cur
  LEFT OUTER JOIN
     (SELECT YEAR(orderdate) AS orderyear,
        COUNT(DISTINCT custid) AS numcusts
      FROM Sales.Orders
      GROUP BY YEAR(orderdate)) AS Prv
    ON Cur.orderyear = Prv.orderyear + 1;
```

This query joins two derived tables that are based on the same query. The first derived table, *Cur*, represents current years, and the second derived table, *Prv*, represents previous years. The join condition *Cur.orderyear = Prv.orderyear + 1* ensures that each year from the first derived table matches the previous year of the second. Because the code uses a left outer join, all left years are preserved, including the first, which has no previous year. The *SELECT* clause of the outer query calculates the difference between the number of customers handled in the current and previous years.

Listing 5-3 produces the following output:

```
orderyear   curnumcusts prvnumcusts growth
----------- ----------- ----------- -----------
2014        67          NULL        NULL
2015        86          67          19
2016        81          86          -5
```

The fact that you cannot refer to multiple instances of the same derived table in the same join forces you to maintain multiple copies of the same query definition. This leads to lengthy code that is hard to maintain and prone to errors.

Common table expressions

Common table expressions (CTEs) are another standard form of table expression similar to derived tables, yet with a couple of important advantages.

CTEs are defined by using a *WITH* statement and have the following general form:

```
WITH <CTE_Name>[(<target_column_list>)]
AS
(
  <inner_query_defining_CTE>
)
<outer_query_against_CTE>;
```

The inner query defining the CTE must follow all requirements mentioned earlier to be valid to define a table expression. As a simple example, the following code defines a CTE called *USACusts* based on a query that returns all customers from the United States, and the outer query selects all rows from the CTE:

```
WITH USACusts AS
(
  SELECT custid, companyname
  FROM Sales.Customers
  WHERE country = N'USA'
)
SELECT * FROM USACusts;
```

As with derived tables, as soon as the outer query finishes, the CTE goes out of scope.

> **Note** The *WITH* clause is used in T-SQL for several purposes. For example, it's used to define a table hint in a query to force a certain optimization option or isolation level. To avoid ambiguity, when the *WITH* clause is used to define a CTE, the preceding statement in the same batch—if one exists—must be terminated with a semicolon. And oddly enough, the semicolon for the entire CTE is not required, though I still recommend specifying it—as I do to terminate all T-SQL statements.

Assigning column aliases in CTEs

CTEs also support two forms of column aliasing: inline and external. For the inline form, specify *<expression> AS <column_alias>*; for the external form, specify the target column list in parentheses immediately after the CTE name.

Here's an example of the inline form:

```
WITH C AS
(
  SELECT YEAR(orderdate) AS orderyear, custid
  FROM Sales.Orders
```

```
)
SELECT orderyear, COUNT(DISTINCT custid) AS numcusts
FROM C
GROUP BY orderyear;
```

And here's an example of the external form:

```
WITH C(orderyear, custid) AS
(
  SELECT YEAR(orderdate), custid
  FROM Sales.Orders
)
SELECT orderyear, COUNT(DISTINCT custid) AS numcusts
FROM C
GROUP BY orderyear;
```

The motivations for using one form or the other are similar to those described for derived tables.

Using arguments in CTEs

As with derived tables, you also can use arguments in the inner query used to define a CTE. Here's an example:

```
DECLARE @empid AS INT = 3;

WITH C AS
(
  SELECT YEAR(orderdate) AS orderyear, custid
  FROM Sales.Orders
  WHERE empid = @empid
)
SELECT orderyear, COUNT(DISTINCT custid) AS numcusts
FROM C
GROUP BY orderyear;
```

Defining multiple CTEs

On the surface, the difference between derived tables and CTEs might seem to be merely semantic. However, the fact that you first name and define a CTE and then use it gives it several important advantages over derived tables. One advantage is that if you need to refer to one CTE from another, you don't nest them; rather, you separate them by commas. Each CTE can refer to all previously defined CTEs, and the outer query can refer to all CTEs. For example, the following code is the CTE alternative to the nested derived tables approach in Listing 5-2:

```
WITH C1 AS
(
  SELECT YEAR(orderdate) AS orderyear, custid
  FROM Sales.Orders
),
C2 AS
(
  SELECT orderyear, COUNT(DISTINCT custid) AS numcusts
```

```
  FROM C1
  GROUP BY orderyear
)
SELECT orderyear, numcusts
FROM C2
WHERE numcusts > 70;
```

This modular approach substantially improves the readability and maintainability of the code compared to the nested derived-table approach.

Note that even if you want to, you cannot nest CTEs, nor can you define a CTE within the parentheses of a derived table. I think of this restriction as a good thing.

Multiple references in CTEs

The fact that a CTE is named and defined first and then queried has another advantage: as far as the *FROM* clause of the outer query is concerned, the CTE already exists; therefore, you can refer to multiple instances of the same CTE in table operators like joins. For example, the following code is the CTE alternative to the solution shown earlier in Listing 5-3 with derived tables:

```
WITH YearlyCount AS
(
  SELECT YEAR(orderdate) AS orderyear,
    COUNT(DISTINCT custid) AS numcusts
  FROM Sales.Orders
  GROUP BY YEAR(orderdate)
)
SELECT Cur.orderyear,
  Cur.numcusts AS curnumcusts, Prv.numcusts AS prvnumcusts,
  Cur.numcusts - Prv.numcusts AS growth
FROM YearlyCount AS Cur
  LEFT OUTER JOIN YearlyCount AS Prv
    ON Cur.orderyear = Prv.orderyear + 1;
```

As you can see, the CTE *YearlyCount* is defined only once and accessed twice in the *FROM* clause of the outer query—once as *Cur* and once as *Prv.* You need to maintain only one copy of the inner query (the code inside the CTE). The solution is clearer and less prone to errors.

If you're curious about performance, recall that earlier I mentioned that table expressions typically have no impact on performance because they're not physically materialized anywhere. Both references to the CTE in the previous query are going to be expanded. Internally, this query has a self join between two instances of the *Orders* table, each of which involves scanning the table data and aggregating it before the join—the same physical processing that takes place with the derived-table approach. If you want to avoid the repetition of the work done here, you should persist the inner query's result in a temporary table or a table variable. My focus in this discussion is on coding aspects and not performance, and clearly the ability to specify the inner query only once is a great benefit.

Recursive CTEs

This section is provided as optional reading. It covers subjects that are beyond the fundamentals.

CTEs are unique among table expressions in the sense that they support recursion. Recursive CTEs, like nonrecursive ones, are defined by the SQL standard. A recursive CTE is defined by at least two queries (more are possible)—at least one query known as the anchor member and at least one query known as the recursive member. The general form of a basic recursive CTE looks like the following:

```
WITH <CTE_Name>[(<target_column_list>)]
AS
(
  <anchor_member>
  UNION ALL
  <recursive_member>
)
<outer_query_against_CTE>;
```

The anchor member is a query that returns a valid relational result table—like a query that is used to define a nonrecursive table expression. The anchor member query is invoked only once.

The recursive member is a query that has a reference to the CTE name and is invoked repeatedly until it returns an empty set. The reference to the CTE name represents the previous result set. The first time that the recursive member is invoked, the previous result set represents whatever the anchor member returned. In each subsequent invocation of the recursive member, the reference to the CTE name represents the result set returned by the previous invocation of the recursive member. Both queries must be compatible in terms of the number of columns they return and the data types of the corresponding columns. The reference to the CTE name in the outer query represents the unified result sets of the invocation of the anchor member and all invocations of the recursive member.

If this is your first encounter with recursive CTEs, you might find this explanation hard to understand. They are best explained with an example. The following code demonstrates how to return information about an employee (Don Funk, employee ID 2) and all the employee's subordinates at all levels (direct or indirect):

```
WITH EmpsCTE AS
(
  SELECT empid, mgrid, firstname, lastname
  FROM HR.Employees
  WHERE empid = 2

  UNION ALL

  SELECT C.empid, C.mgrid, C.firstname, C.lastname
  FROM EmpsCTE AS P
    INNER JOIN HR.Employees AS C
      ON C.mgrid = P.empid
)
SELECT empid, mgrid, firstname, lastname
FROM EmpsCTE;
```

The anchor member queries the *HR.Employees* table and simply returns the row for employee 2:

```
SELECT empid, mgrid, firstname, lastname
FROM HR.Employees
WHERE empid = 2
```

The recursive member joins the CTE—representing the previous result set—with the *Employees* table to return the direct subordinates of the employees returned in the previous result set:

```
SELECT C.empid, C.mgrid, C.firstname, C.lastname
FROM EmpsCTE AS P
  INNER JOIN HR.Employees AS C
    ON C.mgrid = P.empid
```

In other words, the recursive member is invoked repeatedly, and in each invocation it returns the next level of subordinates. The first time the recursive member is invoked, it returns the direct subordinates of employee 2—employees 3 and 5. The second time the recursive member is invoked, it returns the direct subordinates of employees 3 and 5—employees 4, 6, 7, 8, and 9. The third time the recursive member is invoked, there are no more subordinates; the recursive member returns an empty set, and therefore recursion stops.

The reference to the CTE name in the outer query represents the unioned result sets—in other words, employee 2 and all the employee's subordinates.

Here's the output of this code:

```
empid       mgrid       firstname  lastname
----------- ----------- ---------- --------------------
2           1           Don        Funk
3           2           Judy       Lew
5           2           Sven       Mortensen
6           5           Paul       Suurs
7           5           Russell    King
9           5           Patricia   Doyle
4           3           Yael       Peled
8           3           Maria      Cameron
```

In the event of a logical error in the join predicate in the recursive member, or if there are problems with the data that result in cycles, the recursive member potentially can be invoked an infinite number of times. As a safety measure, SQL Server restricts the number of times the recursive member can be invoked to 100 by default. The code will fail if the recursive member is invoked more than 100 times. You can change the default maximum recursion limit (that is, the number of times the recursive member can be invoked) by specifying the hint *OPTION(MAXRECURSION* n*)* at the end of the outer query, where *n* is an integer in the range 0 through 32,767. If you want to remove the restriction altogether, specify *MAXRECURSION 0*. Note that SQL Server stores the intermediate result sets returned by the anchor and recursive members in a work table in *tempdb*; if you remove the restriction and have a runaway query, the work table will quickly get very large, and the query will never finish.

Views

Derived tables and CTEs have a single-statement scope, which means they are not reusable. Views and inline table-valued functions (inline TVFs) are two types of table expressions whose definitions are stored as permanent objects in the database, making them reusable. In most other respects, views and inline TVFs are treated like derived tables and CTEs. For example, when querying a view or an inline

TVF, SQL Server expands the definition of the table expression and queries the underlying objects directly, as with derived tables and CTEs. In this section, I describe views; in the next section, I describe inline TVFs.

As an example, the following code creates a view called *USACusts* in the *Sales* schema in the *TSQLV4* database, representing all customers from the United States:

```
DROP VIEW IF EXISTS Sales.USACusts;
GO
CREATE VIEW Sales.USACusts
AS

SELECT
  custid, companyname, contactname, contacttitle, address,
  city, region, postalcode, country, phone, fax
FROM Sales.Customers
WHERE country = N'USA';
GO
```

Note that just as with derived tables and CTEs, instead of using inline column aliasing as shown in the preceding code, you can use external column aliasing by specifying the target column names in parentheses immediately after the view name.

After you create this view, you can query it much like you query other tables in the database:

```
SELECT custid, companyname
FROM Sales.USACusts;
```

Because a view is an object in the database, you can manage access permissions similar to the way you do for tables. (These permissions include *SELECT, INSERT, UPDATE,* and *DELETE.*) You can even deny direct access to the underlying objects while granting access to the view.

Note that the general recommendation to avoid using *SELECT ** has specific relevance in the context of views. The columns are enumerated in the compiled form of the view, and new table columns will not be automatically added to the view. For example, suppose you define a view based on the query *SELECT * FROM dbo.T1*, and at the view creation time the table *T1* has the columns *col1* and *col2*. SQL Server stores information only on those two columns in the view's metadata. If you alter the definition of the table to add new columns, those new columns will not be added to the view. You can refresh the view's metadata by using the stored procedure *sp_refreshview* or *sp_refreshsqlmodule*, but to avoid confusion, the best practice is to explicitly list the column names you need in the definition of the view. If columns are added to the underlying tables and you need them in the view, use the *ALTER VIEW* statement to revise the view definition accordingly.

Views and the *ORDER BY* clause

The query you use to define a view must meet all requirements mentioned earlier with respect to the inner query in the other types of table expressions. The view should not guarantee any order to the rows, all view columns must have names, and all column names must be unique. In this section, I elaborate a bit about the ordering issue, which is a fundamental point that is crucial to understand.

Remember that a presentation *ORDER BY* clause is not allowed in the query defining a table expression because a relation isn't ordered. If you need to return rows from a view sorted for presentation purposes, you should specify a presentation *ORDER BY* clause in the outer query against the view, like this:

```
SELECT custid, companyname, region
FROM Sales.USACusts
ORDER BY region;
```

Try running the following code to create a view with a presentation *ORDER BY* clause:

```
ALTER VIEW Sales.USACusts
AS

SELECT
  custid, companyname, contactname, contacttitle, address,
  city, region, postalcode, country, phone, fax
FROM Sales.Customers
WHERE country = N'USA'
ORDER BY region;
GO
```

This attempt fails, and you get the following error:

```
Msg 1033, Level 15, State 1, Procedure USACusts, Line 249
The ORDER BY clause is invalid in views, inline functions, derived tables, subqueries, and
common table expressions, unless TOP, OFFSET or FOR XML is also specified.
```

The error message indicates that T-SQL allows the *ORDER BY* clause only in exceptional cases—when the *TOP, OFFSET-FETCH,* or *FOR XML* option is used. In those cases, the *ORDER BY* clause serves a purpose other than its usual presentation purpose. Even standard SQL has a similar restriction, with a similar exception when the *OFFSET-FETCH* option is used.

Because T-SQL allows an *ORDER BY* clause in a view when *TOP* or *OFFSET-FETCH* is also specified, some people think they can create "ordered views." One of the ways people try to achieve this is by using *TOP (100) PERCENT,* like the following:

```
ALTER VIEW Sales.USACusts
AS

SELECT TOP (100) PERCENT
  custid, companyname, contactname, contacttitle, address,
  city, region, postalcode, country, phone, fax
FROM Sales.Customers
WHERE country = N'USA'
ORDER BY region;
GO
```

Even though the code is technically valid and the view is created, you should be aware that if an outer query against the view doesn't have an *ORDER BY* clause, presentation order is not guaranteed. For example, run the following query against the view:

```
SELECT custid, companyname, region
FROM Sales.USACusts;
```

Here's the output from one of my executions, showing that the rows are not sorted by region:

```
custid      companyname             region
----------- ----------------------- ---------------
32          Customer YSIQX          OR
36          Customer LVJSO          OR
43          Customer UISOJ          WA
45          Customer QXPPT          CA
48          Customer DVFMB          OR
55          Customer KZQZT          AK
65          Customer NYUHS          NM
71          Customer LCOUJ          ID
75          Customer XOJYP          WY
77          Customer LCYBZ          OR
78          Customer NLTYP          MT
82          Customer EYHKM          WA
89          Customer YBQTI          WA
```

If the outer query doesn't have an *ORDER BY* clause but the result seems to be ordered, it could be because of certain physical conditions and optimization choices, but those things are not guaranteed to be repeatable. The only way to guarantee presentation order is to have an *ORDER BY* clause in the outer query. Nothing else counts.

In old versions of SQL Server when the inner query had the combination of *TOP (100) PERCENT* and *ORDER BY* and the outer query didn't have an *ORDER BY* clause, you got the rows ordered. It wasn't a guaranteed behavior, but it happened to be the result of the way the optimizer handled things. At some point, Microsoft added smarter optimization that optimizes out this meaningless combination. Unfortunately, the optimizer doesn't yet optimize out the combination when the inner query uses the *OFFSET* clause with *0 ROWS*, and without a *FETCH* clause, like the following:

```
ALTER VIEW Sales.USACusts
AS

SELECT
  custid, companyname, contactname, contacttitle, address,
  city, region, postalcode, country, phone, fax
FROM Sales.Customers
WHERE country = N'USA'
ORDER BY region
OFFSET 0 ROWS;
GO
```

At the moment, when I query the view and don't indicate an *ORDER BY* clause in the outer query, the result rows happen to be sorted by region. But I stress—*do not* assume that's guaranteed. It happens to be the case because of the current optimization. If you need a guarantee that the rows will be returned sorted, you need an *ORDER BY* clause in the outer query.

Do not confuse the behavior of a query that is used to define a table expression with an outer query. An outer query with an *ORDER BY* clause and a *TOP* or *OFFSET-FETCH* option does guarantee presentation order. The simple rule is that if the outer query has an *ORDER BY* clause, you have a presentation ordering guarantee, regardless of whether that *ORDER BY* clause also serves another purpose.

View options

When you create or alter a view, you can specify view attributes and options as part of the view definition. In the header of the view, under the *WITH* clause, you can specify attributes such as *ENCRYPTION* and *SCHEMABINDING*, and at the end of the query you can specify *WITH CHECK OPTION*. The following sections describe the purpose of these options.

The *ENCRYPTION* option

The *ENCRYPTION* option is available when you create or alter views, stored procedures, triggers, and user-defined functions (UDFs). The *ENCRYPTION* option indicates that SQL Server will internally store the text with the definition of the object in an obfuscated format. The obfuscated text is not directly visible to users through any of the catalog objects—only to privileged users through special means.

Before you look at the *ENCRYPTION* option, run the following code to alter the definition of the *USACusts* view to its original version:

```
ALTER VIEW Sales.USACusts
AS

SELECT
  custid, companyname, contactname, contacttitle, address,
  city, region, postalcode, country, phone, fax
FROM Sales.Customers
WHERE country = N'USA';
GO
```

To get the definition of the view, invoke the *OBJECT_DEFINITION* function like this:

```
SELECT OBJECT_DEFINITION(OBJECT_ID('Sales.USACusts'));
```

The text with the definition of the view is available because the view was created without the *ENCRYPTION* option. You get the following output:

```
CREATE VIEW Sales.USACusts
AS

SELECT
  custid, companyname, contactname, contacttitle, address,
  city, region, postalcode, country, phone, fax
FROM Sales.Customers
WHERE country = N'USA';
```

Next, alter the view definition—only this time, include the *ENCRYPTION* option:

```
ALTER VIEW Sales.USACusts WITH ENCRYPTION
AS

SELECT
  custid, companyname, contactname, contacttitle, address,
  city, region, postalcode, country, phone, fax
FROM Sales.Customers
WHERE country = N'USA';
GO
```

Note When you alter a view, if you want to keep options you specified when you created it, you need to repeat those as part of the *ALTER VIEW* command; otherwise, the view will be created without them. Altering a view does retain existing permissions, so you do not need to reassign those.

Try again to get the text with the definition of the view:

```
SELECT OBJECT_DEFINITION(OBJECT_ID('Sales.USACusts'));
```

This time you get a *NULL* back.

As an alternative to the *OBJECT_DEFINITION* function, you can use the *sp_helptext* stored procedure to get object definitions. For example, the following code requests the object definition of the *USA-Custs* view:

```
EXEC sp_helptext 'Sales.USACusts';
```

Because in our case the view was created with the *ENCRYPTION* option, you will not get the object definition back; instead, you'll get the following message:

```
The text for object 'Sales.USACusts' is encrypted.
```

The *SCHEMABINDING* option

The *SCHEMABINDING* option is available to views and UDFs; it binds the schema of referenced objects and columns to the schema of the referencing object. It indicates that referenced objects cannot be dropped and that referenced columns cannot be dropped or altered.

For example, alter the *USACusts* view with the *SCHEMABINDING* option:

```
ALTER VIEW Sales.USACusts WITH SCHEMABINDING
AS

SELECT
  custid, companyname, contactname, contacttitle, address,
  city, region, postalcode, country, phone, fax
FROM Sales.Customers
WHERE country = N'USA';
GO
```

Now try to drop the *address* column from the *Customers* table:

```
ALTER TABLE Sales.Customers DROP COLUMN address;
```

You get the following error:

```
Msg 5074, Level 16, State 1, Line 346
The object 'USACusts' is dependent on column 'address'.
Msg 4922, Level 16, State 9, Line 346
ALTER TABLE DROP COLUMN address failed because one or more objects access this column.
```

Without the *SCHEMABINDING* option, you would have been allowed to make such a schema change, as well as drop the *Customers* table altogether. This can lead to errors at run time when you try to query the view and referenced objects or columns do not exist. If you create the view with the *SCHEMABINDING* option, you can avoid these errors.

To support the *SCHEMABINDING* option, the object definition must meet a couple of requirements. The query is not allowed to use * in the *SELECT* clause; instead, you have to explicitly list column names. Also, you must use schema-qualified two-part names when referring to objects. Both requirements are actually good practices in general.

As you can imagine, creating your objects with the *SCHEMABINDING* option is a good practice.

The *CHECK OPTION* option

The purpose of *CHECK OPTION* is to prevent modifications through the view that conflict with the view's filter.

The query defining the view *USACusts* filters customers from the United States. The view is currently defined without *CHECK OPTION*. This means you can currently insert through the view customers from other countries, and you can update the country of existing customers through the view to one other than the United States. For example, the following code successfully inserts a customer from the United Kingdom through the view:

```
INSERT INTO Sales.USACusts(
  companyname, contactname, contacttitle, address,
  city, region, postalcode, country, phone, fax)
 VALUES(
  N'Customer ABCDE', N'Contact ABCDE', N'Title ABCDE', N'Address ABCDE',
  N'London', NULL, N'12345', N'UK', N'012-3456789', N'012-3456789');
```

The row was inserted through the view into the *Customers* table. However, because the view filters only customers from the United States, if you query the view looking for the new customer, you get an empty set back:

```
SELECT custid, companyname, country
FROM Sales.USACusts
WHERE companyname = N'Customer ABCDE';
```

Query the *Customers* table directly to look for the new customer:

```
SELECT custid, companyname, country
FROM Sales.Customers
WHERE companyname = N'Customer ABCDE';
```

You get the customer in the output, because the new row made it to the *Customers* table:

```
custid      companyname        country
----------- ------------------ ---------------
92          Customer ABCDE     UK
```

Similarly, if you update a customer row through the view, changing the country attribute to a country other than the United States, the update succeeds. But that customer information doesn't show up anymore in the view because it doesn't satisfy the view's query filter.

If you want to prevent modifications that conflict with the view's filter, add *WITH CHECK OPTION* at the end of the query defining the view:

```
ALTER VIEW Sales.USACusts WITH SCHEMABINDING
AS

SELECT
  custid, companyname, contactname, contacttitle, address,
  city, region, postalcode, country, phone, fax
FROM Sales.Customers
WHERE country = N'USA'
WITH CHECK OPTION;
GO
```

Now try to insert a row that conflicts with the view's filter:

```
INSERT INTO Sales.USACusts(
  companyname, contactname, contacttitle, address,
  city, region, postalcode, country, phone, fax)
 VALUES(
  N'Customer FGHIJ', N'Contact FGHIJ', N'Title FGHIJ', N'Address FGHIJ',
  N'London', NULL, N'12345', N'UK', N'012-3456789', N'012-3456789');
```

You get the following error:

```
Msg 550, Level 16, State 1, Line 387
The attempted insert or update failed because the target view either specifies WITH CHECK
OPTION or spans a view that specifies WITH CHECK OPTION and one or more rows resulting from the
operation did not qualify under the CHECK OPTION constraint.
The statement has been terminated.
```

When you're done, run the following code for cleanup:

```
DELETE FROM Sales.Customers
WHERE custid > 91;

DROP VIEW IF EXISTS Sales.USACusts;
```

Inline table-valued functions

Inline TVFs are reusable table expressions that support input parameters. In most respects, except for the support for input parameters, inline TVFs are similar to views. For this reason, I like to think of inline TVFs as parameterized views, even though they are not formally referred to this way.

T-SQL supports another type of table function called multi-statement TVF, which populates and returns a table variable. This type isn't considered a table expression because it's not based on a query.

For example, the following code creates an inline TVF called *GetCustOrders* in the *TSQLV4* database:

```
USE TSQLV4;
DROP FUNCTION IF EXISTS dbo.GetCustOrders;
GO
CREATE FUNCTION dbo.GetCustOrders
  (@cid AS INT) RETURNS TABLE
AS
RETURN
  SELECT orderid, custid, empid, orderdate, requireddate,
    shippeddate, shipperid, freight, shipname, shipaddress, shipcity,
    shipregion, shippostalcode, shipcountry
  FROM Sales.Orders
  WHERE custid = @cid;
GO
```

This inline TVF accepts an input parameter called *@cid*, representing a customer ID, and returns all orders placed by the input customer. You query inline TVFs by using DML statements, which is the same way you query other tables. If the function accepts input parameters, you specify those in parentheses following the function's name. Also, make sure you provide an alias for the table expression. Providing a table expression with an alias is not always a requirement, but it is a good practice because it makes your code more readable and less prone to errors. For example, the following code queries the function to request all orders that were placed by customer 1:

```
SELECT orderid, custid
FROM dbo.GetCustOrders(1) AS O;
```

This code returns the following output:

```
orderid     custid
----------- -----------
10643       1
10692       1
10702       1
10835       1
10952       1
11011       1
```

As with tables, you can refer to an inline TVF as part of a join. For example, the following query joins the inline TVF returning customer 1's orders with the *Sales.OrderDetails* table, matching the orders with their respective order lines:

```
SELECT O.orderid, O.custid, OD.productid, OD.qty
FROM dbo.GetCustOrders(1) AS O
  INNER JOIN Sales.OrderDetails AS OD
    ON O.orderid = OD.orderid;
```

This code returns the following output:

```
orderid     custid      productid   qty
----------- ----------- ----------- ------
10643       1           28          15
10643       1           39          21
```

```
10643       1         46          2
10692       1         63         20
10702       1          3          6
10702       1         76         15
10835       1         59         15
10835       1         77          2
10952       1          6         16
10952       1         28          2
11011       1         58         40
11011       1         71         20
```

When you're done, run the following code for cleanup:

```
DROP FUNCTION IF EXISTS dbo.GetCustOrders;
```

The *APPLY* operator

The *APPLY* operator is a powerful table operator. Like all table operators, *APPLY* is used in the *FROM* clause of a query. There are two supported types of *APPLY*: *CROSS APPLY* and *OUTER APPLY*. Like the *JOIN* table operator, *APPLY* performs its work in logical-query phases. *CROSS APPLY* implements only one logical-query processing phase, whereas *OUTER APPLY* implements two.

> **Note** *APPLY* isn't standard; the standard counterpart is called *LATERAL*, but the standard form wasn't implemented in SQL Server.

The *APPLY* operator operates on two input tables; I'll refer to them as the "left" and "right" tables. The right table is typically a derived table or a TVF. The *CROSS APPLY* operator implements one logical-query processing phase—it applies the right table to each row from the left table and produces a result table with the unified result sets.

It might sound like the *CROSS APPLY* operator is similar to a cross join, and in a sense that's true. For example, the following two queries return the same result sets:

```
SELECT S.shipperid, E.empid
FROM Sales.Shippers AS S
  CROSS JOIN HR.Employees AS E;

SELECT S.shipperid, E.empid
FROM Sales.Shippers AS S
  CROSS APPLY HR.Employees AS E;
```

Remember that a join treats its two inputs as a set, and therefore there's no order between them. This means you cannot refer on one side to elements from the other. With *APPLY*, the left side is evaluated first, and the right side is evaluated per row from the left. So the right side can have references to elements from the left. For example, the following code uses the *CROSS APPLY* operator to return the three most recent orders for each customer:

```
SELECT C.custid, A.orderid, A.orderdate
FROM Sales.Customers AS C
  CROSS APPLY
    (SELECT TOP (3) orderid, empid, orderdate, requireddate
     FROM Sales.Orders AS O
     WHERE O.custid = C.custid
     ORDER BY orderdate DESC, orderid DESC) AS A;
```

You can think of the table expression *A* as a correlated derived table. In terms of logical-query processing, the right table expression (a derived table, in this case) is applied to each row from the *Customers* table. Notice in the inner query's filter the reference to the attribute *C.custid* from the left table. The derived table returns the three most recent orders for the current customer from the left row. Because the derived table is applied to each left row, the *CROSS APPLY* operator returns the three most recent orders for each customer.

Here's the output of this query, shown in abbreviated form:

```
custid      orderid     orderdate
----------- ----------- -----------
1           11011       2016-04-09
1           10952       2016-03-16
1           10835       2016-01-15
2           10926       2016-03-04
2           10759       2015-11-28
2           10625       2015-08-08
3           10856       2016-01-28
3           10682       2015-09-25
3           10677       2015-09-22
...

(263 row(s) affected)
```

Remember that you can use the standard *OFFSET-FETCH* option instead of *TOP*, like this:

```
SELECT C.custid, A.orderid, A.orderdate
FROM Sales.Customers AS C
  CROSS APPLY
    (SELECT orderid, empid, orderdate, requireddate
     FROM Sales.Orders AS O
     WHERE O.custid = C.custid
     ORDER BY orderdate DESC, orderid DESC
     OFFSET 0 ROWS FETCH NEXT 3 ROWS ONLY) AS A;
```

If the right table expression returns an empty set, the *CROSS APPLY* operator does not return the corresponding left row. For example, customers 22 and 57 did not place orders. In both cases, the derived table is an empty set; therefore, those customers are not returned in the output. If you want to return rows from the left side even if there are no matches on the right side, use *OUTER APPLY*. This operator has a second logical phase that preserves all left rows. It keeps the rows from the left side for which there are no matches on the right side, and it uses *NULLs* as placeholders on the right side. You probably noticed that, in the sense that *OUTER APPLY* preserves all left rows, it's similar to a *LEFT OUTER JOIN*. Because of the way *APPLY* works, there's no *APPLY* equivalent of a *RIGHT OUTER JOIN*.

For example, run the following code to return the three most recent orders for each customer and include in the output customers who did not place orders:

```
SELECT C.custid, A.orderid, A.orderdate
FROM Sales.Customers AS C
  OUTER APPLY
    (SELECT TOP (3) orderid, empid, orderdate, requireddate
     FROM Sales.Orders AS O
     WHERE O.custid = C.custid
     ORDER BY orderdate DESC, orderid DESC) AS A;
```

This time, customers 22 and 57 are included in the output, which is shown here in abbreviated form:

```
custid      orderid     orderdate
----------- ----------- -----------
1           11011       2016-04-09
1           10952       2016-03-16
1           10835       2016-01-15
2           10926       2016-03-04
2           10759       2015-11-28
2           10625       2015-08-08
3           10856       2016-01-28
3           10682       2015-09-25
3           10677       2015-09-22
...
22          NULL        NULL
...
57          NULL        NULL
...

(265 row(s) affected)
```

You might find it more convenient to work with inline TVFs instead of derived tables. This way, your code will be simpler to follow and maintain. For example, the following code creates an inline TVF called *TopOrders* that accepts as inputs a customer ID (*@custid*) and a number (*@n*), and returns the *@n* most recent orders for customer *@custid*:

```
DROP FUNCTION IF EXISTS dbo.TopOrders;
GO
CREATE FUNCTION dbo.TopOrders
  (@custid AS INT, @n AS INT)
  RETURNS TABLE
AS
RETURN
  SELECT TOP (@n) orderid, empid, orderdate, requireddate
  FROM Sales.Orders
  WHERE custid = @custid
  ORDER BY orderdate DESC, orderid DESC;
GO
```

You can now substitute the use of the derived table from the previous examples with the new function:

```
SELECT
  C.custid, C.companyname,
  A.orderid, A.empid, A.orderdate, A.requireddate
FROM Sales.Customers AS C
  CROSS APPLY dbo.TopOrders(C.custid, 3) AS A;
```

In terms of physical processing, nothing really changed because, as I stated earlier, the definition of table expressions is expanded, and SQL Server will in any case end up querying the underlying objects directly.

Conclusion

Table expressions can help you simplify your code, improve its maintainability, and encapsulate querying logic. When you need to use table expressions and are not planning to reuse their definitions, use derived tables or CTEs. CTEs have a couple of advantages over derived tables; they are easier to maintain because you do not nest them like you do derived tables. Also, you can refer to multiple instances of the same CTE, which you cannot do with derived tables.

When you need to define reusable table expressions, use views or inline TVFs. When you do not need to support input parameters, use views; otherwise, use inline TVFs.

Use the *APPLY* operator when you want to apply a correlated table expression to each row from a source table and unify all result sets into one result table.

Exercises

This section provides exercises to help you familiarize yourself with the subjects discussed in this chapter. All the exercises in this chapter require your session to be connected to the *TSQLV4* database.

Exercise 1

The following query attempts to filter orders that were not placed on the last day of the year. It's supposed to return the order ID, order date, customer ID, employee ID, and respective end-of-year date for each order:

```
SELECT orderid, orderdate, custid, empid,
  DATEFROMPARTS(YEAR(orderdate), 12, 31) AS endofyear
FROM Sales.Orders
WHERE orderdate <> endofyear;
```

When you try to run this query, you get the following error:

```
Msg 207, Level 16, State 1, Line 233
Invalid column name 'endofyear'.
```

Explain what the problem is, and suggest a valid solution.

Exercise 2-1

Write a query that returns the maximum value in the *orderdate* column for each employee:

- Table involved: *TSQLV4* database, *Sales.Orders* table
- Desired output:

```
empid       maxorderdate
----------- -------------
3           2016-04-30
6           2016-04-23
9           2016-04-29
7           2016-05-06
1           2016-05-06
4           2016-05-06
2           2016-05-05
5           2016-04-22
8           2016-05-06

(9 row(s) affected)
```

Exercise 2-2

Encapsulate the query from Exercise 2-1 in a derived table. Write a join query between the derived table and the *Orders* table to return the orders with the maximum order date for each employee:

- Table involved: *Sales.Orders*
- Desired output:

```
empid       orderdate   orderid     custid
----------- ----------- ----------- -----------
9           2016-04-29  11058       6
8           2016-05-06  11075       68
7           2016-05-06  11074       73
6           2016-04-23  11045       10
5           2016-04-22  11043       74
4           2016-05-06  11076       9
3           2016-04-30  11063       37
2           2016-05-05  11073       58
2           2016-05-05  11070       44
1           2016-05-06  11077       65

(10 row(s) affected)
```

Exercise 3-1

Write a query that calculates a row number for each order based on *orderdate, orderid* ordering:

- Table involved: *Sales.Orders*
- Desired output (abbreviated):

```
orderid     orderdate   custid      empid       rownum
----------- ----------- ----------- ----------- -------
10248       2014-07-04  85          5           1
10249       2014-07-05  79          6           2
10250       2014-07-08  34          4           3
10251       2014-07-08  84          3           4
10252       2014-07-09  76          4           5
10253       2014-07-10  34          3           6
10254       2014-07-11  14          5           7
10255       2014-07-12  68          9           8
10256       2014-07-15  88          3           9
10257       2014-07-16  35          4           10
...

(830 row(s) affected)
```

Exercise 3-2

Write a query that returns rows with row numbers 11 through 20 based on the row-number definition in Exercise 3-1. Use a CTE to encapsulate the code from Exercise 3-1:

- Table involved: *Sales.Orders*
- Desired output:

```
orderid     orderdate   custid      empid       rownum
----------- ----------- ----------- ----------- -------
10258       2014-07-17  20          1           11
10259       2014-07-18  13          4           12
10260       2014-07-19  56          4           13
10261       2014-07-19  61          4           14
10262       2014-07-22  65          8           15
10263       2014-07-23  20          9           16
10264       2014-07-24  24          6           17
10265       2014-07-25  7           2           18
10266       2014-07-26  87          3           19
10267       2014-07-29  25          4           20

(10 row(s) affected)
```

Exercise 4 (optional, advanced)

Write a solution using a recursive CTE that returns the management chain leading to Patricia Doyle (employee ID 9):

- Table involved: *HR.Employees*
- Desired output:

```
empid       mgrid       firstname  lastname
----------- ----------- ---------- --------------------
9           5           Patricia   Doyle
5           2           Sven       Mortensen
2           1           Don        Funk
1           NULL        Sara       Davis

(4 row(s) affected)
```

Exercise 5-1

Create a view that returns the total quantity for each employee and year:

- Tables involved: *Sales.Orders* and *Sales.OrderDetails*
- When running the following code:

```
SELECT * FROM Sales.VEmpOrders ORDER BY empid, orderyear;
```

- Desired output:

```
empid       orderyear   qty
----------- ----------- -----------
1           2014        1620
1           2015        3877
1           2016        2315
2           2014        1085
2           2015        2604
2           2016        2366
3           2014        940
3           2015        4436
3           2016        2476
4           2014        2212
4           2015        5273
4           2016        2313
5           2014        778
5           2015        1471
5           2016        787
6           2014        963
6           2015        1738
6           2016        826
7           2014        485
7           2015        2292
7           2016        1877
8           2014        923
8           2015        2843
8           2016        2147
9           2014        575
9           2015        955
9           2016        1140

(27 row(s) affected)
```

Exercise 5-2 (optional, advanced)

Write a query against *Sales.VEmpOrders* that returns the running total quantity for each employee and year:

- Table involved: *Sales.VEmpOrders* view
- Desired output:

```
empid       orderyear   qty         runqty
----------- ----------- ----------- -----------
1           2014        1620        1620
1           2015        3877        5497
1           2016        2315        7812
2           2014        1085        1085
2           2015        2604        3689
2           2016        2366        6055
3           2014        940         940
3           2015        4436        5376
3           2016        2476        7852
4           2014        2212        2212
4           2015        5273        7485
4           2016        2313        9798
5           2014        778         778
5           2015        1471        2249
5           2016        787         3036
6           2014        963         963
6           2015        1738        2701
6           2016        826         3527
7           2014        485         485
7           2015        2292        2777
7           2016        1877        4654
8           2014        923         923
8           2015        2843        3766
8           2016        2147        5913
9           2014        575         575
9           2015        955         1530
9           2016        1140        2670

(27 row(s) affected)
```

Exercise 6-1

Create an inline TVF that accepts as inputs a supplier ID (*@supid AS INT*) and a requested number of products (*@n AS INT*). The function should return *@n* products with the highest unit prices that are supplied by the specified supplier ID:

- Table involved: *Production.Products*
- When issuing the following query:

```
SELECT * FROM Production.TopProducts(5, 2);
```

- Desired output:

```
productid   productname        unitprice
----------- ------------------ ---------------
12          Product OSFNS      38.00
11          Product QMVUN      21.00

(2 row(s) affected)
```

Exercise 6-2

Using the *CROSS APPLY* operator and the function you created in Exercise 6-1, return the two most expensive products for each supplier:

- Table involved: *Production.Suppliers*
- Desired output (shown here in abbreviated form):

```
supplierid  companyname       productid   productname     unitprice
----------- ----------------- ----------- --------------- ----------
8           Supplier BWGYE    20          Product QHFFP   81.00
8           Supplier BWGYE    68          Product TBTBL   12.50
20          Supplier CIYNM    43          Product ZZZHR   46.00
20          Supplier CIYNM    44          Product VJIEO   19.45
23          Supplier ELCRN    49          Product FPYPN   20.00
23          Supplier ELCRN    76          Product JYGFE   18.00
5           Supplier EQPNC    12          Product OSFNS   38.00
5           Supplier EQPNC    11          Product QMVUN   21.00
...

(55 row(s) affected)
```

- When you're done, run the following code for cleanup:

```
DROP VIEW IF EXISTS Sales.VEmpOrders;
DROP FUNCTION IF EXISTS Production.TopProducts;
```

Solutions

This section provides solutions to the exercises in the preceding section.

Exercise 1

The problem is that in terms of logical-query processing, the *SELECT* clause is evaluated after the *WHERE* clause. This means you're not allowed to refer to an alias you create in the *SELECT* clause within the *WHERE* clause. One solution that doesn't require you to repeat lengthy expressions is to define a table expression such as a CTE based on a query that defines the alias, and then refer to the alias multiple times in the outer query. In our case, the solution looks like this:

```
WITH C AS
(
  SELECT *,
    DATEFROMPARTS(YEAR(orderdate), 12, 31) AS endofyear
  FROM Sales.Orders
)
SELECT orderid, orderdate, custid, empid, endofyear
FROM C
WHERE orderdate <> endofyear;
```

Exercise 2-1

This exercise is just a preliminary step required for the next exercise. This step involves writing a query that returns the maximum order date for each employee:

```
USE TSQLV4;

SELECT empid, MAX(orderdate) AS maxorderdate
FROM Sales.Orders
GROUP BY empid;
```

Exercise 2-2

This exercise requires you to use the query from the previous step to define a derived table and join this derived table with the *Orders* table to return the orders with the maximum order date for each employee, like the following:

```
SELECT O.empid, O.orderdate, O.orderid, O.custid
FROM Sales.Orders AS O
  INNER JOIN (SELECT empid, MAX(orderdate) AS maxorderdate
              FROM Sales.Orders
              GROUP BY empid) AS D
    ON O.empid = D.empid
    AND O.orderdate = D.maxorderdate;
```

Exercise 3-1

This exercise is a preliminary step for the next exercise. It requires you to query the *Orders* table and calculate row numbers based on *orderdate, orderid* ordering, like the following:

```
SELECT orderid, orderdate, custid, empid,
  ROW_NUMBER() OVER(ORDER BY orderdate, orderid) AS rownum
FROM Sales.Orders;
```

Exercise 3-2

This exercise requires you to define a CTE based on the query from the previous step and filter only rows with row numbers in the range 11 through 20 from the CTE, like the following:

```
WITH OrdersRN AS
(
```

```
  SELECT orderid, orderdate, custid, empid,
    ROW_NUMBER() OVER(ORDER BY orderdate, orderid) AS rownum
  FROM Sales.Orders
)
SELECT * FROM OrdersRN WHERE rownum BETWEEN 11 AND 20;
```

You might wonder why you need a table expression here. Window functions (such as the *ROW_NUMBER* function) are allowed only in the *SELECT* and *ORDER BY* clauses of a query, and not directly in the *WHERE* clause. By using a table expression, you can invoke the *ROW_NUMBER* function in the *SELECT* clause, assign an alias to the result column, and refer to that alias in the *WHERE* clause of the outer query.

Exercise 4

You can think of this exercise as the inverse of the request to return an employee and all subordinates in all levels. Here, the anchor member is a query that returns the row for employee 9. The recursive member joins the CTE (call it *C*)—representing the subordinate/child from the previous level—with the *Employees* table (call it *P*)—representing the manager/parent in the next level. This way, each invocation of the recursive member returns the manager from the next level, until no next-level manager is found (in the case of the CEO).

Here's the complete solution query:

```
WITH EmpsCTE AS
(
  SELECT empid, mgrid, firstname, lastname
  FROM HR.Employees
  WHERE empid = 9

  UNION ALL

  SELECT P.empid, P.mgrid, P.firstname, P.lastname
  FROM EmpsCTE AS C
    INNER JOIN HR.Employees AS P
      ON C.mgrid = P.empid
)
SELECT empid, mgrid, firstname, lastname
FROM EmpsCTE;
```

Exercise 5-1

This exercise is a preliminary step for the next exercise. Here you are required to define a view based on a query that joins the *Orders* and *OrderDetails* tables, group the rows by employee ID and order year, and return the total quantity for each group. The view definition should look like the following:

```
USE TSQLV4;
DROP VIEW IF EXISTS Sales.VEmpOrders;
GO
CREATE VIEW  Sales.VEmpOrders
AS
```

```
SELECT
  empid,
  YEAR(orderdate) AS orderyear,
  SUM(qty) AS qty
FROM Sales.Orders AS O
  INNER JOIN Sales.OrderDetails AS OD
    ON O.orderid = OD.orderid
GROUP BY
  empid,
  YEAR(orderdate);
GO
```

Exercise 5-2

In this exercise, you query the *VEmpOrders* view and return the running total quantity for each employee and order year. To achieve this, you can write a query against the *VEmpOrders* view (calling it *V1*) that returns from each row the employee ID, order year, and quantity. In the *SELECT* list, you can incorporate a subquery against a second instance of *VEmpOrders* (calling it *V2*), that returns the sum of all quantities from the rows where the employee ID is equal to the one in *V1*, and the order year is smaller than or equal to the one in *V1*. The complete solution query looks like the following:

```
SELECT empid, orderyear, qty,
  (SELECT SUM(qty)
   FROM  Sales.VEmpOrders AS V2
   WHERE V2.empid = V1.empid
     AND V2.orderyear <= V1.orderyear) AS runqty
FROM  Sales.VEmpOrders AS V1
ORDER BY empid, orderyear;
```

Note that in Chapter 7, "Beyond the fundamentals of querying," you'll learn techniques to compute running totals by using window functions.

Exercise 6-1

This exercise requires you to define an inline TVF called *TopProducts* that accepts a supplier ID (*@supid*) and a number (*@n*) and is supposed to return the *@n* most expensive products supplied by the input supplier ID. Here's how the function definition should look:

```
USE TSQLV4;
DROP FUNCTION IF EXISTS Production.TopProducts;
GO
CREATE FUNCTION Production.TopProducts
  (@supid AS INT, @n AS INT)
  RETURNS TABLE
AS
RETURN
  SELECT TOP (@n) productid, productname, unitprice
  FROM Production.Products
  WHERE supplierid = @supid
  ORDER BY unitprice DESC;
GO
```

Alternatively, you can use the *OFFSET-FETCH* filter. You replace the inner query in the function with the following one:

```
SELECT productid, productname, unitprice
FROM Production.Products
WHERE supplierid = @supid
ORDER BY unitprice DESC
OFFSET 0 ROWS FETCH NEXT @n ROWS ONLY;
```

Exercise 6-2

In this exercise, you write a query against the *Production.Suppliers* table and use the *CROSS APPLY* operator to apply the function you defined in the previous step to each supplier. Your query is supposed to return the two most expensive products for each supplier. Here's the solution query:

```
SELECT S.supplierid, S.companyname, P.productid, P.productname, P.unitprice
FROM Production.Suppliers AS S
  CROSS APPLY Production.TopProducts(S.supplierid, 2) AS P;
```

CHAPTER 6

Set operators

Set operators are operators that combine rows from two query result sets (or multisets). Some of the operators remove duplicates from the result, and hence return a set, whereas others don't, and hence return a multiset. T-SQL supports the following operators: *UNION*, *UNION ALL*, *INTERSECT*, and *EXCEPT*. In this chapter, I first introduce the general form and requirements of these operators, and then I describe each operator in detail.

The general form of a query with a set operator is as follows:

```
Input Query1
<set_operator>
Input Query2
[ORDER BY ...];
```

A set operator compares complete rows between the results of the two input queries involved. Whether a row will be returned in the result of the operator depends on the outcome of the comparison and the operator used. Because a set operator expects multisets as inputs, the two queries involved cannot have *ORDER BY* clauses. Remember that a query with an *ORDER BY* clause does not return a multiset—it returns a cursor. However, although the queries involved cannot have *ORDER BY* clauses, you can optionally add an *ORDER BY* clause to the result of the operator. If you're wondering how you apply a set operator to queries with *TOP* and *OFFSET-FETCH* filters, I'll get to this later in the chapter in the section "Circumventing unsupported logical phases."

In terms of logical-query processing, each of the individual queries can have all logical-query processing phases except for a presentation *ORDER BY*, as I just explained. The operator is applied to the results of the two queries, and the outer *ORDER BY* clause (if one exists) is applied to the result of the operator.

The two input queries must produce results with the same number of columns, and corresponding columns must have compatible data types. By *compatible data types*, I mean that the data type that is lower in terms of data-type precedence must be implicitly convertible to the higher data type. Of course, you also can explicitly convert the data type of a column in one query to the data type of the corresponding column in the other query using the *CAST* or *CONVERT* function.

The names of the columns in the result are determined by the first query; therefore, if you need to assign aliases to result columns, you should assign those in the first query.

Interestingly, when a set operator compares rows between the two inputs, it doesn't use an equality operator; rather, it uses a so-called *distinct predicate*. This predicate produces a *TRUE* when comparing two *NULLs*. I'll demonstrate the importance of this point later in the chapter.

Standard SQL supports two "flavors" of each operator—*DISTINCT* (the default) and *ALL*. The *DISTINCT* flavor eliminates duplicates and returns a set. *ALL* doesn't attempt to remove duplicates and therefore returns a multiset. All three operators in T-SQL support an implicit distinct version, but only the *UNION* operator supports the *ALL* version. In terms of syntax, T-SQL doesn't allow you to specify the *DISTINCT* clause explicitly. Instead, it's implied when you don't specify *ALL*. I'll provide alternatives to the missing *INTERSECT ALL* and *EXCEPT ALL* operators in the "The *INTERSECT ALL* operator" and "The *EXCEPT ALL* operator" sections later in this chapter.

The *UNION* operator

The *UNION* operator unifies the results of two input queries. If a row appears in any of the input sets, it will appear in the result of the *UNION* operator. T-SQL supports both the *UNION ALL* and *UNION* (implicit *DISTINCT*) flavors of the *UNION* operator.

Figure 6-1 illustrates the *UNION* operator. The shaded area represents the result of the operator. The nonshaded areas reflect the fact that the operator doesn't have to include all attributes of the original relations.

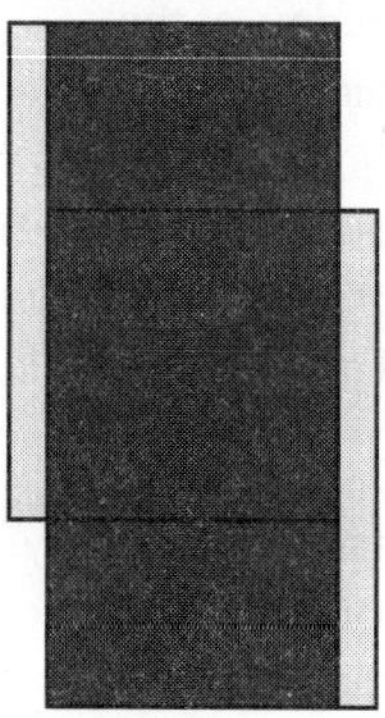

FIGURE 6-1 The *UNION* operator.

The *UNION ALL* operator

The *UNION ALL* operator unifies the two input query results without attempting to remove duplicates from the result. Assuming that *Query1* returns *m* rows and *Query2* returns *n* rows, *Query1 UNION ALL Query2* returns *m* + *n* rows.

For example, the following code uses the *UNION ALL* operator to unify employee locations and customer locations:

```
USE TSQLV4;

SELECT country, region, city FROM HR.Employees
UNION ALL
SELECT country, region, city FROM Sales.Customers;
```

The result has 100 rows—9 from the *Employees* table and 91 from the *Customers* table—and is shown here in abbreviated form:

```
country         region          city
--------------- --------------- ---------------
USA             WA              Seattle
USA             WA              Tacoma
USA             WA              Kirkland
USA             WA              Redmond
UK              NULL            London
UK              NULL            London
UK              NULL            London
...
Finland         NULL            Oulu
Brazil          SP              Resende
USA             WA              Seattle
Finland         NULL            Helsinki
Poland          NULL            Warszawa

(100 row(s) affected)
```

Because *UNION ALL* doesn't eliminate duplicates, the result is a multiset and not a set. The same row can appear multiple times in the result, as is the case with *(UK, NULL, London)* in the result of this query.

The *UNION* (*DISTINCT*) operator

The *UNION* (implicit *DISTINCT*) operator unifies the results of the two queries and eliminates duplicates. Note that if a row appears in both input sets, it will appear only once in the result; in other words, the result is a set and not a multiset.

For example, the following code returns distinct locations that are either employee locations or customer locations:

```
SELECT country, region, city FROM HR.Employees
UNION
SELECT country, region, city FROM Sales.Customers;
```

This code returns 71 distinct rows (unlike the 100 rows in the result with the duplicates), as shown here in abbreviated form:

```
country         region          city
--------------- --------------- ---------------
Argentina       NULL            Buenos Aires
Austria         NULL            Graz
Austria         NULL            Salzburg
Belgium         NULL            Bruxelles
Belgium         NULL            Charleroi
```

```
...
USA            WY              Lander
Venezuela      DF              Caracas
Venezuela      Lara            Barquisimeto
Venezuela      Nueva Esparta   I. de Margarita
Venezuela      Táchira         San Cristóbal

(71 row(s) affected)
```

So when should you use *UNION ALL* and when should you use *UNION*? If duplicates are possible in the unified result and you do not need to return them, use *UNION*. Otherwise, use *UNION ALL*. If duplicates cannot exist when unifying the inputs, *UNION* and *UNION ALL* will return the same result. However, in such a case I recommend you use *UNION ALL* so that you don't pay the unnecessary performance penalty related to checking for duplicates.

The *INTERSECT* Operator

The *INTERSECT* operator returns only the rows that are common to the results of the two input queries. Figure 6-2 illustrates this operator.

FIGURE 6-2 The *INTERSECT* operator.

The *INTERSECT* (*DISTINCT*) operator

The *INTERSECT* operator (implied *DISTINCT*) returns only distinct rows that appear in both input query results. As long as a row appears at least once in both query results, it's returned only once in the operator's result.

For example, the following code returns distinct locations that are both employee locations and customer locations:

```
SELECT country, region, city FROM HR.Employees
INTERSECT
SELECT country, region, city FROM Sales.Customers;
```

This query returns the following output:

```
country         region          city
--------------- --------------- ---------------
UK              NULL            London
USA             WA              Kirkland
USA             WA              Seattle
```

I mentioned earlier that when these operators compare rows, they use an implied distinct predicate, which returns a *TRUE* when comparing two *NULLs*. For example, observe that the location *(UK, NULL, London)* appears in the result of the intersection. If instead of using the *INTERSECT* operator you use an alternative tool like an inner join or a correlated subquery, you need to add special treatment for *NULLs*—for example, assuming the alias *E* for *Employees* and *C* for *Customers*, using the predicate *E.region = C.region OR (E.region IS NULL AND C.region IS NULL)*. Using the *INTERSECT* operator, the solution is much simpler—you don't need to explicitly compare corresponding attributes, and you don't need to add special treatment for *NULLs*.

The *INTERSECT ALL* operator

I provide this section as optional reading for those who feel comfortable with the material covered so far in this chapter. Standard SQL supports an *ALL* flavor of the *INTERSECT* operator, but this flavor has not been implemented in T-SQL. However, you can write your own logical equivalent with T-SQL.

Remember the meaning of the *ALL* keyword in the *UNION ALL* operator: it returns all duplicate rows. Similarly, the keyword *ALL* in the *INTERSECT ALL* operator means that duplicate intersections will not be removed. *INTERSECT ALL* returns the number of duplicate rows matching the lower of the counts in both input multisets. It's as if this operator looks for matches for each occurrence of each row. If there are *x* occurrences of a row R in the first input multiset and *y* occurrences of R in the second, R appears *minimum(x, y)* times in the result. For example, the location *(UK, NULL, London)* appears four times in *Employees* and six times in *Customers*; hence, *INTERSECT ALL* returns four occurrences in the output.

Even though T-SQL does not support a built-in *INTERSECT ALL* operator, you can write your own alternative solution that produces the same result. You can use the *ROW_NUMBER* function to number the occurrences of each row in each input query. To achieve this, specify all participating attributes in the *PARTITION BY* clause of the function, and use *(SELECT <constant>)* in the *ORDER BY* clause of the function to indicate that order doesn't matter. Window functions, including the *ROW_NUMBER* function, are covered in Chapter 7, "Beyond the fundamentals of querying."

> **Tip** A window order clause is mandatory in window ranking functions like *ROW_NUMBER*. As a trick, when you don't care about ordering, use *ORDER BY (SELECT <constant>)* as the window order clause. Microsoft SQL Server realizes in such a case that order doesn't matter.

Then apply the *INTERSECT* operator between the two queries with the *ROW_NUMBER* function. Because the occurrences of the rows are numbered, the intersection is based on the row numbers in addition to the original attributes. For example, in the *Employees* table the four occurrences of the location *(UK, NULL, London)* are numbered 1 through 4. In the *Customers* table the six occurrences of the same row are numbered 1 through 6. Occurrences 1 through 4 intersect between the two.

Here's the complete solution code:

```
SELECT
  ROW_NUMBER()
    OVER(PARTITION BY country, region, city
         ORDER     BY (SELECT 0)) AS rownum,
  country, region, city
FROM HR.Employees

INTERSECT

SELECT
  ROW_NUMBER()
    OVER(PARTITION BY country, region, city
         ORDER     BY (SELECT 0)),
  country, region, city
FROM Sales.Customers;
```

This code produces the following output.

```
rownum               country         region          city
-------------------- --------------- --------------- ---------------
1                    UK              NULL            London
1                    USA             WA              Kirkland
1                    USA             WA              Seattle
2                    UK              NULL            London
3                    UK              NULL            London
4                    UK              NULL            London
```

The standard *INTERSECT ALL* operator is not supposed to return any row numbers. To exclude those from the output, define a table expression based on this query, and in the outer query select only the attributes you want to return. Here's the complete solution code:

```
WITH INTERSECT_ALL
AS
(
  SELECT
    ROW_NUMBER()
      OVER(PARTITION BY country, region, city
           ORDER     BY (SELECT 0)) AS rownum,
    country, region, city
  FROM HR.Employees

  INTERSECT

  SELECT
    ROW_NUMBER()
      OVER(PARTITION BY country, region, city
           ORDER     BY (SELECT 0)),
    country, region, city
  FROM Sales.Customers
```

```
)
SELECT country, region, city
FROM INTERSECT_ALL;
```

This code generates the following output:

```
country         region          city
--------------- --------------- ---------------
UK              NULL            London
USA             WA              Kirkland
USA             WA              Seattle
UK              NULL            London
UK              NULL            London
UK              NULL            London
```

The *EXCEPT* operator

The *EXCEPT* operator implements set differences. It operates on the results of two input queries and returns rows that appear in the first input but not the second. Figure 6-3 illustrates this operator.

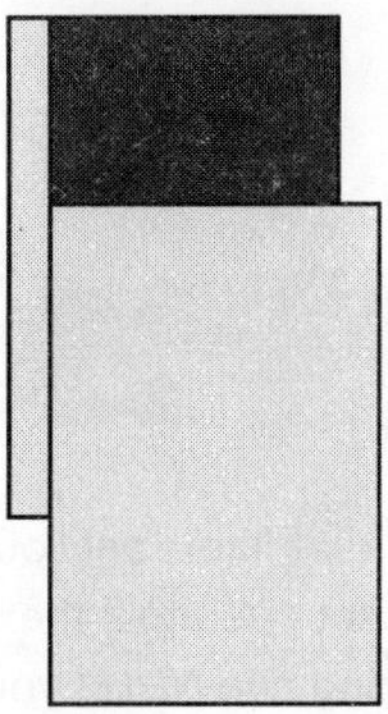

FIGURE 6-3 The *EXCEPT* operator.

The *EXCEPT* (*DISTINCT*) operator

The *EXCEPT* operator (implied *DISTINCT*) returns only distinct rows that appear in the first set but not the second. In other words, a row is returned once in the output as long as it appears at least once in the first input multiset and zero times in the second. Note that unlike *UNION* and *INTERSECT*, *EXCEPT* is noncummutative; that is, the order in which you specify the two input queries matters.

For example, the following code returns distinct locations that are employee locations but not customer locations:

```
SELECT country, region, city FROM HR.Employees
EXCEPT
SELECT country, region, city FROM Sales.Customers;
```

This query returns the following two locations:

```
country         region          city
--------------- --------------- ---------------
USA             WA              Redmond
USA             WA              Tacoma
```

The following query returns distinct locations that are customer locations but not employee locations:

```
SELECT country, region, city FROM Sales.Customers
EXCEPT
SELECT country, region, city FROM HR.Employees;
```

This query returns 66 locations, shown here in abbreviated form:

```
country         region          city
--------------- --------------- ---------------
Argentina       NULL            Buenos Aires
Austria         NULL            Graz
Austria         NULL            Salzburg
Belgium         NULL            Bruxelles
Belgium         NULL            Charleroi
...
USA             WY              Lander
Venezuela       DF              Caracas
Venezuela       Lara            Barquisimeto
Venezuela       Nueva Esparta   I. de Margarita
Venezuela       Táchira         San Cristóbal

(66 row(s) affected)
```

Naturally, there are alternatives to the *EXCEPT* operator. One is an outer join that filters only outer rows, and another is to use the *NOT EXISTS* predicate. However, recall that with set operators the comparison between corresponding columns is implied, and also when comparing two *NULLs* you get a *TRUE*. With joins and subqueries, you need to be explicit about comparisons and you also need to explicitly add special treatment for *NULLs*.

The *EXCEPT ALL* operator

The *EXCEPT ALL* operator is similar to the *EXCEPT* operator, but it also takes into account the number of occurrences of each row. If a row R appears *x* times in the first multiset and *y* times in the second, and $x > y$, R will appear $x - y$ times in *Query1 EXCEPT ALL Query2*. In other words, *EXCEPT ALL* returns only occurrences of a row from the first multiset that do not have a corresponding occurrence in the second.

T-SQL does not provide a built-in *EXCEPT ALL* operator, but you can provide an alternative of your own similar to how you handled *INTERSECT ALL*. Namely, add a *ROW_NUMBER* calculation to each of the input queries to number the occurrences of the rows, and use the *EXCEPT* operator between the two input queries. Only occurrences that don't have matches will be returned.

The following code returns occurrences of employee locations that have no corresponding occurrences of customer locations:

```
WITH EXCEPT_ALL
AS
(
  SELECT
    ROW_NUMBER()
      OVER(PARTITION BY country, region, city
           ORDER     BY (SELECT 0)) AS rownum,
    country, region, city
    FROM HR.Employees

  EXCEPT

  SELECT
    ROW_NUMBER()
      OVER(PARTITION BY country, region, city
           ORDER     BY (SELECT 0)),
    country, region, city
  FROM Sales.Customers
)
SELECT country, region, city
FROM EXCEPT_ALL;
```

This query returns the following output:

```
country         region          city
--------------- --------------- ---------------
USA             WA              Redmond
USA             WA              Tacoma
USA             WA              Seattle
```

Precedence

SQL defines precedence among set operators. The *INTERSECT* operator precedes *UNION* and *EXCEPT*, and *UNION* and *EXCEPT* are evaluated in order of appearance. Using the *ALL* variant doesn't change the precedence. In a query that contains multiple set operators, first *INTERSECT* operators are evaluated, and then operators with the same precedence are evaluated based on their order of appearance.

Consider the following code:

```
SELECT country, region, city FROM Production.Suppliers
EXCEPT
SELECT country, region, city FROM HR.Employees
INTERSECT
SELECT country, region, city FROM Sales.Customers;
```

Because *INTERSECT* precedes *EXCEPT*, the *INTERSECT* operator is evaluated first, even though it appears second in the code. The meaning of this query is, "locations that are supplier locations, but not (locations that are both employee and customer locations)."

This query returns the following output:

```
country         region          city
--------------- --------------- ---------------
Australia       NSW             Sydney
Australia       Victoria        Melbourne
Brazil          NULL            Sao Paulo
Canada          Québec          Montréal
Canada          Québec          Ste-Hyacinthe
Denmark         NULL            Lyngby
Finland         NULL            Lappeenranta
France          NULL            Annecy
France          NULL            Montceau
France          NULL            Paris
Germany         NULL            Berlin
Germany         NULL            Cuxhaven
Germany         NULL            Frankfurt
Italy           NULL            Ravenna
Italy           NULL            Salerno
Japan           NULL            Osaka
Japan           NULL            Tokyo
Netherlands     NULL            Zaandam
Norway          NULL            Sandvika
Singapore       NULL            Singapore
Spain           Asturias        Oviedo
Sweden          NULL            Göteborg
Sweden          NULL            Stockholm
UK              NULL            Manchester
USA             LA              New Orleans
USA             MA              Boston
USA             MI              Ann Arbor
USA             OR              Bend

(28 row(s) affected)
```

To control the order of evaluation of set operators, use parentheses, because they have the highest precedence. Also, using parentheses increases the readability, thus reducing the chance for errors. For example, if you want to return "(locations that are supplier locations but not employee locations) and that are also customer locations," use the following code:

```
(SELECT country, region, city FROM Production.Suppliers
 EXCEPT
 SELECT country, region, city FROM HR.Employees)
INTERSECT
SELECT country, region, city FROM Sales.Customers;
```

This query returns the following output:

```
country         region          city
--------------- --------------- ---------------
Canada          Québec          Montréal
France          NULL            Paris
Germany         NULL            Berlin
```

Circumventing unsupported logical phases

This section can be considered advanced for the book's target audience and is provided here as optional reading. The individual queries that are used as inputs to a set operator support all logical-query processing phases (such as table operators, *WHERE*, *GROUP BY*, and *HAVING*) except for *ORDER BY*. However, only the *ORDER BY* phase is allowed on the result of the operator.

What if you need to apply other logical phases besides *ORDER BY* to the result of the operator? This is not supported directly as part of the query that applies the operator, but you can easily circumvent this restriction by using table expressions. Define a table expression based on a query with a set operator, and apply any logical-query processing phases you want in the outer query. For example, the following query returns the number of distinct locations that are either employee or customer locations in each country:

```
SELECT country, COUNT(*) AS numlocations
FROM (SELECT country, region, city FROM HR.Employees
      UNION
      SELECT country, region, city FROM Sales.Customers) AS U
GROUP BY country;
```

This query returns the following output:

```
country         numlocations
--------------- ------------
Argentina       1
Austria         2
Belgium         2
Brazil          4
Canada          3
Denmark         2
Finland         2
France          9
Germany         11
Ireland         1
Italy           3
Mexico          1
Norway          1
Poland          1
Portugal        1
Spain           3
Sweden          2
Switzerland     2
UK              2
USA             14
Venezuela       4

(21 row(s) affected)
```

This query demonstrates how to group the result of a *UNION* operator; similarly, you can, of course, apply other logical-query phases in the outer query.

Remember that the *ORDER BY* clause is not allowed in the input queries. What if you need to restrict the number of rows in those queries with the *TOP* or *OFFSET-FETCH* filter? Again, you can resolve this problem with table expressions. Recall that an *ORDER BY* clause is allowed in an inner query with *TOP* or *OFFSET-FETCH*. In such a case, the *ORDER BY* clause serves only the filtering-related purpose and has no presentation meaning. For example, the following code uses *TOP* queries to return the two most recent orders for employees 3 and 5:

```
SELECT empid, orderid, orderdate
FROM (SELECT TOP (2) empid, orderid, orderdate
      FROM Sales.Orders
      WHERE empid = 3
      ORDER BY orderdate DESC, orderid DESC) AS D1

UNION ALL

SELECT empid, orderid, orderdate
FROM (SELECT TOP (2) empid, orderid, orderdate
      FROM Sales.Orders
      WHERE empid = 5
      ORDER BY orderdate DESC, orderid DESC) AS D2;
```

This query returns the following output:

```
empid       orderid     orderdate
----------- ----------- -----------
3           11063       2016-04-30
3           11057       2016-04-29
5           11043       2016-04-22
5           10954       2016-03-17
```

Conclusion

In this chapter, I covered the operators *UNION, UNION ALL, EXCEPT*, and *INTERSECT*. I explained that standard SQL also supports operators called *INTERSECT ALL* and *EXCEPT ALL* and explained how to achieve similar functionality in T-SQL. Finally, I introduced precedence among set operators, and I explained how to circumvent unsupported logical-query processing phases by using table expressions.

Exercises

This section provides exercises to help you familiarize yourself with the subjects discussed in Chapter 6. All exercises require you to be connected to the sample database *TSQLV4*.

Exercise 1

Explain the difference between the *UNION ALL* and *UNION* operators. In what cases are the two equivalent? When they are equivalent, which one should you use?

Exercise 2

Write a query that generates a virtual auxiliary table of 10 numbers in the range 1 through 10 without using a looping construct. You do not need to guarantee any order of the rows in the output of your solution:

- Tables involved: None
- Desired output:

```
n
-----------
1
2
3
4
5
6
7
8
9
10

(10 row(s) affected)
```

Exercise 3

Write a query that returns customer and employee pairs that had order activity in January 2016 but not in February 2016:

- Table involved: *Sales.Orders* table
- Desired output:

```
custid      empid
----------- -----------
1           1
3           3
5           8
5           9
6           9
7           6
9           1
12          2
16          7
17          1
20          7
24          8
25          1
26          3
32          4
38          9
39          3
40          2
```

```
41          2
42          2
44          8
47          3
47          4
47          8
49          7
55          2
55          3
56          6
59          8
63          8
64          9
65          3
65          8
66          5
67          5
70          3
71          2
75          1
76          2
76          5
80          1
81          1
81          3
81          4
82          6
84          1
84          3
84          4
88          7
89          4

(50 row(s) affected)
```

Exercise 4

Write a query that returns customer and employee pairs that had order activity in both January 2016 and February 2016:

- Table involved: *Sales.Orders*
- Desired output:

```
custid      empid
----------- -----------
20          3
39          9
46          5
67          1
71          4

(5 row(s) affected)
```

Exercise 5

Write a query that returns customer and employee pairs that had order activity in both January 2016 and February 2016 but not in 2015:

- Table involved: *Sales.Orders*
- Desired output:

```
custid      empid
----------- -----------
67          1
46          5

(2 row(s) affected)
```

Exercise 6 (optional, advanced)

You are given the following query:

```
SELECT country, region, city
FROM HR.Employees

UNION ALL

SELECT country, region, city
FROM Production.Suppliers;
```

You are asked to add logic to the query so that it guarantees that the rows from *Employees* are returned in the output before the rows from *Suppliers*. Also, within each segment, the rows should be sorted by country, region, and city:

- Tables involved: *HR.Employees* and *Production.Suppliers*
- Desired output:

```
country         region          city
--------------- --------------- ---------------
UK              NULL            London
UK              NULL            London
UK              NULL            London
UK              NULL            London
USA             WA              Kirkland
USA             WA              Redmond
USA             WA              Seattle
USA             WA              Seattle
USA             WA              Tacoma
Australia       NSW             Sydney
Australia       Victoria        Melbourne
Brazil          NULL            Sao Paulo
Canada          Québec          Montréal
Canada          Québec          Ste-Hyacinthe
Denmark         NULL            Lyngby
Finland         NULL            Lappeenranta
```

```
France          NULL            Annecy
France          NULL            Montceau
France          NULL            Paris
Germany         NULL            Berlin
Germany         NULL            Cuxhaven
Germany         NULL            Frankfurt
Italy           NULL            Ravenna
Italy           NULL            Salerno
Japan           NULL            Osaka
Japan           NULL            Tokyo
Netherlands     NULL            Zaandam
Norway          NULL            Sandvika
Singapore       NULL            Singapore
Spain           Asturias        Oviedo
Sweden          NULL            Göteborg
Sweden          NULL            Stockholm
UK              NULL            London
UK              NULL            Manchester
USA             LA              New Orleans
USA             MA              Boston
USA             MI              Ann Arbor
USA             OR              Bend

(38 row(s) affected)
```

Solutions

This section provides solutions to the Chapter 6 exercises.

Exercise 1

The *UNION ALL* operator unifies the two input query result sets and doesn't remove duplicates from the result. The *UNION* operator (implied *DISTINCT*) also unifies the two input query result sets, but it does remove duplicates from the result.

The two have different meanings when the result can potentially have duplicates. They have an equivalent meaning when the result can't have duplicates, such as when you're unifying disjoint sets (for example, sales 2015 with sales 2016).

When they do have the same meaning, you need to use *UNION ALL* by default. That's to avoid paying unnecessary performance penalties for the work involved in removing duplicates when they don't exist.

Exercise 2

T-SQL supports a *SELECT* statement based on constants with no *FROM* clause. Such a *SELECT* statement returns a table with a single row. For example, the following statement returns a row with a single column called *n* with the value *1*:

SELECT 1 AS n;

Here's the output of this statement:

```
n
-----------
1

(1 row(s) affected)
```

By using the *UNION ALL* operator, you can unify the result sets of multiple statements like the one just mentioned, each returning a row with a different number in the range 1 through 10, like the following:

```
SELECT 1 AS n
UNION ALL SELECT 2
UNION ALL SELECT 3
UNION ALL SELECT 4
UNION ALL SELECT 5
UNION ALL SELECT 6
UNION ALL SELECT 7
UNION ALL SELECT 8
UNION ALL SELECT 9
UNION ALL SELECT 10;
```

> **Tip** SQL Server supports an enhanced *VALUES* clause you might be familiar with in the context of the *INSERT* statement. The *VALUES* clause is not restricted to representing a single row; it can represent multiple rows. Also, the *VALUES* clause is not restricted to *INSERT* statements but can be used to define a table expression with rows based on constants.
>
> As an example, here's how you can use the *VALUES* clause to provide a solution to this exercise instead of using the *UNION ALL* operator:
>
> ```
> SELECT n
> FROM (VALUES(1),(2),(3),(4),(5),(6),(7),(8),(9),(10)) AS Nums(n);
> ```
>
> I'll provide details about the *VALUES* clause and such table value constructors in Chapter 8, "Data modification," as part of the discussion of the *INSERT* statement.

Exercise 3

You can solve this exercise by using the *EXCEPT* set operator. The left input is a query that returns customer and employee pairs that had order activity in January 2016. The right input is a query that returns customer and employee pairs that had order activity in February 2016. Here's the solution query:

```
USE TSQLV4;

SELECT custid, empid
FROM Sales.Orders
WHERE orderdate >= '20160101' AND orderdate < '20160201'
```

```
EXCEPT

SELECT custid, empid
FROM Sales.Orders
WHERE orderdate >= '20160201' AND orderdate < '20160301';
```

Exercise 4

Whereas Exercise 2 requested customer and employee pairs that had activity in one period but not another, this exercise concerns customer and employee pairs that had activity in both periods. So this time, instead of using the *EXCEPT* operator, you need to use the *INTERSECT* operator, like this:

```
SELECT custid, empid
FROM Sales.Orders
WHERE orderdate >= '20160101' AND orderdate < '20160201'

INTERSECT

SELECT custid, empid
FROM Sales.Orders
WHERE orderdate >= '20160201' AND orderdate < '20160301';
```

Exercise 5

This exercise requires you to combine set operators. To return customer and employee pairs that had order activity in both January 2016 and February 2016, you need to use the *INTERSECT* operator, as in Exercise 4. To exclude customer and employee pairs that had order activity in 2015 from the result, you need to use the *EXCEPT* operator between the result and a third query. The solution query looks like this:

```
SELECT custid, empid
FROM Sales.Orders
WHERE orderdate >= '20160101' AND orderdate < '20160201'

INTERSECT

SELECT custid, empid
FROM Sales.Orders
WHERE orderdate >= '20160201' AND orderdate < '20160301'

EXCEPT

SELECT custid, empid
FROM Sales.Orders
WHERE orderdate >= '20150101' AND orderdate < '20160101';
```

Keep in mind that the *INTERSECT* operator precedes *EXCEPT*. In this case, the default precedence is also the precedence you want, so you don't need to intervene by using parentheses. But you might prefer to add them for clarity, as shown here:

```
(SELECT custid, empid
 FROM Sales.Orders
 WHERE orderdate >= '20160101' AND orderdate < '20160201'

 INTERSECT

 SELECT custid, empid
 FROM Sales.Orders
 WHERE orderdate >= '20160201' AND orderdate < '20160301')

EXCEPT

SELECT custid, empid
FROM Sales.Orders
WHERE orderdate >= '20150101' AND orderdate < '20160101';
```

Exercise 6

The problem here is that the individual queries are not allowed to have *ORDER BY* clauses, and for a good reason. You can solve the problem by adding a result column based on a constant to each of the queries involved in the operator (call it *sortcol*). In the query against *Employees*, specify a smaller constant than the one you specify in the query against *Suppliers*. Define a table expression based on the query with the operator, and in the *ORDER BY* clause of the outer query, specify *sortcol* as the first sort column, followed by *country*, *region*, and *city*. Here's the complete solution query:

```
SELECT country, region, city
FROM (SELECT 1 AS sortcol, country, region, city
      FROM HR.Employees

      UNION ALL

      SELECT 2, country, region, city
      FROM Production.Suppliers) AS D
ORDER BY sortcol, country, region, city;
```

CHAPTER 7

Beyond the fundamentals of querying

This chapter covers querying topics that go beyond the fundamentals and is provided as optional reading. It starts with the powerful window functions, which you can use to apply data-analysis calculations in a flexible and efficient manner. The chapter continues with techniques for pivoting and unpivoting data. Pivoting rotates data from a state of rows to columns, and unpivoting rotates data from columns to rows, similar to pivot tables in Excel. The chapter finishes with a discussion about *grouping sets*, which are the sets of expressions that you group the data by. It covers techniques for defining multiple grouping sets in the same query.

What's common to the features covered in this chapter, beyond being more advanced than other features in this book, is that they're mostly used for analytical purposes. If you need more details about these features beyond what's covered in this chapter, you can find them in the books: *T-SQL Querying* (Microsoft Press, 2015) and *Microsoft SQL Server 2012 High-Performance T-SQL Using Window Functions* (Microsoft Press, 2012).

Window functions

A *window function* is a function that, for each row, computes a scalar result value based on a calculation against a subset of the rows from the underlying query. The subset of rows is known as a *window* and is based on a window descriptor that relates to the current row. The syntax for window functions uses a clause called *OVER*, in which you provide the window specification.

If this sounds too technical, simply think of the need to perform a calculation against a set and return a single value. A classic example is aggregate calculations—such as *SUM*, *COUNT*, and *AVG*—but there are others as well, such as ranking and offset functions. You're familiar already with a couple of ways to apply aggregate calculations—one is by using grouped queries, and another is by using subqueries. However, both options have shortcomings that window functions elegantly resolve.

> **Note** If the upcoming explanations about the design of window functions seem a bit overwhelming, bear with me until I show code samples, which should help clarify things. After you see a couple of code samples, you might want to reread the next several paragraphs.

Grouped queries do provide insights into new information in the form of aggregates, but they also cause you to lose something—the detail. After you group the rows, all computations in the query have to be done in the context of the defined groups. Often, you need to perform calculations that involve both detail and aggregate elements. Window functions are not limited in the same way. A window function is evaluated per detailed row, and it's applied to a subset of rows that is derived from the underlying query result set. The result of the window function is a scalar value, which is added as another column to the query result. In other words, unlike grouped functions, window functions don't cause you to lose the detail. For example, suppose you want to query order values and return the current order value and the percent it constitutes out of the customer total. If you group by the customer, you can get only the customer total. With a window function, you can return the customer total in addition to the detail order value, and you can even compute the percent of the current order value out of the customer total. I'll demonstrate the code to achieve this later in the chapter.

As for subqueries, you can use them to apply a scalar aggregate calculation against a set, but their starting point is a fresh view of the data rather than the underlying query result set. Suppose the underlying query has table operators, filters, and other query elements; those do not affect what a subquery sees as its starting point. If you need the subquery to apply to the underlying query result set as its starting point, you need to repeat all the underlying query logic in the subquery. In contrast, a window function is applied to a subset of rows from the underlying query's result set—not a fresh view of the data. Therefore, anything you add to the underlying query is automatically applicable to all window functions used in the query. If you want, you can further restrict the window.

Another benefit of using window functions is that you gain the ability to define order, when applicable, as part of the specification of the calculation. This does not conflict with relational aspects of the result. That is, order is defined for the calculation and not confused with presentation ordering. The ordering specification for the window function, if applicable, is different from the ordering specification for presentation. If you don't include a presentation *ORDER BY* clause, you have no assurances that the result will be returned in a particular order. If you do decide to force a certain presentation ordering, the resulting ordering can be different than the ordering for the window function.

Following is an example of a query against the *Sales.EmpOrders* view in the *TSQLV4* database that uses a window aggregate function to compute the running-total values for each employee and month:

```
USE TSQLV4;

SELECT empid, ordermonth, val,
  SUM(val) OVER(PARTITION BY empid
                ORDER BY ordermonth
                ROWS BETWEEN UNBOUNDED PRECEDING
                         AND CURRENT ROW) AS runval
FROM Sales.EmpOrders;
```

Here's the output of this query, shown in abbreviated form:

```
empid  ordermonth  val      runval
------ ----------- -------- ----------
1      2014-07-01  1614.88  1614.88
1      2014-08-01  5555.90  7170.78
1      2014-09-01  6651.00  13821.78
1      2014-10-01  3933.18  17754.96
1      2014-11-01  9562.65  27317.61
...
2      2014-07-01  1176.00  1176.00
2      2014-08-01  1814.00  2990.00
2      2014-09-01  2950.80  5940.80
2      2014-10-01  5164.00  11104.80
2      2014-11-01  4614.58  15719.38
...

(192 row(s) affected)
```

There are up to three parts in the definition of a window function, which you specify in a clause called *OVER*: the window-partition clause, window-order clause, and window-frame clause. An empty *OVER()* clause represents the entire underlying query's result set. Then anything you add to the window specification essentially restricts the window.

The window-partition clause (*PARTITION BY*) restricts the window to the subset of rows that have the same values in the partitioning columns as in the current row. In the last query, the window is partitioned by *empid*. For an underlying row with employee ID 1, the window exposed to the function filters only the rows where the employee ID is 1.

The window-order clause (*ORDER BY*) defines ordering, but don't confuse this with presentation ordering. In a window aggregate function, window ordering supports a frame specification. In a window ranking function, window ordering gives meaning to the rank. In our example, the window ordering is based on *ordermonth*.

A window-frame clause (*ROWS BETWEEN <top delimiter> AND <bottom delimiter>*) filters a frame, or a subset, of rows from the window partition between the two specified delimiters. In this example, the frame is defined with no low boundary point (*UNBOUNDED PRECEDING*) and extends until the current row (*CURRENT ROW*). In addition to the window-frame unit *ROWS*, there's another unit called *RANGE*, but it's implemented in T-SQL in a limited capacity.

Putting all these together, you get the running-total values for each employee and month from the function in the example.

Note that because the starting point of a window function is the underlying query's result set, and the underlying query's result set is generated only when you reach the *SELECT* phase, window functions are allowed only in the *SELECT* and *ORDER BY* clauses of a query. Mostly, you'll use window functions in the *SELECT* clause. If you need to refer to a window function in an earlier logical-query processing phase (such as *WHERE*), you need to use a table expression. You specify the window function in the *SELECT* list of the inner query and assign it with an alias. Then, in the outer query, you can refer to that alias anywhere you like.

The windowing concept can take some getting used to, but when you're comfortable with it, you'll realize it's immensely powerful. Beyond being used for the obvious data-analysis calculations, window functions can be used to perform a variety of tasks, typically more elegantly and more efficiently than with alternative methods.

The following sections cover ranking, offset, and aggregate window functions. Because this book is about fundamentals, I will not get into certain topics here. Those topics include the optimization of window functions, distribution functions, and the *RANGE* window frame unit. For details about those items, see my book on the topic, *Microsoft SQL Server 2012 High-Performance T-SQL Using Window Functions* (Microsoft Press, 2012).

Ranking window functions

You use ranking window functions to rank each row with respect to others in the window. T-SQL supports four ranking functions: *ROW_NUMBER*, *RANK*, *DENSE_RANK*, and *NTILE*. The following query demonstrates the use of these functions:

```
SELECT orderid, custid, val,
  ROW_NUMBER() OVER(ORDER BY val) AS rownum,
  RANK()       OVER(ORDER BY val) AS rank,
  DENSE_RANK() OVER(ORDER BY val) AS dense_rank,
  NTILE(100)   OVER(ORDER BY val) AS ntile
FROM Sales.OrderValues
ORDER BY val;
```

This query generates the following output, shown here in abbreviated form:

```
orderid     custid      val       rownum  rank    dense_rank ntile
----------- ----------- --------- ------- ------- ---------- -----
10782       12          12.50     1       1       1          1
10807       27          18.40     2       2       2          1
10586       66          23.80     3       3       3          1
10767       76          28.00     4       4       4          1
10898       54          30.00     5       5       5          1
10900       88          33.75     6       6       6          1
10883       48          36.00     7       7       7          1
11051       41          36.00     8       7       7          1
10815       71          40.00     9       9       8          1
10674       38          45.00     10      10      9          1
...
10691       63          10164.80  821     821     786        10
10540       63          10191.70  822     822     787        10
10479       65          10495.60  823     823     788        10
10897       37          10835.24  824     824     789        10
10817       39          10952.85  825     825     790        10
10417       73          11188.40  826     826     791        10
10889       65          11380.00  827     827     792        10
11030       71          12615.05  828     828     793        10
10981       34          15810.00  829     829     794        10
10865       63          16387.50  830     830     795        10

(830 row(s) affected)
```

The *ROW_NUMBER* function assigns incremental sequential integers to the rows in the query result based on the mandatory window ordering. In the sample query, the ordering is based on the *val* column; therefore, you can see in the output that when the value increases, the row number increases as well. However, even when the ordering value doesn't increase, the row number still must increase. Therefore, if the *ROW_NUMBER* function's *ORDER BY* list is not unique, as in the preceding example, the query is nondeterministic—that is, more than one correct result is possible. For example, observe that two rows with the value 36.00 got the row numbers 7 and 8. Any arrangement of these row numbers would be considered correct. If you want to make a row number calculation deterministic, you need to add a tiebreaker to the *ORDER BY* list to make it unique. For example, you can add the *orderid* column.

As mentioned, the *ROW_NUMBER* function must produce unique values even when there are ties in the ordering values, making it nondeterministic when there are ties. If you want to produce the same rank value given the same ordering value, use the *RANK* or *DENSE_RANK* function instead. The difference between the two is that *RANK* reflects the count of rows that have a lower ordering value than the current row (plus 1), whereas *DENSE_RANK* reflects the count of distinct ordering values that are lower than the current row (plus 1). For example, in the sample query, a rank of 9 indicates eight rows have lower values. In the same row, a dense rank of 8 indicates seven rows that have distinct lower values.

You use the *NTILE* function to associate the rows in the result with tiles (equally sized groups of rows) by assigning a tile number to each row. You specify the number of tiles you are after and window ordering. The sample query has 830 rows and the request was for 10 tiles; therefore, the tile size is 83 (830 divided by 10). Window ordering is based on the *val* column. This means that the 83 rows with the lowest values are assigned tile number 1, the next 83 are assigned tile number 2, the next 83 are assigned tile number 3, and so on. If the number of rows can't be evenly divided by the number of tiles, an extra row is added to each of the first tiles from the remainder. For example, if 102 rows and five tiles were requested, the first two tiles would have 21 rows instead of 20.

Like all window functions, ranking functions support a window partition clause. Remember that window partitioning restricts the window to only those rows that have the same values in the partitioning attributes as in the current row. For example, the expression *ROW_NUMBER() OVER(PARTITION BY custid ORDER BY val)* assigns row numbers independently for each customer. Here's the expression in a query:

```
SELECT orderid, custid, val,
  ROW_NUMBER() OVER(PARTITION BY custid
                    ORDER BY val) AS rownum
FROM Sales.OrderValues
ORDER BY custid, val;
```

This query generates the following output, shown here in abbreviated form:

```
orderid     custid      val          rownum
----------- ----------- ------------ -------
10702       1           330.00       1
10952       1           471.20       2
10643       1           814.50       3
```

```
10835        1          845.80     4
10692        1          878.00     5
11011        1          933.50     6
10308        2          88.80      1
10759        2          320.00     2
10625        2          479.75     3
10926        2          514.40     4
10682        3          375.50     1
...

(830 row(s) affected)
```

Remember that window ordering has nothing to do with presentation ordering and does not change the nature of the result from being relational. If you need to guarantee presentation ordering, you have to add a presentation *ORDER BY* clause, as I did in the last two.

Window functions are logically evaluated as part of the *SELECT* list, before the *DISTINCT* clause is evaluated. If you're wondering why it matters, I'll explain this with an example. Currently, the *OrderValues* view has 830 rows with 795 distinct values in the *val* column. Consider the following query and its output, shown here in abbreviated form:

```
SELECT DISTINCT val, ROW_NUMBER() OVER(ORDER BY val) AS rownum
FROM Sales.OrderValues;

val        rownum
---------- -------
12.50      1
18.40      2
23.80      3
28.00      4
30.00      5
33.75      6
36.00      7
36.00      8
40.00      9
45.00      10
...
12615.05   828
15810.00   829
16387.50   830

(830 row(s) affected)
```

The *ROW_NUMBER* function is processed before the *DISTINCT* clause. First, unique row numbers are assigned to the 830 rows from the *OrderValues* view. Then the *DISTINCT* clause is processed—but there are no duplicate rows to remove. The *DISTINCT* clause has no effect here. If you want to assign row numbers to the 795 unique values, you need to come up with a different solution. For example, because the *GROUP BY* phase is processed before the *SELECT* phase, you can use the following query:

```
SELECT val, ROW_NUMBER() OVER(ORDER BY val) AS rownum
FROM Sales.OrderValues
GROUP BY val;
```

This query generates the following output, shown here in abbreviated form:

```
val       rownum
--------- -------
12.50     1
18.40     2
23.80     3
28.00     4
30.00     5
33.75     6
36.00     7
40.00     8
45.00     9
48.00     10
...
12615.05  793
15810.00  794
16387.50  795

(795 row(s) affected)
```

Here, the *GROUP BY* phase produces 795 groups for the 795 distinct values, and then the *SELECT* phase produces a row for each group, with *val* and a row number based on *val* order. You'll get to work on an alternative solution in this chapter's exercises.

Offset window functions

You use offset window functions to return an element from a row that is at a certain offset from the current row or at the beginning or end of a window frame. T-SQL supports two pairs of offset functions: *LAG* and *LEAD*, and *FIRST_VALUE* and *LAST_VALUE*.

The *LAG* and *LEAD* functions support window partitions and window order clauses. There's no relevance to window framing here. You use these functions to obtain an element from a row that is at a certain offset from the current row within the partition, based on the indicated ordering. The *LAG* function looks before the current row, and the *LEAD* function looks ahead. The first argument to the functions (which is mandatory) is the element you want to return; the second argument (optional) is the offset (1 if not specified); the third argument (optional) is the default value to return if there is no row at the requested offset (which is *NULL* if not specified otherwise).

As an example, the following query returns order information from the *OrderValues* view. For each customer order, the query uses the *LAG* function to return the value of the previous customer's order and the *LEAD* function to return the value of the next customer's order:

```
SELECT custid, orderid, val,
  LAG(val)  OVER(PARTITION BY custid
                 ORDER BY orderdate, orderid) AS prevval,
  LEAD(val) OVER(PARTITION BY custid
                 ORDER BY orderdate, orderid) AS nextval
FROM Sales.OrderValues
ORDER BY custid, orderdate, orderid;
```

Here's the output of this query in abbreviated form:

```
custid  orderid  val      prevval  nextval
------- -------- -------- -------- --------
1       10643    814.50   NULL     878.00
1       10692    878.00   814.50   330.00
1       10702    330.00   878.00   845.80
1       10835    845.80   330.00   471.20
1       10952    471.20   845.80   933.50
1       11011    933.50   471.20   NULL
2       10308    88.80    NULL     479.75
2       10625    479.75   88.80    320.00
2       10759    320.00   479.75   514.40
2       10926    514.40   320.00   NULL
3       10365    403.20   NULL     749.06
3       10507    749.06   403.20   1940.85
3       10535    1940.85  749.06   2082.00
3       10573    2082.00  1940.85  813.37
3       10677    813.37   2082.00  375.50
3       10682    375.50   813.37   660.00
3       10856    660.00   375.50   NULL
...

(830 row(s) affected)
```

Because you didn't indicate the offset, the functions assumed *1* by default. *LAG* obtained the value of the immediately previous customer's order, and *LEAD* obtained it from the next order. Also, because you didn't specify a third argument, *NULL* was assumed by default when there was no previous or next row. The expression *LAG(val, 3, 0)* obtains the value from three rows back and returns 0 if a row wasn't found.

In this example, I just returned the values from the previous and next orders, but normally you compute something based on the returned values. For example, you can compute the difference between the values of the current and previous customers' orders using *val – LAG(val) OVER(...)*. Or you can compute the difference between the current and next customers' orders using *val – LEAD(val) OVER(...)*.

You use the *FIRST_VALUE* and *LAST_VALUE* functions to return an element from the first and last rows in the window frame, respectively. Therefore, these functions support window-partition, window-order, and window-frame clauses. If you want the element from the first row in the window partition, use *FIRST_VALUE* with the window frame extent *ROWS BETWEEN UNBOUNDED PRECEDING AND CURRENT ROW*. If you want the element from the last row in the window partition, use *LAST_VALUE* with the window frame extent *ROWS BETWEEN CURRENT ROW AND UNBOUNDED FOLLOWING*. Note that if you specify *ORDER BY* without a window-frame unit (such as *ROWS*), the bottom delimiter will by default be *CURRENT ROW*, and clearly that's not what you want with *LAST_VALUE*. Also, for performance-related reasons that are beyond the scope of this book, you should be explicit about the window-frame extent even for *FIRST_VALUE*.

As an example, the following query uses the *FIRST_VALUE* function to return the value of the first customer's order and the *LAST_VALUE* function to return the value of the last customer's order:

```
SELECT custid, orderid, val,
  FIRST_VALUE(val) OVER(PARTITION BY custid
                        ORDER BY orderdate, orderid
                        ROWS BETWEEN UNBOUNDED PRECEDING
                                 AND CURRENT ROW) AS firstval,
  LAST_VALUE(val)  OVER(PARTITION BY custid
                        ORDER BY orderdate, orderid
                        ROWS BETWEEN CURRENT ROW
                                 AND UNBOUNDED FOLLOWING) AS lastval
FROM Sales.OrderValues
ORDER BY custid, orderdate, orderid;
```

This query generates the following output, shown here in abbreviated form:

```
custid  orderid  val      firstval  lastval
------- -------- -------- --------- --------
1       10643    814.50   814.50    933.50
1       10692    878.00   814.50    933.50
1       10702    330.00   814.50    933.50
1       10835    845.80   814.50    933.50
1       10952    471.20   814.50    933.50
1       11011    933.50   814.50    933.50
2       10308    88.80    88.80     514.40
2       10625    479.75   88.80     514.40
2       10759    320.00   88.80     514.40
2       10926    514.40   88.80     514.40
3       10365    403.20   403.20    660.00
3       10507    749.06   403.20    660.00
3       10535    1940.85  403.20    660.00
3       10573    2082.00  403.20    660.00
3       10677    813.37   403.20    660.00
3       10682    375.50   403.20    660.00
3       10856    660.00   403.20    660.00
...

(830 row(s) affected)
```

As with *LAG* and *LEAD*, normally you compute something based on the returned values. For example, you can compute the difference between the current and the first customer's order values: *val – FIRST_VALUE(val) OVER(...)*. Or you can compute the difference between the current and last customer's order values: *val – LAST_VALUE(val) OVER(...)*.

Aggregate window functions

You use aggregate window functions to aggregate the rows in the defined window. They support window-partition, window-order, and window-frame clauses.

I'll start with an example that doesn't involve ordering and framing. Recall that using an *OVER* clause with empty parentheses exposes a window of all rows from the underlying query's result set to the function. For example, *SUM(val) OVER()* returns the grand total of all values. If you do add a window-partition clause, you expose a restricted window to the function, with only those rows from the underlying query's result set that share the same values in the partitioning elements as in the current row. For example, *SUM(val) OVER(PARTITION BY custid)* returns the total values for the current customer.

Here's a query against *OrderValues* that returns, along with each order, the grand total of all order values, as well as the customer total:

```
SELECT orderid, custid, val,
  SUM(val) OVER() AS totalvalue,
  SUM(val) OVER(PARTITION BY custid) AS custtotalvalue
FROM Sales.OrderValues;
```

This query returns the following output, shown here in abbreviated form:

```
orderid     custid      val          totalvalue       custtotalvalue
----------- ----------- ------------ ---------------- ---------------
10643       1           814.50       1265793.22       4273.00
10692       1           878.00       1265793.22       4273.00
10702       1           330.00       1265793.22       4273.00
10835       1           845.80       1265793.22       4273.00
10952       1           471.20       1265793.22       4273.00
11011       1           933.50       1265793.22       4273.00
10926       2           514.40       1265793.22       1402.95
10759       2           320.00       1265793.22       1402.95
10625       2           479.75       1265793.22       1402.95
10308       2           88.80        1265793.22       1402.95
10365       3           403.20       1265793.22       7023.98
...

(830 row(s) affected)
```

The *totalvalue* column shows, for each row, the grand total of all values. The column *custtotalvalue* has the total values for the current customer.

> **Important** As mentioned at the beginning of the chapter, one of the great advantages of window functions is that they don't hide the detail. This means you can write expressions that mix detail and aggregates. The next example demonstrates this.

As an example of mixing detail and aggregates, the following query calculates for each row the percentage of the current value out of the grand total, as well as out of the customer total:

```
SELECT orderid, custid, val,
  100. * val / SUM(val) OVER() AS pctall,
  100. * val / SUM(val) OVER(PARTITION BY custid) AS pctcust
FROM Sales.OrderValues;
```

This query returns the following output, shown here in abbreviated form:

```
orderid      custid val         pctall                         pctcust
------------ ------ ----------- ------------------------------ ------------------------------
10643        1      814.50      0.0643470029014691672941       19.0615492628130119354083
10692        1      878.00      0.0693636200705830925528       20.5476246197051252047741
10702        1      330.00      0.0260706089103558320528       7.7229113035338169904048
```

```
10835        1        845.80        0.0668197606556938265161        19.7940556985724315469225
10952        1        471.20        0.0372256694501808123130        11.0273812309852562602387
11011        1        933.50        0.0737482224782338461253        21.8464778843903580622513
10926        2        514.40        0.0406385491620819394181        36.6655974910011048148544
10759        2        320.00        0.0252805904585268674452        22.8090808653195053280587
10625        2        479.75        0.0379011352264945770526        34.1958017035532271285505
10308        2        88.80         0.0070153638522412057160        6.3295199401261627285362
10365        3        403.20        0.0318535439777438529809        5.7403352515240647040566
...

(830 row(s) affected)
```

Aggregate window functions also support a window frame. The frame allows for more sophisticated calculations, such as running and moving aggregates, YTD and MTD calculations, and others. Let's re-examine the query I used in the introduction to the section about window functions:

```
SELECT empid, ordermonth, val,
  SUM(val) OVER(PARTITION BY empid
                ORDER BY ordermonth
                ROWS BETWEEN UNBOUNDED PRECEDING
                         AND CURRENT ROW) AS runval
FROM Sales.EmpOrders;
```

This query generates the following output (abbreviated):

```
empid  ordermonth  val      runval
------ ----------- -------- ----------
1      2014-07-01  1614.88  1614.88
1      2014-08-01  5555.90  7170.78
1      2014-09-01  6651.00  13821.78
1      2014-10-01  3933.18  17754.96
1      2014-11-01  9562.65  27317.61
...
2      2014-07-01  1176.00  1176.00
2      2014-08-01  1814.00  2990.00
2      2014-09-01  2950.80  5940.80
2      2014-10-01  5164.00  11104.80
2      2014-11-01  4614.58  15719.38
...

(192 row(s) affected)
```

Each row in the *EmpOrders* view holds information about the order activity for an employee and month. The query returns for each employee and month the monthly value, plus the running-total values from the beginning of the employee's activity until the current month. To apply the calculation to each employee independently, you partition the window by *empid*. Then you define ordering based on *ordermonth*, giving meaning to the window frame: *ROWS BETWEEN UNBOUNDED PRECEDING AND CURRENT ROW*. This frame means "all activity from the beginning of the partition until the current month."

T-SQL supports other delimiters for the *ROWS* window-frame unit. You can indicate an offset back from the current row as well as an offset forward. For example, to capture all rows from two rows before the current row until one row ahead, you use *ROWS BETWEEN 2 PRECEDING AND 1 FOLLOWING*. Also, if you do not want an upper bound, you can use *UNBOUNDED FOLLOWING*.

Because window functions are so profound and have so many practical uses, I urge you to invest the time and effort to get to know the concept well.

Pivoting data

Pivoting data involves rotating data from a state of rows to a state of columns, possibly aggregating values along the way. In many cases, the pivoting of data is handled by the presentation layer for purposes such as reporting. This section teaches you how to handle pivoting with T-SQL for cases you do decide to handle in the database.

For the rest of the topics in this chapter, I use a sample table called *dbo.Orders* that you create and populate in the *TSQLV4* database by running Listing 7-1.

LISTING 7-1 Code to create and populate the *dbo.Orders* table

```
USE TSQLV4;

DROP TABLE IF EXISTS dbo.Orders;

CREATE TABLE dbo.Orders
(
  orderid   INT        NOT NULL,
  orderdate DATE       NOT NULL,
  empid     INT        NOT NULL,
  custid    VARCHAR(5) NOT NULL,
  qty       INT        NOT NULL,
  CONSTRAINT PK_Orders PRIMARY KEY(orderid)
);

INSERT INTO dbo.Orders(orderid, orderdate, empid, custid, qty)
VALUES
  (30001, '20140802', 3, 'A', 10),
  (10001, '20141224', 2, 'A', 12),
  (10005, '20141224', 1, 'B', 20),
  (40001, '20150109', 2, 'A', 40),
  (10006, '20150118', 1, 'C', 14),
  (20001, '20150212', 2, 'B', 12),
  (40005, '20160212', 3, 'A', 10),
  (20002, '20160216', 1, 'C', 20),
  (30003, '20160418', 2, 'B', 15),
  (30004, '20140418', 3, 'C', 22),
  (30007, '20160907', 3, 'D', 30);

SELECT * FROM dbo.Orders;
```

The query at the end of Listing 7-1 produces the following output:

```
orderid     orderdate  empid          custid    qty
----------- ---------- -------------- --------- -----------
10001       2014-12-24 2              A         12
10005       2014-12-24 1              B         20
10006       2015-01-18 1              C         14
20001       2015-02-12 2              B         12
20002       2016-02-16 1              C         20
30001       2014-08-02 3              A         10
30003       2016-04-18 2              B         15
30004       2014-04-18 3              C         22
30007       2016-09-07 3              D         30
40001       2015-01-09 2              A         40
40005       2016-02-12 3              A         10
```

Suppose you need to query this table and return the total order quantity for each employee and customer. The following grouped query achieves this task:

```
SELECT empid, custid, SUM(qty) AS sumqty
FROM dbo.Orders
GROUP BY empid, custid;
```

This query generates the following output:

```
empid       custid    sumqty
----------- --------- -----------
2           A         52
3           A         20
1           B         20
2           B         27
1           C         34
3           C         22
3           D         30
```

Suppose, however, you have a requirement to produce the output in the form shown in Table 7-1.

TABLE 7-1 Pivoted view of total quantity per employee (on rows) and customer (on columns)

empid	A	B	C	D
1	NULL	20	34	NULL
2	52	27	NULL	NULL
3	20	NULL	22	30

What you see in Table 7-1 is an aggregated and pivoted view of the data; the technique for generating this view is called *pivoting*.

Every pivoting request involves three logical processing phases, each with associated elements:

1. A grouping phase with an associated grouping or *on rows* element
2. A spreading phase with an associated spreading or *on cols* element
3. An aggregation phase with an associated aggregation element and aggregate function

In this example, you need to produce a single row in the result for each unique employee ID. This means the rows from the *dbo.Orders* table need to be grouped by the *empid* attribute (the grouping element).

The *dbo.Orders* table has a single column that holds all customer ID values and a single column that holds their ordered quantities. The pivoting task requires you to produce a different result column for each unique customer ID, holding the aggregated quantities for that customer. You can think of this process as "spreading" the quantities by customer ID. The spreading element in this case is the *custid* attribute.

Finally, because pivoting involves grouping, you need to aggregate data to produce the result values in the "intersection" of the grouping (employee) and spreading (customer) elements. You need to identify the aggregate function (*SUM*, in this case) and the aggregation element (the *qty* attribute, in this case).

To recap, pivoting involves grouping, spreading, and aggregating. In this example, you group by *empid*, spread (quantities) by *custid*, and aggregate with *SUM(qty)*. After you identify the elements involved in pivoting, the rest is just a matter of incorporating those elements in the right places in a generic query template for pivoting.

This chapter presents two solutions for pivoting—one based on an explicit grouped query and another with a table operator called *PIVOT*.

Pivoting with a grouped query

The solution using a grouped query handles all three phases in an explicit and straightforward manner.

The grouping phase is achieved with a *GROUP BY* clause—in this case, *GROUP BY empid*.

The spreading phase is achieved in the *SELECT* clause with a *CASE* expression for each target column. You need to know the spreading element values ahead of time and specify a separate expression for each. Because in this case you need to "spread" the quantities of four customers (A, B, C, and D), there are four *CASE* expressions. For example, here's the *CASE* expression for customer A:

```
CASE WHEN custid = 'A' THEN qty END
```

This expression returns the quantity from the current row only when the current row represents an order for customer A; otherwise, the expression returns a *NULL*. Remember that if an *ELSE* clause is not specified in a *CASE* expression, the implied default is *ELSE NULL*. This means that in the target column for customer A, only quantities associated with customer A appear as column values, and in all other cases the column values are *NULL*.

If you don't know the spreading values ahead of time (the distinct customer IDs in this case), you need to query them from the data, construct the query string yourself by using an aggregate string concatenation method, and use dynamic SQL to execute it. I'll demonstrate how to achieve this in Chapter 11, "Programmable objects."

Finally, the aggregation phase is achieved by applying the relevant aggregate function (*SUM*, in this case) to the result of each *CASE* expression. For example, here's the expression that produces the result column for customer A:

```
SUM(CASE WHEN custid = 'A' THEN qty END) AS A
```

Of course, depending on the request, you might need to use another aggregate function (such as *MAX*, *MIN*, or *COUNT*).

Here's the complete solution query that pivots order data, returning the total quantity for each employee (on rows) and customer (on columns):

```
SELECT empid,
  SUM(CASE WHEN custid = 'A' THEN qty END) AS A,
  SUM(CASE WHEN custid = 'B' THEN qty END) AS B,
  SUM(CASE WHEN custid = 'C' THEN qty END) AS C,
  SUM(CASE WHEN custid = 'D' THEN qty END) AS D
FROM dbo.Orders
GROUP BY empid;
```

This query produces the output shown earlier in Table 7-1. SQL Server also generates the following warning in the Messages pane of SSMS:

```
Warning: Null value is eliminated by an aggregate or other SET operation.
```

The warning notifies you that *NULLs* are ignored by an aggregate function, as we discussed earlier.

Pivoting with the *PIVOT* operator

The solution for pivoting based on an explicit grouped query is standard. T-SQL also supports a proprietary table operator called *PIVOT* that you can use to achieve pivoting in a more concise manner. As a table operator, *PIVOT* operates in the context of the *FROM* clause like any other table operator (for example, *JOIN*). It operates on the source table or table expression provided to it as its left input, pivots the data, and returns a result table. The *PIVOT* operator involves the same logical processing phases as described earlier (grouping, spreading, and aggregating), only it requires less code than the previous solution.

The general form of a query with the *PIVOT* operator is shown here:

```
SELECT ...
FROM <input_table>
  PIVOT(<agg_function>(<aggregation_element>)
          FOR <spreading_element> IN (<list_of_target_columns>)) AS <result_table_alias>
WHERE ...;
```

In the parentheses of the *PIVOT* operator, you specify the aggregate function (*SUM*, in this example), aggregation element (*qty*), spreading element (*custid*), and the list of target column names (*A, B, C, D*). Following the parentheses of the *PIVOT* operator, you specify an alias for the result table.

Note that with the *PIVOT* operator, you do not explicitly specify the grouping elements, removing the need for *GROUP BY* in the query. The *PIVOT* operator figures out the grouping elements implicitly by elimination. The grouping elements are all attributes from the source table that were not specified as either the spreading element or the aggregation element. You must ensure that the source table for the *PIVOT* operator has no attributes other than the grouping, spreading, and aggregation elements so that the implied selection of the grouping elements will be what you want. You achieve this by using a table expression that includes only the attributes you need as the input of the operator. For example, here's the solution query to the original pivoting request, using the *PIVOT* operator:

```
SELECT empid, A, B, C, D
FROM (SELECT empid, custid, qty
      FROM dbo.Orders) AS D
  PIVOT(SUM(qty) FOR custid IN(A, B, C, D)) AS P;
```

Instead of operating directly on the *dbo.Orders* table, the *PIVOT* operator operates on a derived table called *D* that includes only the pivoting elements *empid, custid,* and *qty.* When you account for the spreading element, which is *custid,* and the aggregation element, which is *qty,* what's left is the implied grouping element *empid.*

This query returns the output shown earlier in Table 7-1.

To understand why you're required to use a table expression here, consider the following query that applies the *PIVOT* operator directly to the *dbo.Orders* table:

```
SELECT empid, A, B, C, D
FROM dbo.Orders
  PIVOT(SUM(qty) FOR custid IN(A, B, C, D)) AS P;
```

The *dbo.Orders* table contains the attributes *orderid, orderdate, empid, custid,* and *qty.* Because the query specifies *custid* as the spreading element and *qty* as the aggregation element, the remaining attributes (*orderid, orderdate,* and *empid*) are all considered the grouping elements. This query, therefore, returns the following output:

```
empid       A           B           C           D
----------- ----------- ----------- ----------- -----------
2           12          NULL        NULL        NULL
1           NULL        20          NULL        NULL
1           NULL        NULL        14          NULL
2           NULL        12          NULL        NULL
1           NULL        NULL        20          NULL
3           10          NULL        NULL        NULL
2           NULL        15          NULL        NULL
3           NULL        NULL        22          NULL
3           NULL        NULL        NULL        30
2           40          NULL        NULL        NULL
3           10          NULL        NULL        NULL

(11 row(s) affected)
```

Because *orderid* is part of the grouping elements, you get a row for each order instead of a row for each employee. The logical equivalent of this query that uses the standard solution for pivoting has *orderid, orderdate,* and *empid* listed in the *GROUP BY* list as follows:

```
SELECT empid,
  SUM(CASE WHEN custid = 'A' THEN qty END) AS A,
  SUM(CASE WHEN custid = 'B' THEN qty END) AS B,
  SUM(CASE WHEN custid = 'C' THEN qty END) AS C,
  SUM(CASE WHEN custid = 'D' THEN qty END) AS D
FROM dbo.Orders
GROUP BY orderid, orderdate, empid;
```

As a best practice with the *PIVOT* operator, you should always work with a table expression and not query the underlying table directly. Even if currently the table contains only the columns that are supposed to take part in pivoting, you might add columns to the table in the future, rendering your queries incorrect. It is also important to enumerate the columns both in the table expression's inner query and in the outer query.

As another example of a pivoting request, suppose that instead of returning employees on rows and customers on columns, you want it the other way around: the grouping element is *custid,* the spreading element is *empid,* and the aggregation element and aggregate function remain *SUM(qty).* After you learn the "template" for a pivoting solution (with the grouped query or with the *PIVOT* operator), it's just a matter of fitting those elements in the right places. The following solution query uses the *PIVOT* operator to achieve the result:

```
SELECT custid, [1], [2], [3]
FROM (SELECT empid, custid, qty
      FROM dbo.Orders) AS D
  PIVOT(SUM(qty) FOR empid IN([1], [2], [3])) AS P;
```

The employee IDs 1, 2, and 3 are values in the *empid* column in the source table, but in terms of the result, these values become target column names. You must refer to them as identifiers in the *IN* clause. When identifiers are irregular (for example, when they start with a digit), you need to delimit them—hence, the use of square brackets.

This query returns the following output:

```
custid    1           2           3
--------- ----------- ----------- -----------
A         NULL        52          20
B         20          27          NULL
C         34          NULL        22
D         NULL        NULL        30
```

Unpivoting data

Unpivoting is a technique that rotates data from a state of columns to a state of rows. Usually, it involves querying a pivoted state of the data and producing from each source row multiple result rows, each with a different source column value. A common use case is to unpivot data you imported from a spreadsheet into the database for easier manipulation.

Run the following code to create and populate a table called *EmpCustOrders* in the *TSQLV4* sample database. I'll use this table to demonstrate unpivoting techniques:

```
USE TSQLV4;

DROP TABLE IF EXISTS dbo.EmpCustOrders;

CREATE TABLE dbo.EmpCustOrders
(
  empid INT NOT NULL
    CONSTRAINT PK_EmpCustOrders PRIMARY KEY,
  A VARCHAR(5) NULL,
  B VARCHAR(5) NULL,
  C VARCHAR(5) NULL,
  D VARCHAR(5) NULL
);

INSERT INTO dbo.EmpCustOrders(empid, A, B, C, D)
  SELECT empid, A, B, C, D
  FROM (SELECT empid, custid, qty
        FROM dbo.Orders) AS D
    PIVOT(SUM(qty) FOR custid IN(A, B, C, D)) AS P;

SELECT * FROM dbo.EmpCustOrders;
```

Here's the output of the query against *EmpCustOrders* showing its contents:

```
empid       A           B           C           D
----------- ----------- ----------- ----------- -----------
1           NULL        20          34          NULL
2           52          27          NULL        NULL
3           20          NULL        22          30
```

The table has a row for each employee; a column for each of the four customers *A, B, C,* and *D;* and the order quantity for each employee and customer. Notice that irrelevant intersections (employee-customer combinations that had no intersecting order activity) are represented by *NULLs.* Suppose you get a request to unpivot the data, requiring you to return a row for each employee and customer, along with the order quantity. The result should look like this:

```
empid       custid    qty
----------- --------- -----------
1           B         20
1           C         34
2           A         52
2           B         27
```

```
3           A           20
3           C           22
3           D           30
```

In the following sections, I'll discuss two techniques for solving this problem—one using the *APPLY* operator and another using the *UNPIVOT* operator.

Unpivoting with the *APPLY* operator

Unpivoting involves three logical processing phases: producing copies, extracting values, and eliminating irrelevant rows.

The first step in the solution involves producing multiple copies of each source row—one for each column you need to unpivot. In this case, you need to produce a copy for each of the columns *A, B, C,* and *D,* which represent customer IDs. You can achieve this step by applying a cross join between the *EmpCustOrders* table and a table that has a row for each customer.

If you already have a table of customers in your database, you can use that table in the cross join. If you don't have a table of customers, you can build a virtual one on the fly using a table-value constructor based on the *VALUES* clause. Here's the code that implements this step:

```
SELECT *
FROM dbo.EmpCustOrders
  CROSS JOIN (VALUES('A'),('B'),('C'),('D')) AS C(custid);
```

The *VALUES* clause defines a set of four rows, each with a single customer ID value. The code defines a derived table called *C* based on this clause and names the only column in it *custid.* The code then applies a cross join between *EmpCustOrders* and *C.*

> **Note** If you're not familiar yet with the *VALUES* clause, it's described in detail in Chapter 8, "Data modification."

In this example, the query that implements the first step in the solution returns the following output:

```
empid       A           B           C           D           custid
----------- ----------- ----------- ----------- ----------- ------
1           NULL        20          34          NULL        A
1           NULL        20          34          NULL        B
1           NULL        20          34          NULL        C
1           NULL        20          34          NULL        D
2           52          27          NULL        NULL        A
2           52          27          NULL        NULL        B
2           52          27          NULL        NULL        C
2           52          27          NULL        NULL        D
3           20          NULL        22          30          A
3           20          NULL        22          30          B
3           20          NULL        22          30          C
3           20          NULL        22          30          D
```

As you can see, four copies were produced for each source row—one each for customers *A, B, C,* and *D.*

The second step in the solution is to extract a value from one of the original customer quantity columns (*A*, *B*, *C*, or *D*) to return a single value column (call it *qty* in our case). You need to extract the value from the column that corresponds to the current *custid* value. If *custid* is *'A'*, the *qty* column should return the value from column *A*, if *custid* is *'B'*, *qty* should return the value from column *B*, and so on. To achieve this step, you might think you can simply add the *qty* column as a second column to each row in the table value constructor (the *VALUES* clause), like this:

```
SELECT empid, custid, qty
FROM dbo.EmpCustOrders
  CROSS JOIN (VALUES('A', A),('B', B),('C', C),('D', D)) AS C(custid, qty);
```

However, remember that a join treats its two inputs as a set; hence, there's no order between those inputs. You can't refer to the elements of either of the inputs when constructing the other. In our case, the table-value constructor on the right side of the join has references to the columns *A*, *B*, *C*, and *D* from the left side of the join (*EmpCustOrders*). Consequently, when you try to run this code, you get the following errors:

```
Msg 207, Level 16, State 1, Line 222
Invalid column name 'A'.
Msg 207, Level 16, State 1, Line 222
Invalid column name 'B'.
Msg 207, Level 16, State 1, Line 222
Invalid column name 'C'.
Msg 207, Level 16, State 1, Line 222
Invalid column name 'D'.
```

The solution is to use the *CROSS APPLY* operator instead of the *CROSS JOIN* operator. They are similar, but the former evaluates the left side first and then applies the right side to each left row, making the left side's elements accessible to the right side. Here's the code implementing this step with the *CROSS APPLY* operator:

```
SELECT empid, custid, qty
FROM dbo.EmpCustOrders
  CROSS APPLY (VALUES('A', A),('B', B),('C', C),('D', D)) AS C(custid, qty);
```

This query runs successfully, returning the following output:

```
empid       custid    qty
----------- --------- -----------
1           A         NULL
1           B         20
1           C         34
1           D         NULL
2           A         52
2           B         27
2           C         NULL
2           D         NULL
3           A         20
3           B         NULL
3           C         22
3           D         30
```

Recall that in the original table *NULLs* represent irrelevant intersections. In the result, there's typically no reason to keep irrelevant rows where *qty* is *NULL*. The nice thing in our case is that the *CROSS APPLY* operator, which created the column *qty*, was processed in the *FROM* clause, and the *FROM* clause is evaluated before the *WHERE* clause. This means that the *qty* column is accessible to expressions in the *WHERE* clause. To remove irrelevant rows, add a filter in the *WHERE* clause that discards rows with a *NULL* in the *qty* column, like this:

```
SELECT empid, custid, qty
FROM dbo.EmpCustOrders
  CROSS APPLY (VALUES('A', A),('B', B),('C', C),('D', D)) AS C(custid, qty)
WHERE qty IS NOT NULL;
```

This query returns the following output:

```
empid      custid    qty
---------- --------- -----------
1          B         20
1          C         34
2          A         52
2          B         27
3          A         20
3          C         22
3          D         30
```

Unpivoting with the *UNPIVOT* operator

Unpivoting data involves producing two result columns from any number of source columns—one to hold the source column names as strings and another to hold the source column values. In this example, you need to unpivot the source columns *A, B, C,* and *D,* producing the result names column *custid* and values column *qty*. Similar to the *PIVOT* operator, T-SQL also supports the *UNPIVOT* operator to enable you to unpivot data. The general form of a query with the *UNPIVOT* operator is as follows:

```
SELECT ...
FROM <input_table>
  UNPIVOT(<values_column> FOR <names_column> IN(<source_columns>)) AS <result_table_alias>
WHERE ...;
```

Like the *PIVOT* operator, *UNPIVOT* was also implemented as a table operator in the context of the *FROM* clause. It operates on a source table or table expression (*EmpCustOrders* in this case). Within the parentheses of the *UNPIVOT* operator, you specify the name you want to assign to the column that will hold the source-column values (*qty* here), the name you want to assign to the column that will hold the source-column names (*custid*), and the list of source-column names (*A, B, C,* and *D*). Following the parentheses, you provide an alias to the table resulting from the table operator.

Here's the query that uses the *UNPIVOT* operator to handle our unpivoting task:

```
SELECT empid, custid, qty
FROM dbo.EmpCustOrders
  UNPIVOT(qty FOR custid IN(A, B, C, D)) AS U;
```

Note that the *UNPIVOT* operator implements the same logical-processing phases described earlier—generating copies, extracting elements, and eliminating *NULL* intersections. However, the last phase is not optional as in the solution with the *APPLY* operator. When you need to apply the third phase, it's convenient to use the solution with the *UNPIVOT* operator because it's more concise. When you need to keep the rows with the *NULLs*, use the solution with the *APPLY* operator.

When you're done, run the following code for cleanup:

```
DROP TABLE IF EXISTS dbo.EmpCustOrders;
```

Grouping sets

This section describes what a grouping set is and the features in T-SQL that support grouping sets.

A *grouping set* is a set of expressions you group the data by in a grouped query (a query with a *GROUP BY* clause). The reason for using the term "set" here is that there's no significance to the order in which you specify the expressions in the *GROUP BY* clause. Traditionally in SQL, a single grouped query defines a single grouping set. For example, each of the following four queries defines a single grouping set:

```
SELECT empid, custid, SUM(qty) AS sumqty
FROM dbo.Orders
GROUP BY empid, custid;

SELECT empid, SUM(qty) AS sumqty
FROM dbo.Orders
GROUP BY empid;

SELECT custid, SUM(qty) AS sumqty
FROM dbo.Orders
GROUP BY custid;

SELECT SUM(qty) AS sumqty
FROM dbo.Orders;
```

The first query defines the grouping set *(empid, custid)*; the second *(empid)*, the third *(custid)*, and the last query defines what's known as the empty grouping set, *()*. This code returns four result sets—one for each of the four queries.

Suppose, for reporting purposes, that instead of wanting four separate result sets returned, you want a single unified result set. You can achieve this by using the *UNION ALL* operator between the queries, after planting *NULLs* as placeholders for columns that appear in one query but not others. Here's what the code looks like:

```
SELECT empid, custid, SUM(qty) AS sumqty
FROM dbo.Orders
GROUP BY empid, custid

UNION ALL
```

```
SELECT empid, NULL, SUM(qty) AS sumqty
FROM dbo.Orders
GROUP BY empid

UNION ALL

SELECT NULL, custid, SUM(qty) AS sumqty
FROM dbo.Orders
GROUP BY custid

UNION ALL

SELECT NULL, NULL, SUM(qty) AS sumqty
FROM dbo.Orders;
```

This code generates a single result set with the aggregates for all four groupings:

```
empid       custid    sumqty
----------- --------- -----------
2           A         52
3           A         20
1           B         20
2           B         27
1           C         34
3           C         22
3           D         30
1           NULL      54
2           NULL      79
3           NULL      72
NULL        A         72
NULL        B         47
NULL        C         56
NULL        D         30
NULL        NULL      205

(15 row(s) affected)
```

Even though you managed to get what you were after, this solution has two main problems—the length of the code and performance. It's long because you have a separate query for each grouping set. Also, SQL Server needs to apply a separate scanning of the data for each query.

T-SQL supports standard features you can use to define multiple grouping sets in the same query. Those are the *GROUPING SETS*, *CUBE*, and *ROLLUP* subclauses of the *GROUP BY* clause, and the *GROUPING* and *GROUPING_ID* functions. The main use cases are reporting and data analysis. These features usually need the presentation layer to use more sophisticated GUI controls to display the data than the typical grid control with its columns and rows. But this book's focus is the T-SQL code in the database and not the presentation layer.

The *GROUPING SETS* subclause

The *GROUPING SETS* subclause is a powerful enhancement to the *GROUP BY* clause. You can use it to define multiple grouping sets in the same query. Simply list the grouping sets you want, separated by commas within the parentheses of the *GROUPING SETS* subclause, and for each grouping set list the members, separated by commas, within parentheses. For example, the following query defines four grouping sets: *(empid, custid)*, *(empid)*, *(custid)*, and *()*:

```
SELECT empid, custid, SUM(qty) AS sumqty
FROM dbo.Orders
GROUP BY
  GROUPING SETS
  (
    (empid, custid),
    (empid),
    (custid),
    ()
  );
```

The last grouping set is the empty grouping set representing the grand total. This query is a logical equivalent of the previous solution that unified the result sets of four aggregate queries. Only this one is much shorter, plus it gets optimized better. SQL Server typically needs fewer scans of the data than the number of grouping sets because it can roll up aggregates internally.

The *CUBE* subclause

The *CUBE* subclause of the *GROUP BY* clause provides an abbreviated way to define multiple grouping sets. In the parentheses of the *CUBE* subclause, you provide a set of members separated by commas, and you get all possible grouping sets that can be defined based on the input members. For example, *CUBE(a, b, c)* is equivalent to *GROUPING SETS((a, b, c), (a, b), (a, c), (b, c), (a), (b), (c), ())*. In set theory, the set of all subsets of elements that can be produced from a particular set is called the *power set*. You can think of the *CUBE* subclause as producing the power set of grouping sets that can be formed from the given set of elements.

Instead of using the *GROUPING SETS* subclause in the previous query to define the four grouping sets *(empid, custid)*, *(empid)*, *(custid)*, and *()*, you can simply use *CUBE(empid, custid)*. Here's the complete query:

```
SELECT empid, custid, SUM(qty) AS sumqty
FROM dbo.Orders
GROUP BY CUBE(empid, custid);
```

The *ROLLUP* subclause

The *ROLLUP* subclause of the *GROUP BY* clause also provides an abbreviated way to define multiple grouping sets. However, unlike the *CUBE* subclause, *ROLLUP* doesn't produce all possible grouping sets. *ROLLUP* assumes a hierarchy among the input members and produces only grouping sets that form leading combinations of the input members. For example, whereas *CUBE(a, b, c)* produces all eight possible grouping sets, *ROLLUP(a, b, c)* produces only four based on the hierarchy a>b>c. It is the equivalent of specifying *GROUPING SETS((a, b, c), (a, b), (a), ())*.

For example, suppose you want to return total quantities for all grouping sets that can be defined based on the time hierarchy of *order year, order month, order day*. You can use the *GROUPING SETS* subclause and explicitly list all four possible grouping sets:

```
GROUPING SETS(
  (YEAR(orderdate), MONTH(orderdate), DAY(orderdate)),
  (YEAR(orderdate), MONTH(orderdate)),
  (YEAR(orderdate)),
  () )
```

The logical equivalent that uses the *ROLLUP* subclause is much more concise:

```
ROLLUP(YEAR(orderdate), MONTH(orderdate), DAY(orderdate))
```

Here's the complete query you need to run:

```
SELECT
  YEAR(orderdate) AS orderyear,
  MONTH(orderdate) AS ordermonth,
  DAY(orderdate) AS orderday,
  SUM(qty) AS sumqty
FROM dbo.Orders
GROUP BY ROLLUP(YEAR(orderdate), MONTH(orderdate), DAY(orderdate));
```

This query produces the following output:

```
orderyear   ordermonth     orderday    sumqty
----------- -------------- ----------- -----------
2014        4              18          22
2014        4              NULL        22
2014        8              2           10
2014        8              NULL        10
2014        12             24          32
2014        12             NULL        32
2014        NULL           NULL        64
2015        1              9           40
2015        1              18          14
2015        1              NULL        54
2015        2              12          12
2015        2              NULL        12
2015        NULL           NULL        66
2016        2              12          10
2016        2              16          20
2016        2              NULL        30
2016        4              18          15
2016        4              NULL        15
2016        9              7           30
2016        9              NULL        30
2016        NULL           NULL        75
NULL        NULL           NULL        205
```

The *GROUPING* and *GROUPING_ID* functions

When you have a single query that defines multiple grouping sets, you might need to associate result rows and grouping sets. As long as all grouping elements are defined as *NOT NULL*, this is easy. For example, consider the following query:

```
SELECT empid, custid, SUM(qty) AS sumqty
FROM dbo.Orders
GROUP BY CUBE(empid, custid);
```

This query produces the following output:

```
empid       custid    sumqty
----------- --------- -----------
2           A         52
3           A         20
NULL        A         72
1           B         20
2           B         27
NULL        B         47
1           C         34
3           C         22
NULL        C         56
3           D         30
NULL        D         30
NULL        NULL      205
1           NULL      54
2           NULL      79
3           NULL      72
```

Because both the *empid* and *custid* columns were defined in the *dbo.Orders* table as *NOT NULL*, a *NULL* in those columns can only represent a placeholder, indicating that the column did not participate in the current grouping set. For example, all rows in which *empid* is not *NULL* and *custid* is not *NULL* are associated with the grouping set *(empid, custid)*. All rows in which *empid* is not *NULL* and *custid* is *NULL* are associated with the grouping set *(empid)*, and so on.

However, if a grouping column allows *NULLs* in the table, you cannot tell for sure whether a *NULL* in the result set originated from the data or is a placeholder for a nonparticipating member in a grouping set. One way to solve this problem is to use the *GROUPING* function. This function accepts a name of a column and returns *0* if it is a member of the current grouping set (a detail element) and *1* otherwise (an aggregate element).

> **Note** I find it counterintuitive that the *GROUPING* function returns *1* when the element isn't part of the grouping set and *0* when it is. To me, it would make more sense to return *1* when the element is part of the grouping set and *0* otherwise. The current perspective is to use *1* to indicate the element is an aggregate element and *0* when it's a detail element. You just need to make sure you realize this fact.

For example, the following query invokes the *GROUPING* function for each of the grouping elements:

```
SELECT
  GROUPING(empid) AS grpemp,
  GROUPING(custid) AS grpcust,
  empid, custid, SUM(qty) AS sumqty
FROM dbo.Orders
GROUP BY CUBE(empid, custid);
```

This query returns the following output:

```
grpemp    grpcust    empid      custid    sumqty
--------- ---------- ---------- --------- ----------
0         0          2          A         52
0         0          3          A         20
1         0          NULL       A         72
0         0          1          B         20
0         0          2          B         27
1         0          NULL       B         47
0         0          1          C         34
0         0          3          C         22
1         0          NULL       C         56
0         0          3          D         30
1         0          NULL       D         30
1         1          NULL       NULL      205
0         1          1          NULL      54
0         1          2          NULL      79
0         1          3          NULL      72

(15 row(s) affected)
```

Now you don't need to rely on the *NULLs* anymore to figure out the association between result rows and grouping sets. For example, all rows in which *grpemp* is *0* and *grpcust* is *0* are associated with the grouping set *(empid, custid)*. All rows in which *grpemp* is *0* and *grpcust* is *1* are associated with the grouping set *(empid)*, and so on.

T-SQL supports another function, called *GROUPING_ID*, that can further simplify the process of associating result rows and grouping sets. You provide the function with all elements that participate in any grouping set as inputs—for example, *GROUPING_ID(a, b, c, d)*—and the function returns an integer bitmap in which each bit represents a different input element—the rightmost element represented by the rightmost bit. For example, the grouping set *(a, b, c, d)* is represented by the integer 0 (0×8 + 0×4 + 0×2 + 0×1). The grouping set *(a, c)* is represented by the integer 5 (0×8 + 1×4 + 0×2 + 1×1), and so on.

Instead of calling the *GROUPING* function for each grouping element as in the previous query, you can call the *GROUPING_ID* function once and provide it with all grouping elements as input, as shown here:

```
SELECT
  GROUPING_ID(empid, custid) AS groupingset,
  empid, custid, SUM(qty) AS sumqty
```

```
FROM dbo.Orders
GROUP BY CUBE(empid, custid);
```

This query produces the following output:

```
groupingset   empid       custid    sumqty
------------- ----------- --------- -----------
0             2           A         52
0             3           A         20
2             NULL        A         72
0             1           B         20
0             2           B         27
2             NULL        B         47
0             1           C         34
0             3           C         22
2             NULL        C         56
0             3           D         30
2             NULL        D         30
3             NULL        NULL      205
1             1           NULL      54
1             2           NULL      79
1             3           NULL      72
```

Now you can easily figure out which grouping set each row is associated with. The integer *0* (binary 00) represents the grouping set *(empid, custid)*; the integer *1* (binary 01) represents *(empid)*; the integer *2* (binary 10) represents *(custid)*; and the integer *3* (binary 11) represents *()*.

Conclusion

This chapter covered window functions, pivoting and unpivoting data, and features related to grouping sets.

You use window functions to perform data-analysis calculations in a more flexible and efficient manner than you can when using alternative methods. Window functions have numerous practical uses, so it's worth your time to get to know them well.

I covered two techniques to handle pivoting: one using a standard grouped query and another using the more concise yet proprietary *PIVOT* operator. I also covered two methods to handle unpivoting: one using the *APPLY* operator, which allows you to control whether to remove rows with *NULLs*, and another using the *UNPIVOT* operator, which is more concise but removes rows with *NULLs* as a mandatory step.

T-SQL supports features that make the handling of grouping sets flexible and efficient: the *GROUPING SETS*, *CUBE*, and *ROLLUP* subclauses and the *GROUPING* and *GROUPING_ID* functions.

Exercises

This section provides exercises to help you familiarize yourself with the subjects discussed in Chapter 7. All exercises for this chapter involve querying the *dbo.Orders* table in the *TSQLV4* database that you created and populated earlier in this chapter by running the code in Listing 7-1.

Exercise 1

Write a query against the *dbo.Orders* table that computes both a rank and a dense rank for each customer order, partitioned by *custid* and ordered by *qty*:

- Table involved: *TSQLV4* database, *dbo.Orders* table
- Desired output:

```
custid orderid     qty         rnk                  drnk
------ ----------- ----------- -------------------- --------------------
A      30001       10          1                    1
A      40005       10          1                    1
A      10001       12          3                    2
A      40001       40          4                    3
B      20001       12          1                    1
B      30003       15          2                    2
B      10005       20          3                    3
C      10006       14          1                    1
C      20002       20          2                    2
C      30004       22          3                    3
D      30007       30          1                    1
```

Exercise 2

Earlier in the chapter in the section "Ranking window functions," I provided the following query against the *Sales.OrderValues* view to return distinct values and their associated row numbers:

```
SELECT val, ROW_NUMBER() OVER(ORDER BY val) AS rownum
FROM Sales.OrderValues
GROUP BY val;
```

Can you think of an alternative way to achieve the same task?

- Table involved: *TSQLV4* database, *Sales.OrderValues* view
- Desired output:

```
val       rownum
--------- -------
12.50     1
18.40     2
23.80     3
28.00     4
30.00     5
33.75     6
```

```
36.00      7
40.00      8
45.00      9
48.00      10
...
12615.05   793
15810.00   794
16387.50   795

(795 row(s) affected)
```

Exercise 3

Write a query against the *dbo.Orders* table that computes for each customer order both the difference between the current order quantity and the customer's previous order quantity *and* the difference between the current order quantity and the customer's next order quantity:

- Table involved: *TSQLV4* database, *dbo.Orders* table
- Desired output:

```
custid orderid     qty         diffprev    diffnext
------ ----------- ----------- ----------- -----------
A      30001       10          NULL        -2
A      10001       12          2           -28
A      40001       40          28          30
A      40005       10          -30         NULL
B      10005       20          NULL        8
B      20001       12          -8          -3
B      30003       15          3           NULL
C      30004       22          NULL        8
C      10006       14          -8          -6
C      20002       20          6           NULL
D      30007       30          NULL        NULL
```

Exercise 4

Write a query against the *dbo.Orders* table that returns a row for each employee, a column for each order year, and the count of orders for each employee and order year:

- Table involved: *TSQLV4* database, *dbo.Orders* table
- Desired output:

```
empid       cnt2014     cnt2015     cnt2016
----------- ----------- ----------- -----------
1           1           1           1
2           1           2           1
3           2           0           2
```

Exercise 5

Run the following code to create and populate the *EmpYearOrders* table:

```
USE TSQLV4;

DROP TABLE IF EXISTS dbo.EmpYearOrders;

CREATE TABLE dbo.EmpYearOrders
(
  empid INT NOT NULL
    CONSTRAINT PK_EmpYearOrders PRIMARY KEY,
  cnt2014 INT NULL,
  cnt2015 INT NULL,
  cnt2016 INT NULL
);

INSERT INTO dbo.EmpYearOrders(empid, cnt2014, cnt2015, cnt2016)
  SELECT empid, [2014] AS cnt2014, [2015] AS cnt2015, [2016] AS cnt2016
  FROM (SELECT empid, YEAR(orderdate) AS orderyear
        FROM dbo.Orders) AS D
    PIVOT(COUNT(orderyear)
          FOR orderyear IN([2014], [2015], [2016])) AS P;

SELECT * FROM dbo.EmpYearOrders;
```

Here's the output for the query:

```
empid       cnt2014     cnt2015     cnt2016
----------- ----------- ----------- -----------
1           1           1           1
2           1           2           1
3           2           0           2
```

Write a query against the *EmpYearOrders* table that unpivots the data, returning a row for each employee and order year with the number of orders. Exclude rows in which the number of orders is 0 (in this example, employee 3 in the year 2015).

- Desired output:

```
empid       orderyear   numorders
----------- ----------- -----------
1           2014        1
1           2015        1
1           2016        1
2           2014        1
2           2015        2
2           2016        1
3           2014        2
3           2016        2
```

Exercise 6

Write a query against the *dbo.Orders* table that returns the total quantities for each of the following: (employee, customer, and order year), (employee and order year), and (customer and order year). Include a result column in the output that uniquely identifies the grouping set with which the current row is associated:

- Table involved: *TSQLV4* database, *dbo.Orders* table
- Desired output:

```
groupingset   empid       custid    orderyear   sumqty
------------- ----------- --------- ----------- -----------
0             2           A         2014        12
0             3           A         2014        10
4             NULL        A         2014        22
0             2           A         2015        40
4             NULL        A         2015        40
0             3           A         2016        10
4             NULL        A         2016        10
0             1           B         2014        20
4             NULL        B         2014        20
0             2           B         2015        12
4             NULL        B         2015        12
0             2           B         2016        15
4             NULL        B         2016        15
0             3           C         2014        22
4             NULL        C         2014        22
0             1           C         2015        14
4             NULL        C         2015        14
0             1           C         2016        20
4             NULL        C         2016        20
0             3           D         2016        30
4             NULL        D         2016        30
2             1           NULL      2014        20
2             2           NULL      2014        12
2             3           NULL      2014        32
2             1           NULL      2015        14
2             2           NULL      2015        52
2             1           NULL      2016        20
2             2           NULL      2016        15
2             3           NULL      2016        40

(29 row(s) affected)
```

When you're done with the exercises in this chapter, run the following code for cleanup:

```
DROP TABLE IF EXISTS dbo.Orders;
```

Solutions

This section provides solutions to the Chapter 7 exercises.

Exercise 1

This exercise is very technical. Figuring it out is just a matter of being familiar with the syntax for window-ranking functions. Here's the solution query, returning for each order both the rank and the dense rank, partitioned by *custid* and ordered by *qty*:

```
SELECT custid, orderid, qty,
  RANK() OVER(PARTITION BY custid ORDER BY qty) AS rnk,
  DENSE_RANK() OVER(PARTITION BY custid ORDER BY qty) AS drnk
FROM dbo.Orders;
```

Exercise 2

Another way to handle this task is to write a query that returns distinct values without a row number computation, define a table expression based on this query, and then compute row numbers in the outer query against the table expression. Here's the solution query:

```
WITH C AS
(
  SELECT DISTINCT val
  FROM Sales.OrderValues
)
SELECT val, ROW_NUMBER() OVER(ORDER BY val) AS rownum
FROM C;
```

Exercise 3

You use the window offset functions *LAG* and *LEAD* to return an element from the previous row and the next row, respectively, based on the indicated partitioning and ordering specification. In this exercise, you need to perform the calculations within each customer's orders; hence, the window partitioning should be based on *custid*. As for ordering, use *orderdate* as the first ordering column and *orderid* as the tiebreaker. Here's the complete solution query:

```
SELECT custid, orderid, qty,
  qty - LAG(qty) OVER(PARTITION BY custid
                      ORDER BY orderdate, orderid) AS diffprev,
  qty - LEAD(qty) OVER(PARTITION BY custid
                       ORDER BY orderdate, orderid) AS diffnext
FROM dbo.Orders;
```

This query is a good example that shows you can mix detail elements from the row with window functions in the same expression.

Exercise 4

Solving a pivoting problem is all about identifying the elements involved: the grouping element, spreading element, aggregation element, and aggregate function. After you identify those, you simply fit them into the "template" query for pivoting—whether it's the solution with the grouped query or the solution using the *PIVOT* operator.

In this exercise, the grouping element is the employee (*empid*), the spreading element is order year (*YEAR(orderdate)*), and the aggregate function is *COUNT*; however, identifying the aggregation element is not that straightforward. You want the *COUNT* aggregate function to count matching rows—you don't really care which attribute it counts. In other words, you can use any attribute you want, as long as the attribute does not allow *NULLs*, because aggregate functions ignore *NULLs*.

If it doesn't really matter which attribute you use as the input to the *COUNT* aggregate, why not use the same attribute you already use as the spreading element? In this case, you can use the order year as both the spreading element and aggregation element.

Now that you've identified all pivoting elements, you're ready to write the complete solution. Here's the solution query without using the *PIVOT* operator:

```
USE TSQLV4;

SELECT empid,
  COUNT(CASE WHEN orderyear = 2014 THEN orderyear END) AS cnt2014,
  COUNT(CASE WHEN orderyear = 2015 THEN orderyear END) AS cnt2015,
  COUNT(CASE WHEN orderyear = 2016 THEN orderyear END) AS cnt2016
FROM (SELECT empid, YEAR(orderdate) AS orderyear
      FROM dbo.Orders) AS D
GROUP BY empid;
```

Recall that if you do not specify an *ELSE* clause in a *CASE* expression, an implicit *ELSE NULL* is assumed. Thus, the *CASE* expression produces non-*NULLs* only for matching orders (orders placed by the current employee in the current order year), and only those matching orders are taken into consideration by the *COUNT* aggregate.

Notice that even though this solution does not require you to use a table expression, I used one here to alias the *YEAR(orderdate)* expression as *orderyear* to avoid repeating the expression.

Here's the solution query that uses the *PIVOT* operator:

```
SELECT empid, [2014] AS cnt2014, [2015] AS cnt2015, [2016] AS cnt2016
FROM (SELECT empid, YEAR(orderdate) AS orderyear
      FROM dbo.Orders) AS D
  PIVOT(COUNT(orderyear)
        FOR orderyear IN([2014], [2015], [2016])) AS P;
```

As you can see, it's just a matter of fitting the pivoting elements in the right places.

If you prefer to use your own target column names and not the ones based on the actual data, you can provide your own aliases in the *SELECT* list. In this query, I aliased the result columns *[2014]*, *[2015]*, and *[2016]* as *cnt2014*, *cnt2015*, and *cnt2016*, respectively.

Exercise 5

This exercise involves a request to unpivot the source columns *cnt2014*, *cnt2015*, and *cnt2016* to two target columns—*orderyear* to hold the year that the source column name represents and *numorders* to hold the source-column value. You can use the solutions I showed in the chapter as the basis for solving this exercise with a couple of small revisions.

In the examples I used in the chapter, *NULLs* in the table represented irrelevant column values. The unpivoting solutions I presented filtered out rows with *NULLs*. The *EmpYearOrders* table has no *NULLs*, but it does have zeros in some cases, and the request is to filter out rows with 0 number of orders. With the solution that is based on the *APPLY* operator, simply use the predicate *numorders* <> 0 instead of using *IS NOT NULL*, like this:

```
SELECT empid, orderyear, numorders
FROM dbo.EmpYearOrders
  CROSS APPLY (VALUES(2014, cnt2014),
                     (2015, cnt2015),
                     (2016, cnt2016)) AS A(orderyear, numorders)
WHERE numorders <> 0;
```

As for the solution that uses the *UNPIVOT* operator, remember that it eliminates *NULLs* as an integral part of its logic. However, it does not eliminate zeros—you have to take care of eliminating zeros yourself by adding a *WHERE* clause, like this:

```
SELECT empid, CAST(RIGHT(orderyear, 4) AS INT) AS orderyear, numorders
FROM dbo.EmpYearOrders
  UNPIVOT(numorders FOR orderyear IN(cnt2014, cnt2015, cnt2016)) AS U
WHERE numorders <> 0;
```

Notice the expression used in the *SELECT* list to produce the *orderyear* result column: *CAST(RIGHT(orderyear, 4) AS INT)*. The original column names that the query unpivots are *cnt2014*, *cnt2015*, and *cnt2016*. These column names become the values *'cnt2014'*, *'cnt2015'*, and *'cnt2016'*, respectively, in the *orderyear* column in the result of the *UNPIVOT* operator. The purpose of this expression is to extract the four rightmost characters representing the order year and convert the value to an integer. This manipulation was not required in the standard solution because the constants used to construct the table expression *A* were specified explicitly.

Exercise 6

You can use the *GROUPING SETS* subclause to list the requested grouping sets and the *GROUPING_ID* function to produce a unique identifier for the grouping sets. Here's the complete solution query:

```
SELECT
  GROUPING_ID(empid, custid, YEAR(Orderdate)) AS groupingset,
  empid, custid, YEAR(Orderdate) AS orderyear, SUM(qty) AS sumqty
FROM dbo.Orders
GROUP BY
  GROUPING SETS
  (
    (empid, custid, YEAR(orderdate)),
```

```
  (empid, YEAR(orderdate)),
  (custid, YEAR(orderdate))
);
```

The requested grouping sets are neither a power set nor a rollup of some set of attributes. Therefore, you cannot use either the *CUBE* or *ROLLUP* subclause to further abbreviate the code.

CHAPTER 8

Data modification

SQL has a set of statements known as Data Manipulation Language (DML) that deals with data manipulation. Some people think that DML involves only data modification, but it also involves data retrieval. DML includes the statements *SELECT, INSERT, UPDATE, DELETE, TRUNCATE,* and *MERGE*. So far I've focused on the *SELECT* statement. This chapter focuses on data-modification statements. In addition to covering standard aspects of data modification, I'll also cover aspects specific to T-SQL.

To avoid changing existing data in your sample database, most of the examples in this chapter create and populate new tables in the *dbo* schema in the *TSQLV4* database.

Inserting data

T-SQL provides several statements for inserting data into tables: *INSERT VALUES, INSERT SELECT, INSERT EXEC, SELECT INTO,* and *BULK INSERT.* I'll first describe those statements, and then I'll talk about tools for generating keys, such as the identity property and the sequence object.

The *INSERT VALUES* statement

You use the standard *INSERT VALUES* statement to insert rows into a table based on specified values. To practice using this statement and others, you will work with a table called *Orders* in the *dbo* schema in the *TSQLV4* database. Run the following code to create the *Orders* table:

```
USE TSQLV4;

DROP TABLE IF EXISTS dbo.Orders;

CREATE TABLE dbo.Orders
(
  orderid   INT         NOT NULL
    CONSTRAINT PK_Orders PRIMARY KEY,
  orderdate DATE        NOT NULL
    CONSTRAINT DFT_orderdate DEFAULT(SYSDATETIME()),
  empid     INT         NOT NULL,
  custid    VARCHAR(10) NOT NULL
);
```

The following example demonstrates how to use the *INSERT VALUES* statement to insert a single row into the *Orders* table:

```
INSERT INTO dbo.Orders(orderid, orderdate, empid, custid)
  VALUES(10001, '20160212', 3, 'A');
```

Specifying the target column names right after the table name is optional, but by doing so, you control the value-column associations instead of relying on the order of the columns in the *CREATE TABLE* statement. In T-SQL, specifying the *INTO* clause is optional.

If you don't specify a value for a column, Microsoft SQL Server will use a default value if one was defined for the column. If a default value isn't defined and the column allows *NULLs*, a *NULL* will be used. If no default is defined and the column does not allow *NULLs* and does not somehow get its value automatically, your *INSERT* statement will fail. The following statement doesn't specify a value for the *orderdate* column; rather, it relies on its default (*SYSDATETIME*):

```
INSERT INTO dbo.Orders(orderid, empid, custid)
  VALUES(10002, 5, 'B');
```

T-SQL supports an enhanced standard *VALUES* clause you can use to specify multiple rows separated by commas. For example, the following statement inserts four rows into the *Orders* table:

```
INSERT INTO dbo.Orders
  (orderid, orderdate, empid, custid)
VALUES
  (10003, '20160213', 4, 'B'),
  (10004, '20160214', 1, 'A'),
  (10005, '20160213', 1, 'C'),
  (10006, '20160215', 3, 'C');
```

This statement is processed as a transaction, meaning that if any row fails to enter the table, none of the rows in the statement enters the table.

There's more to this enhanced *VALUES* clause. You can use it as a table-value constructor to construct a derived table. Here's an example:

```
SELECT *
FROM ( VALUES
         (10003, '20160213', 4, 'B'),
         (10004, '20160214', 1, 'A'),
         (10005, '20160213', 1, 'C'),
         (10006, '20160215', 3, 'C') )
     AS O(orderid, orderdate, empid, custid);
```

Following the parentheses that contain the table value constructor, you assign an alias to the table (*O* in this case), and following the table alias, you assign aliases to the target columns in parentheses. This query generates the following output:

```
orderid     orderdate   empid       custid
----------- ----------- ----------- ------
10003       20160213    4           B
10004       20160214    1           A
```

```
10005        20160213     1          C
10006        20160215     3          C
```

The *INSERT SELECT* statement

The standard *INSERT SELECT* statement inserts a set of rows returned by a *SELECT* query into a target table. The syntax is similar to that of an *INSERT VALUES* statement, but instead of using the *VALUES* clause, you specify a *SELECT* query. For example, the following code inserts into the *dbo.Orders* table the result of a query against the *Sales.Orders* table and returns orders that were shipped to the United Kingdom:

```
INSERT INTO dbo.Orders(orderid, orderdate, empid, custid)
  SELECT orderid, orderdate, empid, custid
  FROM Sales.Orders
  WHERE shipcountry = N'UK';
```

You can also use the *INSERT SELECT* statement to specify the target column names, and the recommendation I gave earlier regarding specifying those names remains the same. The behavior in terms of relying on a default constraint or column nullability is also the same as with the *INSERT VALUES* statement. The *INSERT SELECT* statement is performed as a transaction, so if any row fails to enter the target table, none of the rows enters the table.

> **Note** If you include a system function such as *SYSDATETIME* in the inserted query, the function gets invoked only once for the entire query and not once per row. The exception to this rule is if you generate globally unique identifiers (GUIDs) using the *NEWID* function, which gets invoked per row.

The *INSERT EXEC* statement

You use the *INSERT EXEC* statement to insert a result set returned from a stored procedure or a dynamic SQL batch into a target table. You'll find information about stored procedures, batches, and dynamic SQL in Chapter 11, "Programmable objects." The *INSERT EXEC* statement is similar in syntax and concept to the *INSERT SELECT* statement, but instead of using a *SELECT* statement, you specify an *EXEC* statement.

For example, the following code creates a stored procedure called *Sales.GetOrders*, and it returns orders that were shipped to a specified input country (with the *@country* parameter):

```
DROP PROC IF EXISTS Sales.GetOrders;
GO

CREATE PROC Sales.GetOrders
  @country AS NVARCHAR(40)
AS

SELECT orderid, orderdate, empid, custid
FROM Sales.Orders
```

```
WHERE shipcountry = @country;
GO
```

To test the stored procedure, execute it with the input country *France*:

```
EXEC Sales.GetOrders @country = N'France';
```

You get the following output:

```
orderid     orderdate   empid       custid
----------- ----------- ----------- -----------
10248       2014-07-04  5           85
10251       2014-07-08  3           84
10265       2014-07-25  2           7
10274       2014-08-06  6           85
10295       2014-09-02  2           85
10297       2014-09-04  5           7
10311       2014-09-20  1           18
10331       2014-10-16  9           9
10334       2014-10-21  8           84
10340       2014-10-29  1           9
...

(77 row(s) affected)
```

By using an *INSERT EXEC* statement, you can insert the result set returned from the procedure into the *dbo.Orders* table:

```
INSERT INTO dbo.Orders(orderid, orderdate, empid, custid)
  EXEC Sales.GetOrders @country = N'France';
```

The *SELECT INTO* statement

The *SELECT INTO* statement is a nonstandard T-SQL statement that creates a target table and populates it with the result set of a query. By "nonstandard," I mean that it's not part of the ISO and ANSI SQL standards. You cannot use this statement to insert data into an existing table. In terms of syntax, simply add *INTO <target_table_name>* right before the *FROM* clause of the *SELECT* query you want to use to produce the result set. For example, the following code creates a table called *dbo.Orders* and populates it with all rows from the *Sales.Orders* table:

```
DROP TABLE IF EXISTS dbo.Orders;

SELECT orderid, orderdate, empid, custid
INTO dbo.Orders
FROM Sales.Orders;
```

The target table's structure and data are based on the source table. The *SELECT INTO* statement copies from the source the base structure (such as column names, types, nullability, and identity property) and the data. It does not copy from the source constraints, indexes, triggers, column properties such as SPARSE and FILESTREAM, and permissions. If you need those in the target, you'll need to create them yourself.

One of the benefits of the *SELECT INTO* statement is its efficiency. As long as a database property called *Recovery Model* is not set to *FULL*, this statement uses an optimized mode that applies minimal logging. This translates to a very fast operation compared to a fully logged one. Note that the *INSERT SELECT* statement also can benefit from minimal logging, but the list of requirements it needs to meet is longer. For details, see "Prerequisites for Minimal Logging in Bulk Import" in SQL Server Books Online at the following URL: *http://msdn.microsoft.com/en-us/library/ms190422.aspx*.

If you need to use a *SELECT INTO* statement with set operations, you specify the *INTO* clause right in front of the *FROM* clause of the first query. For example, the following *SELECT INTO* statement creates a table called *Locations* and populates it with the result of an *EXCEPT* set operation, returning locations that are customer locations but not employee locations:

```
DROP TABLE IF EXISTS dbo.Locations;

SELECT country, region, city
INTO dbo.Locations
FROM Sales.Customers

EXCEPT

SELECT country, region, city
FROM HR.Employees;
```

The *BULK INSERT* statement

You use the *BULK INSERT* statement to insert into an existing table data originating from a file. In the statement, you specify the target table, the source file, and options. You can specify many options, including the data file type (for example, *char* or *native*), the field terminator, the row terminator, and others—all of which are fully documented.

For example, the following code bulk inserts the contents of the file *c:\temp\orders.tx*t into the table *dbo.Orders*, specifying that the data file type is *char*, the field terminator is a comma, and the row terminator is the newline character:

```
BULK INSERT dbo.Orders FROM 'c:\temp\orders.txt'
  WITH
    (
       DATAFILETYPE    = 'char',
       FIELDTERMINATOR = ',',
       ROWTERMINATOR   = '\n'
    );
```

Note that if you want to actually run this statement, you need to place the *orders.txt* file provided along with the source code for this book into the c:\temp folder.

You can run the *BULK INSERT* statement in a fast, minimally logged mode in certain scenarios as long as certain requirements are met. For details, see "Prerequisites for Minimal Logging in Bulk Import" in SQL Server Books Online.

The identity property and the sequence object

SQL Server supports two built-in solutions to automatically generate numeric keys: the identity column property and the sequence object. The identity property works well for some scenarios, but it also has many limitations. The sequence object resolves many of the identity property's limitations. I'll start with identity.

Identity

Identity is a standard column property. You can define this property for a column with any numeric type with a scale of zero (no fraction). When defining the property, you can optionally specify a seed (the first value) and an increment (a step value). If you don't provide those, the default is *1* for both. You typically use this property to generate *surrogate keys*, which are keys that are produced by the system and are not derived from the application data.

For example, the following code creates a table called *dbo.T1*:

```
DROP TABLE IF EXISTS dbo.T1;

CREATE TABLE dbo.T1
(
  keycol  INT         NOT NULL IDENTITY(1, 1)
    CONSTRAINT PK_T1 PRIMARY KEY,
  datacol VARCHAR(10) NOT NULL
    CONSTRAINT CHK_T1_datacol CHECK(datacol LIKE '[ABCDEFGHIJKLMNOPQRSTUVWXYZ]%')
);
```

The table contains a column called *keycol* that is defined with an identity property using *1* as the seed and *1* as the increment. The table also contains a character string column called *datacol*, whose data is restricted with a *CHECK* constraint to strings starting with an alphabetical character.

In your *INSERT* statements, you must completely ignore the identity column. For example, the following code inserts three rows into the table, specifying values only for the column *datacol*:

```
INSERT INTO dbo.T1(datacol) VALUES('AAAAA'),('CCCCC'),('BBBBB');
```

SQL Server produced the values for *keycol* automatically. Query the table to see the values that were generated:

```
SELECT * FROM dbo.T1;
```

You get the following output:

```
keycol      datacol
----------- ----------
1           AAAAA
2           CCCCC
3           BBBBB
```

When you query the table, naturally you can refer to the identity column by its name (*keycol* in this case). SQL Server also provides a way to refer to the identity column by using the more generic form *$identity*.

For example, the following query selects the identity column from *T1* by using the generic form:

```
SELECT $identity FROM dbo.T1;
```

This query returns the following output:

```
keycol
-----------
1
2
3
```

When you insert a new row into the table, SQL Server generates a new identity value based on the current identity value in the table and the increment. If you need to obtain the newly generated identity value—for example, to insert child rows into a referencing table—you query one of two functions, called *@@identity* and *SCOPE_IDENTITY*.

The *@@identity* function returns the last identity value generated by the session, regardless of scope (for example, a procedure issuing an *INSERT* statement, and a trigger fired by that statement are in different scopes). *SCOPE_IDENTITY* returns the last identity value generated by the current scope (for example, the same procedure). Except in the rare cases when you don't really care about scope, you should use the *SCOPE_IDENTITY* function.

For example, the following code inserts a new row into the table *T1*, obtains the newly generated identity value and places it into a variable by querying the *SCOPE_IDENTITY* function, and queries the variable:

```
DECLARE @new_key AS INT;

INSERT INTO dbo.T1(datacol) VALUES('AAAAA');

SET @new_key = SCOPE_IDENTITY();

SELECT @new_key AS new_key
```

If you ran all previous code samples provided in this section, this code returns the following output:

```
new_key
-----------
4
```

Remember that both *@@identity* and *SCOPE_IDENTITY* return the last identity value produced by the current session. Neither is affected by inserts issued by other sessions. However, if you want to know the current identity value in a table (the last value produced) regardless of session, you should use the *IDENT_CURRENT* function and provide the table name as input. For example, run the following code from a new session (not the one from which you ran the previous *INSERT* statements):

```
SELECT
  SCOPE_IDENTITY() AS [SCOPE_IDENTITY],
  @@identity AS [@@identity],
  IDENT_CURRENT(N'dbo.T1') AS [IDENT_CURRENT];
```

You get the following output:

```
SCOPE_IDENTITY   @@identity   IDENT_CURRENT
---------------- ------------ -------------
NULL             NULL         4
```

Both *@@identity* and *SCOPE_IDENTITY* returned *NULLs* because no identity values were created in the session in which this query ran. *IDENT_CURRENT* returned the value *4* because it returns the current identity value in the table, regardless of the session in which it was produced.

There's a certain part of the design of the identity property that comes as a surprise to some. The change to the current identity value in a table is not undone if the *INSERT* that generated the change fails or the transaction in which the statement runs is rolled back. For example, run the following *INSERT* statement, which conflicts with the *CHECK* constraint defined in the table:

```
INSERT INTO dbo.T1(datacol) VALUES('12345');
```

The insert fails, and you get the following error:

```
Msg 547, Level 16, State 0, Line 159
The INSERT statement conflicted with the CHECK constraint "CHK_T1_datacol". The conflict
occurred in database "TSQLV4", table "dbo.T1", column 'datacol'.
The statement has been terminated.
```

Even though the insert failed, the current identity value in the table changed from *4* to *5*, and this change was not undone because of the failure. This means that the next insert will produce the value *6*:

```
INSERT INTO dbo.T1(datacol) VALUES('EEEEE');
```

Query the table:

```
SELECT * FROM dbo.T1;
```

Notice a gap between the values *4* and *6* in the output:

```
keycol      datacol
----------- ----------
1           AAAAA
2           CCCCC
3           BBBBB
4           AAAAA
6           EEEEE
```

Also, SQL Server uses a performance cache feature for the identity property, which can result in gaps between the keys when there's an unclean termination of the SQL Server process—for example, because of a power failure. As you might realize, you should use the identity property only if you can allow gaps between the keys. Otherwise, you should implement your own mechanism to generate keys.

One of the shortcomings of the identity property is that you cannot add it to an existing column or remove it from an existing column. If you need to make such a change, it's an expensive and cumbersome offline operation.

With SQL Server, you can specify your own explicit values for the identity column when you insert rows, as long as you enable a session option called *IDENTITY_INSERT* against the table involved. There's no option you can use to update an identity column, though.

For example, the following code demonstrates how to insert a row into *T1* with the explicit value *5* in *keycol*:

```
SET IDENTITY_INSERT dbo.T1 ON;
INSERT INTO dbo.T1(keycol, datacol) VALUES(5, 'FFFFF');
SET IDENTITY_INSERT dbo.T1 OFF;
```

Interestingly, when you turn off the *IDENTITY_INSERT* option, SQL Server changes the current identity value in the table only if the explicit value you provided is greater than the current identity value. Because the current identity value in the table prior to running the preceding code was 6, and the *INSERT* statement in this code used the lower explicit value *5*, the current identity value in the table did not change. So if at this point you query the *IDENT_CURRENT* function for this table, you will get *6* and not *5*. This way, the next *INSERT* statement against the table will produce the value 7:

```
INSERT INTO dbo.T1(datacol) VALUES('GGGGG');
```

Query the current contents of the table *T1*:

```
SELECT * FROM dbo.T1;
```

You get the following output:

```
keycol      datacol
----------- ----------
1           AAAAA
2           CCCCC
3           BBBBB
4           AAAAA
5           FFFFF
6           EEEEE
7           GGGGG
```

You need to understand that the identity property itself does not enforce uniqueness in the column. I already explained that you can provide your own explicit values after setting the *IDENTITY_INSERT* option to *ON*, and those values can be ones that already exist in rows in the table. Also, you can reseed the current identity value in the table by using the *DBCC CHECKIDENT* command—for syntax, see "*DBCC CHECKIDENT* (Transact-SQL)" in SQL Server Books Online at the following URL: *https://msdn.microsoft.com/en-us/library/ms176057.aspx*. If you need to guarantee uniqueness in an identity column, make sure you also define a primary key or a unique constraint on that column.

Sequence

T-SQL supports the standard sequence object as an alternative key-generating mechanism for identity. The sequence object is more flexible than identity in many ways, making it the preferred choice in many cases.

One of the advantages of the sequence object is that, unlike identity, it's not tied to a particular column in a particular table; rather, it's an independent object in the database. Whenever you need to generate a new value, you invoke a function against the object and use the returned value wherever you like. For example, if you have such a use case, you can use one sequence object that will help you maintain keys that will not conflict across multiple tables.

To create a sequence object, use the *CREATE SEQUENCE* command. The minimum required information is just the sequence name, but note that the defaults for the various properties in such a case might not be what you want. If you don't indicate the data type, SQL Server will use *BIGINT* by default. If you want a different type, indicate *AS <type>*. The type can be any numeric type with a scale of zero. For example, if you need your sequence to be of an *INT* type, indicate *AS INT*.

Unlike the identity property, the sequence object supports the specification of a minimum value (*MINVALUE <val>*) and a maximum value (*MAXVALUE <val>*) within the type. If you don't indicate what the minimum and maximum values are, the sequence object will assume the minimum and maximum values supported by the type. For example, for an *INT* type, those would be –2,147,483,648 and 2,147,483,647, respectively.

Also, unlike identity, the sequence object supports cycling. Note, though, that the default is *NO CYCLE*. If you want the sequence object to cycle, you need to be explicit about it by using the *CYCLE* option.

Like identity, the sequence object allows you to specify the starting value (*START WITH <val>*) and the increment (*INCREMENT BY <val>*). If you don't indicate the starting value, the default will be the same as the minimum value (*MINVALUE*). If you don't indicate the increment value, it will be *1* by default.

For example, suppose you want to create a sequence that will help you generate order IDs. You want it to be of an *INT* type, have a minimum value of *1* and a maximum value that is the maximum supported by the type, start with *1*, increment by *1*, and allow cycling. Here's the *CREATE SEQUENCE* command you would use to create such a sequence:

```
CREATE SEQUENCE dbo.SeqOrderIDs AS INT
  MINVALUE 1
  CYCLE;
```

You had to be explicit about the type, minimum value, and cycling option because they are different than the defaults. You didn't need to indicate the maximum, start with, and increment values because you wanted the defaults.

The sequence object also supports a caching option (*CACHE <val> | NO CACHE*) that tells SQL Server how often to write the recoverable value to disk. For example, if you specify a cache value of 10,000, SQL Server will write to disk every 10,000 requests, and in between disk writes, it will maintain the current value and how many values are left in memory. If you write less frequently to disk, you'll get better performance when generating a value (on average), but you'll risk losing more values in case of an unexpected termination of the SQL Server process, such as in a power failure. SQL Server has a default cache value of 50, although this number is not officially documented because Microsoft wants to be able to change it.

You can change any of the sequence properties except the data type with the *ALTER SEQUENCE* command (*MINVAL <val>, MAXVAL <val>, RESTART WITH <val>, INCREMENT BY <val>, CYCLE | NO CYCLE*, or *CACHE <val> | NO CACHE*). For example, suppose you want to prevent the sequence *dbo.SeqOrderIDs* from cycling. You can change the current sequence definition with the following *ALTER SEQUENCE* command:

```
ALTER SEQUENCE dbo.SeqOrderIDs
  NO CYCLE;
```

To generate a new sequence value, you need to invoke the standard function *NEXT VALUE FOR <sequence name>*. Here's an example of invoking the function:

```
SELECT NEXT VALUE FOR dbo.SeqOrderIDs;
```

This code generates the following output:

```
-----------
1
```

Notice that, unlike with identity, you didn't need to insert a row into a table in order to generate a new value. Some applications need to generate the new value before using it. With sequences, you can store the result of the function in a variable and use it later in the code. To demonstrate this, first create a table called *T1* with the following code:

```
DROP TABLE IF EXISTS dbo.T1;

CREATE TABLE dbo.T1
(
  keycol  INT         NOT NULL
    CONSTRAINT PK_T1 PRIMARY KEY,
  datacol VARCHAR(10) NOT NULL
);
```

The following code generates a new sequence value, stores it in a variable, and then uses the variable in an *INSERT* statement to insert a row into the table:

```
DECLARE @neworderid AS INT = NEXT VALUE FOR dbo.SeqOrderIDs;
INSERT INTO dbo.T1(keycol, datacol) VALUES(@neworderid, 'a');

SELECT * FROM dbo.T1;
```

This code returns the following output:

```
keycol      datacol
----------- ----------
2           a
```

If you need to use the new key in related rows that you add to another table, you can use the variable when you insert those rows.

If you don't need to generate the new sequence value before using it, you can specify the *NEXT VALUE FOR* function directly as part of your *INSERT* statement, like this:

```
INSERT INTO dbo.T1(keycol, datacol)
  VALUES(NEXT VALUE FOR dbo.SeqOrderIDs, 'b');

SELECT * FROM dbo.T1;
```

This code returns the following output:

```
keycol      datacol
----------- ----------
2           a
3           b
```

Unlike with identity, you can generate new sequence values in an *UPDATE* statement, like this:

```
UPDATE dbo.T1
  SET keycol = NEXT VALUE FOR dbo.SeqOrderIDs;

SELECT * FROM dbo.T1;
```

This code returns the following output:

```
keycol      datacol
----------- ----------
4           a
5           b
```

To get information about your sequences, query a view called *sys.sequences*. For example, to find the current sequence value in the *SeqOrderIDs* sequence, you use the following code:

```
SELECT current_value
FROM sys.sequences
WHERE OBJECT_ID = OBJECT_ID(N'dbo.SeqOrderIDs');
```

This code generates the following output:

```
current_value
--------------
5
```

SQL Server extends its support for the sequence option with capabilities beyond what the competitors and the standard currently support. One of the extensions enables you to control the order of the assigned sequence values in a multirow insert by using an *OVER* clause. Here's an example:

```
INSERT INTO dbo.T1(keycol, datacol)
  SELECT
    NEXT VALUE FOR dbo.SeqOrderIDs OVER(ORDER BY hiredate),
    LEFT(firstname, 1) + LEFT(lastname, 1)
  FROM HR.Employees;
```

```
SELECT * FROM dbo.T1;
```

This code returns the following output:

```
keycol      datacol
----------- ----------
4           a
5           b
6           JL
7           SD
8           DF
9           YP
10          SM
11          PS
12          RK
13          MC
14          PD
```

Another extension to the standard allows the use of the *NEXT VALUE FOR* function in a default constraint. Here's an example:

```
ALTER TABLE dbo.T1
  ADD CONSTRAINT DFT_T1_keycol
    DEFAULT (NEXT VALUE FOR dbo.SeqOrderIDs)
    FOR keycol;
```

Now when you insert rows into the table, you don't have to indicate a value for *keycol*:

```
INSERT INTO dbo.T1(datacol) VALUES('c');

SELECT * FROM dbo.T1;
```

This code returns the following output:

```
keycol      datacol
----------- ----------
4           a
5           b
6           JL
7           SD
8           DF
9           YP
10          SM
11          PS
12          RK
13          MC
14          PD
15          c
```

Unlike with identity, which you cannot add to or remove from an existing column, you can add or remove a default constraint. The preceding example showed how to add a default constraint to a table and associate it with a column. To remove a constraint, use the syntax: *ALTER TABLE <table_name> DROP CONSTRAINT <constraint_name>*.

There's another extension to the standard you can use to allocate a whole range of sequence values at once by using a stored procedure called *sp_sequence_get_range*. The idea is that if the application needs to assign a range of sequence values, it's efficient to update the sequence only once, incrementing it by the size of the range. You call the procedure, indicate the size of the range you want, and collect the first value in the range, as well as other information, by using output parameters. Here's an example of calling the procedure and asking for a range of 1,000,000 sequence values:

```
DECLARE @first AS SQL_VARIANT;

EXEC sys.sp_sequence_get_range
  @sequence_name     = N'dbo.SeqOrderIDs',
  @range_size        = 1000000,
  @range_first_value = @first OUTPUT ;

SELECT @first;
```

> **Note** *SQL_VARIANT* is a generic data type that can hold within it various base data types. The *sp_sequence_get_range* procedure uses this type for several of its parameters, including the output parameter *@range_first_value*. For details about this data type, see SQL Server Books Online at the following URL: *https://msdn.microsoft.com/en-us/library/ms173829.aspx*.

If you run the code twice, you will find that the returned first value in the second call is greater than the first by 1,000,000.

Note that like with identity, the sequence object does not guarantee you will have no gaps. If a new sequence value was generated by a transaction that failed or intentionally rolled back, the sequence change is not undone. Also, as mentioned earlier with identity, sequence objects support a performance cache feature, which can result in gaps when there's an unclean termination of the SQL Server process.

When you're done, run the following code for cleanup:

```
DROP TABLE IF EXISTS dbo.T1;
DROP SEQUENCE IF EXISTS dbo.SeqOrderIDs;
```

Deleting data

T-SQL provides two statements for deleting rows from a table: *DELETE* and *TRUNCATE*. This section describes those statements. The examples I provide in this section are applied against copies of the *Customers* and *Orders* tables from the *Sales* schema created in the *dbo* schema. Run the following code to create and populate those tables:

```
DROP TABLE IF EXISTS dbo.Orders, dbo.Customers;

CREATE TABLE dbo.Customers
(
```

```
  custid       INT           NOT NULL,
  companyname  NVARCHAR(40) NOT NULL,
  contactname  NVARCHAR(30) NOT NULL,
  contacttitle NVARCHAR(30) NOT NULL,
  address      NVARCHAR(60) NOT NULL,
  city         NVARCHAR(15) NOT NULL,
  region       NVARCHAR(15) NULL,
  postalcode   NVARCHAR(10) NULL,
  country      NVARCHAR(15) NOT NULL,
  phone        NVARCHAR(24) NOT NULL,
  fax          NVARCHAR(24) NULL,
  CONSTRAINT PK_Customers PRIMARY KEY(custid)
);

CREATE TABLE dbo.Orders
(
  orderid        INT           NOT NULL,
  custid         INT           NULL,
  empid          INT           NOT NULL,
  orderdate      DATE          NOT NULL,
  requireddate   DATE          NOT NULL,
  shippeddate    DATE          NULL,
  shipperid      INT           NOT NULL,
  freight        MONEY         NOT NULL
    CONSTRAINT DFT_Orders_freight DEFAULT(0),
  shipname       NVARCHAR(40) NOT NULL,
  shipaddress    NVARCHAR(60) NOT NULL,
  shipcity       NVARCHAR(15) NOT NULL,
  shipregion     NVARCHAR(15) NULL,
  shippostalcode NVARCHAR(10) NULL,
  shipcountry    NVARCHAR(15) NOT NULL,
  CONSTRAINT PK_Orders PRIMARY KEY(orderid),
  CONSTRAINT FK_Orders_Customers FOREIGN KEY(custid)
    REFERENCES dbo.Customers(custid)
);
GO

INSERT INTO dbo.Customers SELECT * FROM Sales.Customers;
INSERT INTO dbo.Orders SELECT * FROM Sales.Orders;
```

The *DELETE* statement

The *DELETE* statement is a standard statement used to delete data from a table based on an optional filter predicate. The standard statement has only two clauses—the *FROM* clause, in which you specify the target table name, and a *WHERE* clause, in which you specify a predicate. Only the subset of rows for which the predicate evaluates to *TRUE* will be deleted.

For example, the following statement deletes, from the *dbo.Orders* table, all orders that were placed prior to 2015:

```
DELETE FROM dbo.Orders
WHERE orderdate < '20150101';
```

Run this statement. SQL Server will report that it deleted 152 rows:

```
(152 row(s) affected)
```

Note that you can suppress returning the message that indicates the number of rows affected by turning on the session option *NOCOUNT*. As you probably noticed, this option is off by default.

The *DELETE* statement tends to be expensive when you delete a large number of rows, mainly because it's a fully logged operation.

The *TRUNCATE* statement

The standard *TRUNCATE* statement deletes all rows from a table. Unlike the *DELETE* statement, *TRUNCATE* has no filter. For example, to delete all rows from a table called *dbo.T1*, you run the following code:

```
TRUNCATE TABLE dbo.T1;
```

The advantage that *TRUNCATE* has over *DELETE* is that the former is minimally logged, whereas the latter is fully logged, resulting in significant performance differences. For example, if you use the *TRUNCATE* statement to delete all rows from a table with millions of rows, the operation will finish in a matter of seconds. If you use the *DELETE* statement, the operation can take many minutes. Note that I said *TRUNCATE* is *minimally* logged, as opposed to not being logged at all. SQL Server records which blocks of data were deallocated by the operation so that it can reclaim those in case the transaction needs to be undone. Both *DELETE* and *TRUNCATE* are transactional.

TRUNCATE and *DELETE* also have a functional difference when the table has an identity column. *TRUNCATE* resets the identity value back to the original seed, but *DELETE* doesn't—even when used without a filter. Interestingly, the standard defines an *identity column restart option* for the *TRUNCATE* statement, which you use to control whether to restart or continue the identity value, but unfortunately T-SQL doesn't support this option.

The *TRUNCATE* statement is not allowed when the target table is referenced by a foreign-key constraint, even if the referencing table is empty and even if the foreign key is disabled. The only way to allow a *TRUNCATE* statement is to drop all foreign keys referencing the table with the *ALTER TABLE DROP CONSTRAINT* command. You can then re-create the foreign keys after truncating the table with the *ALTER TABLE ADD CONSTRAINT* command.

Accidents such as truncating or dropping the incorrect table can happen. For example, let's say you have connections open against both the production and the development environments, and you submit your code in the wrong connection. Both the *TRUNCATE* and *DROP* statements are so fast that the transaction is committed before you realize your mistake. To prevent such accidents, you can protect a production table by simply creating a dummy table with a foreign key pointing to that table. You can even disable the foreign key so that it won't have any impact on performance. As I mentioned earlier, even when disabled, this foreign key prevents you from truncating or dropping the referenced table.

In case you have partitioned tables in your database, SQL Server 2016 enhances the *TRUNCATE* statement by supporting the truncation of individual partitions. You can specify a list of partitions and partition ranges (with the keyword *TO* between the range delimiters). As an example, suppose you had a partitioned table called *T1* and you wanted to truncate partitions 1, 3, 5, and 7 through 10. You would use the following code to achieve this:

```
TRUNCATE TABLE dbo.T1 WITH ( PARTITIONS(1, 3, 5, 7 TO 10) );
```

> **Note** Table partitioning is about dividing your table into multiple units called *partitions*, mainly for manageability purposes. This allows handling processes like importing data into the table and purging historic data to be handled more efficiently. You can find details on the topic in SQL Server Books Online at the following URL: *https://msdn.microsoft.com/en-us/library/ms190787.aspx*.

DELETE based on a join

T-SQL supports a nonstandard *DELETE* syntax based on joins. The join serves a filtering purpose and also gives you access to the attributes of the related rows from the joined tables. This means you can delete rows from one table based on a filter against attributes in related rows from another table.

For example, the following statement deletes orders placed by customers from the United States:

```
DELETE FROM O
FROM dbo.Orders AS O
  INNER JOIN dbo.Customers AS C
    ON O.custid = C.custid
WHERE C.country = N'USA';
```

Much like in a *SELECT* statement, the first clause that is logically processed in a *DELETE* statement is the *FROM* clause (the second one that appears in this statement). Then the *WHERE* clause is processed, and finally the *DELETE* clause. In our case, the statement first joins the *Orders* table (aliased as *O*) with the *Customers* table (aliased as *C*) based on a match between the order's customer ID and the customer's customer ID. It then filters only orders placed by customers from the United States. Finally, the statement deletes all qualifying rows from *O* (the alias representing the *Orders* table).

The two *FROM* clauses in a *DELETE* statement based on a join might be confusing. But when you develop the code, develop it as if it were a *SELECT* statement with a join. That is, start with the *FROM* clause with the joins, move on to the *WHERE* clause, and finally—instead of specifying a *SELECT* clause—specify a *DELETE* clause with the alias of the side of the join that is supposed to be the target for the deletion. Note that the first *FROM* clause is optional. In our example, you can specify *DELETE O* instead of *DELETE FROM O*.

As I mentioned earlier, a *DELETE* statement based on a join is nonstandard. If you want to stick to standard code, you can use subqueries instead of joins. For example, the following *DELETE* statement uses a subquery to achieve the same task:

```
DELETE FROM dbo.Orders
WHERE EXISTS
  (SELECT *
   FROM dbo.Customers AS C
   WHERE Orders.custid = C.custid
     AND C.country = N'USA');
```

This code deletes all rows from the *Orders* table for which a related customer from the United States exists in the *Customers* table.

SQL Server processes the two queries the same way (using the same query execution plan); therefore, you shouldn't expect any performance difference between them. I usually recommend sticking to the standard as much as possible unless you have a compelling reason to do otherwise—for example, in the case of a performance difference.

When you're done, run the following code for cleanup:

```
DROP TABLE IF EXISTS dbo.Orders, dbo.Customers;
```

Updating data

T-SQL supports a standard *UPDATE* statement you can use to update rows in a table. T-SQL also supports nonstandard forms of the *UPDATE* statement with joins and with variables. This section describes the different forms of the statement.

The examples I provide in this section are against copies of the *Orders* and *OrderDetails* tables from the *Sales* schema created in the *dbo* schema. Run the following code to create and populate those tables:

```
DROP TABLE IF EXISTS dbo.OrderDetails, dbo.Orders;

CREATE TABLE dbo.Orders
(
  orderid        INT          NOT NULL,
  custid         INT          NULL,
  empid          INT          NOT NULL,
  orderdate      DATE         NOT NULL,
  requireddate   DATE         NOT NULL,
  shippeddate    DATE         NULL,
  shipperid      INT          NOT NULL,
  freight        MONEY        NOT NULL
    CONSTRAINT DFT_Orders_freight DEFAULT(0),
  shipname       NVARCHAR(40) NOT NULL,
  shipaddress    NVARCHAR(60) NOT NULL,
  shipcity       NVARCHAR(15) NOT NULL,
  shipregion     NVARCHAR(15) NULL,
  shippostalcode NVARCHAR(10) NULL,
  shipcountry    NVARCHAR(15) NOT NULL,
  CONSTRAINT PK_Orders PRIMARY KEY(orderid)
);
```

```
CREATE TABLE dbo.OrderDetails
(
  orderid   INT           NOT NULL,
  productid INT           NOT NULL,
  unitprice MONEY         NOT NULL
    CONSTRAINT DFT_OrderDetails_unitprice DEFAULT(0),
  qty       SMALLINT      NOT NULL
    CONSTRAINT DFT_OrderDetails_qty DEFAULT(1),
  discount  NUMERIC(4, 3) NOT NULL
    CONSTRAINT DFT_OrderDetails_discount DEFAULT(0),
  CONSTRAINT PK_OrderDetails PRIMARY KEY(orderid, productid),
  CONSTRAINT FK_OrderDetails_Orders FOREIGN KEY(orderid)
    REFERENCES dbo.Orders(orderid),
  CONSTRAINT CHK_discount  CHECK (discount BETWEEN 0 AND 1),
  CONSTRAINT CHK_qty  CHECK (qty > 0),
  CONSTRAINT CHK_unitprice CHECK (unitprice >= 0)
);
GO

INSERT INTO dbo.Orders SELECT * FROM Sales.Orders;
INSERT INTO dbo.OrderDetails SELECT * FROM Sales.OrderDetails;
```

The *UPDATE* statement

The *UPDATE* statement is a standard statement you can use to update a subset of rows in a table. To identify the subset of rows you need to update, you specify a predicate in a *WHERE* clause. You specify the assignment of values to columns in a *SET* clause, separated by commas.

For example, the following *UPDATE* statement increases the discount of all order details for product 51 by 5 percent:

```
UPDATE dbo.OrderDetails
  SET discount = discount + 0.05
WHERE productid = 51;
```

Of course, you can run a *SELECT* statement with the same filter before and after the update to see the changes. Later in this chapter, I'll show you another way to see the changes, by using a clause called *OUTPUT* that you can add to modification statements.

T-SQL supports compound assignment operators: += (plus equal), –= (minus equal), *= (multiplication equal), /= (division equal), %= (modulo equal), and others. You can use these operators to shorten assignment expressions such as the one in the preceding query. Instead of the expression *discount = discount + 0.05*, you can use this expression: *discount += 0.05*. The full *UPDATE* statement looks like this:

```
UPDATE dbo.OrderDetails
  SET discount += 0.05
WHERE productid = 51;
```

All-at-once operations are an important aspect of SQL you should keep in mind when writing *UPDATE* statements. I explained the concept in Chapter 2, "Single-table queries," in the context of *SELECT* statements, but it's just as applicable with *UPDATE* statements. Remember that all expressions that appear in the same logical phase are evaluated as a set, logically at the same point in time. Consider the following *UPDATE* statement:

```
UPDATE dbo.T1
  SET col1 = col1 + 10, col2 = col1 + 10;
```

Suppose one row in the table has the value 100 in *col1* prior to the update. Can you determine the values of *col1* and *col2* in that row after the update?

If you do not consider the all-at-once concept, you would think that *col1* will be set to 110 and *col2* to 120, as if the assignments were performed from left to right. However, the assignments take place all at once, meaning that both assignments use the same value of *col1*—the value before the update. The result of this update is that both *col1* and *col2* will end up with the value 110.

With the concept of all-at-once in mind, can you figure out how to write an *UPDATE* statement that swaps the values in the columns *col1* and *col2*? In most programming languages where expressions and assignments are evaluated in some order (typically left to right), you need a temporary variable. However, because in SQL all assignments take place as if they happen at the same point in time, the solution is simple:

```
UPDATE dbo.T1
  SET col1 = col2, col2 = col1;
```

In both assignments, the source column values used are those prior to the update, so you don't need a temporary variable.

UPDATE based on a join

Similar to the *DELETE* statement, the *UPDATE* statement also supports a nonstandard form based on joins. As with *DELETE* statements, the join serves a filtering purpose as well as giving you access to attributes from the joined tables.

The syntax is similar to a *SELECT* statement based on a join; that is, the *FROM* and *WHERE* clauses are the same, but instead of the *SELECT* clause, you specify an *UPDATE* clause. The *UPDATE* keyword is followed by the alias of the table that is the target of the update (you can't update more than one table in the same statement), followed by the *SET* clause with the column assignments.

For example, the *UPDATE* statement in Listing 8-1 increases the discount of all order details of orders placed by customer 1 by 5 percent.

LISTING 8-1 *UPDATE* based on a join

```
UPDATE OD
  SET discount += 0.05
FROM dbo.OrderDetails AS OD
  INNER JOIN dbo.Orders AS O
    ON OD.orderid = O.orderid
WHERE O.custid = 1;
```

In terms of logical processing, you start with the *FROM* clause, move on to the *WHERE* clause, and finally go to the *UPDATE* clause. The query joins the *OrderDetails* table (aliased as *OD*) with the *Orders* table (aliased as *O*) based on a match between the order detail's order ID and the order's order ID. The query then filters only the rows where the order's customer ID is *1*. The query then specifies in the *UPDATE* clause that *OD* (the alias of the *OrderDetails* table) is the target of the update, and it increases the discount by 5 percent. You can also specify the full table name in the *UPDATE* clause if you like.

If you want to achieve the same task by using standard code, you can use a subquery instead of a join, like this:

```
UPDATE dbo.OrderDetails
  SET discount += 0.05
WHERE EXISTS
  (SELECT * FROM dbo.Orders AS O
   WHERE O.orderid = OrderDetails.orderid
     AND O.custid = 1);
```

The query's *WHERE* clause filters only order details in which a related order is placed by customer 1. With this particular task, SQL Server processes both versions the same way (using the same query plan); therefore, you shouldn't expect performance differences between the two. As I mentioned earlier, I recommend sticking to standard code unless you have a compelling reason to do otherwise.

There are cases where the join version has advantages. In addition to filtering, the join also gives you access to attributes from other tables you can use in the column assignments in the *SET* clause. The same access to the joined table is used for both filtering and assignment purposes. However, with the subquery approach, you need separate subqueries for filtering and assignments; plus, you need a separate subquery for each assignment. In SQL Server, each subquery involves separate access to the other table.

For example, consider the following nonstandard *UPDATE* statement based on a join:

```
UPDATE T1
  SET col1 = T2.col1,
      col2 = T2.col2,
      col3 = T2.col3
FROM dbo.T1 JOIN dbo.T2
  ON T2.keycol = T1.keycol
WHERE T2.col4 = 'ABC';
```

This statement joins the tables *T1* and *T2* based on a match between *T1.keycol* and *T2.keycol*. The *WHERE* clause filters only rows where *T2.col4* is equal to 'ABC'. The *UPDATE* statement marks the *T1* table as the target for the *UPDATE*, and the *SET* clause sets the values of the columns *col1*, *col2*, and *col3* in *T1* to the values of the corresponding columns from *T2*.

An attempt to express this task by using standard code with subqueries yields the following lengthy query:

```
UPDATE dbo.T1
  SET col1 = (SELECT col1
              FROM dbo.T2
              WHERE T2.keycol = T1.keycol),
```

```
        col2 = (SELECT col2
                FROM dbo.T2
                WHERE T2.keycol = T1.keycol),

        col3 = (SELECT col3
                FROM dbo.T2
                WHERE T2.keycol = T1.keycol)
WHERE EXISTS
  (SELECT *
   FROM dbo.T2
   WHERE T2.keycol = T1.keycol
     AND T2.col4 = 'ABC');
```

Not only is this version convoluted, but each subquery involves separate access to table *T2*. So this version is less efficient than the join version.

Standard SQL has support for *row constructors* (also known as *vector expressions*) that were only implemented partially in T-SQL. As of SQL Server 2016, many aspects of row constructors have not yet been implemented, including the ability to use them in the *SET* clause of an *UPDATE* statement like this:

```
UPDATE dbo.T1

  SET (col1, col2, col3) =

      (SELECT col1, col2, col3
       FROM dbo.T2
       WHERE T2.keycol = T1.keycol)

WHERE EXISTS
  (SELECT *
   FROM dbo.T2
   WHERE T2.keycol = T1.keycol
     AND T2.col4 = 'ABC');
```

But as you can see, this version would still be more complicated than the join version, because it requires separate subqueries for the filtering part and for obtaining the attributes from the other table for the assignments.

Assignment *UPDATE*

T-SQL supports a proprietary *UPDATE* syntax that both updates data in a table and assigns values to variables at the same time. This syntax saves you the need to use separate *UPDATE* and *SELECT* statements to achieve the same task.

One of the common cases for which you can use this syntax is in maintaining a custom sequence/autonumbering mechanism when the identity column property and the sequence object don't work for you. One example is when you need to guarantee that there are no gaps between the values. To achieve this, you keep the last-used value in a table, and whenever you need a new value, you use the special *UPDATE* syntax to both increment the value in the table and assign it to a variable.

Run the following code to first create the *MySequences* table with the column *val*, and then populate it with a single row with the value 0—one less than the first value you want to use:

```
DROP TABLE IF EXISTS dbo.MySequences;

CREATE TABLE dbo.MySequences
(
  id VARCHAR(10) NOT NULL
    CONSTRAINT PK_MySequences PRIMARY KEY(id),
  val INT NOT NULL
);
INSERT INTO dbo.MySequences VALUES('SEQ1', 0);
```

Now, whenever you need to obtain a new sequence value, use the following code:

```
DECLARE @nextval AS INT;

UPDATE dbo.MySequences
  SET @nextval = val += 1
WHERE id = 'SEQ1';

SELECT @nextval;
```

The code declares a local variable called *@nextval*. Then it uses the special *UPDATE* syntax to increment the column value by 1 and assigns the new value to a variable. The code then presents the value in the variable. First *val* is set to *val* + 1, and then the result (*val* + 1) is set to the variable *@nextval*.

The specialized *UPDATE* syntax is run as a transaction, and it's more efficient than using separate *UPDATE* and *SELECT* statements because it accesses the data only once. Note that variable assignment isn't transactional, though.

When you're done, run the following code for cleanup:

```
DROP TABLE IF EXISTS dbo.MySequences;
```

Merging data

T-SQL supports a statement called *MERGE* you can use to merge data from a source into a target, applying different actions (*INSERT*, *UPDATE*, and *DELETE*) based on conditional logic. The *MERGE* statement is part of the SQL standard, although the T-SQL version adds a few nonstandard extensions.

A task achieved by a single *MERGE* statement typically translates to a combination of several other DML statements (*INSERT*, *UPDATE*, and *DELETE*) without *MERGE*.

To demonstrate the *MERGE* statement, I'll use tables called *dbo.Customers* and *dbo.CustomersStage*. Run Listing 8-2 to create those tables and populate them with sample data.

LISTING 8-2 Code that creates and populates *Customers* and *CustomersStage*

```
DROP TABLE IF EXISTS dbo.Customers, dbo.CustomersStage;
GO

CREATE TABLE dbo.Customers
(
  custid      INT         NOT NULL,
  companyname VARCHAR(25) NOT NULL,
  phone       VARCHAR(20) NOT NULL,
  address     VARCHAR(50) NOT NULL,
  CONSTRAINT PK_Customers PRIMARY KEY(custid)
);

INSERT INTO dbo.Customers(custid, companyname, phone, address)
VALUES
  (1, 'cust 1', '(111) 111-1111', 'address 1'),
  (2, 'cust 2', '(222) 222-2222', 'address 2'),
  (3, 'cust 3', '(333) 333-3333', 'address 3'),
  (4, 'cust 4', '(444) 444-4444', 'address 4'),
  (5, 'cust 5', '(555) 555-5555', 'address 5');

CREATE TABLE dbo.CustomersStage
(
  custid      INT         NOT NULL,
  companyname VARCHAR(25) NOT NULL,
  phone       VARCHAR(20) NOT NULL,
  address     VARCHAR(50) NOT NULL,
  CONSTRAINT PK_CustomersStage PRIMARY KEY(custid)
);

INSERT INTO dbo.CustomersStage(custid, companyname, phone, address)
VALUES
  (2, 'AAAAA', '(222) 222-2222', 'address 2'),
  (3, 'cust 3', '(333) 333-3333', 'address 3'),
  (5, 'BBBBB', 'CCCCC', 'DDDDD'),
  (6, 'cust 6 (new)', '(666) 666-6666', 'address 6'),
  (7, 'cust 7 (new)', '(777) 777-7777', 'address 7');
```

Run the following query to examine the contents of the *Customers* table:

```
SELECT * FROM dbo.Customers;
```

This query returns the following output:

```
custid      companyname      phone                address
----------- ---------------- -------------------- ------------
1           cust 1           (111) 111-1111       address 1
2           cust 2           (222) 222-2222       address 2
3           cust 3           (333) 333-3333       address 3
4           cust 4           (444) 444-4444       address 4
5           cust 5           (555) 555-5555       address 5
```

Run the following query to examine the contents of the *CustomersStage* table:

```
SELECT * FROM dbo.CustomersStage;
```

This query returns the following output:

```
custid      companyname      phone                address
----------- ---------------- -------------------- ------------
2           AAAAA            (222) 222-2222       address 2
3           cust 3           (333) 333-3333       address 3
5           BBBBB            CCCCC                DDDDD
6           cust 6 (new)     (666) 666-6666       address 6
7           cust 7 (new)     (777) 777-7777       address 7
```

Suppose you need to merge the contents of the *CustomersStage* table (the source) into the *Customers* table (the target). More specifically, you need to add customers that do not exist and update the customers that do exist.

If you already feel comfortable with deletions and updates based on joins, you should feel quite comfortable with *MERGE* because it's based on join semantics. You specify the target table name in the *MERGE* clause and the source table name in the *USING* clause. You define a merge condition by specifying a predicate in the *ON* clause. The merge condition defines which rows in the source table have matches in the target and which don't. You define the action to take when a match is found in a clause called *WHEN MATCHED THEN*, and the action to take when a match is not found in the *WHEN NOT MATCHED THEN* clause.

Here's the first example for the *MERGE* statement. It adds nonexistent customers and updates existing ones:

```
MERGE INTO dbo.Customers AS TGT
USING dbo.CustomersStage AS SRC
  ON TGT.custid = SRC.custid
WHEN MATCHED THEN
  UPDATE SET
    TGT.companyname = SRC.companyname,
    TGT.phone = SRC.phone,
    TGT.address = SRC.address
WHEN NOT MATCHED THEN
  INSERT (custid, companyname, phone, address)
  VALUES (SRC.custid, SRC.companyname, SRC.phone, SRC.address);
```

> **Note** It's mandatory to terminate the *MERGE* statement with a semicolon, whereas in most other statements in T-SQL, this is optional. As mentioned, it's a best practice to terminate all statements even when you're not required to.

This *MERGE* statement defines the *Customers* table as the target (in the *MERGE* clause) and the *CustomersStage* table as the source (in the *USING* clause). Notice that you can assign aliases to the target and source tables for brevity (TGT and SRC in this case). The predicate *TGT.custid = SRC.custid* is used to define what is considered a match and what is considered a nonmatch. In this case, if a customer ID that exists in the source also exists in the target, that's a match. If a customer ID in the source does not exist in the target, that's a nonmatch.

This *MERGE* statement defines an *UPDATE* action when a match is found, setting the target *companyname*, *phone*, and *address* values to those of the corresponding row from the source. Notice that the syntax of the *UPDATE* action is similar to a normal *UPDATE* statement, except that you don't need to provide the name of the table that is the target of the update because it was already defined in the *MERGE INTO* clause.

This *MERGE* statement defines an *INSERT* action when a match is not found, inserting the row from the source to the target. Again, the syntax of the *INSERT* action is similar to a normal *INSERT* statement, except that you don't need to provide the name of the target table because it was already defined in the *MERGE INTO* clause.

The *MERGE* statement reports that five rows were modified:

```
(5 row(s) affected)
```

This includes three rows that were updated (customers 2, 3, and 5) and two that were inserted (customers 6 and 7). Query the *Customers* table to get the new contents:

```
SELECT * FROM dbo.Customers;
```

This query returns the following output:

```
custid      companyname         phone                address
----------- ------------------- -------------------- ----------
1           cust 1              (111) 111-1111       address 1
2           AAAAA               (222) 222-2222       address 2
3           cust 3              (333) 333-3333       address 3
4           cust 4              (444) 444-4444       address 4
5           BBBBB               CCCCC                DDDDD
6           cust 6 (new)        (666) 666-6666       address 6
7           cust 7 (new)        (777) 777-7777       address 7
```

The *WHEN MATCHED* clause defines what action to take against the target when a source row is matched by a target row. The *WHEN NOT MATCHED* clause defines what action to take against the target when a source row is not matched by a target row. T-SQL also supports a third clause that defines what action to take when a target row is not matched by a source row; this clause is called *WHEN NOT MATCHED BY SOURCE*. For example, suppose you want to add logic to the *MERGE* example to delete rows from the target when there's no matching source row. To achieve this, add the *WHEN NOT MATCHED BY SOURCE* clause with a *DELETE* action, like this:

```
MERGE dbo.Customers AS TGT
USING dbo.CustomersStage AS SRC
  ON TGT.custid = SRC.custid
WHEN MATCHED THEN
  UPDATE SET
    TGT.companyname = SRC.companyname,
    TGT.phone = SRC.phone,
    TGT.address = SRC.address
```

```
WHEN NOT MATCHED THEN
  INSERT (custid, companyname, phone, address)
  VALUES (SRC.custid, SRC.companyname, SRC.phone, SRC.address)
WHEN NOT MATCHED BY SOURCE THEN
  DELETE;
```

Query the *Customers* table to see the result of this *MERGE* statement:

```
SELECT * FROM dbo.Customers;
```

This query returns the following output, showing that customers 1 and 4 were deleted:

```
custid      companyname         phone                address
----------- ------------------- -------------------- ----------
2           AAAAA               (222) 222-2222       address 2
3           cust 3              (333) 333-3333       address 3
5           BBBBB               CCCCC                DDDDD
6           cust 6 (new)        (666) 666-6666       address 6
7           cust 7 (new)        (777) 777-7777       address 7
```

Going back to the first *MERGE* example, which updates existing customers and adds nonexistent ones, you can see that it doesn't check whether column values are actually different before applying an update. This means that a customer row is modified even when the source and target rows are identical. If you want to apply the update only if at least one column value is different, there is a way to achieve this.

The *MERGE* statement supports adding a predicate to the different action clauses by using the *AND* option; the action will take place only if the additional predicate evaluates to *TRUE*. In this case, you need to add a predicate under the *WHEN MATCHED AND* clause that checks that at least one of the column values is different to justify the *UPDATE* action. The complete *MERGE* statement looks like this:

```
MERGE dbo.Customers AS TGT
USING dbo.CustomersStage AS SRC
  ON TGT.custid = SRC.custid
WHEN MATCHED AND
       (   TGT.companyname <> SRC.companyname
        OR TGT.phone       <> SRC.phone
        OR TGT.address     <> SRC.address) THEN
  UPDATE SET
    TGT.companyname = SRC.companyname,
    TGT.phone = SRC.phone,
    TGT.address = SRC.address
WHEN NOT MATCHED THEN
  INSERT (custid, companyname, phone, address)
  VALUES (SRC.custid, SRC.companyname, SRC.phone, SRC.address);
```

As you can see, the *MERGE* statement is powerful, allowing you to express complex modification logic in a single statement.

Modifying data through table expressions

T-SQL doesn't limit the actions against table expressions to *SELECT* only; it also allows other DML statements (*INSERT*, *UPDATE*, *DELETE*, and *MERGE*) against those. Think about it: as explained in Chapter 5, a table expression doesn't really contain data—it's a reflection of data in underlying tables. With this in mind, think of a modification against a table expression as modifying the data in the underlying tables through the table expression. Just as with a *SELECT* statement against a table expression, a modification statement against a table expression also gets expanded, so in practice the activity is done against the underlying tables.

Modifying data through table expressions has a few restrictions:

- If the query defining the table expression joins tables, you're allowed to affect only one of the sides of the join, not both, in the same modification statement.
- You cannot update a column that is a result of a calculation; SQL Server doesn't try to reverse-engineer the values.
- *INSERT* statements must specify values for any columns in the underlying table that do not get their values implicitly. Examples for cases where a column can get a value implicitly include a column that allows *NULLs*, has a default value, has an identity property, or is typed as *ROWVERSION*.

You can find other requirements in SQL Server Books Online.

One use case for modifying data through table expressions is for better debugging and troubleshooting capabilities. For example, Listing 8-1 contained the following *UPDATE* statement:

```
UPDATE OD
  SET discount += 0.05
FROM dbo.OrderDetails AS OD
  INNER JOIN dbo.Orders AS O
    ON OD.orderid = O.orderid
WHERE O.custid = 1;
```

Suppose, for troubleshooting purposes, you first want to see which rows would be modified by this statement without actually modifying them. One option is to revise the code to a *SELECT* statement, and after troubleshooting the code, change it back to an *UPDATE* statement. But instead of needing to make such revisions, you define a table expression based on a *SELECT* statement with the join query and issue an *UPDATE* statement against the table expression. The following example uses a CTE:

```
WITH C AS
(
  SELECT custid, OD.orderid,
    productid, discount, discount + 0.05 AS newdiscount
  FROM dbo.OrderDetails AS OD
    INNER JOIN dbo.Orders AS O
      ON OD.orderid = O.orderid
  WHERE O.custid = 1
)
UPDATE C
  SET discount = newdiscount;
```

And here's an example using a derived table:

```
UPDATE D
  SET discount = newdiscount
FROM ( SELECT custid, OD.orderid,
         productid, discount, discount + 0.05 AS newdiscount
       FROM dbo.OrderDetails AS OD
         INNER JOIN dbo.Orders AS O
           ON OD.orderid = O.orderid
       WHERE O.custid = 1 ) AS D;
```

With the table expression, troubleshooting is simpler because you can always highlight just the inner *SELECT* statement and run it without making any data changes. With this example, the use of table expressions is for convenience. However, in some cases using a table expression is the only option. To demonstrate such a case, I'll use a table called *T1* that you create and populate by running the following code:

```
DROP TABLE IF EXISTS dbo.T1;
CREATE TABLE dbo.T1(col1 INT, col2 INT);
GO

INSERT INTO dbo.T1(col1) VALUES(20),(10),(30);

SELECT * FROM dbo.T1;
```

This code generates the following output:

```
col1        col2
----------- -----------
20          NULL
10          NULL
30          NULL
```

Suppose you want to update the table, setting *col2* to the result of an expression with the *ROW_NUMBER* function. The problem is that the *ROW_NUMBER* function is not allowed in the *SET* clause of an *UPDATE* statement. Try running the following code:

```
UPDATE dbo.T1
  SET col2 = ROW_NUMBER() OVER(ORDER BY col1);
```

You get the following error:

```
Msg 4108, Level 15, State 1, Line 672
Windowed functions can only appear in the SELECT or ORDER BY clauses.
```

To get around this problem, define a table expression that returns both the column you need to update (*col2*) and a result column based on an expression with the *ROW_NUMBER* function (call it *rownum*). Use an *UPDATE* statement against the table expression to set *col2* to *rownum*. Here's how the code looks when using a CTE:

```
WITH C AS
(
  SELECT col1, col2, ROW_NUMBER() OVER(ORDER BY col1) AS rownum
```

```
  FROM dbo.T1
)
UPDATE C
  SET col2 = rownum;
```

Query the table to see the result of the update:

```
SELECT * FROM dbo.T1;
```

You get the following output:

```
col1        col2
----------- -----------
20          2
10          1
30          3
```

Modifications with *TOP* and *OFFSET-FETCH*

T-SQL supports using the *TOP* option directly in *INSERT, UPDATE, DELETE*, and *MERGE* statements. When you use the *TOP* option with such statements, SQL Server stops processing the modification as soon as the specified number or percentage of rows is processed. Unfortunately, unlike with the *SELECT* statement, you cannot specify an *ORDER BY* clause for the *TOP* filter in modification statements. Essentially, whichever rows SQL Server happens to access first will be modified.

The *OFFSET-FETCH* filter is not allowed directly in modifications because this filter requires an *ORDER BY* clause and modification statements don't support one.

An example for a typical usage scenario for modifications with *TOP* is when you have a large modification, such as a large deletion operation, and you want to split it into multiple smaller chunks.

I'll demonstrate modifications with *TOP* by using a table called *dbo.Orders* that you create and populate by running the following code:

```
DROP TABLE IF EXISTS dbo.OrderDetails, dbo.Orders;

CREATE TABLE dbo.Orders
(
  orderid        INT          NOT NULL,
  custid         INT          NULL,
  empid          INT          NOT NULL,
  orderdate      DATE         NOT NULL,
  requireddate   DATE         NOT NULL,
  shippeddate    DATE         NULL,
  shipperid      INT          NOT NULL,
  freight        MONEY        NOT NULL
    CONSTRAINT DFT_Orders_freight DEFAULT(0),
  shipname       NVARCHAR(40) NOT NULL,
  shipaddress    NVARCHAR(60) NOT NULL,
  shipcity       NVARCHAR(15) NOT NULL,
  shipregion     NVARCHAR(15) NULL,
```

```
  shippostalcode NVARCHAR(10) NULL,
  shipcountry    NVARCHAR(15) NOT NULL,
  CONSTRAINT PK_Orders PRIMARY KEY(orderid)
);
GO

INSERT INTO dbo.Orders SELECT * FROM Sales.Orders;
```

The following example demonstrates the use of a *DELETE* statement with the *TOP* option to delete 50 rows from the *Orders* table:

```
DELETE TOP(50) FROM dbo.Orders;
```

Because the statement doesn't have an *ORDER BY* clause, it deletes whichever 50 rows it stumbles into first. Which rows get chosen is a result of physical data layout and optimization choices.

Similarly, you can use the *TOP* option with *UPDATE* and *INSERT* statements, but again, an *ORDER BY* is not allowed. As an example of an *UPDATE* statement with *TOP*, the following code updates 50 rows from the *Orders* table, increasing their *freight* values by 10:

```
UPDATE TOP(50) dbo.Orders
  SET freight += 10.00;
```

Again, you cannot control which 50 rows will be updated; they are the 50 rows that SQL Server happens to access first.

In practice, you typically do care which rows are affected. To control this, you can rely on the ability to modify data through table expressions. You define a table expression based on a *SELECT* query with the *TOP* filter and an *ORDER BY* clause. You then issue the modification statement against the table expression.

For example, the following code deletes the 50 orders with the lowest order ID values:

```
WITH C AS
(
  SELECT TOP (50) *
  FROM dbo.Orders
  ORDER BY orderid
)
DELETE FROM C;
```

Similarly, the following code updates the 50 orders with the highest order ID values, increasing their *freight* values by 10:

```
WITH C AS
(
  SELECT TOP (50) *
  FROM dbo.Orders
  ORDER BY orderid DESC
)
UPDATE C
  SET freight += 10.00;
```

Alternatively, you can use the *OFFSET-FETCH* option instead of *TOP*, like this:

```
WITH C AS
(
  SELECT *
  FROM dbo.Orders
  ORDER BY orderid
  OFFSET 0 ROWS FETCH NEXT 50 ROWS ONLY
)
DELETE FROM C;
```

And here's the revised *UPDATE* example:

```
WITH C AS
(
  SELECT *
  FROM dbo.Orders
  ORDER BY orderid DESC
  OFFSET 0 ROWS FETCH NEXT 50 ROWS ONLY
)
UPDATE C
  SET freight += 10.00;
```

The *OUTPUT* clause

Normally, a modification statement just modifies data. However, sometimes you might find it useful to return information from the modified rows for troubleshooting, auditing, and archiving. T-SQL supports this capability via a clause called *OUTPUT* that you add to the modification statement. In this clause, you specify attributes you want to return from the modified rows.

The *OUTPUT* clause is designed similarly to the *SELECT* clause, only you need to prefix the attributes with either the *inserted* or *deleted* keyword. In an *INSERT* statement, you refer to *inserted*; in a *DELETE* statement, you refer to *deleted*; and in an *UPDATE* statement, you refer to *deleted* for the old state of the row and *inserted* for the new state.

The *OUTPUT* clause returns a result set, much like a *SELECT* statement does. If you want to direct the result set to a table, add an *INTO* clause with the target table name. If you want to return modified rows back to the caller and also direct a copy to a table, specify two *OUTPUT* clauses: one with the *INTO* clause and one without it.

The following sections provide examples of using the *OUTPUT* clause with the different modification statements.

INSERT with *OUTPUT*

An example for a use case of the *OUTPUT* clause with an *INSERT* statement is when you need to insert a row set into a table with an identity column, and you need to get back all identity values that were generated. The *SCOPE_IDENTITY* function returns only the very last identity value that was generated—not all those generated by the statement. The *OUTPUT* clause makes the task simple. I'll use a table called *T1* to demonstrate the technique. Run the following code to create the table *T1* with an identity column called *keycol* and another column called *datacol*:

```
DROP TABLE IF EXISTS dbo.T1;

CREATE TABLE dbo.T1
(
  keycol  INT          NOT NULL IDENTITY(1, 1) CONSTRAINT PK_T1 PRIMARY KEY,
  datacol NVARCHAR(40) NOT NULL
);
```

Suppose you want to insert into *T1* the result of a query against the *HR.Employees* table and return all newly generated identity values. To achieve this, add the *OUTPUT* clause to the *INSERT* statement and specify the attributes you want to return:

```
INSERT INTO dbo.T1(datacol)
  OUTPUT inserted.keycol, inserted.datacol
    SELECT lastname
    FROM HR.Employees
    WHERE country = N'USA';
```

This statement returns the following result set:

```
keycol      datacol
----------- ---------
1           Davis
2           Funk
3           Lew
4           Peled
5           Cameron

(5 row(s) affected)
```

As you can guess, you can use a similar technique to return sequence values generated for an *INSERT* statement by the *NEXT VALUE FOR* function (either directly or in a default constraint).

As mentioned, you can also direct the result set into a table. The table can be a real table, temporary table, or table variable. When the result set is stored in the target table, you can manipulate the data by querying that table. For example, the following code declares a table variable called *@NewRows*, inserts another result set into *T1*, and directs the result set returned by the *OUTPUT* clause into the table variable. The code then queries the table variable just to show the data that was stored in it:

```
DECLARE @NewRows TABLE(keycol INT, datacol NVARCHAR(40));

INSERT INTO dbo.T1(datacol)
  OUTPUT inserted.keycol, inserted.datacol
  INTO @NewRows(keycol, datacol)
    SELECT lastname
    FROM HR.Employees
    WHERE country = N'UK';

SELECT * FROM @NewRows;
```

This code returns the following output showing the contents of the table variable:

```
keycol      datacol
----------- -------------
6           Mortensen
7           Suurs
8           King
9           Doyle

(4 row(s) affected)
```

DELETE with *OUTPUT*

The next example demonstrates the use of the *OUTPUT* clause with a *DELETE* statement. First, run the following code to create a copy of the *Orders* table from the *Sales* schema in the *dbo* schema:

```
DROP TABLE IF EXISTS dbo.Orders;

CREATE TABLE dbo.Orders
(
  orderid        INT           NOT NULL,
  custid         INT           NULL,
  empid          INT           NOT NULL,
  orderdate      DATE          NOT NULL,
  requireddate   DATE          NOT NULL,
  shippeddate    DATE          NULL,
  shipperid      INT           NOT NULL,
  freight        MONEY         NOT NULL
    CONSTRAINT DFT_Orders_freight DEFAULT(0),
  shipname       NVARCHAR(40) NOT NULL,
  shipaddress    NVARCHAR(60) NOT NULL,
  shipcity       NVARCHAR(15) NOT NULL,
  shipregion     NVARCHAR(15) NULL,
  shippostalcode NVARCHAR(10) NULL,
  shipcountry    NVARCHAR(15) NOT NULL,
  CONSTRAINT PK_Orders PRIMARY KEY(orderid)
);
GO

INSERT INTO dbo.Orders SELECT * FROM Sales.Orders;
```

The following code deletes all orders that were placed prior to 2016 and, using the *OUTPUT* clause, returns attributes from the deleted rows:

```
DELETE FROM dbo.Orders
  OUTPUT
    deleted.orderid,
    deleted.orderdate,
    deleted.empid,
    deleted.custid
WHERE orderdate < '20160101';
```

This *DELETE* statement returns the following result set:

```
orderid     orderdate  empid       custid
----------- ---------- ----------- -----------
10248       2014-07-04 5           85
10249       2014-07-05 6           79
10250       2014-07-08 4           34
10251       2014-07-08 3           84
...
10803       2015-12-30 4           88
10804       2015-12-30 6           72
10805       2015-12-30 2           77
10806       2015-12-31 3           84
10807       2015-12-31 4           27

(560 row(s) affected)
```

If you want to archive the rows that are deleted, add an *INTO* clause and specify the archive table name as the target.

UPDATE with *OUTPUT*

By using the *OUTPUT* clause with an *UPDATE* statement, you can refer to both the state of the modified row before the change (by prefixing the attribute names with the *deleted* keyword) and to the state after the change (by prefixing the attribute names with the *inserted* keyword). This way, you can return both old and new states of the updated attributes.

Before I demonstrate how to use the *OUTPUT* clause in an *UPDATE* statement, you should first run the following code to create a copy of the *Sales.OrderDetails* table from the *Sales* schema in the *dbo* schema:

```
DROP TABLE IF EXISTS dbo.OrderDetails;

CREATE TABLE dbo.OrderDetails
(
  orderid   INT            NOT NULL,
  productid INT            NOT NULL,
  unitprice MONEY          NOT NULL
    CONSTRAINT DFT_OrderDetails_unitprice DEFAULT(0),
  qty       SMALLINT       NOT NULL
    CONSTRAINT DFT_OrderDetails_qty DEFAULT(1),
  discount  NUMERIC(4, 3) NOT NULL
    CONSTRAINT DFT_OrderDetails_discount DEFAULT(0),
  CONSTRAINT PK_OrderDetails PRIMARY KEY(orderid, productid),
  CONSTRAINT CHK_discount  CHECK (discount BETWEEN 0 AND 1),
  CONSTRAINT CHK_qty  CHECK (qty > 0),
  CONSTRAINT CHK_unitprice CHECK (unitprice >= 0)
);
GO

INSERT INTO dbo.OrderDetails SELECT * FROM Sales.OrderDetails;
```

The following *UPDATE* statement increases the discount of all order details for product 51 by 5 percent and uses the *OUTPUT* clause to return the product ID, old discount, and new discount from the modified rows:

```
UPDATE dbo.OrderDetails
  SET discount += 0.05
OUTPUT
  inserted.orderid,
  inserted.productid,
  deleted.discount AS olddiscount,
  inserted.discount AS newdiscount
WHERE productid = 51;
```

This statement returns the following output:

```
orderid     productid   olddiscount  newdiscount
----------- ----------- ------------ ------------
10249       51          0.000        0.050
10250       51          0.150        0.200
10291       51          0.100        0.150
10335       51          0.200        0.250
10362       51          0.000        0.050
10397       51          0.150        0.200
10472       51          0.000        0.050
10484       51          0.000        0.050
10486       51          0.000        0.050
10537       51          0.000        0.050
...

(39 row(s) affected)
```

MERGE with *OUTPUT*

You can also use the *OUTPUT* clause with the *MERGE* statement, but remember that a single *MERGE* statement can invoke multiple different DML actions. To identify which DML action produced each output row, you can invoke a function called *$action* in the *OUTPUT* clause, which will return a string representing the action (*INSERT*, *UPDATE*, or *DELETE*).

To demonstrate *MERGE* with *OUTPUT*, I'll use the tables you created earlier in the section "Merging data" by running Listing 8-2. (Rerun that code listing to follow the example.) The following code merges the contents of *CustomersStage* into *Customers*, updating the attributes of customers who already exist in the target and adding customers who don't:

```
MERGE INTO dbo.Customers AS TGT
USING dbo.CustomersStage AS SRC
  ON TGT.custid = SRC.custid
WHEN MATCHED THEN
  UPDATE SET
    TGT.companyname = SRC.companyname,
    TGT.phone = SRC.phone,
    TGT.address = SRC.address
WHEN NOT MATCHED THEN
```

```
  INSERT (custid, companyname, phone, address)
  VALUES (SRC.custid, SRC.companyname, SRC.phone, SRC.address)
OUTPUT $action AS theaction, inserted.custid,
  deleted.companyname AS oldcompanyname,
  inserted.companyname AS newcompanyname,
  deleted.phone AS oldphone,
  inserted.phone AS newphone,
  deleted.address AS oldaddress,
  inserted.address AS newaddress;
```

This *MERGE* statement uses the *OUTPUT* clause to return the old and new values of the modified rows. Of course, with *INSERT* actions, there are no old values, so all references to deleted attributes return *NULLs*. The *$action* function tells you whether an *UPDATE* action or an *INSERT* action produced the output row. Here's the output of this *MERGE* statement:

```
theaction custid oldcompanyname newcompanyname
--------- ------ -------------- --------------
UPDATE    2      cust 2         AAAAA
UPDATE    3      cust 3         cust 3
UPDATE    5      cust 5         BBBBB
INSERT    6      NULL           cust 6 (new)
INSERT    7      NULL           cust 7 (new)

theaction custid oldphone       newphone       oldaddress newaddress
--------- ------ -------------- -------------- ---------- ----------
UPDATE    2      (222) 222-2222 (222) 222-2222 address 2  address 2
UPDATE    3      (333) 333-3333 (333) 333-3333 address 3  address 3
UPDATE    5      (555) 555-5555 CCCCC          address 5  DDDDD
INSERT    6      NULL           (666) 666-6666 NULL       address 6
INSERT    7      NULL           (777) 777-7777 NULL       address 7

(5 row(s) affected)
```

Nested DML

The *OUTPUT* clause returns an output row for every modified row. But what if you need to direct only a subset of the modified rows to a table, perhaps for auditing purposes? T-SQL supports a feature called *nested DML* you can use to directly insert into the final target table only the subset of rows you need from the full set of modified rows.

To demonstrate this capability, first create a copy of the *Products* table from the *Production* schema in the *dbo* schema, as well as the *dbo.ProductsAudit* table, by running the following code:

```
DROP TABLE IF EXISTS dbo.ProductsAudit, dbo.Products;

CREATE TABLE dbo.Products
(
  productid    INT          NOT NULL,
  productname  NVARCHAR(40) NOT NULL,
  supplierid   INT          NOT NULL,
  categoryid   INT          NOT NULL,
  unitprice    MONEY        NOT NULL
    CONSTRAINT DFT_Products_unitprice DEFAULT(0),
```

```
  discontinued BIT          NOT NULL
    CONSTRAINT DFT_Products_discontinued DEFAULT(0),
  CONSTRAINT PK_Products PRIMARY KEY(productid),
  CONSTRAINT CHK_Products_unitprice CHECK(unitprice >= 0)
);

INSERT INTO dbo.Products SELECT * FROM Production.Products;

CREATE TABLE dbo.ProductsAudit
(
  LSN INT NOT NULL IDENTITY PRIMARY KEY,
  TS DATETIME2 NOT NULL DEFAULT(SYSDATETIME()),
  productid INT NOT NULL,
  colname SYSNAME NOT NULL,
  oldval SQL_VARIANT NOT NULL,
  newval SQL_VARIANT NOT NULL
);
```

Suppose you now need to update all products supplied by supplier 1, increasing their price by 15 percent. You also need to audit the old and new values of updated products, but only those with an old price that was less than 20 and a new price that is greater than or equal to 20.

You can achieve this by using nested DML. You write an *UPDATE* statement with an *OUTPUT* clause and define a derived table based on the *UPDATE* statement. You write an *INSERT SELECT* statement that queries the derived table, filtering only the subset of rows that is needed. Here's the complete solution code:

```
INSERT INTO dbo.ProductsAudit(productid, colname, oldval, newval)
  SELECT productid, N'unitprice', oldval, newval
  FROM (UPDATE dbo.Products
          SET unitprice *= 1.15
        OUTPUT
          inserted.productid,
          deleted.unitprice AS oldval,
          inserted.unitprice AS newval
        WHERE supplierid = 1) AS D
  WHERE oldval < 20.0 AND newval >= 20.0;
```

Recall earlier discussions in the book about table expressions—the result of one query can be used as input to another. Here, the result of the statement with the *OUTPUT* clause is used as the input for the outer *INSERT SELECT* statement.

Run the following code to query the *ProductsAudit* table:

```
SELECT * FROM dbo.ProductsAudit;
```

You get the following output:

```
LSN TS                          ProductID   ColName     OldVal   NewVal
--- -------------------------   ----------- ----------- -------- ------
1   2016-02-12 18:56:04.793     1           unitprice   18.00    20.70
2   2016-02-12 18:56:04.793     2           unitprice   19.00    21.85
```

Three products were updated, but only two were filtered by the outer query; therefore, only those two were written to the audit table.

When you're done, run the following code for cleanup:

```
DROP TABLE IF EXISTS dbo.OrderDetails, dbo.ProductsAudit, dbo.Products,
  dbo.Orders, dbo.Customers, dbo.T1, dbo.MySequences, dbo.CustomersStage;
```

Conclusion

In this chapter, I covered various aspects of data modification. I described inserting, updating, deleting, and merging data. I also discussed identity and sequence, modifying data through table expressions, using *TOP* (and indirectly *OFFSET-FETCH*) with modification statements, and returning information from modified rows using the *OUTPUT* clause.

Exercises

This section provides exercises so that you can practice the subjects discussed in this chapter. The database assumed in the exercise is *TSQLV4*.

Exercise 1

Run the following code to create the *dbo.Customers* table in the *TSQLV4* database:

```
USE TSQLV4;

DROP TABLE IF EXISTS dbo.Customers;

CREATE TABLE dbo.Customers
(
  custid      INT          NOT NULL PRIMARY KEY,
  companyname NVARCHAR(40) NOT NULL,
  country     NVARCHAR(15) NOT NULL,
  region      NVARCHAR(15) NULL,
  city        NVARCHAR(15) NOT NULL
);
```

Exercise 1-1

Insert into the *dbo.Customers* table a row with the following information:

- *custid*: 100
- *companyname*: Coho Winery
- *country*: USA
- *region*: WA
- *city*: Redmond

Exercise 1-2

Insert into the *dbo.Customers* table all customers from *Sales.Customers* who placed orders.

Exercise 1-3

Use a *SELECT INTO* statement to create and populate the *dbo.Orders* table with orders from the *Sales.Orders* table that were placed in the years 2014 through 2016.

Exercise 2

Delete from the *dbo.Orders* table orders that were placed before August 2014. Use the *OUTPUT* clause to return the *orderid* and *orderdate* values of the deleted orders:

- Desired output:

```
orderid     orderdate
----------- -----------
10248       2014-07-04
10249       2014-07-05
10250       2014-07-08
10251       2014-07-08
10252       2014-07-09
10253       2014-07-10
10254       2014-07-11
10255       2014-07-12
10256       2014-07-15
10257       2014-07-16
10258       2014-07-17
10259       2014-07-18
10260       2014-07-19
10261       2014-07-19
10262       2014-07-22
10263       2014-07-23
10264       2014-07-24
10265       2014-07-25
10266       2014-07-26
10267       2014-07-29
10268       2014-07-30
10269       2014-07-31

(22 row(s) affected)
```

Exercise 3

Delete from the *dbo.Orders* table orders placed by customers from Brazil.

Exercise 4

Run the following query against *dbo.Customers*, and notice that some rows have a *NULL* in the region column:

```
SELECT * FROM dbo.Customers;
```

The output from this query is as follows:

```
custid      companyname     country         region     city
----------- --------------- --------------- ---------- ---------------
1           Customer NRZBB  Germany         NULL       Berlin
2           Customer MLTDN  Mexico          NULL       México D.F.
3           Customer KBUDE  Mexico          NULL       México D.F.
4           Customer HFBZG  UK              NULL       London
5           Customer HGVLZ  Sweden          NULL       Luleå
6           Customer XHXJV  Germany         NULL       Mannheim
7           Customer QXVLA  France          NULL       Strasbourg
8           Customer QUHWH  Spain           NULL       Madrid
9           Customer RTXGC  France          NULL       Marseille
10          Customer EEALV  Canada          BC         Tsawassen
...

(90 row(s) affected)
```

Update the *dbo.Customers* table, and change all *NULL* region values to *<None>*. Use the *OUTPUT* clause to show the *custid*, *oldregion*, and *newregion*:

- Desired output:

```
custid      oldregion       newregion
----------- --------------- ---------------
1           NULL            <None>
2           NULL            <None>
3           NULL            <None>
4           NULL            <None>
5           NULL            <None>
6           NULL            <None>
7           NULL            <None>
8           NULL            <None>
9           NULL            <None>
11          NULL            <None>
12          NULL            <None>
13          NULL            <None>
14          NULL            <None>
16          NULL            <None>
17          NULL            <None>
18          NULL            <None>
19          NULL            <None>
20          NULL            <None>
23          NULL            <None>
24          NULL            <None>
25          NULL            <None>
26          NULL            <None>
27          NULL            <None>
28          NULL            <None>
29          NULL            <None>
30          NULL            <None>
39          NULL            <None>
40          NULL            <None>
41          NULL            <None>
```

```
44          NULL            <None>
49          NULL            <None>
50          NULL            <None>
52          NULL            <None>
53          NULL            <None>
54          NULL            <None>
56          NULL            <None>
58          NULL            <None>
59          NULL            <None>
60          NULL            <None>
63          NULL            <None>
64          NULL            <None>
66          NULL            <None>
68          NULL            <None>
69          NULL            <None>
70          NULL            <None>
72          NULL            <None>
73          NULL            <None>
74          NULL            <None>
76          NULL            <None>
79          NULL            <None>
80          NULL            <None>
83          NULL            <None>
84          NULL            <None>
85          NULL            <None>
86          NULL            <None>
87          NULL            <None>
90          NULL            <None>
91          NULL            <None>

(58 row(s) affected)
```

Exercise 5

Update all orders in the *dbo.Orders* table that were placed by United Kingdom customers, and set their *shipcountry*, *shipregion*, and *shipcity* values to the *country*, *region*, and *city* values of the corresponding customers.

Exercise 6

Run the following code to create the tables *Orders* and *OrderDetails* and populate them with data:

```
USE TSQLV4;

DROP TABLE IF EXISTS dbo.OrderDetails, dbo.Orders;

CREATE TABLE dbo.Orders
(
  orderid        INT          NOT NULL,
  custid         INT          NULL,
  empid          INT          NOT NULL,
  orderdate      DATE         NOT NULL,
  requireddate   DATE         NOT NULL,
```

```
  shippeddate    DATE          NULL,
  shipperid      INT           NOT NULL,
  freight        MONEY         NOT NULL
    CONSTRAINT DFT_Orders_freight DEFAULT(0),
  shipname       NVARCHAR(40) NOT NULL,
  shipaddress    NVARCHAR(60) NOT NULL,
  shipcity       NVARCHAR(15) NOT NULL,
  shipregion     NVARCHAR(15) NULL,
  shippostalcode NVARCHAR(10) NULL,
  shipcountry    NVARCHAR(15) NOT NULL,
  CONSTRAINT PK_Orders PRIMARY KEY(orderid)
);

CREATE TABLE dbo.OrderDetails
(
  orderid   INT           NOT NULL,
  productid INT           NOT NULL,
  unitprice MONEY         NOT NULL
    CONSTRAINT DFT_OrderDetails_unitprice DEFAULT(0),
  qty       SMALLINT      NOT NULL
    CONSTRAINT DFT_OrderDetails_qty DEFAULT(1),
  discount  NUMERIC(4, 3) NOT NULL
    CONSTRAINT DFT_OrderDetails_discount DEFAULT(0),
  CONSTRAINT PK_OrderDetails PRIMARY KEY(orderid, productid),
  CONSTRAINT FK_OrderDetails_Orders FOREIGN KEY(orderid)
    REFERENCES dbo.Orders(orderid),
  CONSTRAINT CHK_discount  CHECK (discount BETWEEN 0 AND 1),
  CONSTRAINT CHK_qty  CHECK (qty > 0),
  CONSTRAINT CHK_unitprice CHECK (unitprice >= 0)
);
GO

INSERT INTO dbo.Orders SELECT * FROM Sales.Orders;
INSERT INTO dbo.OrderDetails SELECT * FROM Sales.OrderDetails;
```

Write and test the T-SQL code that is required to truncate both tables, and make sure your code runs successfully.

When you're done, run the following code for cleanup:

```
DROP TABLE IF EXISTS dbo.OrderDetails, dbo.Orders, dbo.Customers;
```

Solutions

This section provides solutions to the preceding exercises.

Exercise 1

This exercise is split into three parts. The following sections provide the solutions to those parts.

Exercise 1-1

Make sure you are connected to the *TSQLV4* database:

```
USE TSQLV4;
```

Use the following *INSERT VALUES* statement to insert a row into the *Customers* table with the values provided in the exercise:

```
INSERT INTO dbo.Customers(custid, companyname, country, region, city)
  VALUES(100, N'Coho Winery', N'USA', N'WA', N'Redmond');
```

Exercise 1-2

One way to identify customers who placed orders is to use the *EXISTS* predicate, as the following query shows:

```
  SELECT custid, companyname, country, region, city
  FROM Sales.Customers AS C
  WHERE EXISTS
    (SELECT * FROM Sales.Orders AS O
     WHERE O.custid = C.custid);
```

To insert the rows returned from this query into the *dbo.Customers* table, you can use an *INSERT SELECT* statement as follows:

```
INSERT INTO dbo.Customers(custid, companyname, country, region, city)
  SELECT custid, companyname, country, region, city
  FROM Sales.Customers AS C
  WHERE EXISTS
    (SELECT * FROM Sales.Orders AS O
     WHERE O.custid = C.custid);
```

Exercise 1-3

The following code first ensures that the session is connected to the *TSQLV4* database, and then it drops the *dbo.Orders* table if it already exists. Finally, it uses the *SELECT INTO* statement to create a new *dbo.Orders* table and populate it with orders from the *Sales.Orders* table placed in the years 2014 through 2016:

```
USE TSQLV4;

DROP TABLE IF EXISTS dbo.Orders;

SELECT *
INTO dbo.Orders
FROM Sales.Orders
WHERE orderdate >= '20140101'
  AND orderdate < '20170101';
```

Exercise 2

To delete orders placed before August 2014, you need a *DELETE* statement with a filter based on the predicate *orderdate < '20140801'*. As requested, use the *OUTPUT* clause to return attributes from the deleted rows:

```
DELETE FROM dbo.Orders
  OUTPUT deleted.orderid, deleted.orderdate
WHERE orderdate < '20140801';
```

Exercise 3

This exercise requires you to write a *DELETE* statement that deletes rows from one table (*dbo.Orders*) based on the existence of a matching row in another table (*dbo.Customers*). One way to handle the task is to use a standard *DELETE* statement with an *EXISTS* predicate in the *WHERE* clause, like this:

```
DELETE FROM dbo.Orders
WHERE EXISTS
  (SELECT *
   FROM dbo.Customers AS C
   WHERE Orders.custid = C.custid
     AND C.country = N'Brazil');
```

This *DELETE* statement deletes the rows from the *dbo.Orders* table for which a related row exists in the *dbo.Customers* table with the same customer ID as the order's customer ID and the customer's country is Brazil.

Another way to handle this task is to use the T-SQL–specific *DELETE* syntax based on a join, like this:

```
DELETE FROM O
FROM dbo.Orders AS O
  INNER JOIN dbo.Customers AS C
    ON O.custid = C.custid
WHERE country = N'Brazil';
```

The join between the *dbo.Orders* and *dbo.Customers* tables serves a filtering purpose. The join matches each order with the customer who placed the order. The *WHERE* clause filters only rows for which the customer's country is Brazil. The *DELETE FROM* clause refers to the alias *O* representing the table *Orders*, indicating that *Orders* is the target of the *DELETE* operation.

As a standard alternative, you can use the *MERGE* statement to handle this task. Even though you normally think of using *MERGE* when you need to apply different actions based on conditional logic, you also can use it when you need to apply only one action. In our case, you can use the *MERGE* statement with the *WHEN MATCHED* clause alone; you don't need to have a *WHEN NOT MATCHED* clause as well. The following *MERGE* statement handles the request in the exercise:

```
MERGE INTO dbo.Orders AS O
USING (SELECT * FROM dbo.Customers WHERE country = N'Brazil') AS C
  ON O.custid = C.custid
WHEN MATCHED THEN DELETE;
```

This *MERGE* statement defines the *dbo.Orders* table as the target. It defines a table expression with customers from the *dbo.Customers* table that are from Brazil as the source. An order is deleted from the target (*dbo.Orders*) when a matching row is found in the source (*dbo.Customers*) with the same customer ID.

Exercise 4

This exercise involves writing an *UPDATE* statement that filters only rows for which the region attribute is *NULL*. Make sure you use the *IS NULL* predicate and not an equality operator when looking for *NULLs*. Use the *OUTPUT* clause to return the requested information. Here's the complete *UPDATE* statement:

```
UPDATE dbo.Customers
  SET region = '<None>'
OUTPUT
  deleted.custid,
  deleted.region AS oldregion,
  inserted.region AS newregion
WHERE region IS NULL;
```

Exercise 5

One way to solve this exercise is to use the T-SQL–specific *UPDATE* syntax based on a join. You can join *dbo.Orders* and *dbo.Customers* based on a match between the order's customer ID and the customer's customer ID. In the *WHERE* clause, you can filter only the rows where the customer's country is the United Kingdom. In the *UPDATE* clause, specify the alias you assigned to the *dbo.Orders* table to indicate that it's the target of the modification. In the *SET* clause, assign the values of the shipping location attributes of the order to the location attributes of the corresponding customer. Here's the complete *UPDATE* statement:

```
UPDATE O
  SET shipcountry = C.country,
      shipregion = C.region,
      shipcity = C.city
FROM dbo.Orders AS O
  INNER JOIN dbo.Customers AS C
    ON O.custid = C.custid
WHERE C.country = N'UK';
```

Another solution is to define a CTE based on a *SELECT* query that joins *dbo.Orders* and *dbo.Customers* and returns both the target location attributes from *dbo.Orders* and the source location attributes from *dbo.Customers*. The outer query would then be an *UPDATE* statement modifying the target attributes with the values of the source attributes. Here's the complete solution statement:

```
WITH CTE_UPD AS
(
  SELECT
    O.shipcountry AS ocountry, C.country AS ccountry,
    O.shipregion  AS oregion,  C.region  AS cregion,
```

```
    O.shipcity    AS ocity,    C.city    AS ccity
  FROM dbo.Orders AS O
    INNER JOIN dbo.Customers AS C
      ON O.custid = C.custid
  WHERE C.country = N'UK'
)
UPDATE CTE_UPD
  SET ocountry = ccountry, oregion = cregion, ocity = ccity;
```

You can also use the *MERGE* statement to achieve this task. As explained earlier, even though in a *MERGE* statement you usually want to specify both the *WHEN MATCHED* and *WHEN NOT MATCHED* clauses, the statement supports specifying only one of the clauses. Using only a *WHEN MATCHED* clause with an *UPDATE* action, you can write a solution that is logically equivalent to the last two solutions. Here's the complete solution statement:

```
MERGE INTO dbo.Orders AS O
USING (SELECT * FROM dbo.Customers WHERE country = N'UK') AS C
  ON O.custid = C.custid
WHEN MATCHED THEN
  UPDATE SET shipcountry = C.country,
             shipregion = C.region,
             shipcity = C.city;
```

Exercise 6

There's a foreign-key relationship between *OrderDetails* and *Orders*. In such a case, you're allowed to truncate the referencing table, but not the referenced table, even if there are no related rows in the referencing table. You will need to drop the foreign-key constraint, truncate the tables, and then re-create the constraint, like this:

```
ALTER TABLE dbo.OrderDetails DROP CONSTRAINT FK_OrderDetails_Orders;

TRUNCATE TABLE dbo.OrderDetails;
TRUNCATE TABLE dbo.Orders;

ALTER TABLE dbo.OrderDetails ADD CONSTRAINT FK_OrderDetails_Orders
  FOREIGN KEY(orderid) REFERENCES dbo.Orders(orderid);
```

When you're done, run the following code for cleanup:

```
DROP TABLE IF EXISTS dbo.OrderDetails, dbo.Orders, dbo.Customers;
```

CHAPTER 9

Temporal tables

When you modify data in tables, normally you lose any trace of the premodified state of the rows. You can access only the current state. What if you need to be able to access historical states of the data? Perhaps you need these states for auditing, point-in-time analysis, comparing current states with older states, slowly changing dimensions (details of which you can find in the Wikipedia article at *https://en.wikipedia.org/wiki/Slowly_changing_dimension*), restoring an older state of rows because of accidental deletion or updating, and so on. You could roll your own customized solution based on triggers. Better yet, starting with Microsoft SQL Server 2016, you can use a built-in feature called *system-versioned temporal tables*. This built-in feature provides a solution that is both simpler and more efficient than a customized one can be.

A system-versioned temporal table has two columns representing the validity period of the row, plus a linked history table with a mirrored schema holding older states of modified rows. When you need to modify data, you interact with the current table, issuing normal data-modification statements. SQL Server automatically updates the period columns and moves older versions of rows to the history table. When you need to query data, if you want the current state, you simply query the current table as usual. If you need access to older states, you still query the current table, but you add a clause indicating that you want to see an older state or period of time. SQL Server queries the current and history tables behind the scenes as needed.

The SQL standard supports three types of temporal tables:

- System-versioned temporal tables rely on the system transaction time to define the validity period of a row.
- Application-time period tables rely on the application's definition of the validity period of a row. This means you can define a validity period that will become effective in the future.
- Bitemporal combines the two types just mentioned (transaction and valid time).

SQL Server 2016 supports only system-versioned temporal tables. I hope Microsoft will add support for application-time period tables and bitemporal tables to future versions of SQL Server.

This chapter covers system-versioned temporal tables in three sections: creating tables, modifying data, and querying data.

Creating tables

When you create a system-versioned temporal table, you need to make sure the table definition has all the following elements:

- A primary key
- Two columns defined as *DATETIME2* with any precision, which are non-nullable and represent the start and end of the row's validity period in the UTC time zone
- A start column that should be marked with the option *GENERATED ALWAYS AS ROW START*
- An end column that should be marked with the option *GENERATED ALWAYS AS ROW END*
- A designation of the period columns with the option *PERIOD FOR SYSTEM_TIME (<startcol>, <endcol>)*
- The table option *SYSTEM_VERSIONING*, which should be set to ON
- A linked history table (which SQL Server can create for you) to hold the past states of modified rows

Optionally, you can mark the period columns as hidden so that when you're querying the table with *SELECT* * they won't be returned and when you're inserting data they'll be ignored.

Run the following code to create a system-versioned temporal table called *Employees* and a linked history table called *EmployeesHistory*:

```
USE TSQLV4;

-- Create Employees table
CREATE TABLE dbo.Employees
(
  empid      INT                          NOT NULL
    CONSTRAINT PK_Employees PRIMARY KEY NONCLUSTERED,
  empname    VARCHAR(25)                  NOT NULL,
  department VARCHAR(50)                  NOT NULL,
  salary     NUMERIC(10, 2)               NOT NULL,
  sysstart   DATETIME2(0)
    GENERATED ALWAYS AS ROW START HIDDEN NOT NULL,
  sysend     DATETIME2(0)
    GENERATED ALWAYS AS ROW END   HIDDEN NOT NULL,
  PERIOD FOR SYSTEM_TIME (sysstart, sysend),
  INDEX ix_Employees CLUSTERED(empid, sysstart, sysend)
)
WITH ( SYSTEM_VERSIONING = ON ( HISTORY_TABLE = dbo.EmployeesHistory ) );
```

Review the list of required elements, and make sure you identify them in the code.

Assuming the history table doesn't exist when you run this code, SQL Server creates it for you. If you do not specify a name for the table, SQL Server assigns one for you using the form *MSSQL_TemporalHistoryFor_<object_id>*, where *object_id* is the object ID of the current table. SQL Server creates the history table with a mirrored schema of the current table, but with the following differences:

- No primary key
- A clustered index on (*<endcol>*, *<startcol>*), with page compression if possible

- Period columns that are not marked with any special options, like *GENERATED ALWAYS AS ROW START/END* or *HIDDEN*
- No designation of the period columns with the option *PERIOD FOR SYSTEM_TIME*
- The history table is not marked with the option *SYSTEM_VERSIONING*

If the history table already exists when you create the current table, SQL Server validates the consistency of both the schema (as just described) and the data (with no overlapping periods). If the history table doesn't pass the consistency checks, SQL Server will produce an error at DDL time and won't create the current table. You can optionally indicate you do not want SQL Server to perform the data-consistency check.

If you browse the object tree in Object Explorer in SQL Server Management Studio (SSMS), you'll find the *Employees* table marked as (System-Versioned) and below it the linked *EmployeesHistory* table marked as (History), as shown in Figure 9-1.

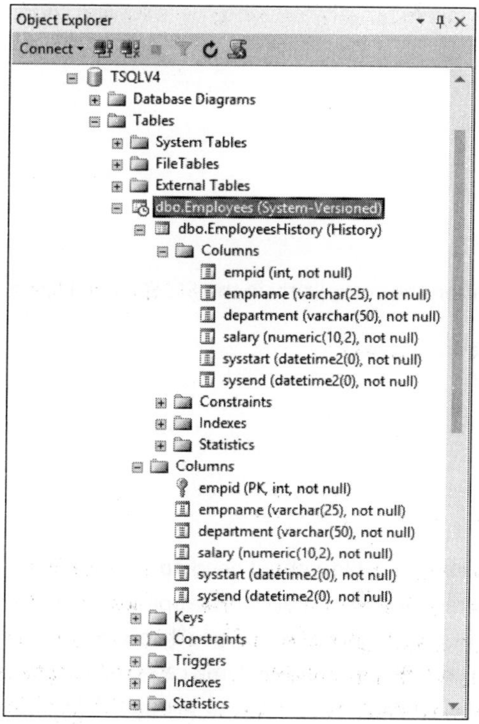

FIGURE 9-1 Temporal table and associated history table in SSMS.

You can also turn an existing nontemporal table that already has data into a temporal one. For example, suppose you have a table called *Employees* in your database and you want to turn it into a temporal table. You first alter the table, adding the period columns and designating them as such using the following code (but don't actually run the code because our *Employees* table is already temporal):

```
ALTER TABLE dbo.Employees ADD
  sysstart DATETIME2(0) GENERATED ALWAYS AS ROW START HIDDEN NOT NULL
    CONSTRAINT DFT_Employees_sysstart DEFAULT('19000101'),
  sysend DATETIME2(0) GENERATED ALWAYS AS ROW END HIDDEN NOT NULL
    CONSTRAINT DFT_Employees_sysend DEFAULT('99991231 23:59:59'),
  PERIOD FOR SYSTEM_TIME (sysstart, sysend);
```

Notice the defaults that set the validity period for the existing rows. You decide what you want the start time of the validity period to be, as long as it's not in the future. The end has to be the maximum supported value in the type.

You then alter the table to enable system versioning and to link it to a history table using the following code (again, don't actually run this code in our case):

```
ALTER TABLE dbo.Employees
  SET ( SYSTEM_VERSIONING = ON ( HISTORY_TABLE = dbo.EmployeesHistory ) );
```

Remember that if you marked the period columns as hidden, when you query the table with *SELECT* * SQL Server won't return them. Try this with our *Employees* table by running the following code:

```
SELECT *
FROM dbo.Employees;
```

You get the following output:

```
empid  empname  department  salary
------ -------- ----------- ---------
```

If you do want to return the period columns, mention them explicitly in the *SELECT* list, like so:

```
SELECT empid, empname, department, salary, sysstart, sysend
FROM dbo.Employees;
```

You get the following output:

```
empid  empname  department  salary    sysstart             sysend
------ -------- ----------- --------- -------------------- --------------------
```

SQL Server supports making schema changes to a temporal table without needing to disable system versioning first. You issue the schema change to the current table, and SQL Server applies it to both the current and history tables. Naturally, if you want to add a non-nullable column, you'll need to add it with a default constraint. For example, suppose you want to add a non-nullable column called *hiredate* to our *Employees* table and use the date January 1st, 1900 as the default. You do so by running the following code:

```
ALTER TABLE dbo.Employees
  ADD hiredate DATE NOT NULL
    CONSTRAINT DFT_Employees_hiredate DEFAULT('19000101');
```

You can then update the hire date of existing employees as needed.

Query the *Employees* table after adding the *hiredate* column:

```
SELECT *
FROM dbo.Employees;
```

You get the following output:

```
empid  empname  department  salary    hiredate
------ -------- ----------- --------- ----------
```

Query the *EmployeesHistory* table:

```
SELECT *
FROM dbo.EmployeesHistory;
```

Notice the output has the *hiredate* column in this table as well:

```
empid  empname  department  salary    sysstart              sysend                hiredate
------ -------- ----------- --------- --------------------- --------------------- -----------
```

SQL Server added the *hiredate* column to both tables, but the default constraint was added only in the current table. Still, if there had been any rows in the history table, SQL Server would have assigned the default value to the *hiredate* column in those rows.

Suppose you want to drop the *hiredate* column from both tables. First you drop the default constraint from the current table by running the following code:

```
ALTER TABLE dbo.Employees
  DROP CONSTRAINT DFT_Employees_hiredate;
```

Second, you drop the column from the current table by running the following code:

```
ALTER TABLE dbo.Employees
  DROP COLUMN hiredate;
```

SQL Server drops the column from both tables.

Modifying data

Modifying temporal tables is similar to modifying regular tables. You modify only the current table with *INSERT, UPDATE, DELETE,* and *MERGE* statements. (There's no support for *TRUNCATE* in SQL Server 2016 temporal tables.) Behind the scenes, SQL Server updates the period columns and moves rows to the history table as needed. Remember that the period columns reflect the validity period of the row in the UTC time zone.

If you defined the period columns as hidden, like in our case, you simply ignore them in *INSERT* statements. If you didn't define them as hidden, as long as you follow best practices and explicitly mention the target column names, you can still ignore them. If you didn't define them as hidden and you do not mention the target column names, you'll need to specify the keyword DEFAULT as the value for them.

In the following examples, I'll demonstrate modifications against the *Employees* table and mention the point in time in the UTC time zone at which I apply them. Naturally, the modification times will be different for you when you run the code samples, so it might be a good idea for you to make a note of those times when you submit them. You can query the *SYSUTCDATETIME* function to get this information.

Run the following code to add a few rows to the *Employees* table (the time was 2016-02-16 17:08:41 when I ran it):

```
INSERT INTO dbo.Employees(empid, empname, department, salary)
  VALUES(1, 'Sara', 'IT'       , 50000.00),
        (2, 'Don' , 'HR'       , 45000.00),
        (3, 'Judy', 'Sales'    , 55000.00),
        (4, 'Yael', 'Marketing', 55000.00),
        (5, 'Sven', 'IT'       , 45000.00),
        (6, 'Paul', 'Sales'    , 40000.00);
```

Query the data in both the current and history tables to see what SQL Server did behind the scenes:

```
SELECT empid, empname, department, salary, sysstart, sysend
FROM dbo.Employees;

SELECT empid, empname, department, salary, sysstart, sysend
FROM dbo.EmployeesHistory;
```

The current table has the six new rows, with the *sysstart* column reflecting the modification time and *sysend* holding the maximum possible value in the type with the chosen precision:

```
empid  empname  department  salary    sysstart             sysend
------ -------- ----------- --------- -------------------- --------------------
1      Sara     IT          50000.00  2016-02-16 17:08:41  9999-12-31 23:59:59
2      Don      HR          45000.00  2016-02-16 17:08:41  9999-12-31 23:59:59
3      Judy     Sales       55000.00  2016-02-16 17:08:41  9999-12-31 23:59:59
4      Yael     Marketing   55000.00  2016-02-16 17:08:41  9999-12-31 23:59:59
5      Sven     IT          45000.00  2016-02-16 17:08:41  9999-12-31 23:59:59
6      Paul     Sales       40000.00  2016-02-16 17:08:41  9999-12-31 23:59:59
```

The validity period indicates that the rows are considered valid since the time they were inserted and with no end limit.

The history table is empty at this point:

```
empid  empname  department  salary    sysstart             sysend
------ -------- ----------- --------- -------------------- --------------------
```

Run the following code to delete the row where the employee ID is 6 (the time was 2016-02-16 17:15:26 when I ran it):

```
DELETE FROM dbo.Employees
WHERE empid = 6;
```

SQL Server moves the deleted row to the history table, setting its *sysend* value to the deletion time. Following is the content of the current table at this point:

```
empid  empname  department  salary    sysstart             sysend
------ -------- ----------- --------- -------------------- --------------------
1      Sara     IT          50000.00  2016-02-16 17:08:41  9999-12-31 23:59:59
2      Don      HR          45000.00  2016-02-16 17:08:41  9999-12-31 23:59:59
3      Judy     Sales       55000.00  2016-02-16 17:08:41  9999-12-31 23:59:59
4      Yael     Marketing   55000.00  2016-02-16 17:08:41  9999-12-31 23:59:59
5      Sven     IT          45000.00  2016-02-16 17:08:41  9999-12-31 23:59:59
```

Following is the content of the history table:

```
empid  empname  department  salary    sysstart             sysend
------ -------- ----------- --------- -------------------- --------------------
6      Paul     Sales       40000.00  2016-02-16 17:08:41  2016-02-16 17:15:26
```

An update of a row is treated as a delete plus an insert. SQL Server moves the old version of the row to the history table with the transaction time as the period end time, and it keeps the current version of the row in the current table with the transaction time as the period start time and the maximum value in the type as the period end time. For example, run the following update to increase the salary of all IT employees by 5 percent (the time was 2016-02-16 17:20:02 when I ran it):

```
UPDATE dbo.Employees
  SET salary *= 1.05
WHERE department = 'IT';
```

Following is the content of the current table after the update:

```
empid  empname  department  salary    sysstart             sysend
------ -------- ----------- --------- -------------------- --------------------
1      Sara     IT          52500.00  2016-02-16 17:20:02  9999-12-31 23:59:59
2      Don      HR          45000.00  2016-02-16 17:08:41  9999-12-31 23:59:59
3      Judy     Sales       55000.00  2016-02-16 17:08:41  9999-12-31 23:59:59
4      Yael     Marketing   55000.00  2016-02-16 17:08:41  9999-12-31 23:59:59
5      Sven     IT          47250.00  2016-02-16 17:20:02  9999-12-31 23:59:59
```

Notice the values in the *salary* and period columns for the IT employees.

Following is the content of the history table:

```
empid  empname  department  salary    sysstart             sysend
------ -------- ----------- --------- -------------------- --------------------
6      Paul     Sales       40000.00  2016-02-16 17:08:41  2016-02-16 17:15:26
1      Sara     IT          50000.00  2016-02-16 17:08:41  2016-02-16 17:20:02
5      Sven     IT          45000.00  2016-02-16 17:08:41  2016-02-16 17:20:02
```

The modification times that SQL Server records in the period columns reflect the transaction start time. If you have a long-running transaction that started at point in time T1 and ended at T2, SQL Server will record T1 as the modification time for all statements. For example, run this code to open an explicit transaction and change the department of employee 5 to Sales (the time was 2016-02-16 17:28:10 when I ran it):

```
BEGIN TRAN;

UPDATE dbo.Employees
  SET department = 'Sales'
WHERE empid = 5;
```

Wait a few seconds, and then run the following code to change the department of employee 3 to IT (the time was 2016-02-16 17:29:22 when I ran it):

```
UPDATE dbo.Employees
  SET department = 'IT'
WHERE empid = 3;

COMMIT TRAN;
```

Following is the content of the current table after running this transaction:

```
empid  empname  department  salary    sysstart             sysend
------ -------- ----------- --------- -------------------- --------------------
1      Sara     IT          52500.00  2016-02-16 17:20:02  9999-12-31 23:59:59
2      Don      HR          45000.00  2016-02-16 17:08:41  9999-12-31 23:59:59
3      Judy     IT          55000.00  2016-02-16 17:28:10  9999-12-31 23:59:59
4      Yael     Marketing   55000.00  2016-02-16 17:08:41  9999-12-31 23:59:59
5      Sven     Sales       47250.00  2016-02-16 17:28:10  9999-12-31 23:59:59
```

Following is the content of the history table at this point:

```
empid  empname  department  salary    sysstart             sysend
------ -------- ----------- --------- -------------------- --------------------
6      Paul     Sales       40000.00  2016-02-16 17:08:41  2016-02-16 17:15:26
1      Sara     IT          50000.00  2016-02-16 17:08:41  2016-02-16 17:20:02
5      Sven     IT          45000.00  2016-02-16 17:08:41  2016-02-16 17:20:02
3      Judy     Sales       55000.00  2016-02-16 17:08:41  2016-02-16 17:28:10
5      Sven     IT          47250.00  2016-02-16 17:20:02  2016-02-16 17:28:10
```

Observe that for all modified rows, the modification time (*sysstart* for current rows and *sysend* for history rows) reflects the transaction start time.

Querying data

Querying data in temporal tables is simple and elegant. If you want to query the current state of the data, you simply query the current table as you would query a normal table. If you want to query a past state of the data, you still query the current table, but you add a clause called *FOR SYSTEM_TIME* and a subclause that indicates the validity point or period of time you're interested in.

Before examining the specifics of querying temporal tables, run the following code to re-create the *Employees* and *EmployeesHistory* tables and to populate them with the same sample data as in my environment, including the values in the period columns:

```
USE TSQLV4;

-- Drop tables if exist
```

```
IF OBJECT_ID(N'dbo.Employees', N'U') IS NOT NULL
BEGIN
  IF OBJECTPROPERTY(OBJECT_ID(N'dbo.Employees', N'U'), N'TableTemporalType') = 2
    ALTER TABLE dbo.Employees SET ( SYSTEM_VERSIONING = OFF );
  DROP TABLE IF EXISTS dbo.EmployeesHistory, dbo.Employees;
END;
GO

-- Create and populate Employees table
CREATE TABLE dbo.Employees
(
  empid      INT             NOT NULL
    CONSTRAINT PK_Employees PRIMARY KEY NONCLUSTERED,
  empname    VARCHAR(25)     NOT NULL,
  department VARCHAR(50)     NOT NULL,
  salary     NUMERIC(10, 2)  NOT NULL,
  sysstart   DATETIME2(0)    NOT NULL,
  sysend     DATETIME2(0)    NOT NULL,
  INDEX ix_Employees CLUSTERED(empid, sysstart, sysend)
);

INSERT INTO dbo.Employees(empid, empname, department, salary, sysstart, sysend) VALUES
  (1 , 'Sara', 'IT'        , 52500.00, '2016-02-16 17:20:02', '9999-12-31 23:59:59'),
  (2 , 'Don' , 'HR'        , 45000.00, '2016-02-16 17:08:41', '9999-12-31 23:59:59'),
  (3 , 'Judy', 'IT'        , 55000.00, '2016-02-16 17:28:10', '9999-12-31 23:59:59'),
  (4 , 'Yael', 'Marketing', 55000.00, '2016-02-16 17:08:41', '9999-12-31 23:59:59'),
  (5 , 'Sven', 'Sales'     , 47250.00, '2016-02-16 17:28:10', '9999-12-31 23:59:59');

-- Create and populate EmployeesHistory table
CREATE TABLE dbo.EmployeesHistory
(
  empid      INT             NOT NULL,
  empname    VARCHAR(25)     NOT NULL,
  department VARCHAR(50)     NOT NULL,
  salary     NUMERIC(10, 2)  NOT NULL,
  sysstart   DATETIME2(0)    NOT NULL,
  sysend     DATETIME2(0)    NOT NULL,
  INDEX ix_EmployeesHistory CLUSTERED(sysend, sysstart)
    WITH (DATA_COMPRESSION = PAGE)
);

INSERT INTO dbo.EmployeesHistory(empid, empname, department, salary, sysstart, sysend) VALUES
  (6 , 'Paul', 'Sales' , 40000.00, '2016-02-16 17:08:41', '2016-02-16 17:15:26'),
  (1 , 'Sara', 'IT'    , 50000.00, '2016-02-16 17:08:41', '2016-02-16 17:20:02'),
  (5 , 'Sven', 'IT'    , 45000.00, '2016-02-16 17:08:41', '2016-02-16 17:20:02'),
  (3 , 'Judy', 'Sales' , 55000.00, '2016-02-16 17:08:41', '2016-02-16 17:28:10'),
  (5 , 'Sven', 'IT'    , 47250.00, '2016-02-16 17:20:02', '2016-02-16 17:28:10');

-- Enable system versioning
ALTER TABLE dbo.Employees ADD PERIOD FOR SYSTEM_TIME (sysstart, sysend);

ALTER TABLE dbo.Employees ALTER COLUMN sysstart ADD HIDDEN;
ALTER TABLE dbo.Employees ALTER COLUMN sysend ADD HIDDEN;

ALTER TABLE dbo.Employees
  SET ( SYSTEM_VERSIONING = ON ( HISTORY_TABLE = dbo.EmployeesHistory ) );
```

This way, the outputs of the queries in your environment will be the same as in the book. Just remember that when a query has no *ORDER BY* cause, there's no guarantee for any specific presentation order in the output. So it is possible that the order of the rows you'll get when you run the queries will be different than in the book.

As mentioned, if you want to query the current state of the rows, simply query the current table:

```
SELECT *
FROM dbo.Employees;
```

This query generates the following output:

```
empid  empname  department  salary
------ -------- ----------- ---------
1      Sara     IT          52500.00
2      Don      HR          45000.00
3      Judy     IT          55000.00
4      Yael     Marketing   55000.00
5      Sven     Sales       47250.00
```

Remember that because the period columns are defined as hidden, a *SELECT ** query doesn't return them. Here I use *SELECT ** for illustration purposes, but I remind you that the best practice is to be explicit about the column list in production code. The same applies to *INSERT* statements. If you do follow best practices, whether the period columns were defined as hidden or not shouldn't really matter to you.

If you want to see a past state of the data, correct to a certain point or period of time, you query the current table followed by the *FOR SYSTEM_TIME* clause, plus a subclause that indicates more specifics. SQL Server will retrieve the data from both the current and history tables as needed. Conveniently, you can specify the *FOR SYSTEM_TIME* clause when querying views, and the clause definition is propagated to underlying objects.

Following is the syntax for using the *FOR SYSTEM_TIME* clause:

```
SELECT ... FROM <table_or_view> FOR SYSTEM_TIME <subclause> AS <alias>;
```

Of the five subclauses that the *SYSTEM_TIME* clause supports, you'll probably use the *AS OF* subclause most often. You use it to request to see the data correct to a specific point in time you specify. The syntax of this subclause is *FOR SYSTEM_TIME AS OF <datetime2 value>*. The input can be either a constant, variable, or parameter. Say the input is a variable called *@datetime*. You'll get back the rows where *@datetime* is on or after *sysstart* and before *sysend*. In other words, the validity period starts on or before *@datetime* and ends after *@datetime*. The following predicate identifies the qualifying rows:

```
sysstart <= @datetime AND sysend > @datetime
```

Run the following code to return the employee rows correct to the point in time 2016-02-16 17:00:00:

```
SELECT *
FROM dbo.Employees FOR SYSTEM_TIME AS OF '2016-02-16 17:00:00';
```

You'll get an empty result because the first insert you issued against the table happened at 2016-02-16 17:08:41:

```
empid  empname  department  salary
------ -------- ----------- ---------
```

Query the table again, this time as of 2016-02-16 17:10:00:

```
SELECT *
FROM dbo.Employees FOR SYSTEM_TIME AS OF '2016-02-16 17:10:00';
```

You get the following output:

```
empid  empname  department  salary
------ -------- ----------- ---------
2      Don      HR          45000.00
4      Yael     Marketing   55000.00
6      Paul     Sales       40000.00
1      Sara     IT          50000.00
5      Sven     IT          45000.00
3      Judy     Sales       55000.00
```

You can also query multiple instances of the same table, comparing different states of the data at different points in time. For example, the following query returns the percentage of increase of salary of employees who had a salary increase between two different points in time:

```
SELECT T2.empid, T2.empname,
  CAST( (T2.salary / T1.salary - 1.0) * 100.0 AS NUMERIC(10, 2) ) AS pct
FROM dbo.Employees FOR SYSTEM_TIME AS OF '2016-02-16 17:10:00' AS T1
  INNER JOIN dbo.Employees FOR SYSTEM_TIME AS OF '2016-02-16 17:25:00' AS T2
    ON T1.empid = T2.empid
   AND T2.salary > T1.salary;
```

This code generates the following output:

```
empid  empname  pct
------ -------- -----
1      Sara     5.00
5      Sven     5.00
```

The subclause *FROM @start TO @end* returns the rows that satisfy the predicate *sysstart < @end AND sysend > @start*. In other words, it returns the rows with a validity period that starts before the input interval ends and that ends after the input interval starts. The following query demonstrates using this subclause:

```
SELECT empid, empname, department, salary, sysstart, sysend
FROM dbo.Employees
  FOR SYSTEM_TIME FROM '2016-02-16 17:15:26' TO '2016-02-16 17:20:02';
```

This query generates the following output:

```
empid  empname  department  salary    sysstart             sysend
------ -------- ----------- --------- -------------------- --------------------
2      Don      HR          45000.00  2016-02-16 17:08:41  9999-12-31 23:59:59
4      Yael     Marketing   55000.00  2016-02-16 17:08:41  9999-12-31 23:59:59
1      Sara     IT          50000.00  2016-02-16 17:08:41  2016-02-16 17:20:02
5      Sven     IT          45000.00  2016-02-16 17:08:41  2016-02-16 17:20:02
3      Judy     Sales       55000.00  2016-02-16 17:08:41  2016-02-16 17:28:10
```

Notice that rows with a *sysstart* value of 2016-02-16 17:20:02 are not included in the output. If you need the input *@end* value to be inclusive, use the *BETWEEN* subclause instead of the *FROM* subclause. The syntax of the *BETWEEN* subclause is *BETWEEN @start AND @end*, and it returns the rows that satisfy the predicate *sysstart <= @end AND sysend > @start*. It returns the rows with a validity period that starts *on or before* the input interval ends and that ends after the input interval starts. The following query demonstrates using this subclause with the same input values as in the previous query:

```
SELECT empid, empname, department, salary, sysstart, sysend
FROM dbo.Employees
  FOR SYSTEM_TIME BETWEEN '2016-02-16 17:15:26' AND '2016-02-16 17:20:02';
```

You get the following output, this time including rows with a *sysstart* value of 2016-02-16 17:20:02:

```
empid  empname  department  salary    sysstart             sysend
------ -------- ----------- --------- -------------------- --------------------
1      Sara     IT          52500.00  2016-02-16 17:20:02  9999-12-31 23:59:59
2      Don      HR          45000.00  2016-02-16 17:08:41  9999-12-31 23:59:59
4      Yael     Marketing   55000.00  2016-02-16 17:08:41  9999-12-31 23:59:59
1      Sara     IT          50000.00  2016-02-16 17:08:41  2016-02-16 17:20:02
5      Sven     IT          45000.00  2016-02-16 17:08:41  2016-02-16 17:20:02
3      Judy     Sales       55000.00  2016-02-16 17:08:41  2016-02-16 17:28:10
5      Sven     IT          47250.00  2016-02-16 17:20:02  2016-02-16 17:28:10
```

The subclause *FOR SYSTEM_TIME CONTAINED IN(@start, @end)* returns the rows that satisfy the predicate *sysstart >= @start AND sysend <= @end*. It returns the rows with a validity period that starts on or after the input interval starts and that ends on or before the input interval ends. In other words, the validity period needs to be completely contained in the input period.

Here's an example demonstrating the use of this clause:

```
SELECT empid, empname, department, salary, sysstart, sysend
FROM dbo.Employees
  FOR SYSTEM_TIME CONTAINED IN('2016-02-16 17:00:00', '2016-02-16 18:00:00');
```

This query generates the following output:

```
empid  empname  department  salary    sysstart             sysend
------ -------- ----------- --------- -------------------- --------------------
6      Paul     Sales       40000.00  2016-02-16 17:08:41  2016-02-16 17:15:26
1      Sara     IT          50000.00  2016-02-16 17:08:41  2016-02-16 17:20:02
5      Sven     IT          45000.00  2016-02-16 17:08:41  2016-02-16 17:20:02
3      Judy     Sales       55000.00  2016-02-16 17:08:41  2016-02-16 17:28:10
5      Sven     IT          47250.00  2016-02-16 17:20:02  2016-02-16 17:28:10
```

Table 9-1 summarizes the aforementioned subclauses and the predicates that represent the qualifying rows.

TABLE 9-1 Qualifying rows for *FOR SYSTEM_TIME* subclauses

Subclause	Qualifying rows
AS OF @datetime	*sysstart <= @datetime AND sysend > @datetime*
FROM @start TO @end	*sysstart < @end AND sysend > @start*
BETWEEN @start AND @end	*sysstart <= @end AND sysend > @start*
CONTAINED IN(@start, @end)	*sysstart >= @start AND sysend <= @end*

Figure 9-2 has a similar summary of the subclauses, with a graphical depiction of the predicates and qualifying rows.

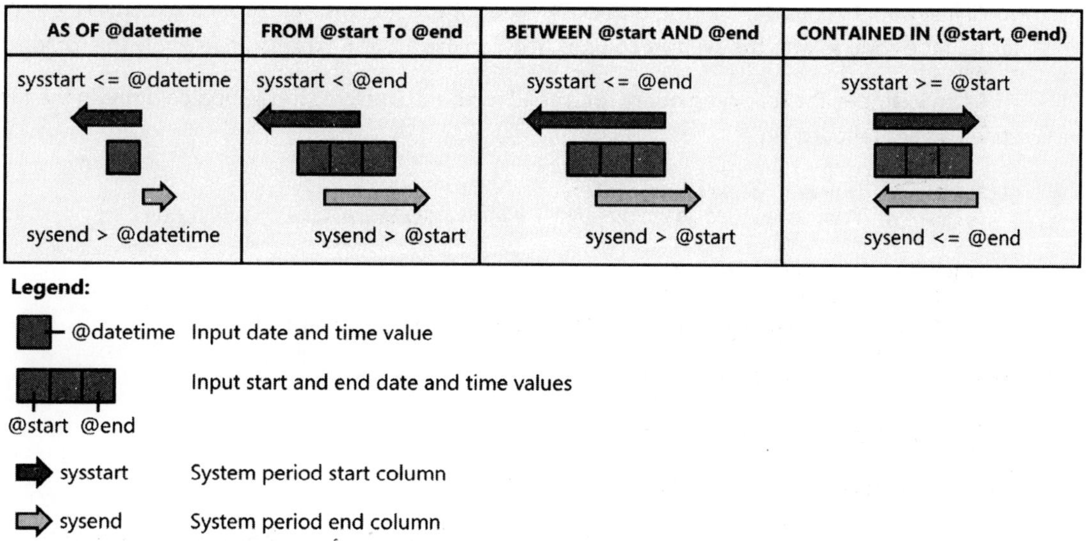

FIGURE 9-2 Illustrations of *FOR SYSTEM_TIME* subclauses.

T-SQL also supports the *ALL* subclause, which simply returns all rows from both tables. The following query demonstrates the use of this subclause:

```
SELECT empid, empname, department, salary, sysstart, sysend
FROM dbo.Employees FOR SYSTEM_TIME ALL;
```

This query generates the following output:

```
empid  empname  department  salary    sysstart             sysend
------ -------- ----------- --------- -------------------- --------------------
1      Sara     IT          52500.00  2016-02-16 17:20:02  9999-12-31 23:59:59
2      Don      HR          45000.00  2016-02-16 17:08:41  9999-12-31 23:59:59
3      Judy     IT          55000.00  2016-02-16 17:28:10  9999-12-31 23:59:59
4      Yael     Marketing   55000.00  2016-02-16 17:08:41  9999-12-31 23:59:59
5      Sven     Sales       47250.00  2016-02-16 17:28:10  9999-12-31 23:59:59
```

```
6       Paul    Sales       40000.00  2016-02-16 17:08:41  2016-02-16 17:15:26
1       Sara    IT          50000.00  2016-02-16 17:08:41  2016-02-16 17:20:02
5       Sven    IT          45000.00  2016-02-16 17:08:41  2016-02-16 17:20:02
3       Judy    Sales       55000.00  2016-02-16 17:08:41  2016-02-16 17:28:10
5       Sven    IT          47250.00  2016-02-16 17:20:02  2016-02-16 17:28:10
```

Remember that the period columns reflect the validity period of the row as *datetime2* values in the UTC time zone. If you want to return those as *datetimeoffset* values in a desired time zone, you can use the *AT TIME ZONE* function. You'll need to use the function twice. Once to convert the input to *datetimeoffset*, indicating that it's in the UTC time zone, and another to convert the value to the target time zone—for example, *sysstart AT TIME ZONE 'UTC' AT TIME ZONE 'Pacific Standard Time'*. If you use only one conversion straight to the target time zone, the function will assume that the source value is already in the target time zone and won't perform the desired switching.

Another thing to consider is that for the *sysend* column, if the value is the maximum in the type, you'll just want to consider it as using the UTC time zone. Otherwise, you'll want to convert it to the target time zone as with the *sysstart* column. You can use a *CASE* expression to apply this logic.

As an example, the following query returns all rows and presents the period columns in the time zone Pacific Standard Time:

```
SELECT empid, empname, department, salary,
  sysstart AT TIME ZONE 'UTC' AT TIME ZONE 'Pacific Standard Time' AS sysstart,
  CASE
    WHEN sysend = '9999-12-31 23:59:59'
      THEN sysend AT TIME ZONE 'UTC'
    ELSE sysend AT TIME ZONE 'UTC' AT TIME ZONE 'Pacific Standard Time'
  END AS sysend
FROM dbo.Employees FOR SYSTEM_TIME ALL;
```

This query generates the following output:

```
empid  empname  department  salary    sysstart                    sysend
------ -------- ----------- --------- --------------------------- ---------------------------
1      Sara     IT          52500.00  2016-02-16 09:20:02 -08:00  9999-12-31 23:59:59 +00:00
2      Don      HR          45000.00  2016-02-16 09:08:41 -08:00  9999-12-31 23:59:59 +00:00
3      Judy     IT          55000.00  2016-02-16 09:28:10 -08:00  9999-12-31 23:59:59 +00:00
4      Yael     Marketing   55000.00  2016-02-16 09:08:41 -08:00  9999-12-31 23:59:59 +00:00
5      Sven     Sales       47250.00  2016-02-16 09:28:10 -08:00  9999-12-31 23:59:59 +00:00
6      Paul     Sales       40000.00  2016-02-16 09:08:41 -08:00  2016-02-16 09:15:26 -08:00
1      Sara     IT          50000.00  2016-02-16 09:08:41 -08:00  2016-02-16 09:20:02 -08:00
5      Sven     IT          45000.00  2016-02-16 09:08:41 -08:00  2016-02-16 09:20:02 -08:00
3      Judy     Sales       55000.00  2016-02-16 09:08:41 -08:00  2016-02-16 09:28:10 -08:00
5      Sven     IT          47250.00  2016-02-16 09:20:02 -08:00  2016-02-16 09:28:10 -08:00
```

When you're done experimenting with the data, run the following code for cleanup:

```
IF OBJECT_ID(N'dbo.Employees', N'U') IS NOT NULL
BEGIN
  IF OBJECTPROPERTY(OBJECT_ID(N'dbo.Employees', N'U'), N'TableTemporalType') = 2
    ALTER TABLE dbo.Employees SET ( SYSTEM_VERSIONING = OFF );
  DROP TABLE IF EXISTS dbo.EmployeesHistory, dbo.Employees;
END;
```

Conclusion

SQL Server's support for system-versioned temporal tables is very powerful. In the past, many systems implemented their own customized solutions to address the same need. With built-in support, the solutions are much simpler and more efficient. This chapter explained how to create, modify, and query temporal tables. Remember that with system-version temporal tables the system transaction time determines the validity period of the row. I hope that in the future we'll see support in SQL Server for application-time period tables where the application can define the validity period, including setting it to a future one, plus bitemporal support, which combines the two types.

Exercises

This section provides exercises to help you familiarize yourself with the subjects discussed in Chapter 9.

Exercise 1

In this exercise, you create a system-versioned temporal table and identify it in SSMS.

Exercise 1-1

Create a system-versioned temporal table called *Departments* with an associated history table called *DepartmentsHistory* in the database *TSQLV4*. The table should have the following columns: *deptid INT*, *deptname VARCHAR(25)*, and *mgrid INT*, all disallowing *NULLs*. Also include columns called *validfrom* and *validto* that define the validity period of the row. Define those with precision zero (1 second), and make them hidden.

Exercise 1-2

Browse the object tree in Object Explorer in SSMS, and identify the *Departments* table and its associated history table.

Exercise 2

In this exercise, you'll modify data in the table *Departments*. Note the point in time in UTC when you submit each statement, and mark those as P1, P2, and so on. You can do so by invoking the *SYSUTC-DATETIME* function in the same batch in which you submit the modification. Another option is to query the *Departments* table and its associated history table and to obtain the point in time from the *validfrom* and *validto* columns.

Exercise 2-1

Insert four rows to the table *Departments* with the following details, and note the time when you apply this insert (call it P1):

- *deptid*: 1, *deptname*: HR, *mgrid*: 7
- *deptid*: 2, *deptname*: IT, *mgrid*: 5
- *deptid*: 3, *deptname*: Sales, *mgrid*: 11
- *deptid*: 4, *deptname*: Marketing, *mgrid*: 13

Exercise 2-2

In one transaction, update the name of department 3 to Sales and Marketing and delete department 4. Call the point in time when the transaction starts P2.

Exercise 2-3

Update the manager ID of department 3 to 13. Call the point in time when you apply this update P2.

Exercise 3

In this exercise, you'll query data from the table *Departments*.

Exercise 3-1

Query the current state of the table *Departments*:

- Desired output:

```
deptid      deptname                  mgrid
----------- ------------------------- -----------
1           HR                        7
2           IT                        5
3           Sales and Marketing       13
```

Exercise 3-2

Query the state of the table *Departments* at a point in time after P2 and before P3:

- Desired output:

```
deptid      deptname                  mgrid
----------- ------------------------- -----------
1           HR                        7
2           IT                        5
3           Sales and Marketing       11
```

Exercise 3-3

Query the state of the table *Departments* in the period between P2 and P3. Be explicit about the column names in the *SELECT* list, and include the *validfrom* and *validto* columns:

- Desired output (with *validfrom* and *validto* reflecting your modification times):

```
deptid  deptname              mgrid  validfrom            validto
------- -------------------- ------ -------------------- --------------------
1       HR                    7      2016-02-18 10:26:07  9999-12-31 23:59:59
2       IT                    5      2016-02-18 10:26:07  9999-12-31 23:59:59
3       Sales and Marketing   13     2016-02-18 10:30:40  9999-12-31 23:59:59
3       Sales and Marketing   11     2016-02-18 10:28:27  2016-02-18 10:30:40
```

Exercise 4

Drop the table *Departments* and its associated history table.

Solutions

This section provides solutions to the Chapter 9 exercises.

Exercise 1

This exercise is split into two parts. The following sections provide the solutions to those parts.

Exercise 1-1

The following code creates the *Departments* table as a system-versioned temporal table with an associated history table called *DepartmentsHistory*:

```
USE TSQLV4;

CREATE TABLE dbo.Departments
(
  deptid    INT                              NOT NULL
    CONSTRAINT PK_Departments PRIMARY KEY,
  deptname  VARCHAR(25)                      NOT NULL,
  mgrid INT                                  NOT NULL,
  validfrom DATETIME2(0)
    GENERATED ALWAYS AS ROW START HIDDEN NOT NULL,
  validto   DATETIME2(0)
    GENERATED ALWAYS AS ROW END   HIDDEN NOT NULL,
  PERIOD FOR SYSTEM_TIME (validfrom, validto)
)
WITH ( SYSTEM_VERSIONING = ON ( HISTORY_TABLE = dbo.DepartmentsHistory ) );
```

Following are the requirements for creating a system-versioned temporal table as they are applied to the *Departments* table:

- A primary key: defined based on the *deptid* column.
- The table option *SYSTEM_VERSIONING* set to *ON*.
- Two non-nullable *DATETIME2* columns, with any precision (in our case 0), representing the start and end of the row's validity period; in our table, the columns are named *validfrom* and *validto*.

- The start column (*validfrom*) marked with the option *GENERATED ALWAYS AS ROW START.*
- The end column (*validto*) marked with the option *GENERATED ALWAYS AS ROW END.*
- A designation of the period columns: *PERIOD FOR SYSTEM_TIME (validfrom, validto)*
- A linked history table called *DepartmentsHistory* (which SQL Server creates for you) to hold the past states of modified rows

Exercise 1-2

In Object Explorer, navigate to Databases, then to the *TSQLV4* database, and then to Tables. Below Tables, you'll find the *Departments* table marked as System-Versioned and, below it, the *DepartmentsHistory* table marked as *History*, as shown in Figure 9-3.

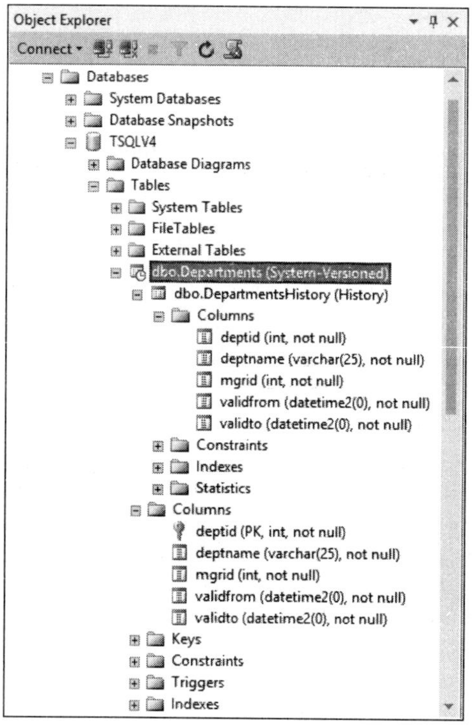

FIGURE 9-3 The *Departments* temporal table and associated history table in SSMS.

Exercise 2

This exercise is split into three parts. The following sections provide the solutions to those parts.

Exercise 2-1

The following code identifies the current point in time as P1 and adds the four requested rows:

```
SELECT CAST(SYSUTCDATETIME() AS DATETIME2(0)) AS P1;
```

```
INSERT INTO dbo.Departments(deptid, deptname, mgrid)
  VALUES(1, 'HR'       , 7 ),
        (2, 'IT'       , 5 ),
        (3, 'Sales'    , 11),
        (4, 'marketing', 13);
```

When I ran this code, I got the following output:

```
P1
---------------------------
2016-02-18 10:26:07
```

Make a note of P1 in your execution, which will be different than in mine.

Exercise 2-2

The following codes identifies the current point in time as P2 and applies the two requested updates in a transaction:

```
SELECT CAST(SYSUTCDATETIME() AS DATETIME2(0)) AS P2;

BEGIN TRAN;

UPDATE dbo.Departments
  SET deptname = 'Sales and Marketing'
WHERE deptid = 3;

DELETE FROM dbo.Departments
WHERE deptid = 4;

COMMIT TRAN;
```

I got the following output when I ran this code:

```
P2
---------------------------
2016-02-18 10:28:27
```

Again, make a note of P2 in your execution.

Exercise 2-3

The following codes identifies the current point in time as P3 and applies the requested update:

```
SELECT CAST(SYSUTCDATETIME() AS DATETIME2(0)) AS P3;

UPDATE dbo.Departments
  SET mgrid = 13
WHERE deptid = 3;
```

I got the following output when I ran this code:

```
P3
---------------------------
2016-02-18 10:30:40
```

Make a note of P3 in your execution.

At this point, I recommend you query both tables, with an explicit reference to the *validfrom* and *validto* columns. Make sure you understand why the values in those columns are what they are.

Exercise 3

This exercise is split into three parts. The following sections provide the solutions to those parts.

Exercise 3-1

Run the following code to query the current state of the table *Departments*, without explicitly referring to the *validfrom* and *validto* columns (using *):

```
SELECT *
FROM dbo.Departments;
```

You get the following output:

```
deptid      deptname                  mgrid
----------- ------------------------- -----------
1           HR                        7
2           IT                        5
3           Sales and Marketing       13
```

Exercise 3-2

Run the following code to query the state of the table *Departments* at a point in time after P2 and before P3 (replace the point in time in this code with one that appears before P2 and P3 that you recorded):

```
SELECT *
FROM dbo.Departments
  FOR SYSTEM_TIME AS OF '2016-02-18 10:29:00'; -- replace this with your time
```

You get the following output:

```
deptid      deptname                  mgrid
----------- ------------------------- -----------
1           HR                        7
2           IT                        5
3           Sales and Marketing       11
```

Notice that the name of department 3 is the new name Sales and Marketing, which was updated at P2. However, the manager ID of department 3 is still 11, because the change to 13 happened at P3.

Exercise 3-3

Run the following code to query the state of the table *Departments* in the period between P2 and P3 (replace the points in time in this code with P2 and P3 that you recorded):

```
SELECT deptid, deptname, mgrid, validfrom, validto
FROM dbo.Departments
  FOR SYSTEM_TIME BETWEEN '2016-02-18 10:28:27'  -- replace this with your P2
                      AND '2016-02-18 10:30:40'; -- replace this with your P3
```

You get the following output (with *validfrom* and *validto* reflecting your modification times):

```
deptid  deptname             mgrid  validfrom            validto
------- -------------------- ------ -------------------- --------------------
1       HR                   7      2016-02-18 10:26:07  9999-12-31 23:59:59
2       IT                   5      2016-02-18 10:26:07  9999-12-31 23:59:59
3       Sales and Marketing  13     2016-02-18 10:30:40  9999-12-31 23:59:59
3       Sales and Marketing  11     2016-02-18 10:28:27  2016-02-18 10:30:40
```

This output shows rows that where valid during the period in which *validfrom* is on or before P3 and *validto* is after P2.

Exercise 4

You cannot drop tables that take part in an enabled system-versioning relationship. You'll need to disable system versioning first. Here's the code to achieve this with the tables in our exercises:

```
ALTER TABLE dbo.Departments SET ( SYSTEM_VERSIONING = OFF );
DROP TABLE dbo.DepartmentsHistory, dbo.Departments;
```

CHAPTER 10

Transactions and concurrency

This chapter covers transactions and their properties and describes how Microsoft SQL Server handles users who are concurrently trying to access the same data. I explain how SQL Server uses locks to isolate inconsistent data, how you can troubleshoot blocking situations, and how you can control the level of consistency when you're querying data with isolation levels. This chapter also covers deadlocks and ways to mitigate their occurrence.

Because this is a book about fundamentals, this chapter focuses on concurrency aspects of traditional data representation in disk-based tables. SQL Server supports a memory-optimized database engine called *In-Memory OLTP*, which holds the data in memory optimized tables. The handling of concurrency for memory-optimized tables is very different than with disk-based tables. Because this feature is an advanced performance-centric feature, it's outside the scope of this book. When you're ready for more advanced aspects of T-SQL with a performance-centric focus, you can find those in the book *T-SQL Querying* (Microsoft Press, 2015). You can also find coverage of the In-Memory OLTP feature in SQL Server Books Online using the following URL: *https://msdn.microsoft.com/en-us/library/dn133186.aspx.*

Transactions

A *transaction* is a unit of work that might include multiple activities that query and modify data and that can also change the data definition.

You can define transaction boundaries either explicitly or implicitly. You define the beginning of a transaction explicitly with a *BEGIN TRAN* (or *BEGIN TRANSACTION*) statement. You define the end of a transaction explicitly with a *COMMIT TRAN* statement if you want to commit it and with a *ROLLBACK TRAN* (or *ROLLBACK TRANSACTION*) statement if you want to undo its changes. Here's an example of marking the boundaries of a transaction with two *INSERT* statements:

```
BEGIN TRAN;
  INSERT INTO dbo.T1(keycol, col1, col2) VALUES(4, 101, 'C');
  INSERT INTO dbo.T2(keycol, col1, col2) VALUES(4, 201, 'X');
COMMIT TRAN;
```

If you do not mark the boundaries of a transaction explicitly, by default, SQL Server treats each individual statement as a transaction; in other words, by default, SQL Server automatically commits the transaction at the end of each statement. You can change the way SQL Server handles implicit transactions with a session option called *IMPLICIT_TRANSACTIONS*. This option is turned off by default. When this option is turned on, you do not have to specify the *BEGIN TRAN* statement to mark the beginning of a transaction, but you have to mark the transaction's end with a *COMMIT TRAN* or *ROLLBACK TRAN* statement.

After one transaction commits or rolls back, unless you open another explicit transaction, the next statement executed implicitly begins another transaction.

Transactions have four properties—atomicity, consistency, isolation, and durability—abbreviated with the acronym *ACID*:

- **Atomicity** A transaction is an atomic unit of work. Either all changes in the transaction take place or none do. If the system fails before a transaction is completed (before the commit instruction is recorded in the transaction log), upon restart, SQL Server undoes the changes that took place. Also, if errors are encountered during the transaction and the error is considered severe enough, such as the target filegroup being full when you try to insert data, SQL Server automatically rolls back the transaction. Some errors, such as primary-key violations and lock-expiration timeouts (discussed later in this chapter, in the "Troubleshooting blocking" section), are not considered severe enough to justify an automatic rollback of the transaction. If you want all errors to abort execution and cause any open transaction to roll back, you can enable a session option called *XACT_ABORT*. You can use error-handling code to capture such errors and apply some course of action (for example, log the error and roll back the transaction). Chapter 11, "Programmable objects," provides an overview of error handling.

> **Tip** At any point in your code, you can tell programmatically whether you're in an open transaction by querying a function called *@@TRANCOUNT*. This function returns *0* if you're not in an open transaction and returns a value greater than 0 if you are.

- **Consistency** The term *consistency* refers to the state of the data that the relational database management system (RDBMS) gives you access to as concurrent transactions modify and query it. As you can probably imagine, consistency is a subjective term, which depends on your application's needs. The "Isolation levels" section later in this chapter explains the level of consistency that SQL Server provides by default and how you can control it if the default behavior is not suitable for your application. Consistency also refers to the fact that the database must adhere to all integrity rules that have been defined within it by constraints (such as primary keys, unique constraints, and foreign keys). The transaction transitions the database from one consistent state to another.

- **Isolation** *Isolation* ensures that transactions access only consistent data. You control what consistency means to your transactions through a mechanism called *isolation levels*. With disk-based tables, SQL Server supports two different models to handle isolation: one based purely on locking, and another based on a combination of locking and row versioning. For simplicity, I'll refer to the latter as just *row versioning*. The model based on locking is the default in a box product. In this model, readers require shared locks. If the current state of the data is inconsistent, readers are blocked until the state of the data becomes consistent. The model based on row versioning is the default in Azure SQL Database. In this model, readers don't take shared locks and don't need to wait. If the current state of the data is inconsistent, the reader gets an older consistent state. The "Isolation levels" section later in this chapter provides more details about both ways of handling isolation.

- **Durability** Data changes are always written to the database's transaction log on disk before they are written to the data portion of the database on disk. After the commit instruction is recorded in the transaction log on disk, the transaction is considered durable even if the change hasn't yet made it to the data portion on disk. When the system starts, either normally or after a system failure, SQL Server inspects the transaction log of each database and runs a recovery process with two phases: redo and undo. The redo phase involves rolling forward (replaying) all the changes from any transaction whose commit instruction is written to the log but whose changes haven't yet made it to the data portion. The undo phase involves rolling back (undoing) the changes from any transaction whose commit instruction was not recorded in the log.

For example, the following code defines a transaction that records information about a new order in the *TSQLV4* database:

```
USE TSQLV4;

-- Start a new transaction
BEGIN TRAN;

  -- Declare a variable
  DECLARE @neworderid AS INT;

  -- Insert a new order into the Sales.Orders table
  INSERT INTO Sales.Orders
      (custid, empid, orderdate, requireddate, shippeddate,
       shipperid, freight, shipname, shipaddress, shipcity,
       shippostalcode, shipcountry)
    VALUES
      (85, 5, '20090212', '20090301', '20090216',
       3, 32.38, N'Ship to 85-B', N'6789 rue de l''Abbaye', N'Reims',
       N'10345', N'France');

  -- Save the new order ID in a variable
  SET @neworderid = SCOPE_IDENTITY();

  -- Return the new order ID
  SELECT @neworderid AS neworderid;

  -- Insert order lines for the new order into Sales.OrderDetails
  INSERT INTO Sales.OrderDetails
      (orderid, productid, unitprice, qty, discount)
    VALUES(@neworderid, 11, 14.00, 12, 0.000),
          (@neworderid, 42, 9.80, 10, 0.000),
          (@neworderid, 72, 34.80, 5, 0.000);

-- Commit the transaction
COMMIT TRAN;
```

The transaction's code inserts a row with the order header information into the *Sales.Orders* table and a few rows with the order lines information into the *Sales.OrderDetails* table. The new order ID is produced automatically by SQL Server because the *orderid* column has an identity property. Immediately after the code inserts the new row into the *Sales.Orders* table, it stores the newly generated order ID in a local variable, and then it uses that local variable when inserting rows into the *Sales.OrderDetails* table. For test purposes, I added a *SELECT* statement that returns the order ID of the newly generated order. Here's the output from the *SELECT* statement after the code runs:

```
neworderid
-----------
11078
```

Note that this example has no error handling and does not make any provision for a *ROLLBACK* in case of an error. To handle errors, you can enclose a transaction in a *TRY/CATCH* construct. You can find an overview of error handling in Chapter 11.

When you're done, run the following code for cleanup:

```
DELETE FROM Sales.OrderDetails
WHERE orderid > 11077;

DELETE FROM Sales.Orders
WHERE orderid > 11077;
```

Locks and blocking

By default, a SQL Server box product uses a pure locking model to enforce the isolation property of transactions. The following sections provide details about locking and explain how to troubleshoot blocking situations that are caused by conflicting lock requests.

As mentioned, Azure SQL Database uses the row-versioning model by default. If you're testing the code in this chapter on Azure SQL Database, you need to turn off the database property *READ_COMMITTED_SNAPSHOT* to switch to the locking model as the default. Use the following code to achieve this:

```
ALTER DATABASE TSQLV4 SET READ_COMMITTED_SNAPSHOT OFF;
```

If you're connected to the *TSQLV4* database, you can alternatively use the keyword *CURRENT* instead of the database name. Also, by default, connections to Azure SQL Database time out quite quickly. So if a demo you're running doesn't work as expected, it could be that a connection involved in that demo timed out.

Locks

Locks are control resources obtained by a transaction to guard data resources, preventing conflicting or incompatible access by other transactions. I'll first cover the important lock modes supported by SQL Server and their compatibility, and then I'll describe the lockable resource types.

Lock modes and compatibility

As you start learning about transactions and concurrency, you should first familiarize yourself with two main lock modes: *exclusive* and *shared*.

When you try to modify data, your transaction requests an exclusive lock on the data resource, regardless of your isolation level. (You'll learn more about isolation levels later in this chapter.) If granted, the exclusive lock is held until the end of the transaction. For single-statement transactions, this means that the lock is held until the statement completes. For multistatement transactions, this means that the lock is held until all statements complete and the transaction is ended by a *COMMIT TRAN* or *ROLLBACK TRAN* command.

Exclusive locks are called "exclusive" because you cannot obtain an exclusive lock on a resource if another transaction is holding any lock mode on the resource, and no lock mode can be obtained on a resource if another transaction is holding an exclusive lock on the resource. This is the way modifications behave by default, and this default behavior cannot be changed—not in terms of the lock mode required to modify a data resource (exclusive) and not in terms of the duration of the lock (until the end of the transaction). In practical terms, this means that if one transaction modifies rows, until the transaction is completed, another transaction cannot modify the same rows. However, whether another transaction can read the same rows or not depends on its isolation level.

As for reading data, the defaults are different for a SQL Server box product and Azure SQL Database. In SQL Server, the default isolation level is called *READ COMMITTED*. In this isolation, when you try to read data, by default your transaction requests a shared lock on the data resource and releases the lock as soon as the read statement is done with that resource. This lock mode is called "shared" because multiple transactions can hold shared locks on the same data resource simultaneously. Although you cannot change the lock mode and duration required when you're modifying data, you can control the way locking is handled when you're reading data by changing your isolation level. As mentioned, I will elaborate on this later in this chapter.

In Azure SQL Database, the default isolation level is called *READ COMMITTED SNAPSHOT*. Instead of relying only on locking, this isolation level relies on a combination of locking and row versioning. Under this isolation level, readers do not require shared locks, and therefore they never wait; they rely on the row-versioning technology to provide the expected isolation. In practical terms, this means that under the *READ COMMITTED* isolation level, if a transaction modifies rows, until the transaction completes, another transaction can't read the same rows. This approach to concurrency control is known as the *pessimistic concurrency* approach. Under the *READ COMMITTED SNAPSHOT* isolation level, if a transaction modifies rows, another transaction trying to read the data will get the last committed state of the rows that was available when the statement started. This approach to concurrency control is known as the *optimistic concurrency* approach.

This lock interaction between transactions is known as *lock compatibility*. Table 10-1 shows the lock compatibility of exclusive and shared locks (when you're working with an isolation level that generates these locks). The columns represent granted lock modes, and the rows represent requested lock modes.

TABLE 10-1 Lock compatibility of exclusive and shared locks

Requested mode	Granted Exclusive (X)	Granted Shared (S)
Exclusive	No	No
Shared	No	Yes

A "No" in the intersection means that the locks are incompatible and the requested mode is denied; the requester must wait. A "Yes" in the intersection means that the locks are compatible and the requested mode is accepted.

The following summarizes lock interaction between transactions in simple terms: data that was modified by one transaction can neither be modified nor read (at least by default in a SQL Server box product) by another transaction until the first transaction finishes. And while data is being read by one transaction, it cannot be modified by another (at least by default in a SQL Server box product).

Lockable resource types

SQL Server can lock different types of resources. Those include rows (RID in a heap, key in an index) pages, objects (for example, tables), databases, and others. Rows reside within pages, and pages are the physical data blocks that contain table or index data. You should first familiarize yourself with these resource types, and at a more advanced stage, you might want to familiarize yourself with other lockable resource types such as extents, allocation units, and heaps or B-trees.

To obtain a lock on a certain resource type, your transaction must first obtain intent locks of the same mode on higher levels of granularity. For example, to get an exclusive lock on a row, your transaction must first acquire intent exclusive locks on the table and the page where the row resides. Similarly, to get a shared lock on a certain level of granularity, your transaction first needs to acquire intent shared locks on higher levels of granularity. The purpose of intent locks is to efficiently detect incompatible lock requests on higher levels of granularity and prevent the granting of those. For example, if one transaction holds a lock on a row and another asks for an incompatible lock mode on the whole page or table where that row resides, it's easy for SQL Server to identify the conflict because of the intent locks that the first transaction acquired on the page and table. Intent locks do not interfere with requests for locks on lower levels of granularity. For example, an intent lock on a page doesn't prevent other transactions from acquiring incompatible lock modes on rows within the page. Table 10-2 expands on the lock compatibility table shown in Table 10-1, adding intent exclusive and intent shared locks.

TABLE 10-2 Lock compatibility including intent locks

Requested mode	Granted Exclusive (X)	Granted Shared (S)	Granted Intent Exclusive (IX)	Granted Intent Shared (IS)
Exclusive	No	No	No	No
Shared	No	Yes	No	Yes
Intent Exclusive	No	No	Yes	Yes
Intent Shared	No	Yes	Yes	Yes

SQL Server determines dynamically which resource types to lock. Naturally, for ideal concurrency, it's best to lock only what needs to be locked—namely, only the affected rows. However, locks require memory resources and internal management overhead. So SQL Server considers both concurrency and system resources when it's choosing which resource types to lock. When SQL Server estimates that a transaction will interact with a small number of rows, it tends to use row locks. With larger numbers of rows, SQL Server tends to use page locks.

SQL Server might first acquire fine-grained locks (such as row or page locks) and, in certain circumstances, try to escalate the fine-grained locks to a table lock to preserve memory. For example, lock escalation is triggered when a single statement acquires at least 5,000 locks against the same object, and then for every 1,250 new locks, if previous attempts at lock escalation were unsuccessful.

You can set a table option called *LOCK_ESCALATION* by using the *ALTER TABLE* statement to control the way lock escalation behaves. You can disable lock escalation if you like, or you can determine whether escalation takes place at a table level (default) or a partition level. (A table can be physically organized into multiple smaller units called *partitions*.)

Troubleshooting blocking

When one transaction holds a lock on a data resource and another transaction requests an incompatible lock on the same resource, the request is blocked and the requester enters a wait state. By default, the blocked request keeps waiting until the blocker releases the interfering lock. Later in this section, I'll explain how you can define a lock expiration time-out in your session if you want to restrict the amount of time that a blocked request waits before it times out.

Blocking is normal in a system as long as requests are satisfied within a reasonable amount of time. However, if some requests end up waiting too long, you might need to troubleshoot the blocking situation and see whether you can do something to prevent such long latencies. For example, long-running transactions result in locks being held for long periods. You can try to shorten such transactions, moving activities that are not supposed to be part of the unit of work outside the transaction. A bug in the application might result in a transaction that remains open in certain circumstances. If you identify such a bug, you can fix it and ensure that the transaction is closed in all circumstances.

The next example demonstrates a blocking situation and how to troubleshoot it. I'm assuming that you're running under the isolation level *READ COMMITTED*. Open three separate query windows in SQL Server Management Studio. (For this example, I'll refer to them as Connection 1, Connection 2, and Connection 3.) Make sure that in all of them you are connected to the sample database *TSQLV4*:

```
USE TSQLV4;
```

Run the following code in Connection 1 to update a row in the *Production.Products* table, adding 1.00 to the current unit price of 19.00 for product 2:

```
BEGIN TRAN;

  UPDATE Production.Products
    SET unitprice += 1.00
  WHERE productid = 2;
```

To update the row, your session had to acquire an exclusive lock, and if the update was successful, SQL Server granted your session the lock. Recall that exclusive locks are kept until the end of the transaction, and because the transaction remains open, the lock is still held.

Run the following code in Connection 2 to try to query the same row:

```
SELECT productid, unitprice
FROM Production.Products
WHERE productid = 2;
```

Your session needs a shared lock to read the data, but because the row is exclusively locked by the other session, and a shared lock is incompatible with an exclusive lock, your session is blocked and has to wait.

Assuming that such a blocking situation happens in your system, and the blocked session ends up waiting for a long time, you probably want to troubleshoot the situation. The rest of this section provides queries against dynamic management objects (objects providing dynamic information about various aspects of your system), including views and functions, that you should run from Connection 3 when you troubleshoot the blocking situation.

To get lock information, including both locks that are currently granted to sessions and locks that sessions are waiting for, query the dynamic management view (DMV) *sys.dm_tran_locks* in Connection 3:

```
SELECT -- use * to explore other available attributes
  request_session_id               AS sid,
  resource_type                    AS restype,
  resource_database_id             AS dbid,
  DB_NAME(resource_database_id)    AS dbname,
  resource_description             AS res,
  resource_associated_entity_id    AS resid,
  request_mode                     AS mode,
  request_status                   AS status
FROM sys.dm_tran_locks;
```

When I run this code in my system (with no other query window open), I get the following output:

```
sid  restype  dbid dbname               res            resid             mode status
---- -------- ---- -------------------- -------------- ----------------- ---- ------
53   DATABASE 8    TSQLV4                              0                 S    GRANT
52   DATABASE 8    TSQLV4                              0                 S    GRANT
51   DATABASE 8    TSQLV4                              0                 S    GRANT
54   DATABASE 8    TSQLV4                              0                 S    GRANT
53   PAGE     8    TSQLV4               1:127          72057594038845440 IS   GRANT
52   PAGE     8    TSQLV4               1:127          72057594038845440 IX   GRANT
53   OBJECT   8    TSQLV4                              133575514         IS   GRANT
52   OBJECT   8    TSQLV4                              133575514         IX   GRANT
52   KEY      8    TSQLV4               (020068e8b274) 72057594038845440 X    GRANT
53   KEY      8    TSQLV4               (020068e8b274) 72057594038845440 S    WAIT
```

Each session is identified by a unique session ID. You can determine your session's ID by querying the function *@@SPID*. If you're working with SQL Server Management Studio, you'll find the session ID in parentheses to the right of the login name in the status bar at the bottom of the query window that has the focus, and also in the caption of the connected query window. For example, Figure 10-1 shows a screenshot of SQL Server Management Studio (SSMS), where the session ID 52 appears to the right of the login name MERU\Gandalf.

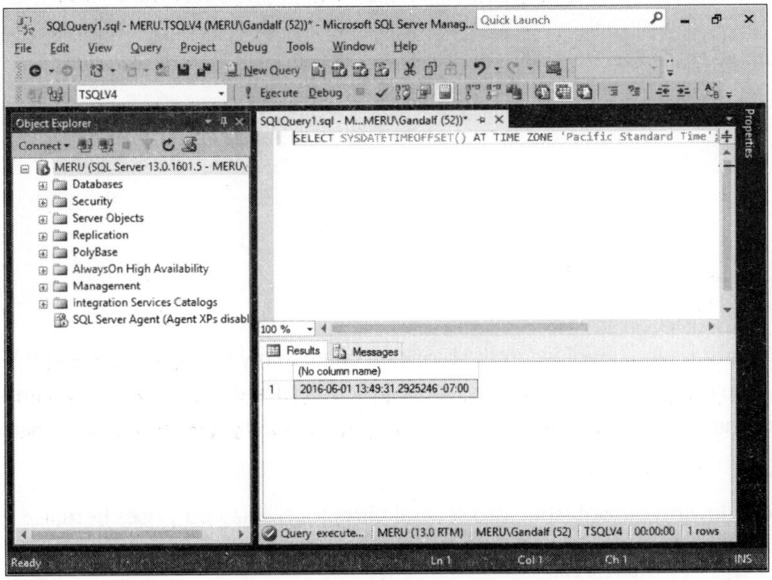

FIGURE 10-1 The session ID shown in SQL Server Management Studio.

As you can see in the output of the query against *sys.dm_tran_locks*, four sessions (51, 52, 53, and 54) are currently holding locks. You can see the following:

- The resource type that is locked (for example, *KEY* for a row in an index)
- The ID of the database in which it is locked, which you can translate to the database name by using the *DB_NAME* function
- The resource and resource ID
- The lock mode
- Whether the lock was granted or the session is waiting for it

Note that this is only a subset of the view's attributes; I recommend that you explore the other attributes of the view to learn what other information about locks is available.

In the output from my query, you can observe that session 53 is waiting for a shared lock on a row in the sample database *TSQLV4*. (The database name is obtained with the *DB_NAME* function.) Notice that session 52 is holding an exclusive lock on the same row. You can determine this by observing that both sessions lock a row with the same *res* and *resid* values. You can figure out which table is involved by moving upward in the lock hierarchy for either session 52 or 53 and inspecting the intent locks on the object (table) where the row resides. You can use the *OBJECT_NAME* function to translate the object ID (133575514 in this example) that appears under the *resid* attribute in the object lock. You will find that the table involved is *Production.Product*.

The *sys.dm_tran_locks* view gives you information about the IDs of the sessions involved in the blocking chain. A *blocking chain* is a chain of two or more sessions that are involved in the blocking situation. You could have session *x* blocking session *y*, session *y* blocking session *z*, and so on—hence the use of the term *chain*. To get information about the connections associated with those session IDs, query a view called *sys.dm_exec_connections* and filter only the session IDs that are involved:

```
SELECT -- use * to explore
  session_id AS sid,
  connect_time,
  last_read,
  last_write,
  most_recent_sql_handle
FROM sys.dm_exec_connections
WHERE session_id IN(52, 53);
```

Note that the session IDs that were involved in the blocking chain in my system were 52 and 53. Depending on what else you're doing in your system, you might get different ones. When you run the queries that I demonstrate here in your system, make sure that you substitute the session IDs with those you find involved in your blocking chain.

This query returns the following output (split into several parts for display purposes here):

```
sid    connect_time             last_read
------ ------------------------ -----------------------
52     2016-06-25 15:20:03.360  2016-06-25 15:20:15.750
53     2016-06-25 15:20:07.300  2016-06-25 15:20:20.950

sid    last_write               most_recent_sql_handle
------ ------------------------ ------------------------------------------------
52     2016-06-25 15:20:15.817  0x01000800DE2DB71FB0936F05000000000000000000000000
53     2016-06-25 15:20:07.327  0x0200000063FC7D052E09844778CDD615CFE7A2D1FB411802
```

The information that this query gives you about the connections includes

- The time they connected.
- The time of their last read and write.
- A binary value holding a handle to the most recent SQL batch run by the connection. You provide this handle as an input parameter to a table function called *sys.dm_exec_sql_text*, and the function returns the batch of code represented by the handle. You can query the table function passing the binary handle explicitly, but you'll probably find it more convenient to use the *APPLY* table operator described in Chapter 5, "Table expressions," to apply the table function to each connection row like this (run in Connection 3):

```
SELECT session_id, text
FROM sys.dm_exec_connections
  CROSS APPLY sys.dm_exec_sql_text(most_recent_sql_handle) AS ST
WHERE session_id IN(52, 53);
```

When I run this query, I get the following output, showing the last batch of code invoked by each connection involved in the blocking chain:

```
session_id  text
----------- -------------------------------------
52          BEGIN TRAN;

              UPDATE Production.Products
                SET unitprice += 1.00
              WHERE productid = 2;

53          (@1 tinyint)
            SELECT [productid],[unitprice]
            FROM [Production].[Products]
            WHERE [productid]=@1
```

The blocked session—53—shows the query that is waiting because that's the last thing the session ran. As for the blocker, in this example, you can see the statement that caused the problem, but keep in mind that the blocker might continue working and that the last thing you see in the code isn't necessarily the statement that caused the trouble.

In SQL Server 2016, you can use the function *sys.dm_exec_input_buffer* instead of *sys.dm_exec_sql_text* to get the code that the sessions of interest submitted last. The function accepts a session ID and request ID (from *sys.dm_exec_requests*, which is described shortly), or a *NULL* instead of a request ID if the ID is not relevant. Here's the code to replace the last example using the new function:

```
SELECT session_id, event_info
FROM sys.dm_exec_connections
  CROSS APPLY sys.dm_exec_input_buffer(session_id, NULL) AS IB
WHERE session_id IN(52, 53);
```

You can also find a lot of useful information about the sessions involved in a blocking situation in the DMV *sys.dm_exec_sessions*. The following query returns only a small subset of the attributes available about those sessions:

```
SELECT -- use * to explore
  session_id AS sid,
  login_time,
  host_name,
  program_name,
  login_name,
  nt_user_name,
  last_request_start_time,
  last_request_end_time
FROM sys.dm_exec_sessions
WHERE session_id IN(52, 53);
```

This query returns the following output in this example, split here into several parts:

```
sid  login_time                host_name
---- ------------------------- ---------
52   2016-06-25 15:20:03.407   K2
53   2016-06-25 15:20:07.303   K2
```

```
sid    program_name                                      login_name
------ ------------------------------------------------- ---------------
52     Microsoft SQL Server Management Studio - Query    K2\Gandalf
53     Microsoft SQL Server Management Studio - Query    K2\Gandalf

sid    nt_user_name   last_request_start_time   last_request_end_time
------ -------------- ------------------------- -----------------------
52     Gandalf        2016-06-25 15:20:15.703   2016-06-25 15:20:15.750
53     Gandalf        2016-06-25 15:20:20.693   2016-06-25 15:20:07.320
```

This output contains information such as the session's logon time, the host name, the program name, the login name, the Windows user name (the *nt_user_name* column), the time that the last request started, and the time that the last request ended. This kind of information gives you a good idea of what those sessions are doing.

Another DMV you'll probably find useful for troubleshooting blocking situations is *sys.dm_exec_requests*. This view has a row for each active request, including blocked requests. In fact, you can easily isolate blocked requests because the attribute *blocking_session_id* is greater than zero. For example, the following query filters only blocked requests:

```
SELECT -- use * to explore
  session_id AS sid,
  blocking_session_id,
  command,
  sql_handle,
  database_id,
  wait_type,
  wait_time,
  wait_resource
FROM sys.dm_exec_requests
WHERE blocking_session_id > 0;
```

This query returns the following output, split across several lines:

```
sid    blocking_session_id  command
------ -------------------- -------
53     52                   SELECT

sid    sql_handle                                          database_id
------ --------------------------------------------------- -----------
53     0x0200000063FC7D052E09844778CDD615CFE7A2D1FB411802  8

sid    wait_type   wait_time   wait_resource
------ ----------- ----------- ---------------------------------------
53     LCK_M_S     1383760     KEY: 8:72057594038845440 (020068e8b274)
```

You can easily identify the sessions that participate in the blocking chain, the resource in dispute, how long the blocked session is waiting in milliseconds, and more.

Alternatively, you can query a DMV called *sys.dm_os_waiting_tasks*, which has only tasks that are currently waiting. It also has an attribute called *blocking_session_id*, and to troubleshoot blocking you'll filter only the waiting tasks where this attribute is greater than zero. Some information in this view overlaps with that in the *sys.dm_exec_requests* view, but it does provide a few attributes that are unique to it with some more information, like the resource description that is in conflict.

If you need to terminate the blocker—for example, if you realize that as a result of a bug in the application the transaction remained open and nothing in the application can close it—you can do so by using the KILL <*session_id*> command. (Don't do so yet.)

Earlier, I mentioned that by default the session has no lock timeout set. If you want to restrict the amount of time your session waits for a lock, you can set a session option called *LOCK_TIMEOUT*. You specify a value in milliseconds—such as 5000 for 5 seconds, 0 for an immediate timeout, and –1 for no timeout (which is the default). To see how this option works, first stop the query in Connection 2 by choosing Cancel Executing Query from the Query menu (or by pressing Alt+Break). Note that if you had an explicit transaction open, canceling the executing query wouldn't cancel the transaction automatically. Run the following code to set the lock timeout to five seconds, and run the query again:

```
SET LOCK_TIMEOUT 5000;

SELECT productid, unitprice
FROM Production.Products
WHERE productid = 2;
```

The query is still blocked because Connection 1 hasn't yet ended the update transaction, but if after 5 seconds the lock request is not satisfied, SQL Server terminates the query and you get the following error:

```
Msg 1222, Level 16, State 51, Line 3
Lock request time out period exceeded.
```

Note that lock timeouts do not roll back transactions.

To remove the lock timeout value, set it back to the default (no timeout), issue the query again, and run the following code in Connection 2:

```
SET LOCK_TIMEOUT -1;

SELECT productid, unitprice
FROM Production.Products
WHERE productid = 2;
```

To terminate the update transaction in Connection 1, run the following code from Connection 3:

```
KILL 52;
```

This statement causes a rollback of the transaction in Connection 1, meaning that the price change of product 2 from 19.00 to 20.00 is undone, and the exclusive lock is released. Go to Connection 2. The query that was blocked until now is able to acquire the lock, and you get the data after the change is undone—namely, before the price change:

```
productid   unitprice
----------- ---------------------
2           19.00
```

Note If you try to close a query window while a transaction is still open, SSMS will prompt you to choose between committing or rolling back the open transaction.

Isolation levels

Isolation levels determine the level of consistency you get when you interact with data. In the default isolation level in a box product, a reader uses shared locks on the target resources and a writer uses exclusive locks. You cannot control the way writers behave in terms of the locks they acquire and the duration of the locks, but you can control the way readers behave. Also, as a result of controlling the behavior of readers, you can have an implicit influence on the behavior of writers. You do so by setting the isolation level, either at the session level with a session option or at the query level with a table hint.

SQL Server supports four isolation levels that are based on the pure locking model: *READ UNCOMMITTED*, *READ COMMITTED* (the default in a SQL Server box product), *REPEATABLE READ*, and *SERIALIZABLE*. SQL Server also supports two isolation levels that are based on a combination of locking and row versioning: *SNAPSHOT* and *READ COMMITTED SNAPSHOT* (the default in Azure SQL Database). *SNAPSHOT* and *READ COMMITTED SNAPSHOT* are in a sense the row-versioning counterparts of *READ COMMITTED* and *SERIALIZABLE*, respectively.

Some texts refer to *READ COMMITTED* and *READ COMMITTED SNAPSHOT* as one isolation level with two different semantic treatments.

You can set the isolation level of the whole session by using the following command:

```
SET TRANSACTION ISOLATION LEVEL <isolation name>;
```

You can use a table hint to set the isolation level of a query:

```
SELECT ... FROM <table> WITH (<isolationname>);
```

Note You cannot explicitly set the isolation level name *READ COMMITTED SNAPSHOT* as a session or query option. To use this isolation level, you need a database flag to be enabled. I provide details on this later in the chapter in the section "Isolation levels based on row versioning."

With the session option, you specify a space between the words in case the name of the isolation level is made of more than one word, such as *REPEATABLE READ*. With the query hint, you don't specify a space between the words—for example, *WITH (REPEATABLEREAD)*. Also, some isolation-level names used as table hints have synonyms. For example, *NOLOCK* is the equivalent of specifying *READUNCOMMITTED*, and *HOLDLOCK* is the equivalent of specifying *SERIALIZABLE*.

The default isolation level in a SQL Server box product instance is *READ COMMITTED* (based on locking). The default in Azure SQL Database is *READ COMMITTED SNAPSHOT* (based on locking and row versioning). By changing the isolation level, you affect both the concurrency of the database users and the consistency they get from the data.

With the first four isolation levels, the higher the isolation level, the stricter the locks are that readers request and the longer their duration is; therefore, the higher the isolation level is, the higher the consistency is and the lower the concurrency is.

With the two rows-versioning-based isolation levels, SQL Server is able to store previous committed versions of rows in *tempdb*. Readers do not request shared locks; instead, if the current version of the rows is not what they are supposed to see, SQL Server provides them with an older version.

The following sections describe each of the six supported isolation levels and demonstrate their behavior.

The *READ UNCOMMITTED* isolation level

READ UNCOMMITTED is the lowest available isolation level. In this isolation level, a reader doesn't ask for a shared lock. A reader that doesn't ask for a shared lock can never be in conflict with a writer that is holding an exclusive lock. This means that the reader can read uncommitted changes (also known as *dirty reads*). It also means the reader won't interfere with a writer that asks for an exclusive lock. In other words, a writer can change data while a reader that is running under the *READ UNCOMMITTED* isolation level reads data.

To see how an uncommitted read (dirty read) works, open two query windows. (I'll refer to them as Connection 1 and Connection 2.) Make sure that in all connections your database context is that of the sample database *TSQLV4*. To avoid confusion, make sure that this is the only activity in the instance.

Run the following code in Connection 1 to open a transaction, update the unit price of product 2 by adding 1.00 to its current price (19.00), and then query the product's row:

```
BEGIN TRAN;

  UPDATE Production.Products
    SET unitprice += 1.00
  WHERE productid = 2;

  SELECT productid, unitprice
  FROM Production.Products
  WHERE productid = 2;
```

Note that the transaction remains open, meaning that the product's row is locked exclusively by Connection 1. The code in Connection 1 returns the following output showing the product's new price:

```
productid   unitprice
----------- ---------------------
2           20.00
```

In Connection 2, run the following code to set the isolation level to *READ UNCOMMITTED* and query the row for product 2:

```
SET TRANSACTION ISOLATION LEVEL READ UNCOMMITTED;

SELECT productid, unitprice
FROM Production.Products
WHERE productid = 2;
```

Because the query did not request a shared lock, it was not in conflict with the other transaction. This query returned the state of the row after the change, even though the change was not committed:

```
productid   unitprice
----------- ---------------------
2           20.00
```

Keep in mind that Connection 1 might apply further changes to the row later in the transaction or even roll back at some point. For example, run the following code in Connection 1 to roll back the transaction:

```
ROLLBACK TRAN;
```

This rollback undoes the update of product 2, changing its price back to 19.00. The value 20.00 that the reader got was never committed. That's an example of a dirty read.

The *READ COMMITTED* isolation level

If you want to prevent readers from reading uncommitted changes, you need to use a stronger isolation level. The lowest isolation level that prevents dirty reads is *READ COMMITTED*, which is also the default isolation level in SQL Server (the box product). As the name indicates, this isolation level allows readers to read only committed changes. It prevents uncommitted reads by requiring a reader to obtain a shared lock. This means that if a writer is holding an exclusive lock, the reader's shared lock request will be in conflict with the writer, and it has to wait. As soon as the writer commits the transaction, the reader can get its shared lock, but what it reads are necessarily only committed changes.

The following example demonstrates that, in this isolation level, a reader can read only committed changes.

Run the following code in Connection 1 to open a transaction, update the price of product 2, and query the row to show the new price:

```
BEGIN TRAN;

  UPDATE Production.Products
    SET unitprice += 1.00
  WHERE productid = 2;

  SELECT productid, unitprice
  FROM Production.Products
  WHERE productid = 2;
```

This code returns the following output:

```
productid   unitprice
----------- ---------------------
2           20.00
```

Connection 1 now locks the row for product 2 exclusively.

Run the following code in Connection 2 to set the session's isolation level to *READ COMMITTED* and query the row for product 2:

```
SET TRANSACTION ISOLATION LEVEL READ COMMITTED;

SELECT productid, unitprice
FROM Production.Products
WHERE productid = 2;
```

Keep in mind that this isolation level is the default, so unless you previously changed the session's isolation level, you don't need to set it explicitly. The *SELECT* statement is currently blocked because it needs a shared lock to be able to read the row, and this shared lock request is in conflict with the exclusive lock held by the writer in Connection 1.

Next, run the following code in Connection 1 to commit the transaction:

```
COMMIT TRAN;
```

Now go to Connection 2 and notice that you get the following output:

```
productid   unitprice
----------- ---------------------
2           20.00
```

Unlike in *READ UNCOMMITTED*, in the *READ COMMITTED* isolation level, you don't get dirty reads. Instead, you can read only committed changes.

In terms of the duration of locks, in the *READ COMMITTED* isolation level, a reader holds the shared lock only until it's done with the resource. It doesn't keep the lock until the end of the transaction; in fact, it doesn't even keep the lock until the end of the statement. This means that in between two reads of the same data resource in the same transaction, no lock is held on the resource. Therefore, another transaction can modify the resource in between those two reads, and the reader might get different values in each read. This phenomenon is called *nonrepeatable reads* or *inconsistent analysis*. For many applications, this phenomenon is acceptable, but for some it isn't.

When you're done, run the following code for cleanup in any of the open connections:

```
UPDATE Production.Products
  SET unitprice = 19.00
WHERE productid = 2;
```

Also, ensure any open transactions in all windows are closed.

The *REPEATABLE READ* isolation level

If you want to ensure that no one can change values in between reads that take place in the same transaction, you need to move up in the isolation levels to *REPEATABLE READ*. In this isolation level, not only does a reader need a shared lock to be able to read, but it also holds the lock until the end of the transaction. This means that as soon as the reader acquires a shared lock on a data resource to read it, no one can obtain an exclusive lock to modify that resource until the reader ends the transaction. This way, you're guaranteed to get repeatable reads, or consistent analysis.

The following example demonstrates getting repeatable reads. Run the following code in Connection 1 to set the session's isolation level to *REPEATABLE READ*, open a transaction, and read the row for product 2:

```
SET TRANSACTION ISOLATION LEVEL REPEATABLE READ;

BEGIN TRAN;

  SELECT productid, unitprice
  FROM Production.Products
  WHERE productid = 2;
```

This code returns the following output showing the current price of product 2:

```
productid   unitprice
----------- ---------------------
2           19.00
```

Connection 1 still holds a shared lock on the row for product 2 because in *REPEATABLE READ*, shared locks are held until the end of the transaction. Run the following code from Connection 2 to try to modify the row for product 2:

```
UPDATE Production.Products
  SET unitprice += 1.00
WHERE productid = 2;
```

Notice that the attempt is blocked because the modifier's request for an exclusive lock is in conflict with the reader's granted shared lock. If the reader was running under the *READ UNCOMMITTED* or *READ COMMITTED* isolation level, it wouldn't hold the shared lock at this point, and the attempt to modify the row would be successful.

Back in Connection 1, run the following code to read the row for product 2 a second time and commit the transaction:

```
  SELECT productid, unitprice
  FROM Production.Products
  WHERE productid = 2;

COMMIT TRAN;
```

This code returns the following output:

```
productid   unitprice
----------- ---------------------
2           19.00
```

Notice that the second read got the same unit price for product 2 as the first read. Now that the reader's transaction has been committed and the shared lock is released, the modifier in Connection 2 can obtain the exclusive lock it was waiting for and update the row.

Another phenomenon prevented by *REPEATABLE READ* but not by lower isolation levels is called a *lost update*. A lost update happens when two transactions read a value, make calculations based on what they read, and then update the value. Because in isolation levels lower than *REPEATABLE READ* no lock is held on the resource after the read, both transactions can update the value, and whichever transaction updates the value last "wins," overwriting the other transaction's update. In *REPEATABLE READ*, both sides keep their shared locks after the first read, so neither can acquire an exclusive lock later in order to update. The situation results in a deadlock, and the update conflict is prevented. I'll provide more details on deadlocks later in this chapter, in the "Deadlocks" section.

When you're done, run the following code for cleanup:

```
UPDATE Production.Products
  SET unitprice = 19.00
WHERE productid = 2;
```

The *SERIALIZABLE* isolation level

Running under the *REPEATABLE READ* isolation level, readers keep shared locks until the end of the transaction. Therefore, you're guaranteed to get a repeatable read of the rows that you read the first time in the transaction. However, your transaction locks only resources (for example, rows) that the query found the first time it ran, not rows that weren't there when the query ran. Therefore, a second read in the same transaction might return new rows as well. Those new rows are called *phantoms*, and such reads are called *phantom reads*. This happens if, in between the reads, another transaction inserts new rows that satisfy the reader's query filter.

To prevent phantom reads, you need to move up in the isolation levels to *SERIALIZABLE*. For the most part, the *SERIALIZABLE* isolation level behaves similarly to *REPEATABLE READ*: namely, it requires a reader to obtain a shared lock to be able to read, and it keeps the lock until the end of the transaction. But the *SERIALIZABLE* isolation level adds another facet—logically, this isolation level causes a reader to lock the whole range of keys that qualify for the query's filter. This means that the reader locks not only the existing rows that qualify for the query's filter, but also future ones. Or, more accurately, it blocks attempts made by other transactions to add rows that qualify for the reader's query filter.

The following example demonstrates that the *SERIALIZABLE* isolation level prevents phantom reads. Run the following code in Connection 1 to set the transaction isolation level to *SERIALIZABLE*, open a transaction, and query all products with category 1:

```
SET TRANSACTION ISOLATION LEVEL SERIALIZABLE;

BEGIN TRAN

  SELECT productid, productname, categoryid, unitprice
  FROM Production.Products
  WHERE categoryid = 1;
```

You get the following output, showing 12 products in category 1:

```
productid   productname    categoryid  unitprice
----------- -------------- ----------- ---------------------
1           Product HHYDP  1           18.00
2           Product RECZE  1           19.00
24          Product QOGNU  1           4.50
34          Product SWNJY  1           14.00
35          Product NEVTJ  1           18.00
38          Product QDOMO  1           263.50
39          Product LSOFL  1           18.00
43          Product ZZZHR  1           46.00
67          Product XLXQF  1           14.00
70          Product TOONT  1           15.00
75          Product BWRLG  1           7.75
76          Product JYGFE  1           18.00

(12 row(s) affected)
```

From Connection 2, run the following code in an attempt to insert a new product with category 1:

```
INSERT INTO Production.Products
    (productname, supplierid, categoryid,
     unitprice, discontinued)
  VALUES('Product ABCDE', 1, 1, 20.00, 0);
```

In all isolation levels that are lower than *SERIALIZABLE*, such an attempt would be successful. In the *SERIALIZABLE* isolation level, the attempt is blocked.

Back in Connection 1, run the following code to query products with category 1 a second time and commit the transaction:

```
  SELECT productid, productname, categoryid, unitprice
  FROM Production.Products
  WHERE categoryid = 1;

COMMIT TRAN;
```

You get the same output as before, with no phantoms. Now that the reader's transaction is committed and the shared key-range lock is released, the modifier in Connection 2 can obtain the exclusive lock it was waiting for and insert the row.

When you're done, run the following code for cleanup:

```
DELETE FROM Production.Products
WHERE productid > 77;
```

Run the following code in all open connections to set the isolation level back to the default:

```
SET TRANSACTION ISOLATION LEVEL READ COMMITTED;
```

Isolation levels based on row versioning

With the row-versioning technology, SQL Server can store previous versions of committed rows in *tempdb*. SQL Server supports two isolation levels, called *SNAPSHOT* and *READ COMMITTED SNAPSHOT*, that are based on this row-versioning technology. The *SNAPSHOT* isolation level is logically similar to the *SERIALIZABLE* isolation level in terms of the types of consistency problems that can or cannot happen; the *READ COMMITTED SNAPSHOT* isolation level is similar to the *READ COMMITTED* isolation level. However, readers using isolation levels based on row versioning do not acquire shared locks, so they don't wait when the requested data is exclusively locked. In other words, readers don't block writers and writers don't block readers. Readers still get levels of consistency similar to *SERIALIZABLE* and *READ COMMITTED.* SQL Server provides readers with an older version of the row if the current version is not the one they are supposed to see.

Note that if you enable any of the row-versioning-based isolation levels (which are enabled in Azure SQL Database by default), the *DELETE* and *UPDATE* statements need to copy the version of the row before the change to *tempdb*; *INSERT* statements don't need to be versioned in *tempdb* because no earlier version of the row exists. But it's important to be aware that enabling any of the isolation levels that are based on row versioning might have a negative impact on the performance of updates and deletes. The performance of readers usually improves, sometimes dramatically, because they do not acquire shared locks and don't need to wait when data is exclusively locked or its version is not the expected one.

The *SNAPSHOT* isolation level

Under the *SNAPSHOT* isolation level, when the reader is reading data, it's guaranteed to get the last committed version of the row that was available when the transaction started. This means you're guaranteed to get committed reads and repeatable reads, and you're also guaranteed not to get phantom reads—just as in the *SERIALIZABLE* isolation level. But instead of using shared locks, this isolation level relies on row versioning.

As mentioned, row versioning incurs a performance penalty, mainly when updating and deleting data, regardless of whether or not the modification is executed from a session running under one of the row-versioning-based isolation levels. For this reason, to allow your transactions to work with the *SNAPSHOT* isolation level in a SQL Server box product instance (a behavior that is enabled by default in Azure SQL Database), you need to first enable the option at the database level by running the following code in any open query window:

```
ALTER DATABASE TSQLV4 SET ALLOW_SNAPSHOT_ISOLATION ON;
```

The following example demonstrates the behavior of the *SNAPSHOT* isolation level. Run the following code from Connection 1 to open a transaction, update the price of product 2 by adding 1.00 to its current price of 19.00, and query the product's row to show the new price:

```
BEGIN TRAN;

  UPDATE Production.Products
    SET unitprice += 1.00
  WHERE productid = 2;
```

```
  SELECT productid, unitprice
  FROM Production.Products
  WHERE productid = 2;
```

Here the output of this code shows that the product's price was updated to 20.00:

```
productid   unitprice
----------- ---------------------
2           20.00
```

Note that even if the transaction in Connection 1 runs under the *READ COMMITTED* isolation level, SQL Server has to copy the version of the row before the update (with the price of 19.00) to *tempdb*. That's because the *SNAPSHOT* isolation level is enabled at the database level. If someone begins a transaction using the *SNAPSHOT* isolation level, that session can request the version before the update. For example, run the following code from Connection 2 to set the isolation level to *SNAPSHOT*, open a transaction, and query the row for product 2:

```
SET TRANSACTION ISOLATION LEVEL SNAPSHOT;

BEGIN TRAN;
  FROM Production.Products

  SELECT productid, unitprice
  WHERE productid = 2;
```

If your transaction was under the *SERIALIZABLE* isolation level, the query would be blocked. But because it's running under *SNAPSHOT*, you get the last committed version of the row that was available when the transaction started. That version (with the price of 19.00) is not the current version (with the price of 20.00), so SQL Server pulls the appropriate version from the version store, and the code returns the following output:

```
productid   unitprice
----------- ---------------------
2           19.00
```

Go back to Connection 1, and commit the transaction that modified the row:

```
COMMIT TRAN;
```

At this point, the current version of the row with the price of 20.00 is a committed version. However, if you read the data again in Connection 2, you should still get the last committed version of the row that was available when the transaction started (with a price of 19.00). Run the following code in Connection 2 to read the data again, and then commit the transaction:

```
  SELECT productid, unitprice
  FROM Production.Products
  WHERE productid = 2;

COMMIT TRAN;
```

As expected, you get the following output with a price of 19.00:

```
productid   unitprice
----------- ---------------------
2           19.00
```

Run the following code in Connection 2 to open a new transaction, query the data, and commit the transaction:

```
BEGIN TRAN

  SELECT productid, unitprice
  FROM Production.Products
  WHERE productid = 2;

COMMIT TRAN;
```

This time, the last committed version of the row that was available when the transaction started is the one with a price of 20.00. Therefore, you get the following output:

```
productid   unitprice
----------- ---------------------
2           20.00
```

Now that no transaction needs the version of the row with the price of 19.00, a cleanup thread that runs once a minute can remove it from *tempdb* the next time it runs. As you can imagine, very long transactions prevent SQL Server from being able to clean up row versions, and can cause *tempdb* to fill up.

When you're done, run the following code for cleanup:

```
UPDATE Production.Products
  SET unitprice = 19.00
WHERE productid = 2;
```

Conflict detection

The *SNAPSHOT* isolation level prevents update conflicts, but unlike the *REPEATABLE READ* and *SERIALIZABLE* isolation levels that do so by generating a deadlock, the *SNAPSHOT* isolation level fails the transaction, indicating that an update conflict was detected. The *SNAPSHOT* isolation level can detect update conflicts by examining the version store. It can figure out whether another transaction modified the data between a read and a write that took place in your transaction.

The following example demonstrates a scenario with no update conflict, followed by an example of a scenario with an update conflict.

Run the following code in Connection 1 to set the transaction isolation level to *SNAPSHOT*, open a transaction, and read the row for product 2:

```
SET TRANSACTION ISOLATION LEVEL SNAPSHOT;

BEGIN TRAN;

  SELECT productid, unitprice
  FROM Production.Products
```

```
  WHERE productid = 2;
```

You get the following output:

```
productid   unitprice
----------- ---------------------
2           19.00
```

Assuming you made some calculations based on what you read, run the following code while still in Connection 1 to update the price of the product you queried previously to 20.00, and commit the transaction:

```
  UPDATE Production.Products
    SET unitprice = 20.00
  WHERE productid = 2;

COMMIT TRAN;
```

No other transaction modified the row between your read, calculation, and write; therefore, there was no update conflict and SQL Server allowed the update to take place.

Run the following code to modify the price of product 2 back to 19.00:

```
UPDATE Production.Products
  SET unitprice = 19.00
WHERE productid = 2;
```

Next, run the following code in Connection 1, again, to open a transaction, and read the row for product 2:

```
BEGIN TRAN;

  SELECT productid, unitprice
  FROM Production.Products
  WHERE productid = 2;
```

You get the following output, indicating that the price of the product is 19.00:

```
productid   unitprice
----------- ---------------------
2           19.00
```

This time, run the following code in Connection 2 to update the price of product 2 to 25.00:

```
UPDATE Production.Products
  SET unitprice = 25.00
WHERE productid = 2;
```

Assume you made calculations in Connection 1 based on the price of 19.00 that you read. Based on your calculations, try to update the price of the product to 20.00 in Connection 1:

```
  UPDATE Production.Products
    SET unitprice = 20.00
  WHERE productid = 2;
```

SQL Server detected that this time another transaction modified the data between your read and write; therefore, it fails your transaction with the following error:

```
Msg 3960, Level 16, State 2, Line 1
Snapshot isolation transaction aborted due to update conflict. You cannot use snapshot isolation
to access table 'Production.Products' directly or indirectly in database 'TSQLV4' to update,
delete, or insert the row that has been modified or deleted by another transaction. Retry the
transaction or change the isolation level for the update/delete statement.
```

Of course, you can use error-handling code to retry the whole transaction when an update conflict is detected.

When you're done, run the following code for cleanup:

```
UPDATE Production.Products
  SET unitprice = 19.00
WHERE productid = 2;
```

Close all connections. Note that if all connections aren't closed, your example results might not match those in the chapter examples.

The *READ COMMITTED SNAPSHOT* isolation level

The *READ COMMITTED SNAPSHOT* isolation level is also based on row versioning. It differs from the *SNAPSHOT* isolation level in that instead of providing a reader with a transaction-level consistent view of the data, it provides the reader with a statement-level consistent view of the data. The *READ COMMITTED SNAPSHOT* isolation level also does not detect update conflicts. This results in logical behavior similar to the *READ COMMITTED* isolation level, except that readers do not acquire shared locks and do not wait when the requested resource is exclusively locked. If under *READ COMMITTED SNAPSHOT* you want a reader to acquire a shared lock, you need to add a table hint called *READCOMMITTEDLOCK* to your *SELECT* statements, as in *SELECT * FROM dbo.T1 WITH (READCOMMITTEDLOCK)*.

To enable the use of the *READ COMMITTED SNAPSHOT* isolation level in a SQL Server box product (a behavior that is enabled by default in Azure SQL Database), you need to turn on a database option called *READ_COMMITTED_SNAPSHOT*. Run to following code to enable this option in the *TSQLV4* database:

```
ALTER DATABASE TSQLV4 SET READ_COMMITTED_SNAPSHOT ON;
```

Note that for this code to run successfully, you need exclusive access to the *TSQLV4* database.

An interesting aspect of enabling this database flag is that, unlike with the *SNAPSHOT* isolation level, this flag actually changes the meaning, or semantics, of the *READ COMMITTED* isolation level to *READ COMMITTED SNAPSHOT*. This means that when this database flag is turned on, unless you explicitly change the session's isolation level, *READ COMMITTED SNAPSHOT* is the default.

For a demonstration of using the *READ COMMITTED SNAPSHOT* isolation level, open two connections. Run the following code in Connection 1 to open a transaction, update the row for product 2, and read the row, leaving the transaction open:

```
USE TSQLV4;

BEGIN TRAN;

  UPDATE Production.Products
    SET unitprice += 1.00
  WHERE productid = 2;

  SELECT productid, unitprice
  FROM Production.Products
  WHERE productid = 2;
```

You get the following output, indicating that the product's price was changed to 20.00:

```
productid   unitprice
----------- ---------------------
2           20.00
```

In Connection 2, open a transaction and read the row for product 2, leaving the transaction open:

```
BEGIN TRAN;

  SELECT productid, unitprice
  FROM Production.Products
  WHERE productid = 2;
```

You get the last committed version of the row that was available when the statement started (19.00):

```
productid   unitprice
----------- ---------------------
2           19.00
```

Run the following code in Connection 1 to commit the transaction:

```
COMMIT TRAN;
```

Now run the code in Connection 2 to read the row for product 2 again, and commit the transaction:

```
  SELECT productid, unitprice
  FROM Production.Products
  WHERE productid = 2;

COMMIT TRAN;
```

If this code was running under the *SNAPSHOT* isolation level, you would get a price of 19.00; however, because the code is running under the *READ COMMITTED SNAPSHOT* isolation level, you get the last committed version of the row that was available when the statement started (20.00) and not when the transaction started (19.00):

```
productid   unitprice
----------- ---------------------
2           20.00
```

Recall that this phenomenon is called a nonrepeatable read, or inconsistent analysis.

When you're done, run the following code for cleanup:

```
UPDATE Production.Products
  SET unitprice = 19.00
WHERE productid = 2;
```

Close all connections. Open a new connection, and run the following code to disable the isolation levels that are based on row versioning in the *TSQLV4* database:

```
ALTER DATABASE TSQLV4 SET ALLOW_SNAPSHOT_ISOLATION OFF;
ALTER DATABASE TSQLV4 SET READ_COMMITTED_SNAPSHOT OFF;
```

Summary of isolation levels

Table 10-3 provides a summary of the logical consistency problems that can or cannot happen in each isolation level, and it indicates whether the isolation level detects update conflicts for you and whether the isolation level uses row versioning.

TABLE 10-3 Summary of isolation levels

Isolation level	Allows uncommitted reads?	Allows nonrepeatable reads?	Allows lost updates?	Allows phantom reads?	Detects update conflicts?	Uses row versioning?
READ UNCOMMITTED	Yes	Yes	Yes	Yes	No	No
READ COMMITTED	No	Yes	Yes	Yes	No	No
READ COMMITTED SNAPSHOT	No	Yes	Yes	Yes	No	Yes
REPEATABLE READ	No	No	No	Yes	No	No
SERIALIZABLE	No	No	No	No	No	No
SNAPSHOT	No	No	No	No	Yes	Yes

Deadlocks

A *deadlock* is a situation in which two or more sessions block each other. An example of a two-session deadlock is when session A blocks session B and session B blocks session A. An example of a deadlock involving more than two sessions is when session A blocks session B, session B blocks session C, and session C blocks session A. In any of these cases, SQL Server detects the deadlock and intervenes by terminating one of the transactions. If SQL Server did not intervene, the sessions involved would remain deadlocked forever.

Unless otherwise specified, SQL Server chooses to terminate the transaction that did the least work (based on the activity written to the transaction log), because rolling that transaction's work back is the cheapest option. However, with SQL Server you can set a session option called *DEADLOCK_PRIORITY* to one of 21 values in the range *–10* through *10.* The session with the lowest deadlock priority is chosen as the deadlock "victim" regardless of how much work is done; in the event of a tie, the amount of work is used as a tiebreaker. If the same amount of work is estimated for all sessions involved, a coin toss is used as the final tiebreaker.

The following example demonstrates a simple deadlock. After presenting the example, I'll explain how you can mitigate deadlock occurrences in the system.

Open two connections, and make sure you're connected to the *TSQLV4* database in both. Run the following code in Connection 1 to open a new transaction, update a row in the *Production.Products* table for product 2, and leave the transaction open:

```
USE TSQLV4;

BEGIN TRAN;

  UPDATE Production.Products
    SET unitprice += 1.00
  WHERE productid = 2;
```

Run the following code in Connection 2 to open a new transaction, update a row in the *Sales.OrderDetails* table for product 2, and leave the transaction open:

```
BEGIN TRAN;

  UPDATE Sales.OrderDetails
    SET unitprice += 1.00
  WHERE productid = 2;
```

At this point, the transaction in Connection 1 is holding an exclusive lock on the row for product 2 in the *Production.Products* table, and the transaction in Connection 2 is now holding locks on the rows for product 2 in the *Sales.OrderDetails* table. Both queries succeed, and no blocking has occurred yet.

Run the following code in Connection 1 to attempt to query the rows for product 2 in the *Sales.OrderDetails* table, and commit the transaction:

```
  SELECT orderid, productid, unitprice
  FROM Sales.OrderDetails
  WHERE productid = 2;

COMMIT TRAN;
```

The transaction in Connection 1 needs a shared lock to be able to perform its read. Because the other transaction holds an exclusive lock on the same resource, the transaction in Connection 1 is blocked. At this point, you have a blocking situation, not yet a deadlock. Of course, a chance remains that Connection 2 will end the transaction, releasing all locks and allowing the transaction in Connection 1 to get the requested locks.

Next, run the following code in Connection 2 to attempt to query the row for product 2 in the *Product.Production* table and commit the transaction:

```
  SELECT productid, unitprice
  FROM Production.Products
  WHERE productid = 2;

COMMIT TRAN;
```

To be able to perform its read, the transaction in Connection 2 needs a shared lock on the row for product 2 in the *Product.Production* table, so this request is now in conflict with the exclusive lock held on the same resource by Connection 1. Each of the sessions blocks the other—you have a deadlock. SQL Server identifies the deadlock (typically within a few seconds), chooses one of the sessions involved as the deadlock victim, and terminates its transaction with the following error:

```
Msg 1205, Level 13, State 51, Line 1
Transaction (Process ID 52) was deadlocked on lock resources with another process and has been
chosen as the deadlock victim. Rerun the transaction.
```

In this example, SQL Server chose to terminate the transaction in Connection 1 (shown here as process ID 52). Because you didn't set a deadlock priority and both transactions did a similar amount of work, either transaction could have been terminated.

Deadlocks are expensive because they involve undoing work that has already been done and then, usually with some error-handling logic, redoing the work. You can follow a few practices to mitigate deadlock occurrences in your system.

Obviously, the longer the transactions are, the longer locks are kept, increasing the probability of deadlocks. You should try to keep transactions as short as possible, taking activities out of the transaction that aren't logically supposed to be part of the same unit of work. For example, don't use transactions that require user input to finish!

One typical deadlock, also called a *deadly embrace* deadlock, happens when transactions access resources in inverse order. In the example just given, Connection 1 first accessed a row in *Production.Products* and then accessed a row in *Sales.OrderDetails*, whereas Connection 2 first accessed a row in *Sales.OrderDetails* and then accessed a row in *Production.Products*. This type of deadlock can't happen if both transactions access resources in the same order. By swapping the order in one of the transactions, you can prevent this type of deadlock from happening—assuming that it makes no logical difference to your application.

The deadlock example has a real logical conflict because both sides try to access the same rows. However, deadlocks often happen when there is no real logical conflict, because of a lack of good indexing to support query filters. For example, suppose both statements in the transaction in Connection 2 filtered product 5. Now that the statements in Connection 1 handle product 2 and the statements in Connection 2 handle product 5, there shouldn't be any conflict. However, if you don't have indexes defined on the *productid* column in the tables to support the filter, SQL Server has to scan (and lock) all rows in the table. This, of course, can lead to a deadlock. In short, good index design can help mitigate the occurrences of deadlocks that have no real logical conflict.

Another option to consider to mitigate deadlock occurrences is the choice of isolation level. The *SELECT* statements in the example needed shared locks because they ran under the *READ COMMITTED* isolation level. If you use the *READ COMMITTED SNAPSHOT* isolation level, readers will not need shared locks, and deadlocks that evolve because of the involvement of shared locks can be eliminated.

When you're done, run the following code for cleanup in any connection:

```
UPDATE Production.Products
  SET unitprice = 19.00
WHERE productid = 2;

UPDATE Sales.OrderDetails
  SET unitprice = 19.00
WHERE productid = 2
  AND orderid >= 10500;

UPDATE Sales.OrderDetails
  SET unitprice = 15.20
WHERE productid = 2
  AND orderid < 10500;
```

Conclusion

This chapter introduced you to transactions and concurrency. I described what transactions are and how SQL Server manages them. I explained how SQL Server isolates data accessed by one transaction from inconsistent use by other transactions, and how to troubleshoot blocking scenarios. I described how you can control the level of consistency you get from the data by choosing an isolation level, and the impact your choice has on concurrency. I described four isolation levels that do not rely on row versioning and two that do. Finally, I covered deadlocks and explained practices you can follow to reduce the frequency of their occurrence.

To practice what you learned, perform the following exercises.

Exercises

This section provides exercises to help you familiarize yourself with the subjects discussed in this chapter. The exercises for most of the previous chapters involve requests for which you have to figure out a solution in the form of a T-SQL query or statement. The exercises for this chapter are different. You'll be provided with instructions to follow to troubleshoot blocking and deadlock situations, and to observe the behavior of different isolation levels. Therefore, this chapter's exercises have no separate "Solutions" section as in other chapters. Exercises 1, 2, and 3 are independent of each other.

For all exercises in this chapter, make sure you're connected to the *TSQLV4* sample database by running the following code:

```
USE TSQLV4;
```

Exercises 1-1 through 1-6 deal with blocking. They assume you're using the isolation level *READ COMMITTED* (locking). Remember that this is the default isolation level in a SQL Server box product. To perform these exercises on Azure SQL Database, you need to turn versioning off.

Exercise 1-1

Open three connections in SQL Server Management Studio. (The exercises will refer to them as Connection 1, Connection 2, and Connection 3.) Run the following code in Connection 1 to update rows in *Sales.OrderDetails*:

```
BEGIN TRAN;

  UPDATE Sales.OrderDetails
    SET discount = 0.05
  WHERE orderid = 10249;
```

Exercise 1-2

Run the following code in Connection 2 to query *Sales.OrderDetails*; Connection 2 will be blocked:

```
SELECT orderid, productid, unitprice, qty, discount
FROM Sales.OrderDetails
WHERE orderid = 10249;
```

Exercise 1-3

Run the following code in Connection 3, and identify the locks and session IDs involved in the blocking chain:

```
SELECT -- use * to explore
  request_session_id            AS sid,
  resource_type                 AS restype,
  resource_database_id          AS dbid,
  resource_description          AS res,
  resource_associated_entity_id AS resid,
  request_mode                  AS mode,
  request_status                AS status
FROM sys.dm_tran_locks;
```

Exercise 1-4

Replace the session IDs 52 and 53 with the ones you found to be involved in the blocking chain in the previous exercise. Run the following code to obtain connection, session, and blocking information about the processes involved in the blocking chain:

```
-- Connection info:
SELECT -- use * to explore
  session_id AS sid,
  connect_time,
  last_read,
  last_write,
  most_recent_sql_handle
FROM sys.dm_exec_connections
WHERE session_id IN(52, 53);
```

```
-- Session info
SELECT -- use * to explore
  session_id AS sid,
  login_time,
  host_name,
  program_name,
  login_name,
  nt_user_name,
  last_request_start_time,
  last_request_end_time
FROM sys.dm_exec_sessions
WHERE session_id IN(52, 53);

-- Blocking
SELECT -- use * to explore
  session_id AS sid,
  blocking_session_id,
  command,
  sql_handle,
  database_id,
  wait_type,
  wait_time,
  wait_resource
FROM sys.dm_exec_requests
WHERE blocking_session_id > 0;
```

Exercise 1-5

Run the following code to obtain the SQL text of the connections involved in the blocking chain:

```
SELECT session_id, text
FROM sys.dm_exec_connections
  CROSS APPLY sys.dm_exec_sql_text(most_recent_sql_handle) AS ST
WHERE session_id IN(52, 53);
```

Exercise 1-6

Run the following code in Connection 1 to roll back the transaction:

```
ROLLBACK TRAN;
```

Observe in Connection 2 that the *SELECT* query returned the two order detail rows, and that those rows were not modified.

Remember that if you need to terminate the blocker's transaction, you can use the KILL command. Close all connections.

Exercises 2-1 through 2-6 deal with isolation levels.

Exercise 2-1

In this exercise, you'll practice using the *READ UNCOMMITTED* isolation level.

Exercise 2-1a

Open two new connections. (This exercise will refer to them as Connection 1 and Connection 2.)

Exercise 2-1b

Run the following code in Connection 1 to update rows in *Sales.OrderDetails* and query it:

```
BEGIN TRAN;

  UPDATE Sales.OrderDetails
    SET discount += 0.05
  WHERE orderid = 10249;

  SELECT orderid, productid, unitprice, qty, discount
  FROM Sales.OrderDetails
  WHERE orderid = 10249;
```

Exercise 2-1c

Run the following code in Connection 2 to set the isolation level to *READ UNCOMMITTED* and query *Sales.OrderDetails*:

```
SET TRANSACTION ISOLATION LEVEL READ UNCOMMITTED;

SELECT orderid, productid, unitprice, qty, discount
FROM Sales.OrderDetails
WHERE orderid = 10249;
```

Notice that you get the modified, uncommitted version of the rows.

Exercise 2-1d

Run the following code in Connection 1 to roll back the transaction:

```
ROLLBACK TRAN;
```

Exercise 2-2

In this exercise, you'll practice using the *READ COMMITTED* isolation level.

Exercise 2-2a

Run the following code in Connection 1 to update rows in *Sales.OrderDetails* and query it:

```
BEGIN TRAN;

  UPDATE Sales.OrderDetails
    SET discount += 0.05
  WHERE orderid = 10249;

  SELECT orderid, productid, unitprice, qty, discount
```

```
  FROM Sales.OrderDetails
  WHERE orderid = 10249;
```

Exercise 2-2b

Run the following code in Connection 2 to set the isolation level to *READ COMMITTED* and query *Sales.OrderDetails*:

```
SET TRANSACTION ISOLATION LEVEL READ COMMITTED;

SELECT orderid, productid, unitprice, qty, discount
FROM Sales.OrderDetails
WHERE orderid = 10249;
```

Notice that you're now blocked.

Exercise 2-2c

Run the following code in Connection 1 to commit the transaction:

```
COMMIT TRAN;
```

Exercise 2-2d

Go to Connection 2, and notice that you get the modified, committed version of the rows.

Exercise 2-2e

Run the following code for cleanup:

```
UPDATE Sales.OrderDetails
  SET discount = 0.00
WHERE orderid = 10249;
```

Exercise 2-3

In this exercise, you'll practice using the *REPEATABLE READ* isolation level.

Exercise 2-3a

Run the following code in Connection 1 to set the isolation level to *REPEATABLE READ*, open a transaction, and read data from *Sales.OrderDetails*:

```
SET TRANSACTION ISOLATION LEVEL REPEATABLE READ;

BEGIN TRAN;

  SELECT orderid, productid, unitprice, qty, discount
  FROM Sales.OrderDetails
  WHERE orderid = 10249;
```

You get two rows with discount values of 0.00.

Exercise 2-3b

Run the following code in Connection 2, and notice that you're blocked:

```
UPDATE Sales.OrderDetails
  SET discount += 0.05
WHERE orderid = 10249;
```

Exercise 2-3c

Run the following code in Connection 1 to read the data again and commit the transaction:

```
  SELECT orderid, productid, unitprice, qty, discount
  FROM Sales.OrderDetails
  WHERE orderid = 10249;

COMMIT TRAN;
```

You get the two rows with discount values of 0.00 again, giving you repeatable reads. Note that if your code was running under a lower isolation level (such as *READ UNCOMMITTED* or *READ COMMITTED*), the *UPDATE* statement wouldn't be blocked, and you would get nonrepeatable reads.

Exercise 2-3d

Go to Connection 2, and notice that the update has finished.

Exercise 2-3e

Run the following code for cleanup:

```
UPDATE Sales.OrderDetails
  SET discount = 0.00
WHERE orderid = 10249;
```

Exercise 2-4

In this exercise, you'll practice using the *SERIALIZABLE* isolation level.

Exercise 2-4a

Run the following code in Connection 1 to set the isolation level to *SERIALIZABLE* and query *Sales.OrderDetails*:

```
SET TRANSACTION ISOLATION LEVEL SERIALIZABLE;

BEGIN TRAN;

  SELECT orderid, productid, unitprice, qty, discount
  FROM Sales.OrderDetails
  WHERE orderid = 10249;
```

Exercise 2-4b

Run the following code in Connection 2 to attempt to insert a row to *Sales.OrderDetails* with the same order ID that is filtered by the previous query, and notice that you're blocked:

```
INSERT INTO Sales.OrderDetails
    (orderid, productid, unitprice, qty, discount)
  VALUES(10249, 2, 19.00, 10, 0.00);
```

Note that in lower isolation levels (such as *READ UNCOMMITTED*, *READ COMMITTED*, or *REPEATABLE READ*), this *INSERT* statement wouldn't be blocked.

Exercise 2-4c

Run the following code in Connection 1 to query *Sales.OrderDetails* again and commit the transaction:

```
  SELECT orderid, productid, unitprice, qty, discount
  FROM Sales.OrderDetails
  WHERE orderid = 10249;

COMMIT TRAN;
```

You get the same result set you got from the previous query in the same transaction, and because the *INSERT* statement was blocked, you get no phantom reads.

Exercise 2-4d

Go back to Connection 2, and notice that the *INSERT* statement has finished.

Exercise 2-4e

Run the following code for cleanup:

```
DELETE FROM Sales.OrderDetails
WHERE orderid = 10249
  AND productid = 2;
```

Exercise 2-4f

Run the following code in both Connection 1 and Connection 2 to set the isolation level to the default:

```
SET TRANSACTION ISOLATION LEVEL READ COMMITTED;
```

Exercise 2-5

In this exercise, you'll practice using the *SNAPSHOT* isolation level.

Exercise 2-5a

Run the following code to allow the *SNAPSHOT* isolation level in the *TSQLV4* database:

```
ALTER DATABASE TSQLV4 SET ALLOW_SNAPSHOT_ISOLATION ON;
```

Exercise 2-5b

Run the following code in Connection 1 to open a transaction, update rows in *Sales.OrderDetails*, and query it:

```
BEGIN TRAN;

  UPDATE Sales.OrderDetails
    SET discount += 0.05
  WHERE orderid = 10249;

  SELECT orderid, productid, unitprice, qty, discount
  FROM Sales.OrderDetails
  WHERE orderid = 10249;
```

Exercise 2-5c

Run the following code in Connection 2 to set the isolation level to *SNAPSHOT* and query *Sales.OrderDetails*. Notice that you're not blocked—instead, you get an earlier, consistent version of the data that was available when the transaction started (with discount values of 0.00):

```
SET TRANSACTION ISOLATION LEVEL SNAPSHOT;

BEGIN TRAN;

  SELECT orderid, productid, unitprice, qty, discount
  FROM Sales.OrderDetails
  WHERE orderid = 10249;
```

Exercise 2-5d

Go to Connection 1 and commit the transaction:

```
COMMIT TRAN;
```

Exercise 2-5e

Go to Connection 2 and query the data again; notice that you still get discount values of 0.00:

```
  SELECT orderid, productid, unitprice, qty, discount
  FROM Sales.OrderDetails
  WHERE orderid = 10249;
```

Exercise 2-5f

In Connection 2, commit the transaction and query the data again; notice that now you get discount values of 0.05:

```
COMMIT TRAN;
```

```
SELECT orderid, productid, unitprice, qty, discount
FROM Sales.OrderDetails
WHERE orderid = 10249;
```

Exercise 2-5g

Run the following code for cleanup:

```
UPDATE Sales.OrderDetails
  SET discount = 0.00
WHERE orderid = 10249;
```

Close all connections.

Exercise 2-6

In this exercise, you'll practice using the *READ COMMITTED SNAPSHOT* isolation level.

Exercise 2-6a

Turn on *READ_COMMITTED_SNAPSHOT* in the *TSQLV4* database:

```
ALTER DATABASE TSQLV4 SET READ_COMMITTED_SNAPSHOT ON;
```

Exercise 2-6b

Open two new connections. (This exercise will refer to them as Connection 1 and Connection 2.)

Exercise 2-6c

Run the following code in Connection 1 to open a transaction, update rows in *Sales.OrderDetails*, and query it:

```
BEGIN TRAN;

  UPDATE Sales.OrderDetails
    SET discount += 0.05
  WHERE orderid = 10249;

  SELECT orderid, productid, unitprice, qty, discount
  FROM Sales.OrderDetails
  WHERE orderid = 10249;
```

Exercise 2-6d

Run the following code in Connection 2, which is now running under the *READ COMMITTED SNAPSHOT* isolation level because the database flag *READ_COMMITTED_SNAPSHOT* is turned on. Notice that you're not blocked—instead, you get an earlier, consistent version of the data that was available when the statement started (with discount values of 0.00):

```
BEGIN TRAN;

  SELECT orderid, productid, unitprice, qty, discount
  FROM Sales.OrderDetails
  WHERE orderid = 10249;
```

Exercise 2-6e

Go to Connection 1 and commit the transaction:

```
COMMIT TRAN;
```

Exercise 2-6f

Go to Connection 2, query the data again, and commit the transaction. Notice that you get the new discount values of 0.05:

```
  SELECT orderid, productid, unitprice, qty, discount
  FROM Sales.OrderDetails
  WHERE orderid = 10249;

COMMIT TRAN;
```

Exercise 2-6g

Run the following code for cleanup:

```
UPDATE Sales.OrderDetails
  SET discount = 0.00
WHERE orderid = 10249;
```

Close all connections.

Exercise 2-6h

Change the database flags back to the defaults in a box product, disabling isolation levels based on row versioning:

```
ALTER DATABASE TSQLV4 SET ALLOW_SNAPSHOT_ISOLATION OFF;
ALTER DATABASE TSQLV4 SET READ_COMMITTED_SNAPSHOT OFF;
```

Note that if you want to change these settings back to the defaults in Azure SQL Database, you'll need to set both to ON.

Exercise 3 (steps 1 through 7) deals with deadlocks. It assumes that versioning is turned off.

Exercise 3-1

Open two new connections. (This exercise will refer to them as Connection 1 and Connection 2.)

Exercise 3-2

Run the following code in Connection 1 to open a transaction and update the row for product 2 in *Production.Products*:

```
BEGIN TRAN;

  UPDATE Production.Products
    SET unitprice += 1.00
  WHERE productid = 2;
```

Exercise 3-3

Run the following code in Connection 2 to open a transaction and update the row for product 3 in *Production.Products*:

```
BEGIN TRAN;

  UPDATE Production.Products
    SET unitprice += 1.00
  WHERE productid = 3;
```

Exercise 3-4

Run the following code in Connection 1 to query product 3. You will be blocked.

```
  SELECT productid, unitprice
  FROM Production.Products
  WHERE productid = 3;

COMMIT TRAN;
```

Exercise 3-5

Run the following code in Connection 2 to query product 2. You will be blocked, and a deadlock error will be generated either in Connection 1 or Connection 2:

```
  SELECT productid, unitprice
  FROM Production.Products
  WHERE productid = 2;

COMMIT TRAN;
```

Exercise 3-6

Can you suggest a way to prevent this deadlock? Hint: Refer back to what you read in the "Deadlocks" section.

Exercise 3-7

Run the following code for cleanup:

```
UPDATE Production.Products
  SET unitprice = 19.00
WHERE productid = 2;

UPDATE Production.Products
  SET unitprice = 10.00
WHERE productid = 3;
```

CHAPTER 11

Programmable objects

This chapter provides a brief overview of programmable objects to familiarize you with the capabilities of T-SQL in this area and with the concepts involved. The chapter covers variables; batches; flow elements; cursors; temporary tables; routines such as user-defined functions, stored procedures, and triggers; and dynamic SQL.

Variables

You use variables to temporarily store data values for later use in the same batch in which they were declared. I describe batches later in this chapter, but for now, the important thing for you to know is that a batch is one T-SQL statement or more sent to Microsoft SQL Server for execution as a single unit.

Use a *DECLARE* statement to declare one or more variables, and use a *SET* statement to assign a value to a single variable. For example, the following code declares a variable called *@i* of an *INT* data type and assigns it the value *10*:

```
DECLARE @i AS INT;
SET @i = 10;
```

Alternatively, you can declare and initialize a variable in the same statement, like this:

```
DECLARE @i AS INT = 10;
```

When you assign a value to a scalar variable, the value must be the result of a scalar expression. The expression can be a scalar subquery. For example, the following code declares a variable called *@empname* and assigns it the result of a scalar subquery that returns the full name of the employee with an ID of 3:

```
USE TSQLV4;

DECLARE @empname AS NVARCHAR(61);

SET @empname = (SELECT firstname + N' ' + lastname
                FROM HR.Employees
                WHERE empid = 3);

SELECT @empname AS empname;
```

This code returns the following output:

```
empname
----------
Judy Lew
```

The *SET* statement can operate on only one variable at a time, so if you need to assign values to multiple variables, you need to use multiple *SET* statements. This approach can involve unnecessary overhead when you need to pull multiple attribute values from the same row. For example, the following code uses two separate *SET* statements to pull both the first and last names of the employee with the ID of 3 to two separate variables:

```
DECLARE @firstname AS NVARCHAR(20), @lastname AS NVARCHAR(40);

SET @firstname = (SELECT firstname
                  FROM HR.Employees
                  WHERE empid = 3);
SET @lastname = (SELECT lastname
                 FROM HR.Employees
                 WHERE empid = 3);

SELECT @firstname AS firstname, @lastname AS lastname;
```

This code returns the following output:

```
firstname  lastname
---------- ---------
Judy       Lew
```

T-SQL also supports a nonstandard assignment *SELECT* statement, which you use to query data and assign multiple values obtained from the same row to multiple variables by using a single statement. Here's an example:

```
DECLARE @firstname AS NVARCHAR(20), @lastname AS NVARCHAR(40);

SELECT
  @firstname = firstname,
  @lastname  = lastname
FROM HR.Employees
WHERE empid = 3;

SELECT @firstname AS firstname, @lastname AS lastname;
```

The assignment *SELECT* has predictable behavior when exactly one row qualifies. However, note that if the query has more than one qualifying row, the code doesn't fail. The assignments take place per qualifying row, and with each row accessed, the values from the current row overwrite the existing values in the variables. When the assignment *SELECT* finishes, the values in the variables are those from the last row that SQL Server happened to access. For example, the following assignment *SELECT* has two qualifying rows:

```
DECLARE @empname AS NVARCHAR(61);
```

```
SELECT @empname = firstname + N' ' + lastname
FROM HR.Employees
WHERE mgrid = 2;

SELECT @empname AS empname;
```

The employee information that ends up in the variable after the assignment *SELECT* finishes depends on the order in which SQL Server happens to access those rows—and you have no control over this order. When I ran this code, I got the following output:

```
empname
---------------
Sven Mortensen
```

The *SET* statement is safer than the assignment *SELECT* because it requires you to use a scalar subquery to pull data from a table. Remember that a scalar subquery fails at run time if it returns more than one value. For example, the following code fails:

```
DECLARE @empname AS NVARCHAR(61);

SET @empname = (SELECT firstname + N' ' + lastname
                FROM HR.Employees
                WHERE mgrid = 2);

SELECT @empname AS empname;
```

Because the variable was not assigned a value, it remains *NULL*, which is the default for variables that were not initialized. This code returns the following output:

```
Msg 512, Level 16, State 1, Line 71
Subquery returned more than 1 value. This is not permitted when the subquery follows =, !=, <,
<= , >, >= or when the subquery is used as an expression.
empname
--------
NULL
```

Batches

A batch is one or more T-SQL statements sent by a client application to SQL Server for execution as a single unit. The batch undergoes parsing (syntax checking), resolution/binding (checking the existence of referenced objects and columns, permissions checking), and optimization as a unit.

Don't confuse *transactions* and *batches*. A transaction is an atomic unit of work. A batch can have multiple transactions, and a transaction can be submitted in parts as multiple batches. When a transaction is canceled or rolled back, SQL Server undoes the partial activity that has taken place since the beginning of the transaction, regardless of where the batch began.

Client application programming interfaces (APIs) such as ADO.NET provide you with methods for submitting a batch of code to SQL Server for execution. SQL Server utilities such as SQL Server

Management Studio (SSMS), SQLCMD, and OSQL provide a client tool command called *GO* that signals the end of a batch. Note that the *GO* command is a client tool command and not a T-SQL server command.

A batch as a unit of parsing

A batch is a set of commands that are parsed and executed as a unit. If the parsing is successful, SQL Server then attempts to execute the batch. In the event of a syntax error in the batch, the whole batch is not submitted to SQL Server for execution. For example, the following code has three batches, the second of which has a syntax error (*FOM* instead of *FROM* in the second query):

```
-- Valid batch
PRINT 'First batch';
USE TSQLV4;
GO
-- Invalid batch
PRINT 'Second batch';
SELECT custid FROM Sales.Customers;
SELECT orderid FOM Sales.Orders;
GO
-- Valid batch
PRINT 'Third batch';
SELECT empid FROM HR.Employees;
```

Because the second batch has a syntax error, the whole batch is not submitted to SQL Server for execution. The first and third batches pass syntax validation and therefore are submitted for execution. This code produces the following output showing that the whole second batch was not executed:

```
First batch
Msg 102, Level 15, State 1, Line 91
Incorrect syntax near 'Sales'.
Third batch
empid
-----------
2
7
1
5
6
8
3
9
4

(9 row(s) affected)
```

Batches and variables

A variable is local to the batch in which it's defined. If you refer to a variable that was defined in another batch, you'll get an error saying that the variable was not defined. For example, the following code declares a variable and prints its content in one batch, and then it tries to print its content from another batch:

```
DECLARE @i AS INT;
SET @i = 10;
-- Succeeds
PRINT @i;
GO

-- Fails
PRINT @i;
```

The reference to the variable in the first *PRINT* statement is valid because it appears in the same batch where the variable was declared, but the second reference is invalid. Therefore, the first *PRINT* statement returns the variable's value (*10*), whereas the second fails. Here's the output returned from this code:

```
10
Msg 137, Level 15, State 2, Line 106
Must declare the scalar variable "@i".
```

Statements that cannot be combined in the same batch

The following statements cannot be combined with other statements in the same batch: *CREATE DEFAULT, CREATE FUNCTION, CREATE PROCEDURE, CREATE RULE, CREATE SCHEMA, CREATE TRIGGER,* and *CREATE VIEW.* For example, the following code has a *DROP* statement followed by a *CREATE VIEW* statement in the same batch and therefore is invalid:

```
DROP VIEW IF EXISTS Sales.MyView;

CREATE VIEW Sales.MyView
AS

SELECT YEAR(orderdate) AS orderyear, COUNT(*) AS numorders
FROM Sales.Orders
GROUP BY YEAR(orderdate);
GO
```

An attempt to run this code generates the following error:

```
Msg 111, Level 15, State 1, Line 113
'CREATE VIEW' must be the first statement in a query batch.
```

To get around the problem, separate the *DROP VIEW* and *CREATE VIEW* statements into different batches by adding a *GO* command after the *DROP VIEW* statement.

A batch as a unit of resolution

A batch is a unit of resolution (also known as *binding*). This means that checking the existence of objects and columns happens at the batch level. Keep this fact in mind when you're designing batch boundaries. When you apply schema changes to an object and try to manipulate the object data in the same batch, SQL Server might not be aware of the schema changes yet and fail the data-manipulation statement with a resolution error. I'll demonstrate the problem through an example and then recommend best practices.

Run the following code to create a table called *T1* in the current database, with one column called *col1*:

```
DROP TABLE IF EXISTS dbo.T1;
CREATE TABLE dbo.T1(col1 INT);
```

Next, try to add a column called *col2* to *T1* and query the new column in the same batch:

```
ALTER TABLE dbo.T1 ADD col2 INT;
SELECT col1, col2 FROM dbo.T1;
```

Even though the code might seem to be perfectly valid, the batch fails during the resolution phase with the following error:

```
Msg 207, Level 16, State 1, Line 130
Invalid column name 'col2'.
```

At the time the *SELECT* statement was resolved, *T1* had only one column, and the reference to the *col2* column caused the error. One best practice you can follow to avoid such problems is to separate data-definition language (DDL) and Data-Manipulation Language (DML) statements into different batches, as in the following example:

```
ALTER TABLE dbo.T1 ADD col2 INT;
GO
SELECT col1, col2 FROM dbo.T1;
```

The *GO n* option

The *GO* command is not really a T-SQL command; it's actually a command used by SQL Server's client tools, such as SSMS, to denote the end of a batch. This command supports an argument indicating how many times you want to execute the batch. To see how the *GO* command with the argument works, first create the table *T1* by using the following code:

```
DROP TABLE IF EXISTS dbo.T1;
CREATE TABLE dbo.T1(col1 INT IDENTITY);
```

The *col1* column gets its values automatically from an identity property. Note that the demo works just as well if you use a default constraint to generate values from a sequence object. Next, run the following code to suppress the default output produced by DML statements that indicates how many rows were affected:

```
SET NOCOUNT ON;
```

Finally, run the following code to define a batch with an *INSERT DEFAULT VALUES* statement and to execute the batch 100 times:

```
INSERT INTO dbo.T1 DEFAULT VALUES;
GO 100

SELECT * FROM dbo.T1;
```

The query returns 100 rows with the values *1* through *100* in *col1*.

Flow elements

You use flow elements to control the flow of your code. T-SQL provides basic forms of control with flow elements, including the *IF . . . ELSE* element and the *WHILE* element.

The *IF . . . ELSE* flow element

You use the *IF . . . ELSE* element to control the flow of your code based on the result of a predicate. You specify a statement or statement block that is executed if the predicate is *TRUE*, and optionally a statement or statement block that is executed if the predicate is *FALSE* or *UNKNOWN*.

For example, the following code checks whether today is the last day of the year (in other words, whether today's year is different than tomorrow's year). If this is true, the code prints a message saying that today is the last day of the year; if it's not true ("else"), the code prints a message saying that today is not the last day of the year:

```
IF YEAR(SYSDATETIME()) <> YEAR(DATEADD(day, 1, SYSDATETIME()))
  PRINT 'Today is the last day of the year.';
ELSE
  PRINT 'Today is not the last day of the year.';
```

In this example, I use *PRINT* statements to demonstrate which parts of the code were executed and which weren't, but of course you can specify other statements as well.

Keep in mind that T-SQL uses three-valued logic and that the *ELSE* block is activated when the predicate is either *FALSE* or *UNKNOWN*. In cases for which both *FALSE* and *UNKNOWN* are possible outcomes of the predicate (for example, when *NULL*s are involved) and you need different treatment for each case, make sure you have an explicit test for *NULL*s with the *IS NULL* predicate.

If the flow you need to control involves more than two cases, you can nest *IF . . . ELSE* elements. For example, the next code I'll show you handles the following three cases differently:

- Today is the last day of the year.
- Today is the last day of the month but not the last day of the year.
- Today is not the last day of the month.

```
IF YEAR(SYSDATETIME()) <> YEAR(DATEADD(day, 1, SYSDATETIME()))
  PRINT 'Today is the last day of the year.';
ELSE
  IF MONTH(SYSDATETIME()) <> MONTH(DATEADD(day, 1, SYSDATETIME()))
    PRINT 'Today is the last day of the month but not the last day of the year.';
  ELSE
    PRINT 'Today is not the last day of the month.';
```

If you need to run more than one statement in the *IF* or *ELSE* sections, you need to use a statement block. You mark the boundaries of a statement block with the *BEGIN* and *END* keywords. For example, the following code shows how to run one type of process if it's the first day of the month and another type of process if it isn't:

```
IF DAY(SYSDATETIME()) = 1
BEGIN
  PRINT 'Today is the first day of the month.';
  PRINT 'Starting first-of-month-day process.';
  /* ... process code goes here ... */
  PRINT 'Finished first-of-month-day database process.';
END;
ELSE
BEGIN
  PRINT 'Today is not the first day of the month.';
  PRINT 'Starting non-first-of-month-day process.';
  /* ... process code goes here ... */
  PRINT 'Finished non-first-of-month-day process.';
END;
```

The *WHILE* flow element

T-SQL provides the *WHILE* element, which you can use to execute code in a loop. The *WHILE* element executes a statement or statement block repeatedly while the predicate you specify after the *WHILE* keyword is *TRUE*. When the predicate is *FALSE* or *UNKNOWN*, the loop terminates.

T-SQL doesn't provide a built-in looping element that executes a predetermined number of times, but it's easy to mimic such an element with a *WHILE* loop and a variable. For example, the following code demonstrates how to write a loop that iterates 10 times:

```
DECLARE @i AS INT = 1;
WHILE @i <= 10
BEGIN
  PRINT @i;
  SET @i = @i + 1;
END;
```

The code declares an integer variable called *@i* that serves as the loop counter and initializes it with the value *1*. The code then enters a loop that iterates while the variable is smaller than or equal to *10*. In each iteration, the code in the loop's body prints the current value of *@i* and then increments it by 1. This code returns the following output showing that the loop iterated 10 times:

```
1
2
```

```
3
4
5
6
7
8
9
10
```

If at some point in the loop's body you want to break out of the current loop and proceed to execute the statement that appears after the loop's body, use the *BREAK* command. For example, the following code breaks from the loop if the value of *@i* is equal to *6*:

```
DECLARE @i AS INT = 1;
WHILE @i <= 10
BEGIN
  IF @i = 6 BREAK;
  PRINT @i;
  SET @i = @i + 1;
END;
```

This code produces the following output showing that the loop iterated five times and terminated at the beginning of the sixth iteration:

```
1
2
3
4
5
```

Of course, this code is not very sensible; if you want the loop to iterate only five times, you should simply specify the predicate *@i <= 5*. Here I just wanted to demonstrate the use of the *BREAK* command with a simple example.

If at some point in the loop's body you want to skip the rest of the activity in the current iteration and evaluate the loop's predicate again, use the *CONTINUE* command. For example, the following code demonstrates how to skip the activity of the sixth iteration of the loop from the point where the *IF* statement appears and until the end of the loop's body:

```
DECLARE @i AS INT = 0;
WHILE @i < 10
BEGIN
  SET @i = @i + 1;
  IF @i = 6 CONTINUE;
  PRINT @i;
END;
```

The output of this code shows that the value of *@i* was printed in all iterations except the sixth:

```
1
2
3
4
```

```
5
7
8
9
10
```

As another example of using a *WHILE* loop, the following code creates a table called *dbo.Numbers* and populates it with 1,000 rows with the values *1* through *1,000* in the column *n*:

```
SET NOCOUNT ON;
DROP TABLE IF EXISTS dbo.Numbers;
CREATE TABLE dbo.Numbers(n INT NOT NULL PRIMARY KEY);
GO

DECLARE @i AS INT = 1;
WHILE @i <= 1000
BEGIN
  INSERT INTO dbo.Numbers(n) VALUES(@i);
  SET @i = @i + 1;
END;
```

Cursors

In Chapter 2, "Single-table queries," I explained that a query without an *ORDER BY* clause returns a set (or a multiset), whereas a query with an *ORDER BY* clause returns what standard SQL calls a *cursor*—a nonrelational result with order guaranteed among rows. In the context of the discussion in Chapter 2, the use of the term "cursor" was conceptual. SQL and T-SQL also supports an object called *cursor* you can use to process rows from a result of a query one at a time and in a requested order. This is in contrast to using set-based queries—normal queries without a cursor for which you manipulate the set or multiset as a whole and cannot rely on order.

I want to stress that your default choice should be to use set-based queries; only when you have a compelling reason to do otherwise should you consider using cursors. This recommendation is based on several factors, including the following:

- First and foremost, when you use cursors you pretty much go against the relational model, which is based on set theory.
- The record-by-record manipulation done by the cursor has overhead. A certain extra cost is associated with each record manipulation by the cursor compared to set-based manipulation. Given a set-based query and cursor code that do similar physical processing behind the scenes, the cursor code is usually many times slower than the set-based code.
- With cursors, you write imperative solutions—in other words, you're responsible for defining how to process the data (declaring the cursor, opening it, looping through the cursor records, closing the cursor, and deallocating the cursor). With set-based solutions, you write declarative code where you mainly focus on the logical aspects of the solution—in other words, on what to

get instead of on how to get it. Therefore, cursor solutions tend to be longer, less readable, and harder to maintain than set-based solutions.

For most people, it's not simple to think in relational terms immediately when they start learning SQL. It's more intuitive for most people to think in terms of cursors—processing one record at a time in a certain order. As a result, cursors are widely used, and in most cases they are misused; that is, they are used even when much better set-based solutions exist. Make a conscious effort to adopt the set-based state of mind and to truly think in terms of sets. It can take time—in some cases years—but as long as you're working with a language that is based on the relational model, that's the right way to think.

Every rule has exceptions. One example is when you need to apply a certain task to each row from some table or view. For example, you might need to execute some administrative task for each index or table in your database. In such a case, it makes sense to use a cursor to iterate through the index or table names one at a time and execute the relevant task for each of those.

Another example of when you should consider cursors is when your set-based solution performs badly and you exhaust your tuning efforts using the set-based approach. As mentioned, set-based solutions tend to be much faster, but in some exceptional cases the cursor solution is faster. One such example is computing running aggregates using T-SQL code that is compatible with legacy versions of SQL Server that don't support the frame option in window functions. Relational solutions to running aggregates using joins or subqueries are extremely slow. An iterative solution, such as one based on a cursor, is usually the optimal one. If there are no compatibility restrictions, using a relational solution with window functions is the optimal way to compute running totals.

Working with a cursor generally involves the following steps:

1. Declare the cursor based on a query.
2. Open the cursor.
3. Fetch attribute values from the first cursor record into variables.
4. As long as you haven't reached the end of the cursor (while the value of a function called *@@FETCH_STATUS* is *0*), loop through the cursor records; in each iteration of the loop, perform the processing needed for the current row, and then fetch the attribute values from the next row into the variables.
5. Close the cursor.
6. Deallocate the cursor.

The following example with cursor code calculates the running total quantity for each customer and month from the *Sales.CustOrders* view:

```
SET NOCOUNT ON;

DECLARE @Result AS TABLE
(
  custid     INT,
  ordermonth DATE,
```

```
  qty        INT,
  runqty     INT,
  PRIMARY KEY(custid, ordermonth)
);

DECLARE
  @custid     AS INT,
  @prvcustid  AS INT,
  @ordermonth AS DATE,
  @qty        AS INT,
  @runqty     AS INT;

DECLARE C CURSOR FAST_FORWARD /* read only, forward only */ FOR
  SELECT custid, ordermonth, qty
  FROM Sales.CustOrders
  ORDER BY custid, ordermonth;

OPEN C;

FETCH NEXT FROM C INTO @custid, @ordermonth, @qty;

SELECT @prvcustid = @custid, @runqty = 0;

WHILE @@FETCH_STATUS = 0
BEGIN
  IF @custid <> @prvcustid
    SELECT @prvcustid = @custid, @runqty = 0;

  SET @runqty = @runqty + @qty;

  INSERT INTO @Result VALUES(@custid, @ordermonth, @qty, @runqty);

  FETCH NEXT FROM C INTO @custid, @ordermonth, @qty;
END;

CLOSE C;

DEALLOCATE C;

SELECT
  custid,
  CONVERT(VARCHAR(7), ordermonth, 121) AS ordermonth,
  qty,
  runqty
FROM @Result
ORDER BY custid, ordermonth;
```

The code declares a cursor based on a query that returns the rows from the *CustOrders* view ordered by customer ID and order month, and it iterates through the records one at a time. The code keeps track of the current running-total quantity in a variable called *@runqty* that is reset every time a new customer is found. For each row, the code calculates the current running total by adding the current month's quantity (*@qty*) to *@runqty*, and it inserts a row with the customer ID, order month, current month's quantity, and running quantity into a table variable called *@Result*. When the code is done processing all cursor records, it queries the table variable to present the running aggregates.

Here's the output returned by this code, shown in abbreviated form:

```
custid      ordermonth qty         runqty
----------- ---------- ----------- -----------
1           2015-08    38          38
1           2015-10    41          79
1           2016-01    17          96
1           2016-03    18          114
1           2016-04    60          174
2           2014-09    6           6
2           2015-08    18          24
2           2015-11    10          34
2           2016-03    29          63
3           2014-11    24          24
3           2015-04    30          54
3           2015-05    80          134
3           2015-06    83          217
3           2015-09    102         319
3           2016-01    40          359
...
89          2014-07    80          80
89          2014-11    105         185
89          2015-03    142         327
89          2015-04    59          386
89          2015-07    59          445
89          2015-10    164         609
89          2015-11    94          703
89          2016-01    140         843
89          2016-02    50          893
89          2016-04    90          983
89          2016-05    80          1063
90          2015-07    5           5
90          2015-09    15          20
90          2015-10    34          54
90          2016-02    82          136
90          2016-04    12          148
91          2014-12    45          45
91          2015-07    31          76
91          2015-12    28          104
91          2016-02    20          124
91          2016-04    81          205

(636 row(s) affected)
```

As explained in Chapter 7, "Beyond the fundamentals of querying," T-SQL supports window functions you can use to provide elegant and highly efficient solutions to running aggregates, freeing you from needing to use cursors. Here's how you address the same task with a window function:

```
SELECT custid, ordermonth, qty,
  SUM(qty) OVER(PARTITION BY custid
              ORDER BY ordermonth
              ROWS UNBOUNDED PRECEDING) AS runqty
FROM Sales.CustOrders
ORDER BY custid, ordermonth;
```

Temporary tables

When you need to temporarily store data in tables, in certain cases you might prefer not to work with permanent tables. Suppose you need the data to be visible only to the current session, or even only to the current batch. As an example, suppose you need to store temporary data during data processing, as in the cursor example in the previous section. Another case where people use temporary tables is when they don't have permissions to create permanent tables in a user database.

SQL Server supports three kinds of temporary tables you might find more convenient to work with than permanent tables in such cases: local temporary tables, global temporary tables, and table variables. The following sections describe the three kinds and demonstrate their use with code samples.

Local temporary tables

You create a local temporary table by naming it with a single pound sign as a prefix, such as *#T1*. All three kinds of temporary tables are created in the *tempdb* database.

A local temporary table is visible only to the session that created it, in the creating level and all inner levels in the call stack (inner procedures, triggers, and dynamic batches). A local temporary table is destroyed automatically by SQL Server when the creating level in the call stack goes out of scope. For example, suppose a stored procedure called *Proc1* calls a procedure called *Proc2*, which in turn calls a procedure called *Proc3*, which in turn calls a procedure called *Proc4*. *Proc2* creates a temporary table called *#T1* before calling *Proc3*. The table *#T1* is visible to *Proc2*, *Proc3*, and *Proc4* but not to *Proc1*, and it's destroyed automatically by SQL Server when *Proc2* finishes. If the temporary table is created in an ad-hoc batch in the outermost nesting level of the session (in other words, when the value of the *@@NESTLEVEL* function is *0*), it's visible to all subsequent batches as well and is destroyed by SQL Server automatically only when the creating session disconnects.

You might wonder how SQL Server prevents name conflicts when two sessions create local temporary tables with the same name. SQL Server internally adds a suffix to the table name that makes it unique in *tempdb*. As a developer, you shouldn't care—you refer to the table using the name you provided without the internal suffix, and only your session has access to your table.

One obvious scenario for which local temporary tables are useful is when you have a process that needs to store intermediate results temporarily—such as during a loop—and later query the data.

Another scenario is when you need to access the result of some expensive processing multiple times. For example, suppose you need to join the *Sales.Orders* and *Sales.OrderDetails* tables, aggregate order quantities by order year, and join two instances of the aggregated data to compare each year's total quantity with the previous year. The *Orders* and *OrderDetails* tables in the sample database are very small, but in real-life situations such tables can have millions of rows. One option is to use table expressions, but remember that table expressions are virtual. The expensive work involving scanning all the data, joining the *Orders* and *OrderDetails* tables, and aggregating the data would have to happen twice with table expressions. Instead, it makes sense to do all the expensive work only once—storing the result in a local temporary table—and then join two instances of the temporary table, especially because the result of the expensive work is a tiny set with only one row per order year.

The following code illustrates this scenario using a local temporary table:

```
DROP TABLE IF EXISTS #MyOrderTotalsByYear;
GO

CREATE TABLE #MyOrderTotalsByYear
(
  orderyear INT NOT NULL PRIMARY KEY,
  qty       INT NOT NULL
);

INSERT INTO #MyOrderTotalsByYear(orderyear, qty)
  SELECT
    YEAR(O.orderdate) AS orderyear,
    SUM(OD.qty) AS qty
  FROM Sales.Orders AS O
    INNER JOIN Sales.OrderDetails AS OD
      ON OD.orderid = O.orderid
  GROUP BY YEAR(orderdate);

SELECT Cur.orderyear, Cur.qty AS curyearqty, Prv.qty AS prvyearqty
FROM #MyOrderTotalsByYear AS Cur
  LEFT OUTER JOIN #MyOrderTotalsByYear AS Prv
    ON Cur.orderyear = Prv.orderyear + 1;
```

This code produces the following output:

```
orderyear   curyearqty  prvyearqty
----------- ----------- -----------
2014        9581        NULL
2015        25489       9581
2016        16247       25489
```

To verify that the local temporary table is visible only to the creating session, try accessing it from another session:

```
SELECT orderyear, qty FROM #MyOrderTotalsByYear;
```

You get the following error:

```
Msg 208, Level 16, State 0, Line 1
Invalid object name '#MyOrderTotalsByYear'.
```

When you're done, go back to the original session and drop the temporary table:

```
DROP TABLE IF EXISTS #MyOrderTotalsByYear;
```

It's generally recommended that you clean up resources as soon as you're done working with them.

Global temporary tables

> **Note** At the date of this writing, global temporary tables are not supported by Azure SQL Database. If you want to run the code samples from this section, you need to connect to a SQL Server box product.

When you create a global temporary table, it's visible to all other sessions. Global temporary tables are destroyed automatically by SQL Server when the creating session disconnects and there are no active references to the table. You create a global temporary table by naming it with two pound signs as a prefix, such as *##T1*.

Global temporary tables are useful when you want to share temporary data with everyone. No special permissions are required, and everyone has full DDL and DML access. Of course, the fact that everyone has full access means that anyone can change or even drop the table, so consider the alternatives carefully.

For example, the following code creates a global temporary table called *##Globals* with columns called *id* and *val*:

```
CREATE TABLE ##Globals
(
  id  sysname     NOT NULL PRIMARY KEY,
  val SQL_VARIANT NOT NULL
);
```

The table in this example is intended to mimic global variables, which are not supported in T-SQL. The *id* column is of a *sysname* data type (the type that SQL Server uses internally to represent identifiers), and the *val* column is of a *SQL_VARIANT* data type (a generic type that can store within it a value of almost any base type).

Anyone can insert rows into the table. For example, run the following code to insert a row representing a variable called *i* and initialize it with the integer value *10*:

```
INSERT INTO ##Globals(id, val) VALUES(N'i', CAST(10 AS INT));
```

Anyone can modify and retrieve data from the table. For example, run the following code from any session to query the current value of the variable *i*:

```
SELECT val FROM ##Globals WHERE id = N'i';
```

This code returns the following output:

```
val
-----------
10
```

Note Keep in mind that as soon as the session that created the global temporary table disconnects and there are no active references to the table, SQL Server automatically destroys the table.

If you want a global temporary table to be created every time SQL Server starts, and you don't want SQL Server to try to destroy it automatically, you need to create the table from a stored procedure that is marked as a startup procedure. (For details, see "sp_procoption" in SQL Server Books Online at the following URL: *http://msdn.microsoft.com/en-us/library/ms181720.aspx*.)

Run the following code from any session to explicitly destroy the global temporary table:

```
DROP TABLE IF EXISTS ##Globals;
```

Table variables

Table variables are similar to local temporary tables in some ways and different in others. You declare table variables much like you declare other variables, by using the *DECLARE* statement.

As with local temporary tables, table variables have a physical presence as a table in the *tempdb* database, contrary to the common misconception that they exist only in memory. Like local temporary tables, table variables are visible only to the creating session, but because they are variables they have a more limited scope: only the current batch. Table variables are visible neither to inner batches in the call stack nor to subsequent batches in the session.

If an explicit transaction is rolled back, changes made to temporary tables in that transaction are rolled back as well; however, changes made to table variables by statements that completed in the transaction aren't rolled back. Only changes made by the active statement that failed or that was terminated before completion are undone.

Temporary tables and table variables also have optimization differences, but those topics are outside the scope of this book. For now, I'll just say that in terms of performance, usually it makes more sense to use table variables with small volumes of data (only a few rows) and to use local temporary tables otherwise.

For example, the following code uses a table variable instead of a local temporary table to compare total order quantities of each order year with the year before:

```
DECLARE @MyOrderTotalsByYear TABLE
(
  orderyear INT NOT NULL PRIMARY KEY,
  qty       INT NOT NULL
);

INSERT INTO @MyOrderTotalsByYear(orderyear, qty)
  SELECT
    YEAR(O.orderdate) AS orderyear,
    SUM(OD.qty) AS qty
```

```
  FROM Sales.Orders AS O
    INNER JOIN Sales.OrderDetails AS OD
      ON OD.orderid = O.orderid
  GROUP BY YEAR(orderdate);

SELECT Cur.orderyear, Cur.qty AS curyearqty, Prv.qty AS prvyearqty
FROM @MyOrderTotalsByYear AS Cur
  LEFT OUTER JOIN @MyOrderTotalsByYear AS Prv
    ON Cur.orderyear = Prv.orderyear + 1;
```

This code returns the following output:

```
orderyear   curyearqty  prvyearqty
----------- ----------- -----------
2014        9581        NULL
2015        25489       9581
2016        16247       25489
```

Note that instead of using a table variable or a temporary table and a self-join here, this particular task can be handled alternatively with the *LAG* function, like this:

```
SELECT
  YEAR(O.orderdate) AS orderyear,
  SUM(OD.qty) AS curyearqty,
  LAG(SUM(OD.qty)) OVER(ORDER BY YEAR(orderdate)) AS prvyearqty
FROM Sales.Orders AS O
  INNER JOIN Sales.OrderDetails AS OD
    ON OD.orderid = O.orderid
GROUP BY YEAR(orderdate);
```

Table types

You can use a table type to preserve a table definition as an object in the database. Later you can reuse it as the table definition of table variables and input parameters of stored procedures and user-defined functions. Table types are required for table-valued parameters (TVPs).

For example, the following code creates a table type called *dbo.OrderTotalsByYear* in the current database:

```
DROP TYPE IF EXISTS dbo.OrderTotalsByYear;

CREATE TYPE dbo.OrderTotalsByYear AS TABLE
(
  orderyear INT NOT NULL PRIMARY KEY,
  qty       INT NOT NULL
);
```

After the table type is created, whenever you need to declare a table variable based on the table type's definition, you won't need to repeat the code—instead, you can simply specify *dbo.OrderTotalsByYear* as the variable's type, like this:

```
DECLARE @MyOrderTotalsByYear AS dbo.OrderTotalsByYear;
```

As a more complete example, the following code declares a variable called *@MyOrderTotalsByYear* of the new table type, queries the *Orders* and *OrderDetails* tables to calculate total order quantities by order year, stores the result of the query in the table variable, and queries the variable to present its contents:

```
DECLARE @MyOrderTotalsByYear AS dbo.OrderTotalsByYear;

INSERT INTO @MyOrderTotalsByYear(orderyear, qty)
  SELECT
    YEAR(O.orderdate) AS orderyear,
    SUM(OD.qty) AS qty
  FROM Sales.Orders AS O
    INNER JOIN Sales.OrderDetails AS OD
      ON OD.orderid = O.orderid
  GROUP BY YEAR(orderdate);

SELECT orderyear, qty FROM @MyOrderTotalsByYear;
```

This code returns the following output:

```
orderyear   qty
----------- -----------
2014        9581
2015        25489
2016        16247
```

The benefit of the table type feature extends beyond just helping you shorten your code. As I mentioned, you can use it as the type of input parameters of stored procedures and functions, which is a useful capability.

Dynamic SQL

With SQL Server, you can construct a batch of T-SQL code as a character string and then execute that batch. This capability is called *dynamic SQL*. SQL Server provides two ways of executing dynamic SQL: using the *EXEC* (short for *EXECUTE*) command, and using the *sp_executesql* stored procedure. I will explain the difference between the two and provide examples for using each.

Dynamic SQL is useful for several purposes, including the following ones:

- **Automating administrative tasks** For example, querying metadata and constructing and executing a *BACKUP DATABASE* statement for each database in the instance
- **Improving performance of certain tasks** For example, constructing parameterized ad-hoc queries that can reuse previously cached execution plans (more on this later)
- **Constructing elements of the code based on querying the actual data** For example, constructing a *PIVOT* query dynamically when you don't know ahead of time which elements should appear in the *IN* clause of the *PIVOT* operator

Note Be extremely careful when concatenating user input as part of your code. Hackers can attempt to inject code you did not intend to run. The best measure you can take against SQL injection is to avoid concatenating user input as part of your code (for example, by using parameters). If you do concatenate user input as part of your code, make sure you thoroughly inspect the input and look for SQL injection attempts. You can find an article on the subject in SQL Server Books Online using the following URL: *https://technet.microsoft.com/en-us/library/ms161953(v=sql.105).aspx.*

The *EXEC* command

The *EXEC* command accepts a character string in parentheses as input and executes the batch of code within the character string. *EXEC* supports both regular and Unicode character strings as input. This command can also be used to execute a stored procedure, as I will demonstrate later in the chapter.

The following example stores a character string with a *PRINT* statement in the variable *@sql* and then uses the *EXEC* command to invoke the batch of code stored within the variable:

```
DECLARE @sql AS VARCHAR(100);
SET @sql = 'PRINT ''This message was printed by a dynamic SQL batch.'';';
EXEC(@sql);
```

Notice the use of two single quotes to represent one single quote in a string within a string. This code returns the following output:

```
This message was printed by a dynamic SQL batch.
```

The *sp_executesql* stored procedure

The *sp_executesql* stored procedure is an alternative tool to the *EXEC* command for executing dynamic SQL code. It's more secure and more flexible in the sense that it has an interface; that is, it supports input and output parameters. Note that unlike *EXEC*, *sp_executesql* supports only Unicode character strings as the input batch of code.

The fact that you can use input and output parameters in your dynamic SQL code can help you write more secure and more efficient code. In terms of security, parameters that appear in the code cannot be considered part of the code—they can only be considered operands in expressions. So, by using parameters, you can eliminate your exposure to SQL injection.

The *sp_executesql* stored procedure can perform better than *EXEC* because its parameterization aids in reusing cached execution plans. An execution plan is the physical processing plan SQL Server produces for a query, with the set of instructions describing which objects to access, in what order, which indexes to use, how to access them, which join algorithms to use, and so on. One of the requirements for reusing a previously cached plan is that the query string be the same as the one for which the cached plan was created. The best way to efficiently reuse query execution plans is to use stored procedures with parameters. This way, even when parameter values change, the query string remains the same. But if you decide to use ad-hoc code instead of stored procedures, at least you can still work with parameters if you use *sp_executesql* and therefore increase the chances for plan reuse.

The *sp_executesql* procedure has two input parameters and an assignments section. You specify the Unicode character string holding the batch of code you want to run in the first parameter, which is called *@stmt*. You provide a Unicode character string holding the declarations of input and output parameters in the second input parameter, which is called *@params*. Then you specify the assignments of input and output parameters separated by commas.

The following example constructs a batch of code with a query against the *Sales.Orders* table. The example uses an input parameter called *@orderid* in the query's filter:

```
DECLARE @sql AS NVARCHAR(100);

SET @sql = N'SELECT orderid, custid, empid, orderdate
FROM Sales.Orders
WHERE orderid = @orderid;';

EXEC sp_executesql
  @stmt = @sql,
  @params = N'@orderid AS INT',
  @orderid = 10248;
```

This code generates the following output:

```
orderid     custid      empid       orderdate
----------- ----------- ----------- -----------
10248       85          5           2014-07-04
```

This code assigns the value *10248* to the input parameter, but even if you run it again with a different value, the code string remains the same. This way, you increase the chances for reusing a previously cached plan.

Using *PIVOT* with Dynamic SQL

This section is advanced and optional, and it's intended for readers who feel very comfortable with pivoting techniques and dynamic SQL. In Chapter 7, I explained how to use the *PIVOT* operator to pivot data. I mentioned that in a static query, you have to know ahead of time which values to specify in the *IN* clause of the *PIVOT* operator. Following is an example of a static query with the *PIVOT* operator:

```
SELECT *
FROM (SELECT shipperid, YEAR(orderdate) AS orderyear, freight
      FROM Sales.Orders) AS D
  PIVOT(SUM(freight) FOR orderyear IN([2014],[2015],[2016])) AS P;
```

This example queries the *Sales.Orders* table and pivots the data so that it returns shipper IDs in the rows, order years in the columns, and the total freight in the intersection of each shipper and order year. This code returns the following output:

```
shipperid   2014         2015          2016
----------- ------------ ------------- -------------
3           4233.78      11413.35      4865.38
1           2297.42      8681.38       5206.53
2           3748.67      12374.04      12122.14
```

With the static query, you have to know ahead of time which values (order years in this case) to specify in the *IN* clause of the *PIVOT* operator. This means you need to revise the code every year. Instead, you can query the distinct order years from the data, construct a batch of dynamic SQL code based on the years you queried, and execute the dynamic SQL batch like this:

```
DECLARE
  @sql       AS NVARCHAR(1000),
  @orderyear AS INT,
  @first     AS INT;

DECLARE C CURSOR FAST_FORWARD FOR
  SELECT DISTINCT(YEAR(orderdate)) AS orderyear
  FROM Sales.Orders
  ORDER BY orderyear;

SET @first = 1;

SET @sql = N'SELECT *
FROM (SELECT shipperid, YEAR(orderdate) AS orderyear, freight
      FROM Sales.Orders) AS D
  PIVOT(SUM(freight) FOR orderyear IN(';

OPEN C;

FETCH NEXT FROM C INTO @orderyear;

WHILE @@fetch_status = 0
BEGIN
  IF @first = 0
    SET @sql += N','
  ELSE
    SET @first = 0;

  SET @sql += QUOTENAME(@orderyear);

  FETCH NEXT FROM C INTO @orderyear;
END;

CLOSE C;

DEALLOCATE C;

SET @sql += N')) AS P;';

EXEC sp_executesql @stmt = @sql;
```

> **Note** There are more efficient ways to concatenate strings than using a cursor, such as using Common Language Runtime (CLR) aggregates and the *FOR XML PATH* option, but they are more advanced and are beyond the scope of this book.

Routines

Routines are programmable objects that encapsulate code to calculate a result or to execute activity. SQL Server supports three types of routines: user-defined functions, stored procedures, and triggers.

With SQL Server, you can choose whether to develop a routine with T-SQL or with Microsoft .NET code based on the CLR integration in the product. Because this book's focus is T-SQL, the examples here use T-SQL. When the task at hand mainly involves data manipulation, T-SQL is usually a better choice. When the task is more about iterative logic, string manipulation, or computationally intensive operations, .NET code is usually a better choice.

User-defined functions

The purpose of a user-defined function (UDF) is to encapsulate logic that calculates something, possibly based on input parameters, and return a result.

SQL Server supports scalar and table-valued UDFs. *Scalar UDFs* return a single value; *table-valued UDFs* return a table. One benefit of using UDFs is that you can incorporate them into queries. Scalar UDFs can appear anywhere in the query where an expression that returns a single value can appear (for example, in the *SELECT* list). Table UDFs can appear in the *FROM* clause of a query. The example in this section is a scalar UDF.

UDFs are not allowed to have any side effects. This obviously means UDFs are not allowed to apply any schema or data changes in the database. But other ways of causing side effects are less obvious.

For example, invoking the *RAND* function to return a random value or the *NEWID* function to return a globally unique identifier (GUID) have side effects. Whenever you invoke the *RAND* function without specifying a seed, SQL Server generates a random seed that is based on the previous invocation of *RAND*. For this reason, SQL Server needs to store information internally whenever you invoke the *RAND* function. Similarly, whenever you invoke the *NEWID* function, the system needs to set some information aside to be taken into consideration in the next invocation of *NEWID*. Because *RAND* and *NEWID* have side effects, you're not allowed to use them in your UDFs.

For example, the following code creates a UDF called *dbo.GetAge* that returns the age of a person with a specified birth date (*@birthdate argument*) at a specified event date (*@eventdate argument*):

```
DROP FUNCTION IF EXISTS dbo.GetAge;
GO

CREATE FUNCTION dbo.GetAge
(
  @birthdate AS DATE,
```

```
  @eventdate AS DATE
)
RETURNS INT
AS
BEGIN
  RETURN
    DATEDIFF(year, @birthdate, @eventdate)
    - CASE WHEN 100 * MONTH(@eventdate) + DAY(@eventdate)
              < 100 * MONTH(@birthdate) + DAY(@birthdate)
           THEN 1 ELSE 0
      END;
END;
GO
```

The function calculates the age as the difference, in terms of years, between the birth year and the event year, minus 1 year in cases where the event month and day are smaller than the birth month and day. The expression *100 * month + day* is simply a trick to concatenate the month and day. For example, for the twelfth day in the month of February, the expression yields the integer 212.

Note that a function can have more than just a *RETURN* clause in its body. It can have code with flow elements, calculations, and more. But the function must have a *RETURN* clause that returns a value.

To demonstrate using a UDF in a query, the following code queries the *HR.Employees* table and invokes the *GetAge* function in the *SELECT* list to calculate the age of each employee today:

```
SELECT
  empid, firstname, lastname, birthdate,
  dbo.GetAge(birthdate, SYSDATETIME()) AS age
FROM HR.Employees;
```

For example, if you were to run this query on February 12, 2016, you would get the following output:

```
empid       firstname  lastname             birthdate  age
----------- ---------- -------------------- ---------- -----------
1           Sara       Davis                1968-12-08 47
2           Don        Funk                 1972-02-19 43
3           Judy       Lew                  1983-08-30 32
4           Yael       Peled                1957-09-19 58
5           Sven       Mortensen            1975-03-04 40
6           Paul       Suurs                1983-07-02 32
7           Russell    King                 1980-05-29 35
8           Maria      Cameron              1978-01-09 38
9           Patricia   Doyle                1986-01-27 30

(9 row(s) affected)
```

Note that if you run the query in your system, the values you get in the age column depend on the date on which you run the query.

Stored procedures

Stored procedures are routines that encapsulate code. They can have input and output parameters, they can return result sets of queries, and they are allowed to have side effects. Not only can you modify data through stored procedures, you can also apply schema changes through them.

Compared to using ad-hoc code, the use of stored procedures gives you many benefits:

- **Stored procedures encapsulate logic.** If you need to change the implementation of a stored procedure, you apply the change in one place using the *ALTER PROC* command, and all users of the procedure will use the new version from that point.
- **Stored procedures give you better control of security.** You can grant a user permissions to execute the procedure without granting the user direct permissions to perform the underlying activities. For example, suppose you want to allow certain users to delete a customer from the database, but you don't want to grant them direct permissions to delete rows from the *Customers* table. You want to ensure that requests to delete a customer are validated—for example, by checking whether the customer has open orders or open debts—and you might also want to audit the requests. By not granting direct permissions to delete rows from the *Customers* table but instead granting permissions to execute a procedure that handles the task, you ensure that all the required validations and auditing always take place. In addition, stored procedures with parameters can help prevent SQL injection, especially when they replace ad-hoc SQL submitted from the client application.
- **You can incorporate all error-handling code within a procedure, silently taking corrective action where relevant.** I discuss error handling later in this chapter.
- **Stored procedures give you performance benefits.** Earlier I talked about reuse of previously cached execution plans. Queries in stored procedure are usually parameterized and therefore have a high likelihood to reuse previously cached plans. Another performance benefit of using stored procedures is a reduction in network traffic. The client application needs to submit only the procedure name and its arguments to SQL Server. The server processes all the procedure's code and returns only the output back to the caller. No back-and-forth traffic is associated with intermediate steps of the procedure.

As a simple example, the following code creates a stored procedure called *Sales.GetCustomerOrders*. The procedure accepts a customer ID (*@custid*) and a date range (*@fromdate* and *@todate*) as inputs. The procedure returns rows from the *Sales.Orders* table representing orders placed by the requested customer in the requested date range as a result set, and the number of affected rows as an output parameter (*@numrows*):

```
DROP PROC IF EXISTS Sales.GetCustomerOrders;
GO

CREATE PROC Sales.GetCustomerOrders
  @custid   AS INT,
  @fromdate AS DATETIME = '19000101',
  @todate   AS DATETIME = '99991231',
  @numrows  AS INT OUTPUT
```

```
AS
SET NOCOUNT ON;

SELECT orderid, custid, empid, orderdate
FROM Sales.Orders
WHERE custid = @custid
  AND orderdate >= @fromdate
  AND orderdate < @todate;

SET @numrows = @@rowcount;
GO
```

When executing the procedure, if you don't specify a value in the *@fromdate* parameter, the procedure will use the default *19000101*, and if you don't specify a value in the *@todate* parameter, the procedure will use the default *99991231*. Notice the use of the keyword *OUTPUT* to indicate that the parameter *@numrows* is an output parameter. The *SET NOCOUNT ON* command is used to suppress messages indicating how many rows were affected by DML statements, such as the *SELECT* statement within the procedure.

Here's an example of executing the procedure, requesting information about orders placed by the customer with the ID of 1 in the year 2015. The code absorbs the value of the output parameter *@numrows* in the local variable *@rc* and returns it to show how many rows were affected by the query:

```
DECLARE @rc AS INT;

EXEC Sales.GetCustomerOrders
  @custid   = 1,
  @fromdate = '20150101',
  @todate   = '20160101',
  @numrows  = @rc OUTPUT;

SELECT @rc AS numrows;
```

The code returns the following output showing three qualifying orders:

```
orderid     custid      empid       orderdate
----------- ----------- ----------- -----------
10643       1           6           2015-08-25
10692       1           4           2015-10-03
10702       1           4           2015-10-13

numrows
-----------
3
```

Run the code again, providing a customer ID that doesn't exist in the *Orders* table (for example, customer ID 100). You get the following output indicating that there are zero qualifying orders:

```
orderid     custid      empid       orderdate
----------- ----------- ----------- -----------------------

numrows
-----------
0
```

Triggers

A *trigger* is a special kind of stored procedure—one that cannot be executed explicitly. Instead, it's attached to an event. Whenever the event takes place, the trigger fires and the trigger's code runs. SQL Server supports the association of triggers with two kinds of events: data manipulation events (DML triggers) such as *INSERT*, and data definition events (DDL triggers) such as *CREATE TABLE*.

You can use triggers for many purposes, including auditing, enforcing integrity rules that cannot be enforced with constraints, and enforcing policies.

A trigger is considered part of the transaction that includes the event that caused the trigger to fire. Issuing a *ROLLBACK TRAN* command within the trigger's code causes a rollback of all changes that took place in the trigger, and also of all changes that took place in the transaction associated with the trigger.

Triggers in SQL Server fire per statement and not per modified row.

DML triggers

SQL Server supports two kinds of DML triggers: *after* and *instead of*. An *after* trigger fires after the event it's associated with finishes and can be defined only on permanent tables. An *instead of* trigger fires instead of the event it's associated with and can be defined on permanent tables and views.

In the trigger's code, you can access pseudo tables called *inserted* and *deleted* that contain the rows that were affected by the modification that caused the trigger to fire. The inserted table holds the new image of the affected rows in the case of *INSERT* and *UPDATE* actions. The deleted table holds the old image of the affected rows in the case of *DELETE* and *UPDATE* actions. Remember that *INSERT*, *UPDATE*, and *DELETE* actions can be invoked by the *INSERT*, *UPDATE*, and *DELETE* statements, as well as by the *MERGE* statement. In the case of *instead of* triggers, the inserted and deleted tables contain the rows that were supposed to be affected by the modification that caused the trigger to fire.

The following simple example of an *after* trigger audits inserts to a table. Run the following code to create a table called *dbo.T1* in the current database, and another table called *dbo.T1_Audit* that holds audit information for insertions to *T1*:

```
DROP TABLE IF EXISTS dbo.T1_Audit, dbo.T1;

CREATE TABLE dbo.T1
(
  keycol  INT         NOT NULL PRIMARY KEY,
  datacol VARCHAR(10) NOT NULL
);

CREATE TABLE dbo.T1_Audit
(
  audit_lsn  INT          NOT NULL IDENTITY PRIMARY KEY,
  dt         DATETIME2(3) NOT NULL DEFAULT(SYSDATETIME()),
  login_name sysname      NOT NULL DEFAULT(ORIGINAL_LOGIN()),
  keycol     INT          NOT NULL,
  datacol    VARCHAR(10)  NOT NULL
);
```

In the audit table, the *audit_lsn* column has an identity property and represents an audit log serial number. The *dt* column represents the date and time of the insertion, using the default expression *SYSDATETIME()*. The *login_name* column represents the name of the login that performed the insertion, using the default expression *ORIGINAL_LOGIN()*.

Next, run the following code to create the *AFTER INSERT* trigger *trg_T1_insert_audit* on the *T1* table to audit insertions:

```
CREATE TRIGGER trg_T1_insert_audit ON dbo.T1 AFTER INSERT
AS
SET NOCOUNT ON;

INSERT INTO dbo.T1_Audit(keycol, datacol)
  SELECT keycol, datacol FROM inserted;
GO
```

As you can see, the trigger simply inserts into the audit table the result of a query against the inserted table. The values of the columns in the audit table that are not listed explicitly in the *INSERT* statement are generated by the default expressions described earlier. To test the trigger, run the following code:

```
INSERT INTO dbo.T1(keycol, datacol) VALUES(10, 'a');
INSERT INTO dbo.T1(keycol, datacol) VALUES(30, 'x');
INSERT INTO dbo.T1(keycol, datacol) VALUES(20, 'g');
```

The trigger fires after each statement. Next, query the audit table:

```
SELECT audit_lsn, dt, login_name, keycol, datacol
FROM dbo.T1_Audit;
```

You get the following output, only with *dt* and *login_name* values that reflect the date and time when you ran the inserts, and the login you used to connect to SQL Server:

```
audit_lsn   dt                          login_name       keycol      datacol
----------- --------------------------- ---------------- ----------- ----------
1           2016-02-12 09:04:27.713 K2\Gandalf       10          a
2           2016-02-12 09:04:27.733 K2\Gandalf       30          x
3           2016-02-12 09:04:27.733 K2\Gandalf       20          g
```

When you're done, run the following code for cleanup:

```
DROP TABLE dbo.T1_Audit, dbo.T1;
```

DDL triggers

SQL Server supports DDL triggers, which can be used for purposes such as auditing, policy enforcement, and change management. SQL Server box product supports the creation of DDL triggers at two scopes, the database scope and the server scope, depending on the scope of the event. Azure SQL Database currently supports only database triggers.

You create a *database* trigger for events with a database scope, such as *CREATE TABLE*. You create an *all server* trigger for events with a server scope, such as *CREATE DATABASE*. SQL Server supports only *after* DDL triggers; it doesn't support *instead of* DDL triggers.

Within the trigger, you obtain information about the event that caused the trigger to fire by querying a function called *EVENTDATA*, which returns the event information as an XML instance. You can use XQuery expressions to extract event attributes such as post time, event type, and login name from the XML instance.

The following code creates the *dbo.AuditDDLEvents* table, which holds the audit information:

```
DROP TABLE IF EXISTS dbo.AuditDDLEvents;

CREATE TABLE dbo.AuditDDLEvents
(
  audit_lsn        INT          NOT NULL IDENTITY,
  posttime         DATETIME2(3) NOT NULL,
  eventtype        sysname      NOT NULL,
  loginname        sysname      NOT NULL,
  schemaname       sysname      NOT NULL,
  objectname       sysname      NOT NULL,
  targetobjectname sysname      NULL,
  eventdata        XML          NOT NULL,
  CONSTRAINT PK_AuditDDLEvents PRIMARY KEY(audit_lsn)
);
```

Notice that the table has a column called *eventdata* that has an XML data type. In addition to the individual attributes that the trigger extracts from the event information and stores in individual attributes, it also stores the full event information in the *eventdata* column.

Run the following code to create the *trg_audit_ddl_events* audit trigger on the database by using the event group *DDL_DATABASE_LEVEL_EVENTS*, which represents all DDL events at the database level:

```
CREATE TRIGGER trg_audit_ddl_events
  ON DATABASE FOR DDL_DATABASE_LEVEL_EVENTS
AS
SET NOCOUNT ON;

DECLARE @eventdata AS XML = eventdata();

INSERT INTO dbo.AuditDDLEvents(
  posttime, eventtype, loginname, schemaname,
  objectname, targetobjectname, eventdata)
  VALUES(
    @eventdata.value('(/EVENT_INSTANCE/PostTime)[1]',         'VARCHAR(23)'),
    @eventdata.value('(/EVENT_INSTANCE/EventType)[1]',        'sysname'),
    @eventdata.value('(/EVENT_INSTANCE/LoginName)[1]',        'sysname'),
    @eventdata.value('(/EVENT_INSTANCE/SchemaName)[1]',       'sysname'),
    @eventdata.value('(/EVENT_INSTANCE/ObjectName)[1]',       'sysname'),
    @eventdata.value('(/EVENT_INSTANCE/TargetObjectName)[1]', 'sysname'),
    @eventdata);
GO
```

The trigger's code first stores the event information obtained from the *EVENTDATA* function in the *@eventdata* variable. The code then inserts a row into the audit table with the attributes extracted by using XQuery expressions by the *.value* method from the event information, plus the XML instance with the full event information. (For details about the XQuery language, see the following Wikipedia article: *https://en.wikipedia.org/wiki/XQuery.*)

To test the trigger, run the following code, which contains a few DDL statements:

```
CREATE TABLE dbo.T1(col1 INT NOT NULL PRIMARY KEY);
ALTER TABLE dbo.T1 ADD col2 INT NULL;
ALTER TABLE dbo.T1 ALTER COLUMN col2 INT NOT NULL;
CREATE NONCLUSTERED INDEX idx1 ON dbo.T1(col2);
```

Next, run the following code to query the audit table:

```
SELECT * FROM dbo.AuditDDLEvents;
```

You get the following output (split here into two sections for display purposes), but with values in the *posttime* and *loginname* attributes that reflect the post time and logon name in your environment:

```
audit_lsn posttime                  eventtype      loginname
--------- ------------------------- -------------- ----------------
1         2016-02-12 09:06:18.293   CREATE_TABLE   K2\Gandalf
2         2016-02-12 09:06:18.413   ALTER_TABLE    K2\Gandalf
3         2016-02-12 09:06:18.423   ALTER_TABLE    K2\Gandalf
4         2016-02-12 09:06:18.423   CREATE_INDEX   K2\Gandalf

audit_lsn   schemaname    objectname    targetobjectname  eventdata
----------- ------------- ------------- ----------------- -------------------
1           dbo           T1            NULL              <EVENT_INSTANCE>...
2           dbo           T1            NULL              <EVENT_INSTANCE>...
3           dbo           T1            NULL              <EVENT_INSTANCE>...
4           dbo           idx1          T1                <EVENT_INSTANCE>...
```

When you're done, run the following code for cleanup:

```
DROP TRIGGER IF EXISTS trg_audit_ddl_events ON DATABASE;
DROP TABLE IF EXISTS dbo.AuditDDLEvents;
```

Error handling

SQL Server provides you with tools to handle errors in your T-SQL code. The main tool used for error handling is a construct called *TRY...CATCH*. SQL Server also provides a set of functions you can invoke to get information about the error. I'll start with a basic example demonstrating the use of *TRY...CATCH*, followed by a more detailed example demonstrating the use of the error functions.

You work with the *TRY...CATCH* construct by placing the usual T-SQL code in a *TRY* block (between the *BEGIN TRY* and *END TRY* keywords) and placing all the error-handling code in the adjacent *CATCH* block (between the *BEGIN CATCH* and *END CATCH* keywords). If the *TRY* block has no error, the *CATCH* block is simply skipped. If the *TRY* block has an error, control is passed to the corresponding *CATCH* block. Note that if a *TRY...CATCH* block captures and handles an error, as far as the caller is concerned, there was no error.

Run the following code to demonstrate a case with no error in the *TRY* block:

```
BEGIN TRY
  PRINT 10/2;
  PRINT 'No error';
END TRY
BEGIN CATCH
  PRINT 'Error';
END CATCH;
```

All code in the *TRY* block completed successfully; therefore, the *CATCH* block was skipped. This code generates the following output:

```
5
No error
```

Next, run similar code, but this time divide by zero. An error occurs:

```
BEGIN TRY
  PRINT 10/0;
  PRINT 'No error';
END TRY
BEGIN CATCH
  PRINT 'Error';
END CATCH;
```

When the *divide by zero* error happened in the first *PRINT* statement in the *TRY* block, control was passed to the corresponding *CATCH* block. The second *PRINT* statement in the *TRY* block was not executed. Therefore, this code generates the following output:

```
Error
```

Typically, error handling involves some work in the *CATCH* block investigating the cause of the error and taking a course of action. SQL Server gives you information about the error via a set of functions. The *ERROR_NUMBER* function returns an integer with the number of the error. The *CATCH* block usually includes flow code that inspects the error number to determine what course of action to take. The *ERROR_MESSAGE* function returns error-message text. To get the list of error numbers and messages, query the *sys.messages* catalog view. The *ERROR_SEVERITY* and *ERROR_STATE* functions return the error severity and state. The *ERROR_LINE* function returns the line number in the code where the error happened. Finally, the *ERROR_PROCEDURE* function returns the name of the procedure in which the error happened and returns *NULL* if the error did not happen within a procedure.

To demonstrate a more detailed error-handling example including the use of the error functions, first run the following code, which creates a table called *dbo.Employees* in the current database:

```
DROP TABLE IF EXISTS dbo.Employees;

CREATE TABLE dbo.Employees
(
```

```
  empid   INT         NOT NULL,
  empname VARCHAR(25) NOT NULL,
  mgrid   INT         NULL,
  CONSTRAINT PK_Employees PRIMARY KEY(empid),
  CONSTRAINT CHK_Employees_empid CHECK(empid > 0),
  CONSTRAINT FK_Employees_Employees
    FOREIGN KEY(mgrid) REFERENCES dbo.Employees(empid)
);
```

The following code inserts a new row into the *Employees* table in a *TRY* block, and if an error occurs, shows how to identify the error by inspecting the *ERROR_NUMBER* function in the *CATCH* block. The code uses flow control to identify and handle errors you want to deal with in the *CATCH* block, and it re-throws the error otherwise.

The code also prints the values of the other error functions simply to show what information is available to you when an error occurs:

```
BEGIN TRY

  INSERT INTO dbo.Employees(empid, empname, mgrid)
    VALUES(1, 'Emp1', NULL);
  -- Also try with empid = 0, 'A', NULL

END TRY
BEGIN CATCH

  IF ERROR_NUMBER() = 2627
  BEGIN
    PRINT '    Handling PK violation...';
  END;
  ELSE IF ERROR_NUMBER() = 547
  BEGIN
    PRINT '    Handling CHECK/FK constraint violation...';
  END;
  ELSE IF ERROR_NUMBER() = 515
  BEGIN
    PRINT '    Handling NULL violation...';
  END;
  ELSE IF ERROR_NUMBER() = 245
  BEGIN
    PRINT '    Handling conversion error...';
  END;
  ELSE
  BEGIN
    PRINT 'Re-throwing error...';
    THROW;
  END;

  PRINT '    Error Number  : ' + CAST(ERROR_NUMBER() AS VARCHAR(10));
  PRINT '    Error Message : ' + ERROR_MESSAGE();
  PRINT '    Error Severity: ' + CAST(ERROR_SEVERITY() AS VARCHAR(10));
  PRINT '    Error State   : ' + CAST(ERROR_STATE() AS VARCHAR(10));
  PRINT '    Error Line    : ' + CAST(ERROR_LINE() AS VARCHAR(10));
  PRINT '    Error Proc    : ' + COALESCE(ERROR_PROCEDURE(), 'Not within proc');

END CATCH;
```

When you run this code for the first time, the new row is inserted into the *Employees* table successfully, and therefore the *CATCH* block is skipped. You get the following output:

```
(1 row(s) affected)
```

When you run the same code a second time, the *INSERT* statement fails, control is passed to the *CATCH* block, and a primary-key-violation error is identified. You get the following output:

```
Handling PK violation...
Error Number  : 2627
Error Message : Violation of PRIMARY KEY constraint 'PK_Employees'. Cannot insert duplicate key
in object 'dbo.Employees'.
Error Severity: 14
Error State   : 1
Error Line    : 3
Error Proc    : Not within proc
```

To see other errors, run the code with the values *0*, *'A'*, and *NULL* as the employee ID.

Here, for demonstration purposes, I used *PRINT* statements as the actions when an error was identified. Of course, error handling usually involves more than just printing a message indicating that the error was identified.

Note that you can create a stored procedure that encapsulates reusable error-handling code like this:

```
DROP PROC IF EXISTS dbo.ErrInsertHandler;
GO

CREATE PROC dbo.ErrInsertHandler
AS
SET NOCOUNT ON;

IF ERROR_NUMBER() = 2627
BEGIN
  PRINT 'Handling PK violation...';
END;
ELSE IF ERROR_NUMBER() = 547
BEGIN
  PRINT 'Handling CHECK/FK constraint violation...';
END;
ELSE IF ERROR_NUMBER() = 515
BEGIN
  PRINT 'Handling NULL violation...';
END;
ELSE IF ERROR_NUMBER() = 245
BEGIN
  PRINT 'Handling conversion error...';
END;

PRINT 'Error Number  : ' + CAST(ERROR_NUMBER() AS VARCHAR(10));
PRINT 'Error Message : ' + ERROR_MESSAGE();
PRINT 'Error Severity: ' + CAST(ERROR_SEVERITY() AS VARCHAR(10));
PRINT 'Error State   : ' + CAST(ERROR_STATE() AS VARCHAR(10));
PRINT 'Error Line    : ' + CAST(ERROR_LINE() AS VARCHAR(10));
```

```
PRINT 'Error Proc    : ' + COALESCE(ERROR_PROCEDURE(), 'Not within proc');
GO
```

In your *CATCH* block, you check whether the error number is one of those you want to deal with locally. If it is, you simply execute the stored procedure; otherwise, you re-throw the error:

```
BEGIN TRY

  INSERT INTO dbo.Employees(empid, empname, mgrid)
    VALUES(1, 'Emp1', NULL);

END TRY
BEGIN CATCH

  IF ERROR_NUMBER() IN (2627, 547, 515, 245)
    EXEC dbo.ErrInsertHandler;
  ELSE
    THROW;

END CATCH;
```

This way, you can maintain the reusable error-handling code in one place.

Conclusion

This chapter provided a high-level overview of programmable objects and, as such, doesn't include an exercises section. Its goal is to make you aware of SQL Server's programmability capabilities. This chapter covered variables, batches, flow elements, cursors, temporary tables, dynamic SQL, user-defined functions, stored procedures, triggers, and error handling—quite a few subjects. This chapter also concludes the book. When you're ready to tackle more advanced T-SQL topics including query-tuning coverage, the next natural step is to read my book *T-SQL Querying* (Microsoft Press, 2015).

APPENDIX

Getting started

The purpose of this appendix is to help you get started and set up your environment so that you have everything you need to get the most out of this book.

You can run all code samples in this book on a Microsoft SQL Server box product, and most of the examples can be run on Microsoft Azure SQL Database. For details about the differences between the flavors, see the section "The ABCs of Microsoft RDBMS flavors" in Chapter 1, "Background to T-SQL querying and programming."

The first section, "Getting started with Azure SQL Database," provides a link to the website where you can find the information you need to get started with Azure SQL Database.

The second section, "Installing a SQL Server box product," assumes you want to connect to a SQL Server box product instance to run the code samples in this book, and that you don't have an instance to connect to already. This section walks you through the installation process for a SQL Server 2016 instance. If you already have an instance of SQL Server to connect to, feel free to skip this section.

The third section, "Downloading and installing SQL Server Management Studio," provides instructions to download and install SQL Server Management Studio (SSMS).

The fourth section, "Downloading source code and installing the sample database," points you to the website where you can get the downloadable source code for the book and provides instructions for installing the book's sample database on both a SQL Server box product and Azure SQL Database.

The fifth section, "Working with SQL Server Management Studio," explains how to develop and execute T-SQL code in SQL Server by using SSMS.

The last section, "Working with SQL Server Books Online," describes SQL Server Books Online and explains its importance in helping you get information about T-SQL.

Getting started with Azure SQL Database

If you want to run the code samples in this book on Azure SQL Database, you need access to an Azure SQL Database server, with an account that has privileges to create a new database (or ask an administrator to create the sample database for you). If you don't already have access to Azure SQL Database, you can find useful information on how to get started on the Microsoft Azure main page at *https://azure.microsoft.com*.

You need a Microsoft account to create a Microsoft Azure subscription. If you don't already have an account, you can create one at *https://signup.live.com*. When you have a Microsoft Azure subscription, you can connect to the Microsoft Azure Portal at *https://portal.azure.com*, from which you can manage your Azure SQL Database servers and databases.

The Microsoft Azure main page offers different options for getting started (by buying a subscription or getting a free trial), and it provides access to resources such as the management portal, community, and support.

When you have access to Azure SQL Database, proceed to the instructions on how to download the source code and install the sample database later in this appendix.

Installing a SQL Server box product

This section is relevant for those who want to run the code samples in this book and practice the exercises against a SQL Server box product and don't already have access to one. You can use any edition of SQL Server 2016 or later. Assuming you don't already have an instance of SQL Server to connect to, the following sections describe where you can obtain SQL Server and how to install it.

1. Obtain SQL Server

As I mentioned, you can use any edition of SQL Server 2016 or later to practice the materials in this book. If you have a subscription to the Microsoft Developer Network (MSDN), you can use the SQL Server 2016 Developer edition for learning purposes. You can download it from *https://msdn.microsoft.com/subscriptions/downloads*. The SQL Server Developer edition is also available for free for Visual Studio Dev Essentials members. For details, see *https://blogs.technet.microsoft.com/dataplatforminsider/2016/03/31/microsoft-sql-server-developer-edition-is-now-free*. Another option is to use the free trial software of SQL Server 2016, which you can download from *https://www.microsoft.com/sql*. In this appendix, I demonstrate the installation of the SQL Server 2016 Evaluation edition.

2. Install the database engine

Assuming you have the SQL Server installation software available, you can proceed to installing the product.

To install the database engine

1. Start the setup.exe program from the SQL Server installation folder. You should see the SQL Server Installation Center dialog box shown in Figure A-1.

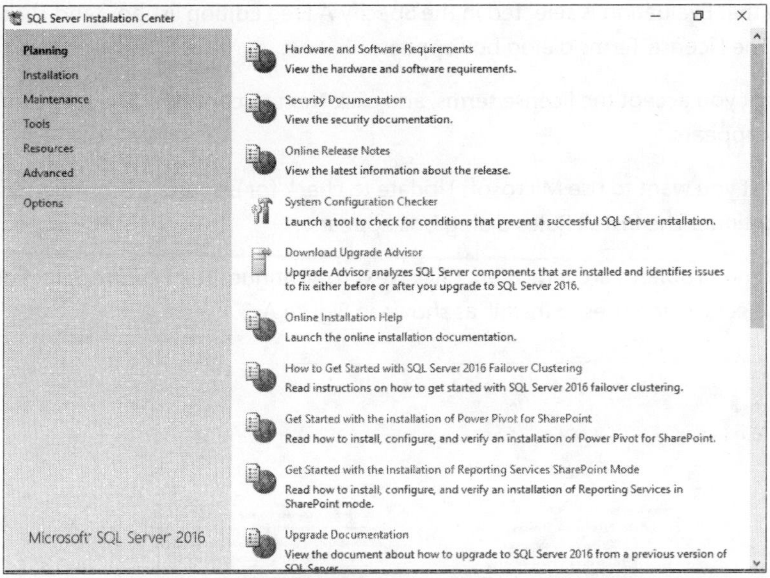

FIGURE A-1 SQL Server Installation Center.

2. In the left pane, choose Installation. Note that the screen changes.
3. In the right pane, choose New SQL Server Stand-Alone Installation Or Add Features To An Existing Installation. The Product Key dialog box appears, as shown in Figure A-2.

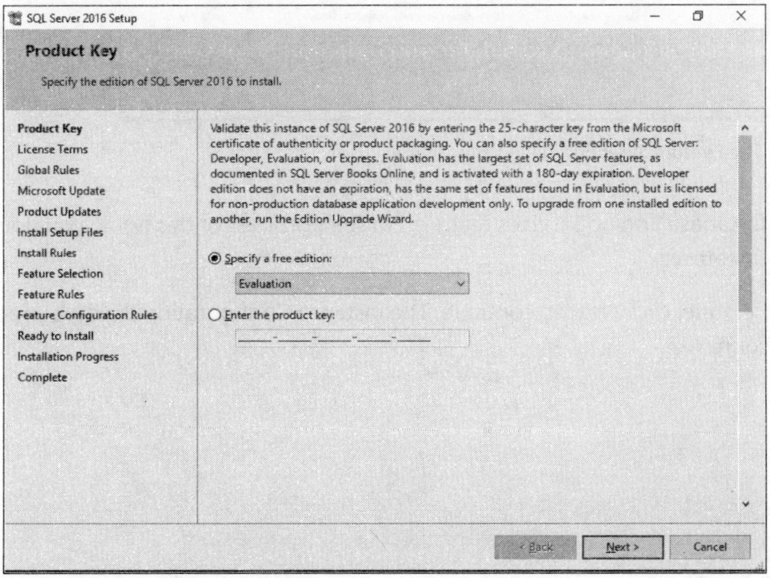

FIGURE A-2 The Product Key dialog box.

4. Make sure that Evaluation is selected in the Specify A Free Edition list box, and click Next to continue. The License Terms dialog box appears.

5. Confirm that you accept the license terms, and click Next to continue. The Microsoft Update dialog box appears.

6. Confirm that you want to use Microsoft Update to check for updates (recommended), and click Next to continue. The Install Rules dialog box appears.

7. Ensure that no problems are indicated. Click Next to continue. The Feature Selection dialog box appears. Select the features to install, as shown in Figure A-3.

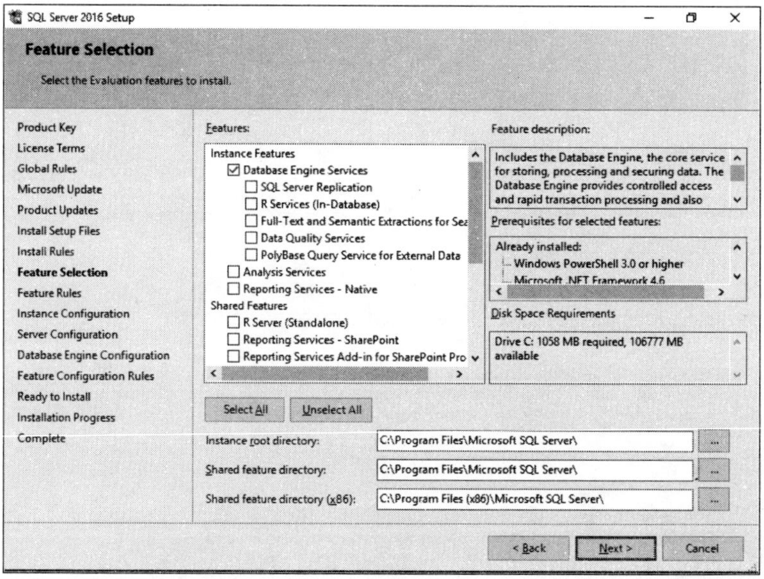

FIGURE A-3 The Feature Selection dialog box.

8. Select the Database Engine Services feature. For the purposes of this book, you don't need any of the other features.

9. When you're done, click Next to continue. The Instance Configuration dialog box appears, as shown in Figure A-4.

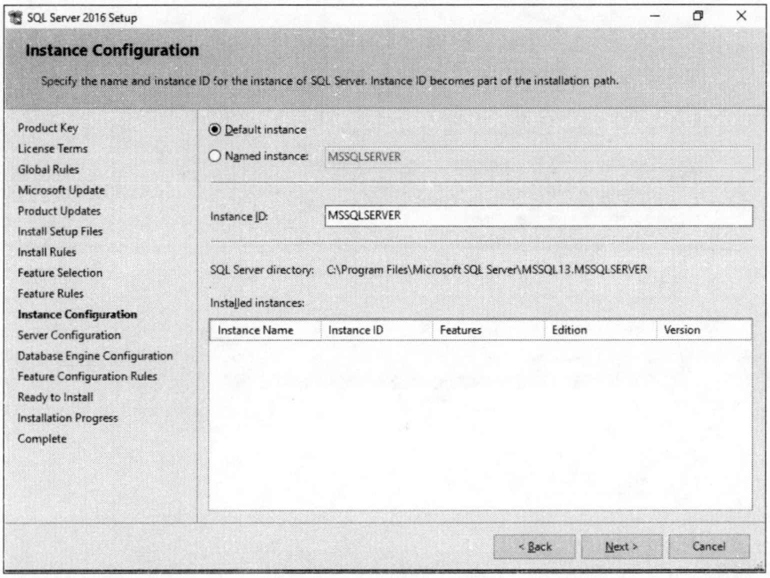

FIGURE A-4 The Instance Configuration dialog box.

If you're not familiar with the concept of SQL Server instances, you can find details in Chapter 1, in the "SQL Server architecture" section.

10. If a default instance of SQL Server is not installed on your computer and you would like to configure the new instance as the default, simply confirm that the Default Instance option is selected. If you want to configure the new instance as a named instance, make sure the Named Instance option is selected and that you specify a name for the new instance (for example, **SQL2016**). When you later connect to SQL Server, you'll specify only the computer name for a default instance (for example, **MERU**), and the computer name\instance name for a named instance (for example, **MERU\SQL2016**).

11. When you're done, click Next to continue. The Server Configuration dialog box appears.

    For the purposes of this book, you do not need to change the default choices in the Service Accounts and Collation dialog boxes. If you want to know more about collation, you can find details in Chapter 2, "Single-table queries," in the "Working with character data" section.

12. Click Next to continue. The Database Engine Configuration dialog box appears.

13. On the Server Configuration tab, ensure that under Authentication Mode the Windows Authentication Mode option is selected. Under Specify SQL Server Administrators, click Add Current User to assign the current logged-on user with the System Administrator (sysadmin) server role, as shown in Figure A-5. SQL Server administrators have unrestricted access to the SQL Server database engine.

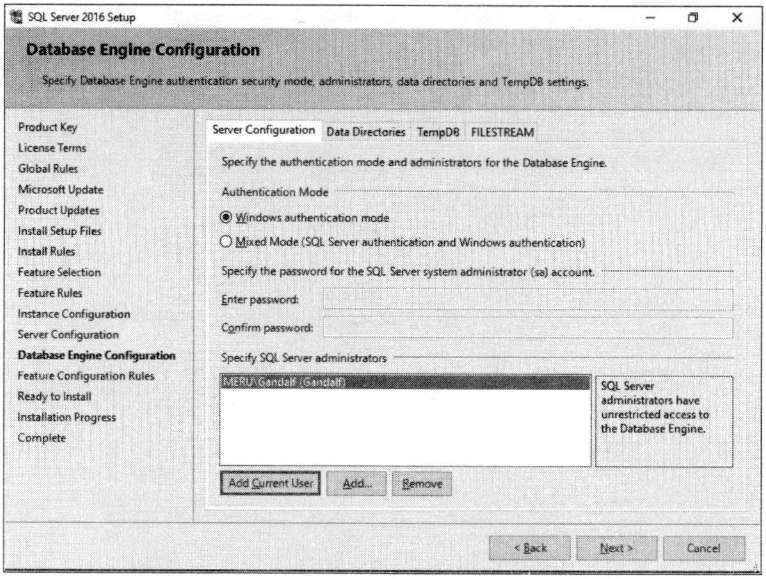

FIGURE A-5 The Database Engine Configuration dialog box.

Of course, in your case, your current user name will appear instead of *MERU\Gandalf*.

If you want to change the setup program's defaults in terms of data directories, you can do so on the Data Directories tab. For the purposes of the book, you don't need to configure anything on the TempDB and FILESTREAM tabs.

14. Click Next to continue. The Ready To Install dialog box appears with a summary of the installation choices.
15. Ensure that the summary indicates your choices correctly, and click Install to start the actual installation process. The Installation Progress dialog box appears and remains open throughout the remainder of the installation process. This dialog box provides a general progress bar as well as indicating the status of each feature that is being installed. (See Figure A-6.)

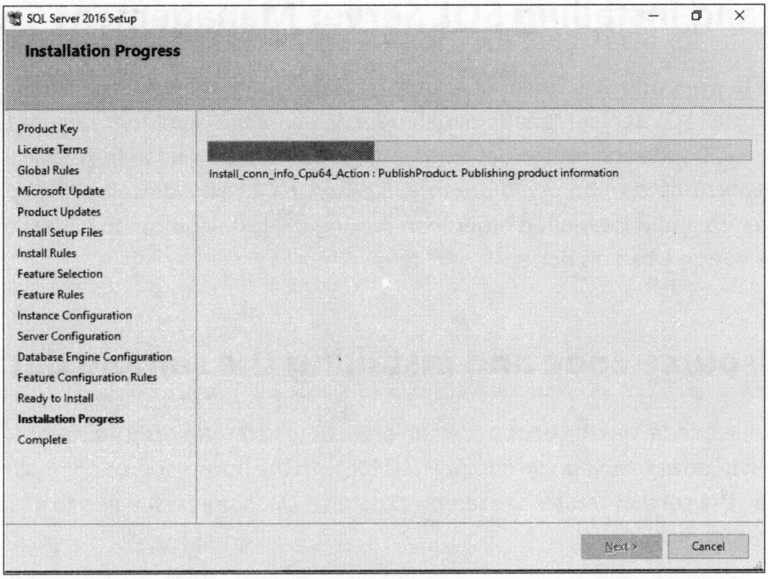

FIGURE A-6 The Installation Progress dialog box.

16. When the installation is complete, the Complete dialog box appears, as shown in Figure A-7.

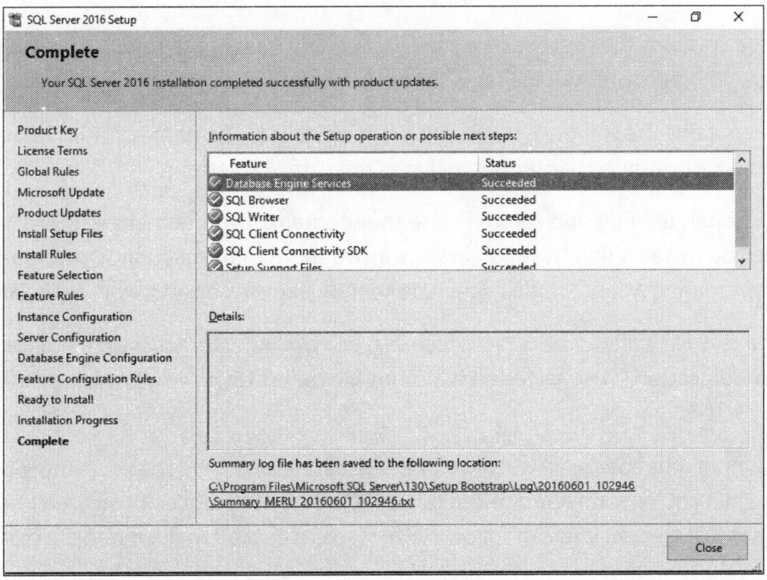

FIGURE A-7 The Complete dialog box.

This dialog box should indicate the successful completion of the installation.

17. Click Close to finish.

Downloading and installing SQL Server Management Studio

Whether you plan to work with SQL Server or Azure SQL Database as the database engine, you need to download and install SQL Server Management Studio (SSMS)—the client tool you use to develop and execute your T-SQL code against the database engine. You can download the installation software from *https://msdn.microsoft.com/en-us/library/mt238290.aspx*. Once the download completes, run the setup program. No user input is required other than clicking the Install button to initiate the installation and the Close button when it's done.

Downloading source code and installing the sample database

To download the source code, visit the book's companion website here: *http://tsql.solidq.com/books/tf3*. This page has a link to download a single compressed file with the book's source code, as well as a script file called TSQLV4.sql that creates the sample database. Decompress the files to a local folder (for example, C:\TSQLFundamentals).

You'll find up to three .sql script files associated with each chapter of the book:

- One file contains the source code for the corresponding chapter. It's provided for your convenience, in case you don't want to type the code that appears in the book. The name of this file matches the title of the corresponding chapter.
- A second file contains the exercises for the chapter. The name of this file also matches the title of the corresponding chapter but includes the suffix "Exercises."
- A third file contains the solutions to the chapter's exercises. The name of this file matches the title of the corresponding chapter but includes the suffix "Solutions."

You use SSMS to open the files and run the code they contain. If you don't have SSMS installed already, make sure you install it first by following the instructions in the section "Downloading and installing SQL Server Management Studio." The next section explains how to work with SSMS.

You'll also find a text file called orders.txt, which you can use when practicing the materials from Chapter 8, "Data modification." Also included is a script file called TSQLV4.sql, which creates the book's sample database, *TSQLV4*.

To create the sample database in an instance of a SQL Server box product, you simply need to run this script file while you're connected to the target SQL Server instance. If you aren't familiar with running script files in SQL Server, you can follow these steps to complete the database creation.

To create and populate the sample database in a SQL Server box product

1. Double-click the TSQLV4.sql file name in File Explorer to open the file in SSMS. The Connect To Database Engine dialog box appears.

2. In the Server Name box, ensure that the name of the instance you want to connect to appears. For example, you would type the name **MERU** if your instance was installed as the default instance in a computer called **MERU**, or **MERU\SQL2016** if your instance was installed as a named instance called *SQL2016* in a computer called *MERU*.

3. In the Authentication box, make sure Windows Authentication is selected. Click Connect.

4. When you're connected to SQL Server, press F5 to run the script. When the execution is done, the Command(s) Completed Successfully message should appear in the Messages pane. You should see the *TSQLV4* database in the Available Databases box.

5. When you're done, you can close SSMS.

To create and populate the sample database in Azure SQL Database

1. Double-click the file name in File Explorer to open the file in SSMS. The Connect To Database Engine dialog box appears.

2. In the Server Name box, ensure that the name of the Azure SQL Database server you want to connect to appears—for example, *myserver.database.windows.net*.

3. In the Authentication box, make sure SQL Authentication is selected and the correct logon name and password are entered. Click Options.

4. On the Connection Properties tab, type **master** in the Connect To Database text box, and then click Connect.

5. Skip the instructions under Section A in the script (for a SQL Server box product), and follow the instructions under Section B in the script (for Azure SQL Database). The most important instruction is the one telling you to run the following command to create the *TSQLV4* database:

   ```
   CREATE DATABASE TSQLV4;
   ```

6. Right-click any empty area in the query pane, and choose Connection | Change Connection. The Connect To Database Engine dialog box appears. Specify **TSQLV4** as the database to connect to, and click Connect. You should see the *TSQLV4* database in the Available Databases box.

   As an alternative, you can simply select the *TSQLV4* database from the Available Databases box.

7. Highlight the code in Section C (beginning with Create Schemas and continuing all the way to the end of the script file). Press F5 to run the script. When the execution is done, the Command(s) Completed Successfully message should appear in the Messages pane. Note that on slow connections it might take the code a few minutes to complete.

8. When you're done, you can close SSMS.

The data model of the *TSQLV4* database is provided in Figure A-8 for your convenience.

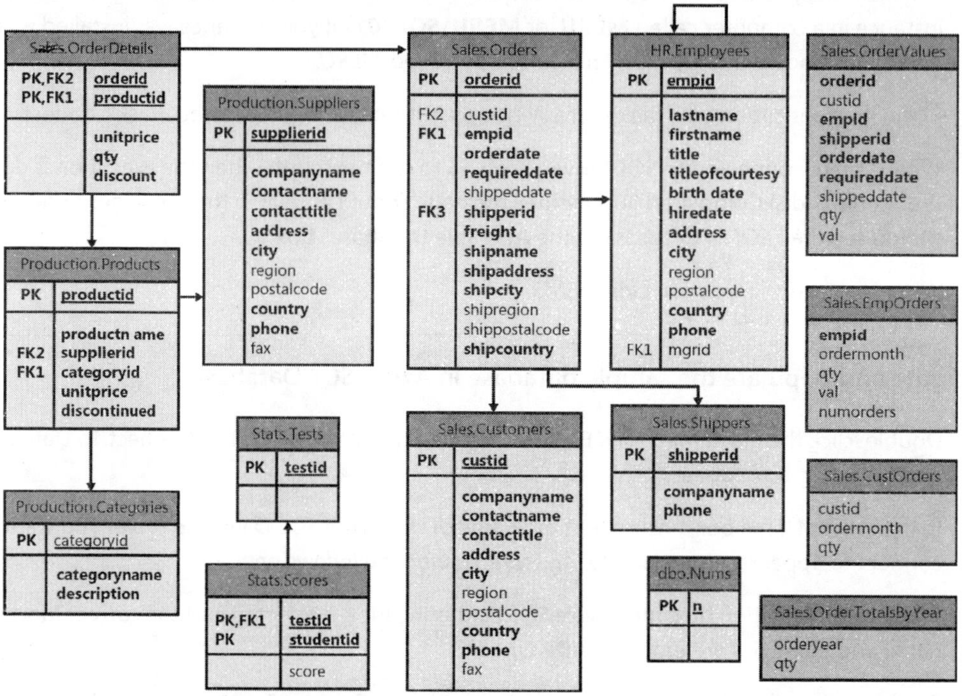

FIGURE A-8 The data model of the *TSQLV4* database.

Working with SQL Server Management Studio

SQL Server Management Studio (SSMS) is the client tool you use to develop and execute T-SQL code against SQL Server. The purpose of this section is not to provide a complete guide to working with SSMS, but rather just to help you get started.

Note SSMS is updated periodically, so your experience might vary from the screenshots in this appendix.

To start working with SSMS

1. Start SSMS from the Microsoft SQL Server program group.
2. If this is the first time you have run SSMS, I recommend specifying the startup options so that the environment is set up the way you want it.
    a. If a Connect To Server dialog box appears, click Cancel for now.

b. Choose the Tools | Options menu item to open the Options dialog box. Under Environment | Startup, set the At Startup option to Open Object Explorer And Query Window. This choice tells SSMS that whenever it starts, it should open the Object Explorer and a new query window.

   The Object Explorer is the tool you use to manage SQL Server and graphically inspect object definitions, and a query window is where you develop and execute T-SQL code against SQL Server. Feel free to navigate the tree to explore the options you can set, but few of them are likely to mean much at this point. After you gain some experience with SSMS, you'll find many of the options more meaningful and probably want to change some of them.

c. When you're done exploring the Options dialog box, click OK to confirm your choices.

3. Close SSMS and start it again to verify that it actually opens the Object Explorer and a new query window. You should see the Connect To Server dialog box, as shown in Figure A-9.

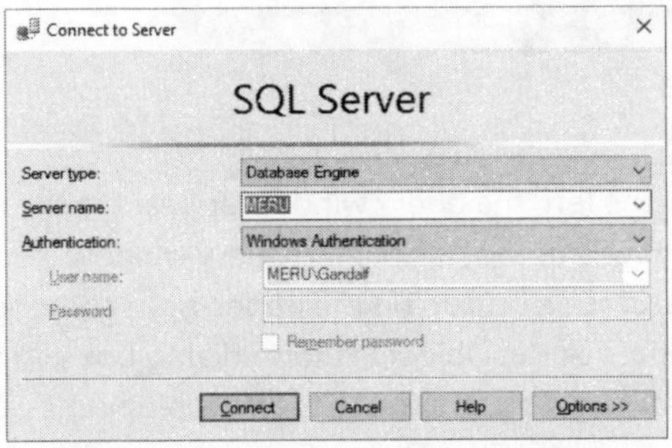

FIGURE A-9 The Connect To Server dialog box.

4. In this dialog box, you specify the details of the SQL Server instance you want to connect to.

5. Type the name of the server you want to connect to in the Server Name box, or select it from the list if you've already connected to it successfully in the past. For Azure SQL Database you will need to specify the full DNS server name in the form *yourserver.database.windows.net* (replacing *yourserver* with your server name).

6. Choose the authentication mode in the Authentication list box according to the type of login you are connecting with (Windows Authentication or SQL Server Authentication). If you use the former (recommended), you don't need to specify the login name and password. If you use the latter, specify the SQL authenticated login name and password information. For Azure SQL Database, also click Options and specify **TSQLV4** in the Connect To Dataset box in the Connection Properties dialog box.

7. Click Connect. SSMS should start, as shown in Figure A-10.

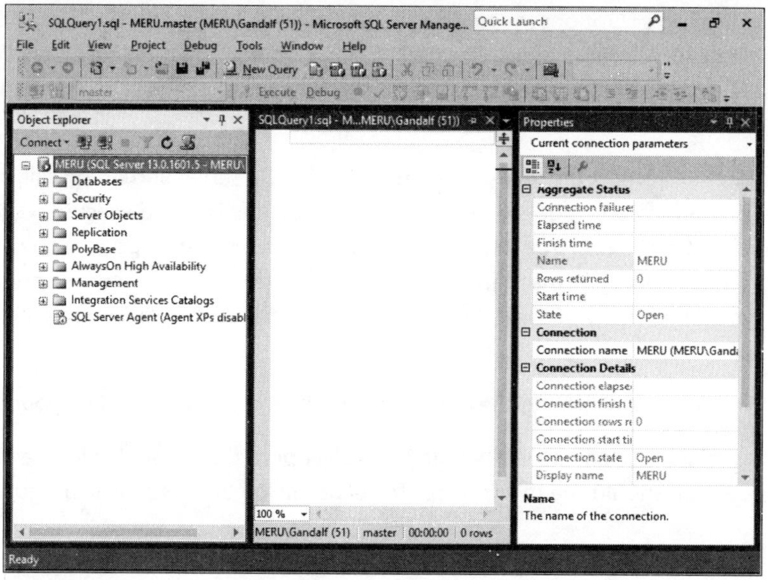

FIGURE A-10 The opening screen of SSMS.

The Object Explorer window appears on the left, the query window appears to the right of Object Explorer, and the Properties window is to the right of the query window. You can hide the Properties window by clicking the Auto Hide button (in the upper-right corner of the window, to the left of the X). Adjust the sizes of the Object Explorer dialog box and the query window as convenient to you. Although the focus of this book is on developing T-SQL code and not SQL Server management, I urge you to explore the Object Explorer by navigating the tree and by right-clicking the various nodes. You'll find the Object Explorer to be a convenient tool for graphically inspecting your databases and database objects, as shown in Figure A-11.

Note that you can drag items from the Object Explorer to the query window.

> **Tip** If you drag the Columns folder of a table from the Object Explorer to the query window, SQL Server will list all table columns separated by commas.

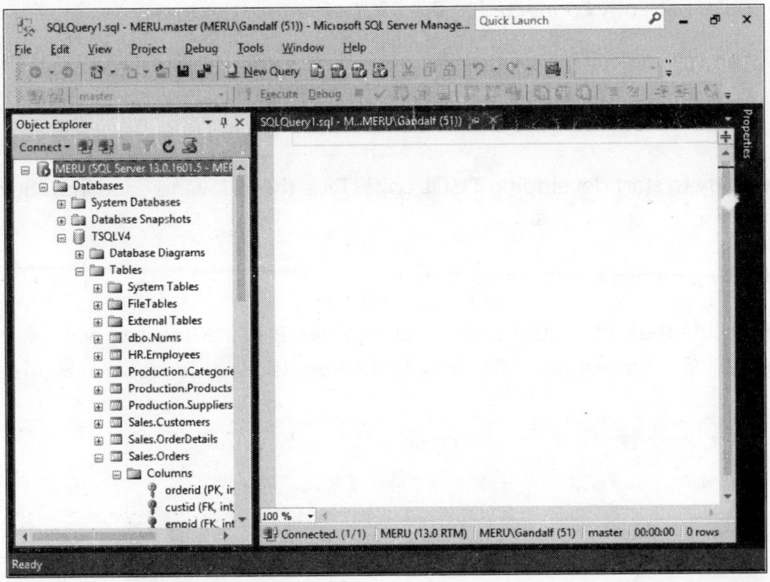

FIGURE A-11 The Object Explorer.

In the query window, you develop and execute T-SQL code. The code you run is executed against the database you're connected to. You can choose the database you want to connect to from the Available Databases combo box, as shown in Figure A-12.

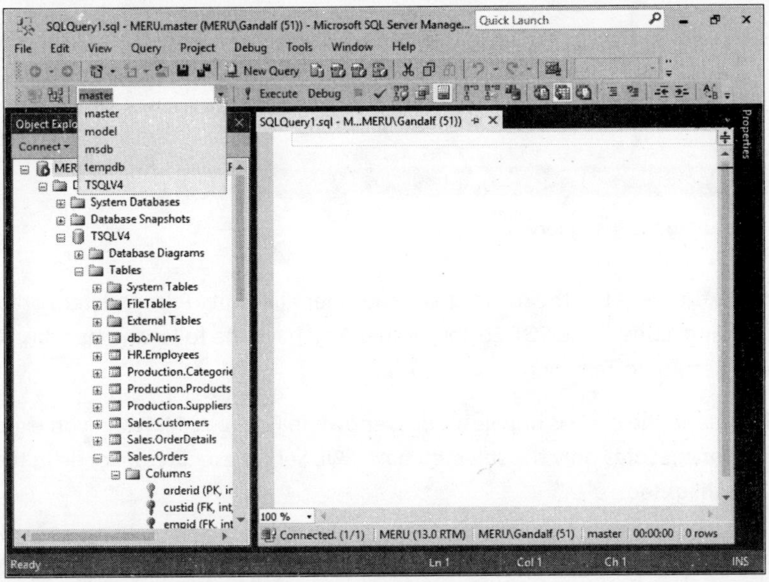

FIGURE A-12 The Available Databases combo box.

8. Make sure you're currently connected to the *TSQLV4* sample database.

   Note that, at any point, you can change the server and database you're connected to by right-clicking an empty area in the query window and then choosing Connection | Change Connection.

9. You're now ready to start developing T-SQL code. Type the following code into the query window:

```
SELECT orderid, orderdate FROM Sales.Orders;
```

10. Press F5 to execute the code. Alternatively, you can click Execute (the icon with the red exclamation point). You'll get the output of the code in the Results pane, as shown in Figure A-13.

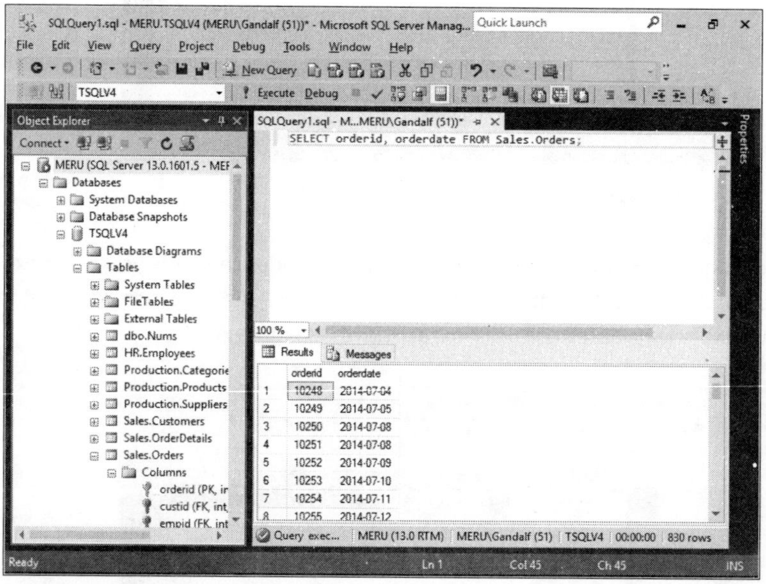

FIGURE A-13 Executing the first query.

You can control the target of the results from the Query | Results To menu item or by clicking the corresponding icons in the SQL Editor toolbar. You have the following options: Results To Grid (default), Results To Text, and Results To File.

Note that if some of the code is highlighted, as shown in Figure A-14, when you execute the code, SQL Server executes only the selected part. SQL Server executes all code in the script only if no code is highlighted.

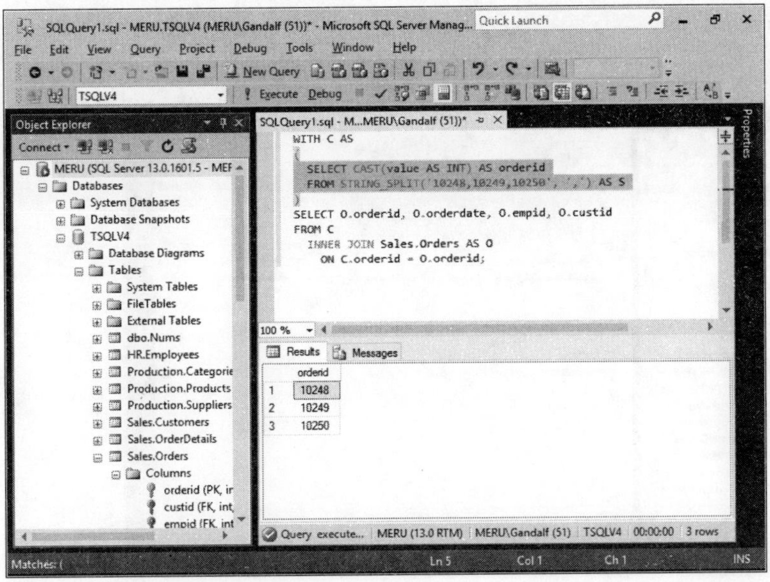

FIGURE A-14 Executing only selected code.

> **Tip** If you press and hold the Alt button before you start highlighting code, you can highlight a rectangular block that doesn't necessarily start at the beginning of the lines of code, for purposes of copying or executing, as shown in Figure A-15. Pressing Tab or Shift+Tab will shift the whole rectangle forward or backward, respectively. If at this point you start typing something, what you type gets repeated in all highlighted lines. Try it!

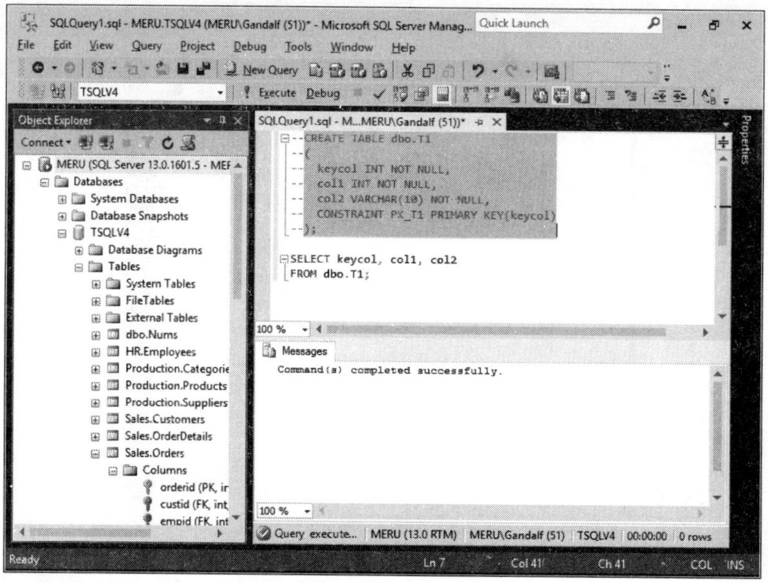

FIGURE A-15 Highlighting a rectangular block.

Finally, before I leave you to your own explorations, I'd like to remind you that all the source code for the book is available for download from the book's website. The previous section in this appendix, "Downloading source code and installing the sample database," provides the details. Assuming you downloaded the source code and extracted the compressed files to a local folder, you can open the script file you want to work with from File | Open | File or by clicking the Open File icon on the standard toolbar. Alternatively, you can double-click the script file's name in File Explorer to open the script file within SSMS.

Working with SQL Server Books Online

Microsoft SQL Server Books Online is the online documentation that Microsoft provides for SQL Server. It contains a huge amount of useful information. When you're developing T-SQL code, think of Books Online as your best friend—besides this T-SQL fundamentals book, of course.

You can access Books Online from the Help menu in SSMS by clicking View Help. By default, SSMS goes to the Internet to get help content. You can also install and access help locally from the Help Viewer, which you start by choosing Add and Remove Help Content from the Help menu, or by clicking Ctrl+Alt+F1. Install new content from the Manage Content tab. I installed all the items with SQL in their name.

Learning to use Books Online is not rocket science, and I don't want to insult anyone's intelligence by explaining the obvious. Dedicating a section to Books Online in the "Getting started" appendix is more about making you aware of its existence and emphasizing its importance rather than explaining how to use it. Too often, people ask others for help about a topic related to SQL Server when they can easily find the answer if they only put a little effort into searching for it in Books Online.

I'll explain a few of the ways to get information from Books Online. One of the windows I use most in Help Viewer to search for information is the Index tab, shown in Figure A-16.

Type what you're looking for in the search box. As you type the letters of the subject you're looking for (for example, **window function**), Help Viewer places the first qualifying item at the top of the sorted list of subjects. You can type T-SQL keywords for which you need syntax information, for example, or any other subject of interest.

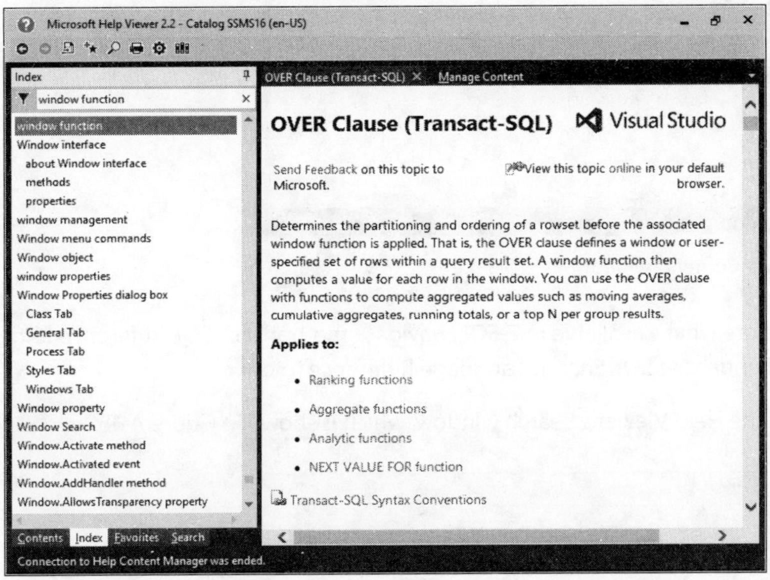

FIGURE A-16 The Help Viewer Index window.

You can add the topic to the Help Favorites by clicking the Add To Favorites button from the toolbar, making it easy to get back to later. You can also sync the current help item with the respective topic on the Content tab by clicking the Show Topic In Contents button.

You can also look for an item through the Contents tab by navigating the tree of topics, as shown in Figure A-17.

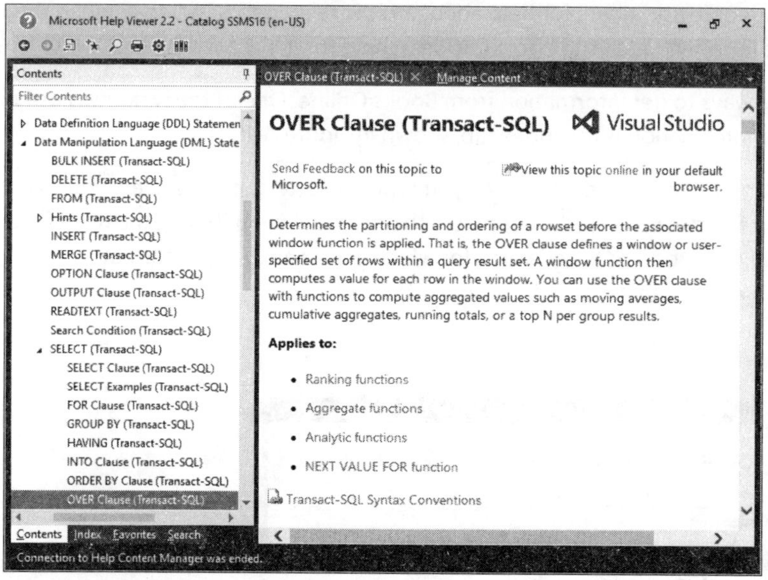

FIGURE A-17 The Help Viewer Contents window.

If you just want to explore what's available in T-SQL, navigate the Transact-SQL Reference folder tree, which can be found under the SQL Shared Language Reference folder.

Another useful tool is the Help Viewer's Search window, which is shown in Figure A-18.

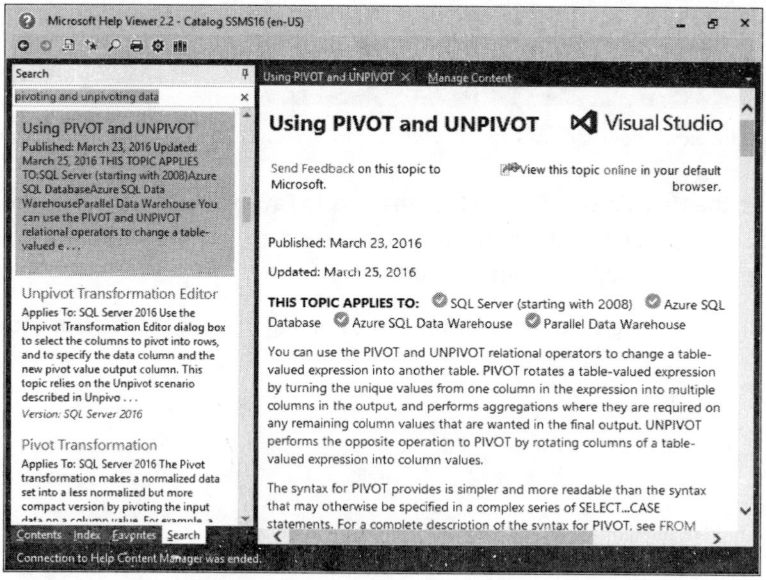

FIGURE A-18 The Help Viewer Search window.

You use the search box when looking for articles that contain words you're looking for. This search is more abstract than a search on the Index tab—somewhat similar to a search performed by an Internet search engine. Note that if you want to find a certain word in an open article, click the Find In Topic button on the toolbar or press Ctrl+F to activate the Find bar.

> **Tip** Finally, let me add a last tip. If you need help with a syntax element while writing code in SQL Server Management Studio, make sure your cursor is positioned somewhere in that code element and then press F1. This will load Books Online and open the syntax page for that element, assuming that such a Help item exists.

Index

Symbols and Numbers

A

B

C

D

E

F

G

H

I

J

K

L

P

Q

R

S

T

X

Y

About the author

ITZIK BEN-GAN is a mentor with and co-founder of SolidQ. A Microsoft Data Platform MVP since 1999, Itzik has taught numerous training events around the world focused on T-SQL querying, query tuning, and programming. Itzik is the author of several books about T-SQL. He has written many articles for *SQL Server Pro* as well as articles and white papers for MSDN and *The SolidQ Journal*. Itzik's speaking engagements include Tech-Ed, SQL PASS, SQL Server Connections, presentations to various SQL Server user groups, and SolidQ events.

Itzik is a subject-matter expert within SolidQ for its T-SQL related activities. He authored SolidQ's Advanced T-SQL and T-SQL Fundamentals courses and delivers them regularly worldwide. You can learn more about Itzik at *http://tsql.solidq.com/*.

From technical overviews to drilldowns on special topics, get *free* ebooks from Microsoft Press at:

www.microsoftvirtualacademy.com/ebooks

Download your free ebooks in PDF, EPUB, and/or Mobi for Kindle formats.

Look for other great resources at Microsoft Virtual Academy, where you can learn new skills and help advance your career with free Microsoft training delivered by experts.

Microsoft Press

Get the latest news from Microsoft Press sent to your inbox.

- New and upcoming books
- Special offers
- Free eBooks
- How-to articles

Sign up today at MicrosoftPressStore.com/Newsletters

Microsoft

Now that you've read the book...

Tell us what you think!

Was it useful?
Did it teach you what you wanted to learn?
Was there room for improvement?

Let us know at http://aka.ms/tellpress

Your feedback goes directly to the staff at Microsoft Press, and we read every one of your responses. Thanks in advance!

Microsoft